NATIONAL GEOGRAPHIC

COMPLETE GUIDE TO
PET HEALTH, BEHAVIOR, AND HAPPINESS

COMPLETE GUIDE TO
PET HEALTH, BEHAVIOR, AND HAPPINESS

The Veterinarian's Approach to At-Home Animal Care

Gary Weitzman, DVM, MPH, CAWA

NATIONAL GEOGRAPHIC

WASHINGTON, D.C.

Since 1888, the National Geographic Society has funded more than 13,000 research, exploration, and preservation projects around the world. National Geographic Partners distributes a portion of the funds it receives from your purchase to National Geographic Society to support programs including the conservation of animals and their habitats.

National Geographic Partners
1145 17th Street NW
Washington, DC 20036-4688 USA

Get closer to National Geographic explorers and photographers, and connect with our global community. Join us today at nationalgeographic.com/join

For information about special discounts for bulk purchases, please contact National Geographic Books Special Sales: specialsales@natgeo.com

For rights or permissions inquiries, please contact National Geographic Books Subsidiary Rights: bookrights@natgeo.com

Library of Congress Cataloging-in-Publication Data
Names: Weitzman, Gary, author. | National Geographic Society (U.S.)
Title: National Geographic complete guide to pet health, behavior, and
    happiness : the veterinarian's approach to at-home animal care / Gary
    Weitzman, DVM, MPH, CAWA.
Description: Washington, D.C. : National Geographic, [2019] | Includes
    bibliographical references and index.
Identifiers: LCCN 2018027275 | ISBN 9781426219658
Subjects: LCSH: Pets--Health. | Pets--Behavior. | Pets--Psychology.
Classification: LCC SF413 .W38 2019 | DDC 636.088/7--dc23
LC record available at https://lccn.loc.gov_2018027275

Interior design: Katie Olsen

Printed in China

18/RRDS/1

Questioner: "How are we to treat others?"
Ramana Maharshi: "There are no others."

For all the selfless shelter and rescue workers making new
lives possible for homeless and neglected animals

CONTENTS

PART 6 | Diagnostics, Aging, and Holistic Medicine 350

Introduction

The human–animal relationship is one of the cornerstones of a just and compassionate society. Beginning in childhood and continuing throughout life, the bonds we form with our companion animals can provide the basis of respect and regard for all living things.

— Gus W. Thornton, former president of MSPCA-Angell
and the World Society for the Protection of Animals

Barbara had a bad night. At 2:15 a.m., the Seattle-based human resources manager awoke to what sounded like a scuffle downstairs in her living room, followed by a loud, single bark. It was unusual for Zoe, her six-year-old German shepherd, to wake her during the night. Even more unusual was what she found in the living room.

When Barbara got to the scene of the crime, she took a moment to register what she saw, then opened the kitchen door in hopes Zoe would finish outside what she started in the living room.

In four different spots, Barbara could see exactly what Zoe ate for dinner; in three other places were what appeared to be the remnants of the meals Zoe had eaten the day before. That wasn't the really bad part, though. Worse than the mess, which would take the carpet cleaner the better part of a day to deep clean, was what was on top of the mess: a thick trail of slime with a few bloody spots that led from the corner of the living room, over the rug, onto the sofa, and back to the door. Bloodstains aside, this was highly unusual for her well-trained, healthy dog so Barbara took Zoe to an emergency veterinary hospital.

Hours later, Barbara had a bill exceeding $750—her regret over not purchasing pet health insurance was palpable—and she was exhausted and emotionally drained. Should Barbara have made a different decision? After all, in spite of the horrible mess, Zoe had been alert and acting as if nothing was wrong. What was going on?

As it turned out, Zoe had eaten something she was sensitive to and pulled that least coveted of gastrointestinal tickets: winning a three-day bout of hemorrhagic colitis. Although this seemed like an emergency (and for the rugs, it certainly was), Barbara could have waited until the morning to take Zoe to her regular vet, saving some stress, sleep, and, of course, money. Certainly the sight of blood coming anywhere from your dog is scary, but Zoe was still bright-eyed so it wasn't necessarily a true emergency. Lots of pet owners find themselves in similar positions as Barbara: a sick pet in the middle of the night or on a Sunday evening and no idea of what to do. Knowing how your pet acts, looks, and feels when healthy is key to understanding when he is and when he is not facing a true emergency.

If only you could text your vet in the middle of the night for help and get an answer right away. If you're very lucky, you might actually have an amazing veterinarian who answers texts at 2 a.m. For the rest of us, think of this book as your 24-hour on-call vet, bringing the veterinary office to your home with expert advice on common health, behavior, and training issues.

I've filled these pages with everything a responsible pet owner needs to know, such as comprehensive information about medical conditions, injuries, and emergencies. But this book is much more than a medical reference. Here you will find everything you need to become the best pet owner you can be, including how to find your next best friend, how to choose and use the best pet supplies, behavior tips and training techniques you need to know, dietary recommendations, basic first-aid skills, how to determine if a trip to the vet is necessary or if an over-the-counter remedy is available, and much more.

In the nearly three decades I've been working with animals, I've had a chance to see a lot of dogs like Barbara's, as well as other dogs, cats, horses, birds, chinchillas and, rabbits, for emergencies and non-emergencies at all hours of the day and night. In addition to being a licensed veterinarian, I'm the president of the San Diego Humane Society, one of the largest and most comprehensive animal shelters in the country. I'm a lucky guy. In my career, I've owned and operated a veterinary clinic, practiced public health and preventive medicine as an Air Force officer, and worked in West Africa on diseases affecting animals and people. I couldn't have imagined where my career in medicine would take me when I first read

their animals, we will always have pet homelessness and suffering.

A few years ago, I cohosted a nationally distributed weekly public radio show that explored the latest in animal science, pet health and behavior, and wildlife conservation. I took calls from people all over the country who loved their pets but had problems they needed help with, sometimes after exhausting all the resources of their own veterinarians, referral vets, and the internet. This show was a challenge, but a good one, and a constant reminder of how often problems arise that are sometimes tough, but more often than not can be handled pretty easily with some practice, some patience, and a little knowledge. Much of what's gone into this book comes from six years of those conversations with people who loved their pets enough to call into a national radio show for help.

My own two wonderful dogs, Jake and Betty, are constant reminders of what all pet owners face when their animals are sick, injured, or just acting badly. Jake is a German shepherd, so I can sympathize with Barbara's 2 a.m. plight. Despite being a sturdy-looking, take-charge, everything-needs-to-be-barked-at kind of dog, German shepherds are actually big babies with a gastrointestinal fragility inconsistent with their appearance and behavior. Or perhaps that's why they are sensitive. Jake, like most other shepherds, is too smart for his own good (or mine). With those smarts comes a sensitivity that his vocal predilection belies and can lead to great anxiety and even stomach and intestinal issues. The anxiety leads to behavioral quirks that

British veterinarian James Herriot's book *All Creatures Great and Small* when I was eight years old. I thought I would be getting up in the middle of the night to help a cow give birth in a frozen barn; that's where Herriot seemed to end up more often than not.

These days, I crawl around in very few frozen barns. My life now is more about animal welfare in general, including animal sheltering, population medicine, behavior, conservation, and pet homelessness. But it's also very much about finding ways for people to get accessible and affordable veterinary care, the lack of which is nothing short of a crisis for animals and the progress of animal welfare in this country. Until we can ensure that every animal owner has access to affordable spay or neuter and medical services for nearly every German shepherd owner will recognize (as do all my staff at the shelter who see, and hear, Jake every day). These are chatty dogs who want nothing more than to get their point across no matter how long it takes. So Barbara is probably very used to Zoe's laser-tuned focus on her, as well as her sensitive GI tract. And she knows that her smart dog would never have an accident in the house unless something very unusual was happening.

At the other end of the spectrum is my younger dog, Betty. A pit bull mix rescued from a poorly resourced shelter with few adopters in West Virginia, Betty is nearly the perfect dog. Sweet as sugar, her only goal is to make humans happy. As a side note, if everyone who likes dogs would adopt one well-behaved pit bull mix to go with their purebred dog, we would probably end pet homelessness in this country. That's because our real last frontier of dog overpopulation is the much misunderstood pit bull. In fact, pit bulls aren't a breed in themselves, any more than they're a particular temperament type. They're just another mix. But we'll get to that later. Suffice it to say that once you get to know a pit bull, you might just shed those preconceived notions of the stereotypical "vicious" dog. Sure, like any dog, there are good and not so good ones, but these can be great family dogs, who were actually called "nanny dogs" in the early 1900s.

Back to Zoe. The holy grail for veterinarians and shelter directors is to keep our pets healthy and happy. In animal rehab, that combination of physical and mental health is what we so fervently hope to achieve: keep pets in homes healthy and rehabilitate the animals who end up in shelters. Better yet, fix the issues that push many people into relinquishing their pets long before they ever end up in need of new homes. No one is perfect, least of all our animals, but in many cases, "not quite perfect" is more than enough to keep everyone, human and animal, happy. This book is my effort to maintain that bond, keeping everyone in the relationship between human and animal happy. It's worth it. These creatures give everything of themselves to us. Taking the best possible care of them is the least we can do in return, even, as Barbara discovered, when that care occurs in the middle of the night. ■

The author and his dogs, Jake (left) and Betty (right)

PART 1

Animal Happiness and Responsible Pet Ownership

To open our hearts and homes to another species for the sole prospect of companionship is the simplest expression of the important bond between humans and animals.

CHAPTER 1

Human Happiness

I'm a firm believer that the closest thing to perfection in the universe is the dog. Nothing else comes close to a canine in terms of absolute design gold. They are a work of art. They come in all shapes and sizes, so they fit in anywhere; we've bred them to do all sorts of jobs, from herding to hunting to vermin control and even simply being a constant companion; they're gorgeous and soft or bristly or smooth; and they live to please us. Dogs lighten the load of life and show emotion through their eyes and mouths, and in case we miss the point, they wag their tails. Ingenious! Most of all, dogs love us unconditionally.

CHOOSING THE RIGHT PET

Dogs are just one of the many wonderful species you can choose for a pet. I've spent most of my professional life trying to answer the question, "What pet do you think would be best for my family?" It's a tough question to answer because only you really know what pet will be best. To figure it out, look within yourself and ask what you want most in an animal companion and what you would like to avoid. Then consider what pet best meets your criteria.

Here's an example. Let's say you came to my shelter at the San Diego Humane Society looking for a family pet that would be a good choice for your children. You've narrowed your list down to Labradoodles because you heard they have great temperaments (they do) and they are hypoallergenic (they aren't entirely; no dog is, but more about that later). What if, after hearing your top criteria, I introduced you to a litter of golden retriever puppies, arguably the "perfect" dog because they check the box as a great family pet, but they do produce a lot of dander. You'd probably fall in love at first sight. I can't predict how many of these puppies will actually behave (or shed) the way we expect golden retrievers to, since on average, one in five purebred puppies is an outlier. Although they all might have certain physical and behavioral similarities, they're all unique beings with their own motivations, intellect, personalities, and desires.

BRAIN SCANS SHOW SIMILARITIES BETWEEN DOGS AND HUMANS

A 2014 study published in the journal *Current Biology* described how a group of noted Hungarian ethologists and behaviorists from Eötvös Loránd University scanned the brains of 11 golden retrievers and border collies and determined that their brains responded in exactly the same manner toward emotional sound stimuli as did humans. This study objectively demonstrated that our two species share a region for emotional processing and that dogs are finely attuned to human voices. This had not previously been described in any nonprimates. Both findings were heralded as "very cool" by fellow scientists at Emory University. Fittingly, the study was entirely voluntary for the dogs. Only dogs who enjoyed going into the MRI machine participated. (They're better patients than I am.) Their reward: a big dog biscuit.

Matchmaking is alive and well in the animal sheltering world. The animal your local shelter suggests could be the perfect pet for you, even though he might not be exactly what you envisioned. Don't tighten your requirements so much that you take all the fun out of it. For example, despite negative stereotypes, pit bulls are the marshmallows of the dog world when they are well raised and socialized: They are short-haired, loyal, and incredibly affectionate. Animal welfare professionals know that properly raised pit bulls are among the best dogs you can ever have. One of the best parts about facilitating adoptions at an animal shelter is seeing the hearts flow from the eyes of both species when the right match happens.

It's good to keep in mind during your search that there is no such thing as the perfect pet. There is perfect love for your imperfect pet, but none of us have perfection mastered—especially at the beginning of any relationship, and don't kid yourself, this is a relationship. You can't go into pet ownership halfhearted and conditionally. You have to set yourself up for the long-term commitment. Once you do, this could be the best relationship you'll ever have.

So while I can't really tell you what pet you should get, I can tell you that you'll have the time of your life finding out for yourself. Just don't be surprised if it turns out to be one that never crossed your mind.

OWNING PETS IS GOOD FOR YOUR HEALTH

There is a reason dogs have been considered man's best friend, and it might be more than just loyalty. In the past decade, multiple studies have cited the physiological and psychological effects of pets on humans. One study found that simply petting an animal lowers blood pressure, cortisol levels, and heart rate. In a 2015 article published in *Science,* researchers noted that oxytocin released during contact between humans and animals caused a dramatic bonding effect, along with lowered levels of cortisol. We all know pets make us feel good emotionally; now we know they improve our physical health too.

QUESTIONS TO ASK YOURSELF BEFORE GETTING A PET

Every person is different, and every animal is different, so a little introspection before you choose a pet can help a lot. Making a firm list about your habits, interests, free time, and how you want to spend time with your pet will allow you to identify the best pet for you. Consider these criteria when searching for your one-of-a-kind pet:

1   Activity level: Do you want a running companion or just a buddy to watch TV with you? Or maybe you want to be motivated to get out of the house and onto the hiking trail you drive by on your way to work every day. Regardless, you must balance the pet's needs and your own. If you adopt a lively

dog to be a weekend trail-running companion, don't expect him to enjoy lying around the house all day while you're at work.

2   Organization: Some pets are messier than others. Who will be responsible for cleaning up after the dog? Do you have a housekeeper? If not, how important is the word *clean* to you? In other words, how much fur can you tolerate on the upholstery, or carpets, or anywhere else?

3   Time management: How much time are you at home? Dogs were bred to be our companions, and often we are their only company. I don't recommend leaving any dog at home alone for more than a half-day. The same goes for cats, but their tolerance is probably a full day. We all know life happens, though. Also, if you work full time (most of us do), your pet will probably be home alone unless you can bring him to work. The benefits of pets in the workplace are real and have been cited in peer-reviewed journals. Many modern workplaces recognize these benefits and encourage their employees to bring their pets to work. If you can't bring your pet to work with you, consider using a dog walker or doggie day care (see Chapter 9).

4   Space: How big is your house? If you're considering a dog, will the dog have access to a safe, enclosed outdoor space? Some pets need more space than others. You might be surprised to learn that a cat and a greyhound need roughly the same amount of house space—not much!

5   Family dynamics: Do you have other pets? Have you considered how they will react

to a new pet in the house? Some pets don't enjoy the company of other animals, but many do. Do you have children? Are they developmentally ready to interact safely with a pet and share the responsibility of pet ownership with you? Many shelters and breeders recommend waiting to get a pet until children are five years old.

6   Climate: Do you live in a dry, hot desert or a colder climate where you get snow? Consider the needs of the animal you wish to bring home. For instance, a Saint Bernard, with its heavy coat, is not ideal if your summers are sweltering. Hairless or thin-coated breeds are much happier living in a temperate climate rather than a place with

long, cold winters. With some preparation, it's possible to make extremes work, but it's definitely easier to keep a short-haired pet warm with sweaters than to keep a large, fluffy animal cool in the summer heat.

7 Finances: Have you considered budget? For example, keeping a horse and keeping a hamster are very different financial commitments. (See "Budgeting for Your Pet" in Chapter 5.) On average, keeping a dog is estimated to run between $1,000 and $1,500 per year.

8 Commitment: Are you in it for the long haul? A pet is a lifelong commitment. A guinea pig lives on average five years; an African gray parrot can live nearly 80 years. Dogs and cats can live 10 to 15 years or more. Make sure you're ready before starting your pet search.

DOGS

This is the "big time" in terms of pet ownership. Dogs are a commitment, but they give back in spades. For my money, life is worthless without commitment, so why not give it all you've got? Dog owners know that no one will love you the way a dog does. Sometimes this can be a burden. For instance, my dog Jake is absolutely obsessed with me, to the point that he never takes his eyes off me if we're in the same room. And when I'm out of sight, I know that he's waiting to hear me come back. It's wonderful and heartbreaking all at the same time. It also sums up what you should expect if you want a dog.

Life Span and General Care

The old adage that dogs live a year for every seven of ours is still pretty accurate. Thanks to

KIDS AND DOGS

No child should grow up without a pet. But if you're thinking of getting your kid a pet, do one thing: Wait until he or she is at least five years old. Most kids younger than five lack the maturity and impulse control needed to interact safely with pets. When you decide to get a pet, first check your local shelter, where a good adoptions counselor will help match your family with an appropriate pet. A small kindergartner might not be well matched with a boisterous boxer, for example. Dog trainer Colleen Pelar's book *Living With Kids and Dogs* is invaluable and teaches how to safely and successfully introduce your children to the joy of pets. Check out her website: *livingwithkidsanddogs.com*.

recent advances in small animal medicine and surgery, dogs and cats are living longer now than ever before. On average, a good age to shoot for is 14 for any dog. Some live longer and some, sadly, live shorter lives. In general, life span is inversely proportional to size, with smaller dogs living well into their teens and larger dogs stopping short, sometimes before 10 years old. For example, giant breeds like Newfoundlands and Bernese mountain dogs might live only to about eight years old. Some toy breeds like miniature pinschers and papillons might live 13 to 15 years, or even longer. There are always exceptions, and we count on those, but in general, size is the key factor here.

It takes work to care for dogs, nurture them, enrich their lives, and be responsible for them for a decade and a half. Dogs need all the things we need in life, except maybe our mortgage and credit card bills. Some, like Australian shepherds and border collies, need jobs to keep them fulfilled. Other dogs are veritable slugs. Yes, I'm looking at you, greyhound. All dogs need exercise, even five-pound Yorkshire terriers living on the 60th floor of a Manhattan co-op. Also, what better reason for us to get out and breathe fresh air than a dog on the other end of the leash?

No dog should live outside. That's just a fact. We bred them to be our companions and helpers, and they deserve to have our company if we're going to take them away from the companionship of their own species. There are a few exceptions. For example, Alaskan sled dogs and other true working dogs enjoy living outside with their pack companions. Same thing goes for working herding breed dogs like border collies or livestock guardians like great

Ask **DR. GARY:**

Should I Get a Purebred or a Mix?

I love purebred dogs. No species has so much variety as the canine. Each breed comes with unique qualities and challenges. On the flip side, shelters are full of mixed-breed dogs. Most of these dogs demonstrate hybrid vigor, being healthier than their purebred counterparts. Interestingly, some shelters have stopped labeling any breed on their dogs because with the recent advent of genetic testing, we're seeing that many dogs are not the breeds we think they are based on appearance alone. If you want a purebred dog because you grew up watching *Lassie,* or you love pugs, go for it. But if you want a great combination of many good attributes, go for a mutt. Either way, you can't go wrong.

AS SEEN ON TV

You might fall in love with a breed you see on TV or in a movie, but the reality of life with that breed might not be what you expect. Some breeds you see in the media might seem like perfect family pets, but in reality, they can be tough to live with, requiring enormous amounts of training, mental stimulation, and exercise. Even the smartest breed, the border collie, which can achieve more athletic feats than an Olympian, does not come preprogrammed that way. The ones you see in the movies are extensively trained by expert handlers. Do your research before falling for a breed to be sure it will fit with your lifestyle.

Pyrenees, who are frequently happiest when they're outside doing their jobs.

If I could ask just one thing of anyone getting a dog, it's this: Give yourself to your dog. Be his companion and substitute for the company of his own. He needs it and you'll never regret it.

CATS

Cats are subtle—until they're not. The funny saying, "To dogs we're family, but to cats we're staff," is tongue in cheek, but that doesn't mean it's not true. I suggest you get a cat if you want a steadfast, if sometimes demanding, companion and because you like the stealthy, primal way cats act. Cats can be mysterious, as anyone who has watched a cat push a paper cup off a table will attest (or sometimes a glass, which is less fun).

But they do very neat things like head butt and purr. What other animal is implanted with an audible motor of approval?

Finally, despite their independent streak, cats need us; never make the mistake of thinking they don't. Cats would not be with people if they didn't want to be. They show it by insisting on getting attention from us even when we're reading the paper, working on the computer, or trying to cook. Seemingly boneless, they can bend around our legs in the kitchen purring and rubbing affectionately on our pant cuffs until we acknowledge there is nothing more important in the world than paying attention to them. In fact, a cat's no-nonsense, utterly honest relationship is downright refreshing.

Are You Ready for a Cat?

The first thing we learn in vet in school is that "cats are not small dogs." Okay, maybe not the first thing, but in describing cats, nothing could be truer. If you're thinking about getting a cat because you don't have time for a dog, think again. You should get a cat because you think they're cool, which they are. There is possibly nothing cooler than a cat. Hence the term *cool cat*.

Cats take as much time and energy as dogs, and don't let anyone tell you otherwise. Sure, some of the work is a little less obvious; you don't have to walk your cat (although I've seen that done), but you do have to scoop the litter box. It's a trade-off. Cats need attention and play as much as dogs do. You can't just plug them in and leave them alone. They need companionship and mind puzzles to be healthy and happy. And if they don't get it, bookmark Chapter 19 on cat behavior for easy reference.

BEST FIRST PETS FOR KIDS

Rabbits are fantastic first pets for kids. They are tame and gentle, easily housetrained, and affectionate. Other ideal starter pets are rats (gentle, clean, and intelligent animals) and guinea pigs. There's nothing sweeter than a "hello" squeak from a guinea pig. But get two of any of these pets because they are all social creatures and need the company of their own kind. Just be careful: Two of the right combo (or wrong depending on your goals) can lead to a dozen more! Remember that your child's first pet is a great way to learn about responsibility, but all pets are a family commitment to ensure they are safe and thriving. That's especially true when you consider that rabbits can live 12 to 15 years and chinchillas even into their 20s!

Life Span and General Care

Cats have shared their lives with humans for about 9,500 years. The average cat life span is about 14 years, although that life span, like that of dogs, is happily increasing thanks to advances in veterinary care. The anecdotal longevity winner is the Siamese, some of whom have been known to live into their late 20s.

Unlike dogs, who get to go to the park with us and enjoy daily walks, cats are safest kept indoors. That means it's up to us to make their lives full. I always tell people that their goal should be to make their homes better than an amusement park for their cats. That's their whole world, after all. We'll go into what supplies you need to do this in Chapter 5, but cats need toys, exercise, and stimulation just as much as dogs do—and in some ways, even more so. There is no such thing as a "cat park" to bring your feline to for exercise, so it's up to you to make one at home.

OTHER PETS

For much of my childhood, my parents had a negative response to my request for a dog, so I instead filled the house with sea monkeys (How could they just be brine shrimp when they built cities?), 40 gerbils, two parakeets, a handful of chameleons, a guinea pig, a rabbit, two hamsters, and a huge iguana. Did I mention that the 40 gerbils weren't always in a cage? My dream came true when my parents finally relented when I was 16 and I got my first dog, Cocoa, a fluffy chow-shepherd mix.

Maybe you're not ready for a dog or cat. Or you might be allergic or not ready for fur. Or you think you might not have enough room for a dog. You have many other pet

Chameleon

Chinchilla

If you do go for one of these pocket pets, know that not all species share our daylight world. Chinchillas and hamsters are nocturnal, as are rats and sugar gliders (yes, that's a real animal). That doesn't mean they won't interact with you during daylight hours, but the real party happens at night. Nocturnal pets thrive at night and need some cover and darkness during the day.

Possibly the most underrated pet in the world is the rabbit. These intelligent, sweet, and beautiful creatures can be housetrained and are terrific companions. And what could be better than those ears? A related option is the softer-than-butter chinchilla, but these animals take a bit of work and have their own unique requirements, which include a daily dust bath.

options. If you're short on space but want to cuddle, play, and delight in the antics of tiny, furry creatures, look to the world of "pocket pets": guinea pigs, chinchillas, hamsters, gerbils, mice, and rats, for example. A quick shout-out to ferrets while we're here is in order. These are the clowns of the pocket pet world. They are illegal in some places (California, Hawaii, Washington, D.C., and New York City, as of this printing), but they're nonetheless wonderful, affectionate, and intelligent companions.

If fur is totally out of the question, reptiles, although not for everyone, are certainly intriguing and have a wonderful seeming disinterest in us. Another "nonfur" option is a fish aquarium. Whether freshwater or saltwater, aquariums are

WHAT TO DO IF YOU FIND AN INJURED WILD ANIMAL

If you find a baby bird that fell out of a nest or an orphaned baby bunny, or if your pet injures a wild animal or disrupts a nest, contact a professional. Most communities have wildlife rehabilitation programs. My shelter in San Diego operates Project Wildlife, which helps more than 10,000 wild animals a year. Wildlife rehab websites can provide step-by-step care of found animals. In most cases, unless a baby animal is clearly injured, the best course of action is to leave it alone, quiet and protected, until mom can find her way back. If that doesn't work after 12 to 24 hours, contact a local wildlife rehabilitator for help.

beautiful and relaxing, and fish actually have distinct personalities!

Finally, birds are magnificent, but some birds are a lifetime responsibility. The cockatoo, for example, can live more than 60 years and Amazon parrots can live as long as 80 years. That's six dog lifetimes!

The only thing I'd steer you away from is buying your furry, scaled, or winged companion from a pet store. There are plenty of other options for all of these pets, including adopting from an animal shelter or local rescue group. We'll get to more on that later.

Exotics

What we typically consider an "exotic pet" is actually a domesticated wild animal, which includes animals ranging from chinchillas to tropical birds, sugar gliders, and pythons. Some are bred in captivity, but they are no different from their wild counterparts. Some states ban certain animals as pets. In California, for example, you can't own gerbils or ferrets for fear these animals may escape and affect the agricultural balance in the state. Know what your own state allows before falling in love with the idea of a pet you can't have. A note of caution: When you have an exotic pet, you need to find a specialty vet who can treat that pet. Exotic animal vets are less common and often more expensive than vets who treat dogs and cats. After all, they are specialists, and rare ones at that.

I'm not a fan of owning any wild animal, domesticated or not, but it can't be denied that a great deal of time and energy has gone into domesticating or taming certain wild animals. These include rabbits, guinea pigs, rats, hamsters, chinchillas, gerbils, ferrets, and most tropical

DON'T SHOP FOR YOUR BIRD. ADOPT.

Birds are one of the most magnificent creatures on the planet. They come in thousands of shapes and sizes, and they can fly. What's better than that? I'll just ask you to do one thing: Try adoption first before going to a breeder. Never go to a pet store and be careful of internet sites where you don't get to meet the breeder. Enforcement has ramped up, but tragically, unethical traders still perpetuate the horrific capture of birds from the wild. Specific bird rescues are the best place to find a bird, but check your local shelter too, as many shelters also have birds. With life spans ranging from 40 to 70 years or more, bringing home any bird is a major commitment.

birds. You should never own nondomesticated wildlife. These include everything else living outside our homes such as raccoons, prairie dogs, opossums, hedgehogs, some fish, most parrots, and many reptiles (unless, of course, they are rescued). They will have a much better life if left in the wild where they belong. Don't go near healthy, active wildlife, and don't acclimate native wildlife to people. It makes them dangerously accustomed to humans and ruins their lives. It's also against the law to keep wildlife in your home. As a good rule of thumb, if an animal would normally run away from you or if it can eat you in the wild, you shouldn't own it as a pet.

One final thought: We humans should not think that we can "own" any animal we think we'd like. We don't have that right. We've coexisted with animals for thousands of years. Some of those animals have been domesticated to be our companions, but many have not. So please, think it through before you get a hedgehog, sugar glider, or baby alligator. Just because we can make them our pets doesn't necessarily make it right to do so.

WHAT TO LOOK FOR IN A DOG

Arguably the riskiest part of owning a puppy or dog is the very first thing to do: select your pet. How can you maximize the chance of a perfect match in the dog you've always dreamed about? Before looking for a puppy or dog, decide what characteristics about dogs you value the most. This will help you determine what type of pet will fit best into your family. Of course, looks are important. (Yes, we're all a little superficial that way.) You have to like the look of a dachshund, or a chow chow, or a shih tzu. But the fact is, we all have preferences. For me, temperament, including energy level, is the most important determinant of all, followed way down the list by size, look, and coat type. Of least importance should be the dog's sex (male or female).

Your Pet Wish List

Use this chart (opposite) to help narrow down what you want or don't want in a canine companion by circling all that apply. When you start looking at dogs, see if their traits fit with your ideal preferences. For help, talk to the shelter staff, rescue volunteer, or breeder about your preferences.

Purebred or a Mixed Breed?

What specifically is it about that breed you think you have to have? For example, you've always loved boxers. But did you know that boxers can jump seven feet straight into the air and have enough energy to pull a cart for 200 feet before eating your couch pillows because they don't love being left at home alone? Then there's the firefighter's favorite, the Dalmatian, whose breed rose to prominence during the 1996 debut of Disney's live-action film *101 Dalmatians,* only to become the most anecdotally relinquished dog breed in America the very next year when new families discovered that each puppy has enough energy to stand up to 101 Cruella de Vils. All breeds have certain genetic

---

DNA TESTING IN DOGS

Genetic testing has come a long way since it was first introduced in 2007. Those early days of low breed inventory were the equivalent of getting the dart near the target rather than hitting a bull's-eye. Today's kits can differentiate hundreds of breeds and more than 20,000 genetic markers. Although this is mostly fun fact material, it can provide valuable information about important health-screening data. Kits are available online and are easy to do from home. The most highly rated tests include the Wisdom Panel, Embark, Orivet Dog DNA, and DNA My Dog. Cat DNA testing isn't as accurate yet as dog DNA testing, but all we need to know about cats is that they're all royalty.

YOUR DOG WISH LIST (CIRCLE ONE BOX PER ROW)

Size	Tiny	Small	Medium	Large	Giant
Exercise needs	Off-the-charts energy	Daily jogging and off-leash running	Two or more brisk walks a day	One daily walk	Lazybones
Personality	Prefers to be alone	Independent but likes attention	Cuddly lap lover	Never met a stranger	Attached to the hip
Shedding	Don't care	Hair doesn't bother me	Less hair is more	Nonshedding	Hairless
Grooming needs	Wash and wear	Occasional brushing	Daily brushing	Professional grooming every few months	Monthly professional grooming
Barking	Don't care	I like barking because it deters burglars	Moderate barking	A little barking is no big deal	Silence
Age	Don't care	Puppy	Young	Adult	Senior

characteristics that you can't wish away. You can read more about purebred dogs in Chapter 3.

Now, let's talk about mixed breeds—the Heinz 57s, the beloved mutts. Although you might be surprised to learn that many animal shelters have plenty of purebreds to choose from, we often champion the mixed breeds. Why settle on one breed when you can benefit from a combination? This is a case of good old hybrid vigor, and it's true. Hybrid vigor is defined as an increase in superior qualities arising from the crossbreeding of genetically different plants or animals. In other words, why select one good breed's attributes when you can have a combination of several? Many genetic traits from many different breeds can add up to a winning combination. Of course, that works both ways, but there's no such thing as a "bad dog."

Personality

Personality is unequivocally the most important thing to consider in a companion, either four-legged or two-legged. Most of us are middle-of-the-road types, meaning we want a dog who will be a companion, have energy when we have energy, and will curl up by

our side when we don't. Basically, the process is easy as long as you focus on personality—yours and your dog's.

Let's break it down. Temperament leads to personality, and personality leads to behavior. Although personality drives temperament, that isn't the same thing as behavior. The saying "everything in moderation" applies equally in your selection of a dog or cat. Animals whose behavior traits lie on the extremes are not always the best choice to fit into the typical un-extreme human family. Extremely shy dogs can be a challenge if you have a busy household or an active social life. Extremely active dogs like the border collie or the Australian shepherd won't want to wait alone all day for you to come home. These are critical behavioral traits you need to consider before choosing a new dog.

There are a few ways to even the odds of a perfect match. In the early 2000s, the American Society for the Prevention of Cruelty to Animals (ASPCA) in New York developed a color-coded pet matching program, Meet Your Match (MYM), which looks at pets' sociability, playfulness, energy level, motivation, and manners and matches your lifestyle with the pet most likely to meet your confessed criteria. It's as scientific as possible while recognizing that love is very hard to put into a spreadsheet. You want a calm, good-natured, happy pup who will sleep on your lap while you watch TV? Look for the purple-coded dogs labeled "Couch Potato." Need a little more energy? Pick the green dog marked "Life of the Party." It works for cats too, although admittedly most cats hide their real behaviors until they arrive at their home.

But it's a good start. Many shelters use MYM or similar color-coding guides to help prospective adopters narrow down the sometimes overwhelming numbers of animals eagerly waiting to go to their new homes.

If the shelter or rescue you're working with doesn't use a formal program, have a conversation with your adoption counselor or rescue volunteer about what your life is like. Maybe you enjoy weekend hikes, walking in the woods, or running on the beach. Or maybe you work all day and like to binge-watch TV on the weekends. These two very different lifestyles would probably do best with two very different canines.

When you meet your potential new dog, whether through an adoption event or at a breeder's, don't expect all to be revealed on that first date. Dogs, like humans, can be extroverts or introverts, and often their level of comfort determines their true personalities. You might not get a good sense of your new dog's true personality for weeks or even months after adoption. This is because many rescued pets need time to become comfortable with their surroundings, including you. But an adoption coordinator or a reputable breeder can give you all the information they know about that pet up to that point, so trust their guidance. If you're looking at a puppy, the sky's the limit on what that personality will be. But you'll get clues, including the general breed traits most associated with that puppy.

Activity Level

It's important to consider the energy level of the new dog you're contemplating. A dog who needs four hours of exercise every day just so he doesn't eat your couch won't work for you if you work long hours away from home. If you're a runner, you need a dog that can keep up with you, not a brachycephalic breed like a pug or short-legged breed like a dachshund.

In my job, I get to see firsthand how many dogs end up at the shelter because people didn't think about activity requirements before they got their dog. All relationships take work, but starting off with the best match possible makes everything easier. True dog love starts with common ground.

PUPPY OR ADULT?

Many people want puppies, but you shouldn't write off an adult dog. Most adult dogs already know or quickly pick up housetraining, and many older dogs are past the destructive puppy phase. What you see is what you get with an adult — the size of your new dog, his coat, and probably his temperament. With puppies, you can only comment on how big his paws are and guess what that will mean in 18 months (I'll fill you in: It means nothing). Only you and your family can really decide what age dog is best, but keep an open mind when searching for your future companion.

Consider what you desire or want to avoid in a dog in terms of energy, and ask the people at the shelter or rescue to help match you with your new dog.

Dogs fall all over the spectrum in terms of energy levels and exercise requirements, so it's all about finding one that fits in best with your lifestyle. When choosing a dog, activity level is one of the most important considerations—it should trump color, looks, sex, and possibly even size, since some large dogs are very low energy and some small dogs are very high energy.

Size

I always smile when asked how big a puppy will get. We have an idea of what certain breeds average, but we don't know exactly where your puppy will land on that spectrum.

My dog Betty, for instance, is a pit bull mix and has six brothers and sisters who are 3 feet tall at the shoulders and weigh in at 85 pounds apiece. Betty is only about 1½ feet tall at the shoulders and is on a strict diet to get down to her ideal weight of 65 pounds. What can I say? She's very food motivated.

Despite what you might have heard, the size of the paws means nothing except that they'll probably continue to have four of them. When looking at an individual puppy, know that the shelter's or rescue's best guess at size might be off by a bit. Still, there are clues. For instance, knowing the predominant breed of your pup will help you make an educated guess about size. Of course, seeing the parents is one of the best indicators, but that too has its limitations, as anyone who has siblings of varying heights will tell you. If you really want predictability in size, choose an adult dog. It doesn't get more predictable than that.

Ask **DR. GARY:**

How Do I Find a Hypoallergenic Dog?

The first thing to understand is that *hypoallergenic* means "less allergic," not "nonallergic." Every dog has saliva, fur, and dander. Some dogs shed less and therefore have lower levels of the things we might react to. Poodles, bichons frises, Maltese, and Portuguese water dogs are just some of the breeds that tend to elicit fewer allergic reactions. But nonallergic they're not. If you or anyone else in your family has allergies, that person should spend time with adults of the breed you're considering to make sure he or she doesn't react. Be careful with mixed breeds, especially "designer breeds" that are crosses between hypoallergenic breeds and other breeds, including all of the "doodles." The individual dogs vary in their level of hypoallergenicity, shedding, and dander.

Coat Type

Expect a lot of fur when you get a dog, and you won't be disappointed. Exactly how much hair you can deal with is something to consider. If less is more for you, look at the Chinese crested dog, which is nearly hairless. If you couldn't care less and just want a giant fur ball to hug, allow me to show you the Newfoundland. Sometimes it's not easy to know how much a dog will shed. In fact, some short-coated dogs shed way more than dogs with long hair. That's when you need to do some research and know that huskies shed and poodles don't. Terriers fall in the middle. Some dogs are wash and wear, meaning a routine bath will do it. Other dogs need monthly trips to a groomer (the cost of this can add up). If you're not sure what level of shedding and coat care to expect from a particular dog you're eyeing, ask the breeder, shelter staff, or rescue volunteers for their take on that pup.

Chinese crested

Male or Female?

The last ballot question to answer in determining what kind of dog is best for you is gender. Does it matter? Maybe. In the most general terms, male dogs can have more wanderlust, can mark more, and might get into dog scuffles more than females do. Female dogs can be less goofy and playful and will go into heat approximately every eight to 14 months if they're not spayed. (We'll talk more about how spaying and neutering can impact many of these traits in Chapter 15.) Basically, gender is the last stop before you put in your application on a dog, and it comes down to personal preference more than anything else. I got my first male dog 11 years ago after having only female dogs previously. Jake has personality, that's

for sure, but I suspect it's more because he was genetically born with it than because he's a male.

One Puppy or Two?

Although those of us in rescue often advise adopters to get two kittens, we never suggest two puppies. That can be a formula for disaster. We used to think that two puppies would bond with each other and not their human. That's not really true. However, it is true that two puppies can bond so closely that they might become stressed or even suffer from anxiety if you separate them. Also, the puppy with the stronger personality can bully the more submissive puppy (which could happen between two dogs even if they aren't puppies). More likely, two puppies will egg each other on and

KITTEN OR ADULT?

The biggest benefit to adopting an adult cat over a kitten is personality: What you see is what you get. A kitten's true personality might be anything but what his adolescence indicates. That kitten who is careening around your house batting a toy mouse might become a sedate adult who excels at curling up on the windowsill and almost never plays with the feathered sticks you bought at your pet store last month. Don't get me wrong; kittens are the most hilarious creatures in the world. But if you want a sure thing regarding personality, get an adult cat. The other advantage? Lots of adult cats are sitting in animal shelters, just waiting for someone to take them home. Help us help them.

get into 10 times more trouble together. Regardless, the math is irrefutable: Two puppies with unique personalities equal two different socialization and training plans—in other words, twice the work for you. One last thing to think about is that two puppies at the same time means you will have two seniors at the same time in about 10 to 15 years—that's twice the medical bills and twice the senior dog incontinence, not to mention the pain of losing two beloved dogs within a short time frame.

In short, I'm worried that you won't want two puppies if you try to raise two puppies at the same time. Trust me. Kittens take work just like puppies do and have their own critical socialization periods just like puppies (up to about four months). But two kittens really take the same amount of work as one kitten—maybe even less since they entertain each other. But two puppies take approximately the same amount of work as 16 puppies. At least you'll feel that way. If you must have two, wait at least six months until your first puppy is a bit older and wiser, or at least housetrained. The height of adolescent behavior challenges is 6 to 18 months of age, so you might want to wait until you're through that before stepping back into the ring.

WHAT TO LOOK FOR IN A CAT

Looking for a cat can be very different from looking for a dog. For starters, everyone who's ever fallen in love with a cat knows that cats pick us, not the other way around. It just works better that way. Should you wish to exercise your own free will in choosing a cat, start with the superficial and then go deeper. What look do you want? Longhaired or short? What color do you like? Follow that with personality. You might glimpse some of this in a shelter environment, but the cat you bring home might not show you her true colors until she's comfortable in her new realm, I mean home. Some breed considerations might come into play (see below), but when it comes to cats, looks and personality are your biggest variables.

The sad fact is that there is no shortage of cats in shelters; in fact, feline homelessness is one of the biggest challenges facing animal welfare today. Part of that is because there are just so many unaltered cats and too many outdoor cats with access to other unaltered cats. The result? Many cats relinquished to shelters and not enough people adopting them.

Purebred or Mix?

Unless you've always been in love with a particular breed like a Persian, Siamese, or ragdoll, chances are that you'll end up at a shelter in your search for a new kitten or cat. Although you might find purebred cats in need of rescue, the vast majority are mixed breeds. The main differentiator to concentrate on is not the breed of the cat necessarily, but the amount of cat. In other words, decide how much fur you want. Generally, cats come in long-haired and short-haired versions. There are also no-haired cats like the sphynx and various rexes as well as other exotic cats, but most of us end up with a simple choice between domestic shorthair (DSH) and domestic longhair (DLH), which are by far the most common cats you will find—so much so that we call them by these descriptions as though they were actual breeds. You might also find cats with hair that's sort of in between short and long, and we throw caution to the wind and call those domestic medium-hairs (DMH).

Personality

Like dogs, personality is the most important characteristic of any cat or kitten. Cats have been living with humans for far less time than dogs

Ask DR. GARY:

Should I Get One Kitten or Two?

At the San Diego Humane Society, we have a full-scale, 24-hour kitten nursery up and running from March to November every year. You can't not like cats when you see a hundred ridiculously cute kittens playing (or terrorizing) each other in their exercise pens all day. It's a marvelous sight. The only adoption requirement is that you have to adopt two of them. And why wouldn't you? Two kittens are three times more fun than one, and they're self-entertaining with half the work. You'll never regret two kittens, and you'll never have the opportunity to get another cat that's as bonded to your own cat as you will when you get them together. One chance, so don't blow it: Get two kittens.

(maybe 9,500 years compared with about 15,000 for dogs), so in many ways, cats are not as domesticated. This is exactly what makes them so appealing to many of us. It also drives their personalities. Many cats keep their distance from even the ones they love, preferring to be admired from afar like a fine art piece. Others are truly lap cats and will follow you around tirelessly ready to literally collapse on your lap unrelentingly (or computer keyboard or newspaper as long as you're trying to read it). Pick the personality that you want. You might luck out and end up with a cat who actually accommodates you.

Coat Type

Remember when I said you have only one decision: how much cat, or fur, you want? An obvious

follow-up to that question is whether you want to groom your cat. This is not a hard one. The longer a cat's fur is, the finer the grade. The finer the fur, the more you have to do to it, which means grooming. When fine-coated, long-haired cats are not groomed, they mat, and a matted cat is not a happy cat. If you want a long-haired cat, plan on thoroughly brushing or combing her anywhere from daily to a few times a week. Most long-haired cats also need a good bath at least twice a year. You can certainly do this yourself, but that's not for the faint of heart. There's a reason domestic short-haired cats are the most common: They're also the easiest, at least from a coat perspective.

Color

I met a wonderful cat lover recently who only looked for black cats to adopt. She had absolutely no interest in having a cat of a particular color. Mostly, that was because she knew that black cats have a harder time getting adopted than cats with other colors.

If you don't have a cat or claim you don't like cats, you might think that most cats look alike. They don't. All cats have distinguishing colors (except my friend's black cats). And most people who love cats love a particular color, whether white, black, gray, orange, or combinations of all four. Does color matter? In this case, it does. Colors seem to be linked to personality traits in cats. Not invariably, but in enough cases that we can guide people to a particular personality using color as a starting place. Orange tabbies are often the friendliest of cats, and tortoiseshells are, well, let's just say confident and headstrong. Interestingly, orange tabbies are nearly always males and calicoes and tortoiseshells are nearly always female. When

Ask **DR. GARY:**

Can I Find a Hypoallergenic Cat?

Devon rex

All cats shed, and you might be allergic to their hair, but the big culprit for cat allergies is that self-grooming shampoo cats use to keep themselves clean: their saliva. Allergies are caused by a protein contained in cats' saliva called Fel d 1. Certain breeds are purported to have less Fel d 1 than others, causing fewer reactions. The Siberian and Balinese, for instance, might cause less sneezing and runny eyes than other cats. Other less allergenic breeds include the Cornish and Devon rexes, Bengal, Oriental shorthair, Russian blue, Siamese, and sphynx. Cat allergies are the most common allergy in people. If you're an allergic cat lover, in time your tolerance may improve. I'd also suggest allergy shots, which did me a world of good through vet school. Of course, for true cat lovers, there are always antihistamines.

exceptions happen, it causes quite the stir in shelters with a celebrity cat. In the end, should color really matter? That's totally up to you. But know which traits land on which colors. When all else fails, go with orange. I've never met an orange tabby who didn't want to be your best friend.

Male or Female?

Should you get a male or female cat? That's totally up to you, but I'll confess I always steer first-time cat adopters to a male cat over a female. Unlike dogs, gender does tend to carry a bit more importance when it comes to a cat's personality. Male cats are usually more gregarious and less "huntery" than females. They're also a bit goofier and even more friendly and outgoing than female cats. Just think back to those old Mutual of Omaha *Wild Kingdom* episodes on the African savanna. Which lions were doing all the work out there? Not the males. The females were all business, doing the hunting and raising the cubs. The males were lounging and taking life easy. Subtract about 690 pounds, and you've got the same situation with our domestic cats. As with anything else, these distinctions won't always hold true, but boy cats are a good bet if you want a lighter-hearted feline pal. ■

CHAPTER 2

Rescue and Adoption

Where, oh where, should you go to get your new companion? I always like to start with a shelter or rescue group since I run a shelter. But there are many other reasons to begin there, including the important fact that we humans have created the problem of pet overpopulation or, more accurately, pet homelessness; so, isn't it up to us to fix it? Shelters and rescues are full of purebred and mixed breeds of all types of animals. Regardless of what kind of animal you want, I believe we should all have a social conscience when deciding where to get a pet. We're all on this planet together, and taking care of it includes the animals we care about.

THE ADOPTION OPTION

We have a lot of homeless animals in this country. According to the ASPCA, an estimated 6.5 million dogs and cats enter U.S. shelters every year. That's a lot of relationships waiting to happen and, more important, a lot of risk for those animals: Approximately 1.5 million of them will be euthanized every year in this country alone.

Even if you must have that tan-and-white Havanese puppy, why not first search your local shelter database for a dog resembling your dream companion? Chances are the pet you desire might be there. Many shelters, mine included, will go on the hunt for that dog, cat, or parrot you're looking for. Even if he or she is not in their adoption database, they may be able to find another shelter or rescue group that has the type of pet you're looking for. It's all part of our common mission to get homeless animals into homes. After all, it works when you're looking for a car, so why not let us do the same thing with your next pet?

If you do happen to strike out with your local shelters, try a breed-specific rescue. If you still can't find what you're looking for, consider a responsible breeder (see Chapter 3). Many reputable breeders also volunteer with breed rescue and might be able to connect you with a homeless purebred.

HOW TO FIND ADOPTABLE PETS ONLINE

Looking for the right pet can be overwhelming, even when you think you know exactly what you want. Adoption websites like Petfinder.com and Adopt-a-Pet.com are great resources to search for

a pet. These sites bring all the available dog and cat "inventory" into one easy-to-navigate resource for people looking for their new best friend. When you search these sites, you will find listings of adoptable animals from both shelters and rescue groups in your area, allowing you to survey all the available pets in your area. From there, you can either visit the pet at the shelter or arrange to meet a pet who is with a rescue group.

These online pet adoption search engines are trustworthy—shelters and rescues sign up for memberships and list their available pets. They are also completely nonprofit sourced, with one notable exception: Adopt-a-Pet, now a Petco partner, has a new service, Rehome, through which private parties can list their own pets for adoption. This is a good thing because there certainly are situations when people can no longer care for their pets and this option allows pets to skip a stay in the shelter completely.

Never rely on resale websites such as Craigslist or classified ads to find an animal. You have no idea of the condition of the animal, the condition of the housing, or the integrity of the seller. Some people post ads for "adoption" but are really breeding and selling animals in an unethical manner. Besides delivering an unhealthy animal, an unethical seller can do considerable amount of damage to the species they are breeding.

Of course, it's perfectly acceptable, and a great idea, to use the internet to research a pet. You can read about the many breeds and mixes, and find out what pet owners feel are the positives and negatives of particular breeds.

MODERN SHELTERS—NOT THE "POUND" ANYMORE!

There are many animal shelters, and they are not all the same, so it can be confusing. Basically, there are two types of shelters: public (government run) and private. The differences can be nonexistent or substantial. Most government jurisdictions have certain public responsibilities, including animal control, an old term that has largely been replaced with the term *animal services*. Modern shelters can perform some to all aspects of animal care and protection, including licensing and enforcement, lost-and-found services, behavior and training, education, and veterinary care. Check online or in person with your local shelter to discover which services they offer.

When you're looking to adopt a pet, it doesn't matter what type of shelter you go to. Just go. I suggest you get the skinny on which shelters have the greatest stresses or needs in your community and start with one of those shelters. One of the best ways to find this out is to look up your local shelter on Facebook. That's a great resource to see what animals are most in need of adoption, issues your community might be facing in protecting animals, and comments by the shelter's followers.

Today there are approximately 3,500 brick-and-mortar animal shelters in the United States. Some are public, some private. The most success happens when the private shelters help out the public shelters by providing the services beyond which the government requires or by transferring animals over so that they don't run out of resources at the public shelters. This public-private partnership is where true zero-euthanasia communities begin.

I work at a private shelter, the San Diego Humane Society, which offers nearly every service available to animals and people looking for animals. We have multiple campuses and care for about 50,000 animals a year. We don't do this alone, however. Good animal stewardship requires good community

WHY THE TERM "NO KILL" DOES HARM

I'm a fan of saving lives, but I dislike the term "no kill." It causes division by implying that some shelters want to save lives while others don't. Nothing could be further from the truth. To call one shelter a "no-kill" shelter labels another as a "kill" shelter that doesn't want to save lives. That's just wrong. I prefer a term my shelter uses: "getting to zero." It means no healthy or treatable animal will be euthanized at any shelter in our community. We got to zero at the San Diego Humane Society in the early 2000s, then got to zero

for the entire county in 2015 thanks to collaboration with our colleagues at other area shelters. It's a good reminder that the language that binds us is far more effective than that which divides.

WHAT'S IN A NAME?

Lots of shelters use the name *humane society* or *SPCA,* but there's no affiliation from one to another. Nor is there an affiliation with national organizations like the Humane Society of the United States in Washington, D.C. (HSUS) or the American Society for the Prevention of Cruelty to Animals (ASPCA) in New York City. Both groups do operate facilities of their own, however. HSUS operates a large animal sanctuary in Texas and several wildlife care centers across the country. The ASPCA operates an animal shelter in Manhattan and a renowned spay/neuter center, the Humane Alliance in Asheville, North Carolina. Like *Xerox* and *Kleenex,* the terms *humane society* and *SPCA* have simply become synonymous with animal shelters. We work together in a common mission, but we're all separate.

collaboration; we have strong partnerships with six other animal shelters, including four government shelters. It's a perfect marriage, if there is such a thing, because we're together for one reason: to help each other save lives, and that is exactly what happens. Moving animals between shelters allows for the best use of resources and the best services for the public. It's a great partnership.

A VISIT TO THE SHELTER

If you haven't visited an animal shelter before or haven't visited one in a long time, you might not know what to expect. Hint: It's not all sadness—

quite the opposite most of the time! When you arrive, first try to meet some of the staff. In progressive animal shelters, you're adopting more than just an animal. You're adopting the adoption counselors, veterinarians, and support staff too. In the best shelters (which thankfully are becoming more common), this is for life—all the support you want as long as you want it.

Request a tour of the shelter. I'm all about education, so if a shelter won't take time with you or show you around, that says a lot about what you might expect once you adopt an animal from that facility. Remember that this is a long-term relationship for both you and your new pet, but also for you and the shelter you adopt from. I'm not a fan of secrets, so any facility that is off-limits to the public is not one I'd want to patronize. Granted, it's all about the animals, which makes it doubly hard if the humans working there don't make it easy or pleasant to adopt them. If you should run into this scenario, ask to speak to a manager. Believe me, everyone working at a shelter wants the experience to be as positive as possible.

ADOPTION COUNSELORS

Think of a shelter adoption counselor as a hotel concierge. A good concierge will set you up with the best dinner in town and tickets to the hottest show. That's what a good adoption counselor will do for you. Consider the counselor your partner in your search for a pet. A short interview about your hopes and dreams for your pet will lead to the best matchmaking service you'll ever have. Unfortunately, many animal shelters barely have enough staff to take care of the animals, never mind adoption specialists. Still, all shelters have staff, and they know their animals best. Do some breed research at home and create your wish list before you walk in. Knowledge is power.

Here's what to look for in a good shelter: a clean visual and olfactory impression as you walk in, open and friendly staff, and animals who seem relatively calm and well cared for. In San Diego, we adopt out about 40,000 animals a year. I often talk to people who are afraid to come into the shelter because they think it's a sad place and too difficult to see the animals waiting to go home. Actually, this is exactly the experience we make sure adopters don't have. Instead, we want people to see hope and joy and beauty in their animal shelter. I tell people we want to make sure our "guests" have an enjoyable day looking for their new best friend.

Note how customer friendly the employees are, and ask about the shelter's return policy. That's right: I encourage people to ask about a return policy. It's better to adopt and realize that a particular animal doesn't fit in with you and your family than not to adopt at all. That's not a failure in any sense of the word: The animal gets a break from the shelter, you've learned more about what you want, and we learn much more about how that pet behaved in a real home.

A few years ago, I realized that I would never want to adopt an animal without doing a test drive at home. That means that all my housemates—human and animal—get an opinion in whether that dog or cat fits in with the pack. And vice versa because an unhappy new pet equals an unhappy new pet owner and pack. After all, it's not just about me. It's also about what the new animal needs, which might not be my house full of crazy dogs. That was realization number one.

Realization number two was that adopters really don't get this luxury. You take a gamble with every animal you take home. Sure, you can always return an animal, but that's not as easy as it sounds. There is often a stigma to doing this, with a lot of disappointed expressions from the shelter staff, not to mention your broken heart.

At the San Diego Humane Society, we have an "adoption guarantee." If your new pet is not absolutely perfect for you and your family, bring him

back, and we'll make it right: no judgment, attitude, or scorn, and full refund (you can donate the fee back if you want). Better yet, we'll find you a different pet, having learned a little more about what you need. We only ask that you tell us everything you learned about that animal because it helps us place him later. A pet is a long-term commitment, so you should know what you're committing to. Our pets will thrive in the right home (and so will you), but they'll languish in the wrong ones. We want to do whatever possible to ensure the former and avoid the latter.

RESCUE GROUPS

Rescue groups are different from animal shelters in that they don't generally have facilities to house their animals. Instead, most rescue groups rely on volunteer foster families to house and care for their animals. That's a great thing; you'll get tons of information from someone already living with that pet—even more than you might get at an animal shelter.

There are many different types of rescue groups, including single-breed rescue (which focus on just one breed, like Labrador retrievers or Persian cats), small-dog rescue, cat-only rescue, senior pet rescue, and more. Adopting from a rescue is a little different from going to a shelter. Rescues are staffed entirely by volunteers and usually have no office to check in with. They help their local shelters by taking animals from the shelters to adopt them out through their network of foster homes. They're a godsend. Without rescue groups, shelters would be even more crowded than they are. Whether you adopt through a shelter or rescue, you're helping the same animals and saving a life.

If you adopt through a rescue, you'll either meet the pet at an arranged meeting place or visit during an adoption event, which are often

RESCUE A RABBIT

Rabbits are the third most popular pet after dogs and cats in the United States. According to the American Pet Products Association, there are approximately three million pet rabbits living in about two million U.S. households. Bunnies make incredible pets, and there are plenty of them in shelters. At the San Diego Humane Society, we usually have at least 100 rabbits available for adoption at any given time. Most rabbits end up in shelters because people don't know how to care for them. Once you understand that you can't just plop them in a cage and call it a day, rabbits are intelligent, trainable, and adorable. To learn everything you need to know about rabbit care, visit House Rabbit Society: *rabbit.org*.

held at pet supply stores. If the meeting goes well and you decide to adopt, you can often take your new pet home that day.

ADOPTION APPLICATIONS AND POLICIES

After meeting the new love of your life, you'll need to fill out an adoption application, which will be specific to the shelter or rescue you select. It could range from listing contact information to full disclosures about other pets, family members, your veterinarian, and what might feel like a full college admissions essay. At my shelter, we ask for contact information, and everything else is a conversation. We think this conversational approach is the best way to make a perfect match for both adopter and pet.

Before adoption, pets are usually examined and treated by a veterinarian, updated on vaccines and dewormers, spayed or neutered, microchipped, and possibly even licensed—all for somewhere between $10 and a few hundred dollars. That's a great deal when you consider that, on average, every animal costs the shelter somewhere between $500 and $1,000 to care for.

ADOPTION PROCESS: OPEN ADOPTIONS

Today, progressive shelters embrace *open adoptions,* which remove most barriers to adoption. An open adoption process is interactive and educational rather than an interrogation. In the past, an adopter might have had to jump through a lot of hoops like providing a letter from their landlord with permission to adopt an animal, handing over previous veterinary records, and scheduling a home visit. Heaven forbid they had a full-time job. The assumption was that we needed to protect animals from the public. With more than 1.5 million homeless animals euthanized every year, we were actually protecting animals to death.

Modern shelters have now realized that there's no point to these barriers. But although this is less

NOT QUITE READY TO ADOPT? FOSTER INSTEAD

If you're not entirely sure you're ready to adopt, fostering a pet is a great way to test-drive the idea. And, yes, we do know it can backfire if you find you can't part with your foster. Unquestionably, the best animal to adopt is the one you already have in your home. You've already cared for that dog or cat, know some of his behaviors, and probably have already fallen in love. Although we lightheartedly call these "foster failures," they're anything but. These animals have already proved they fit into your home and life, and you into theirs. It's a match made in heaven by the angel who fosters.

common than it was a decade ago, it still happens. If you find yourself in the position of being judged and denied as an adopter, let the management know about your experience. That might help the shelter develop more modern protocols. Don't become jaded. Find another shelter or a rescue group. Thankfully, that old process is changing as we all figure out that it does no good to prevent more adoptions than we allow.

When you're with the adoption counselor, have an honest conversation. This will allow the shelter to better find the right match for you. Evaluate the shelter or rescue on the basis of its knowledge of its animals and willingness to offer you helpful advice. Hold them to a high standard of courtesy. A bad adoption experience hurts everyone. Fortunately, these days, that's the rare exception. ■

ADOPT A SENIOR PET

The rescuer-of-the-year award goes to anyone who adopts a senior pet. Nothing is sadder than seeing senior animals in shelters grieving the end of the life they knew. Some of these angels might have medical or behavior issues, but don't let that deter you. Many people adopt senior pets repeatedly because the rewards are so great. Some shelters and senior dog rescues waive adoption fees or even offer financial assistance if you adopt a senior pet who requires medication or ongoing treatment for medical issues. It's true that you'll have less time with a senior pet than a puppy, but for that pet, that extra amount of time is priceless.

CHAPTER 3

Purebred Dogs and Cats

Every era has a celebrity dog breed — a dog that's received renewed attention from the public. Rin Tin Tin was the perfect "spokesdog" for purebred German shepherds in the 1920s. In the 1950s, everyone wanted a long-haired collie just like Lassie, whose name became eponymous with that breed. In the 1990s, no handbag was complete without a Chihuahua, and by the turn of this century, it was all about Labs even though Marley was, let's just say, a challenging dog.

For whatever reason, people fall in love with keeshonden and Maltese, golden retrievers and Portuguese water dogs. With cats, we seem to be far less susceptible to such manipulation, yet Himalayan lovers would never even think about bringing home a "regular" cat. Some of the magic of purebred dogs and cats is their unique genetic morphology. They come in different sizes, look completely unique, have different coat types, and behave differently. Some even have different life spans. Whatever your pet preferences, there's a breed for everyone.

CHOOSE YOUR DOG BREED

Deciding on the right breed for you can be overwhelming, so I'll try to make it easier. The American Kennel Club groups purebred dogs into seven categories according to the original jobs the breeds were created to do: Herding, Hound, Non-Sporting, Sporting, Terrier, Toy, and Working. You'll find similarities among breeds within the same group, so it can be fun to explore related breeds when trying to determine what type of dog you are drawn to. To learn about the different groups and the breeds in each, visit *akc.org*.

Herding

These breeds were developed to—you guessed it—herd! The instinct to herd is very ingrained in many of these dogs. Most love to herd (and not just livestock; they may chase and nip at your other animals and even kids too). Herding dogs need to work—to be exercised and mentally challenged to thrive. They have a ton of energy and make great running or hiking partners. Dog sports like agility can provide the physical and mental challenges they need. Some popular herding breeds are Australian shepherds, collies, Ger-

man shepherds, old English sheepdogs, Pembroke Welsh corgis, and Shetland sheepdogs. Learn as much as you can about them before looking for one. Some herding breeds can be a bit too intense for your average dog lover (the incredibly intelligent border collie comes to mind!).

Hound

One thing you should know about these dogs is that they absolutely love to bark. And howl. A lot! Bred to hunt and chase, hounds have incredible stamina. During the hunt, they bark at their prey, but at dinnertime, their bark might be more about how quickly you put their food down. Many hounds are surprisingly accomplished shedders and can become a little too obsessed with using those great sniffers to check out everything that makes its way to the ground in front of them. But if you can get past their charming exuberance, hounds make wonderful family pets. They historically lived and hunted in large packs, so they are generally quite friendly with other dogs and people, too. Hounds are classified into two types: scent hounds (bred to track and hunt using their exceptional sense of smell) and sight hounds (which hunt using their excellent

Pembroke Welsh corgi

Scottish terrier

eyesight). Some popular scent hound breeds are basset hounds, beagles, and bloodhounds. Well-known sight hounds include Afghan hounds, greyhounds, and whippets.

Non-Sporting

This group is a bit of a catchall for breeds that don't fit precisely into other categories. The non-sporting breeds are as individually different as the other groups are from each other (and some actually do have sporting backgrounds, such as the standard poodle, which was originally a water retriever). You will find great diversity among the breeds in this group, including bichons frises, Boston terriers, Dalmatians, French bulldogs, miniature and standard poodles, and shiba inus.

Sporting

These dogs were created to work seamlessly alongside people as they hunted for birds. They are some of the most loyal and trainable breeds and typically make excellent family dogs. Sporting breeds are energetic companions requiring lots of exercise. Breeds in this group include retrievers, spaniels, and setters, and each is slightly different in terms of shape, size, and personality. Some of the most popular breeds in any home include this category: golden retrievers, Labrador retrievers, cocker spaniels, English springer spaniels, English setters, and Irish setters.

Terrier

Terriers love to dig, and they can be can be tough as nails personality wise. Most terriers are never going to be best friends with your beloved cat. They were bred to hunt and kill rodents like mice and rats, so they are tenacious and feisty, with energy to spare. They are also endlessly entertaining and always up for adventure. This incredibly diverse group includes American Staffordshire terriers, bull terriers, cairn terriers, miniature schnauzers, Scottish terriers, and West Highland white terriers.

Toy

These breeds were created for one reason alone: to be pampered and beloved companions or, as the AKC puts it, simply to "embody sheer delight." Expect them to want to be held. Some toy breeds like the tiny Chihuahua and Yorkshire terrier love to be in charge (and think they are quite a bit bigger than they really are!), while others are more docile. Many toys breeds are delicate and aren't usually recommended for families with kids under the age of five. Some popular toy breeds include Cavalier King Charles spaniels, Maltese, and pugs.

Working

This group contains breeds that were created to perform serious jobs, including pulling heavy carts loaded with goods to market, guarding flocks of livestock from thieves and predators, rescuing people from water or avalanches, and protecting the family farm. You won't be able to "fire" them if you don't like the job they were bred for. They're great companions, but many are very large and extremely strong dogs. Some working breeds should be left to experienced dog owners only. Others are great family dogs. Some popular working breeds are Akitas, Bernese mountain dogs, boxers, Doberman pinschers, great Pyrenees, and Portuguese water dogs.

Narrowing Down Your Breed List

Consider a breed that matches your own personality. Look at disposition, coat type, activity level, and size. If you want an exercise companion, steer clear of the brachycephalic breeds (those with "pushed-in" faces like the pug, bulldog, and Pekingese). And you will need something with legs a little longer than those of a dachshund. If this is your first dog, don't go for a strong guard dog breed like the Doberman pinscher, Tibetan mastiff, or even the Akita, which need expert handling, or at least previous experience.

Learn as much about your prospective new breed as possible. Go to your local dog park to talk to other owners of that breed, check out breed

PUTTING THEM TO WORK

If you're looking for a serious working dog to help manage livestock on your farm or guard your large property, search for a knowledgeable breeder or breed-specific rescue group to help you every step of the way, from affirming that the breed is the right choice for the work, to choosing the best puppy for your needs and environment, and helping you with training, socialization, and even nutrition for your working dog. If it's your first time with a certain working breed, the breeder will probably ask lots of questions about your readiness. Welcome her queries, and take the opportunity to learn. Raising and training a working breed can be a challenge, but one with great rewards.

Border collie at work

forums online, and maybe even visit a local AKC dog show. Dog shows are great fun and a wonderful place to meet local breeders. You can see beautiful examples of many different breeds and at some larger shows they even have special Meet the Breeds booths where you can pet and interact with dogs of every breed imaginable. When attending a dog show, remember one very important rule: Don't touch any dogs without first asking permission. Show dogs are impeccably groomed before going

THE PROBLEM WITH RARE COLORS AND SIZES

Humans get bored. We have a knack for wanting the unusual. Breeding "off standard," as it's called, is a bad idea. Why is going for a nonstandard color or size a problem? Because the process of breeding for such attributes usually jeopardizes other standard traits, most importantly health. For instance, breeding for rare colors not usually found in the breed can introduce genetically linked diseases. Unscrupulous breeders charge more for puppies with these rare traits, even if they might be unhealthy. Responsible breeders care more about the health and vitality of their breed than your checkbook. Don't look for a breeder who advertises rare colors. If you want a truly unique dog, try your local shelter.

into the ring. You don't want to mess up any of that hard work. If you see someone with a breed you're interested in, by all means approach that person and introduce yourself. If the breeder or handler is busy getting her dog ready to show, ask for a business card or a good time to come back later to talk.

A Word About Designer Dogs

It's interesting to me that Labradoodle owners often refer to their dogs as "purebred." That designation is truly impossible since by definition, these dogs are the result of a crossbreeding of a Labrador retriever and a poodle. It's no different from any other mixed breed except that it has a specific name. There are many designer breeds, most involving poodles because of their great temperaments, high intelligence, and low allergic quotient (with traits like that, it's interesting that more people don't just get poodles). We've seen many of these over the years from cockapoos to Lhasapoos to goldendoodles. They can be great dogs, but they're truly mixes—mutts by definition.

Even more interesting to me is the fact that the creator of the Labradoodle, Australian dog breeder Wally Conron, expressed regret on creating the mix in the 1980s as the result of a request for a guide dog who didn't shed. In an interview published in *Psychology Today,* Conron said that ironically, no one would buy the dogs from that first litter of crossbred poodles and Labs because they wanted purebred dogs. Clever marketing rebranded the dogs as a new breed: the Labradoodle. It was nothing more than a gimmick, but the gimmick worked.

Today the Labradoodle is one of the most sought-after dog mixes in the world. Because they are hybrids, their characteristics are not consistent from one dog to the next. This can be seen in

Ask **DR. GARY:**

What Is Health Testing?

Never buy a purebred animal from any breeder who doesn't do health testing. Responsible breeders want to ensure their offspring are protected from genetic health issues specific to that breed. German shepherds are bred to minimize dysplastic hips, cocker spaniels to avoid the tragedy of early-age blindness, and Scottish terriers to avoid blood clotting issues. In the cat world, good breeders of Maine coon cats test for hypertrophic cardiomyopathy. These specialized health tests are performed on adult breeding animals before they're bred. Ask the breeder to provide copies of the parents' test results. For dogs, tests for each breed are listed on the AKC website (visit *akc.org/dog-breeders* and search "health testing requirements"). For cats, check out the University of California, Davis feline genetic testing service (*vgl.ucdavis .edu/services/cat*).

the wildly different appearance of many Labradoodles. Some truly have nonshedding coats, but some do not. Today, Conron laments that he opened up Pandora's box, as he calls it, and now there are thousands of breeders mixing poodles with every breed imaginable, all in the quest for profit and often at the expense of the original breed's integrity. This is misleading to the public, many of whom actually find out that their hypoallergenic dog isn't hypoallergenic at all.

CHOOSE YOUR CAT BREED

Although cats might exhibit less polymorphism than dogs, they are not a one-size-fits-all animal in any way. Cat lovers certainly have their pref-

erences too. I know a wonderful couple who supports my shelter and have always had Cornish rex cats and they always will. Whether you love these unique, personable, and nearly hairless cats like they do or want to curl up next to the mound of soft-as-butter fur that is the Burmese, cats certainly have unique characteristics in both physical appearance and behavior. Ragdolls love to be held, Abyssinians much less so. Himalayans can be aloof, and Siamese love to play—as long as it's with their one selected human. Bengals look like miniature versions of the great cats of the wild. People who have had Munchkins won't go for another type once they discover this charming dwarf breed. Scottish folds have ears that lie flat and forward on their heads, making them look like little owls. No matter your preference, there's probably a cat that can fulfill your wish list. The only caution you really need is to find a responsible breeder or rescue to get your purebred cat. If that's not in the plans, check out your local shelter where, if you're lucky, you just might find one.

Should you decide on a specific breed, make sure you know as much as possible about that cat. Consider not only that breed's looks but also general characteristics about its personality, activity level, and, of course, coat type. If you don't want to ever see a groomer or wield a brush during your cat's lifetime, steer clear of the Persian and Himalayan. If you prefer a cat that is seen and not heard, avoid the Siamese, which is one of the loudest and most talkative breeds.

Talk to your breeder and other cat owners to find out what they like about the breed, as well as the pitfalls they've discovered with their cats. You can even explore online communities where you can chat with owners of the breeds you're looking at to hear their firsthand experiences and opinions.

Finally, if you can, attend a local cat show to learn about the breeds you're interested in. Cat shows are very laid-back and lots of fun. They are also an excellent place to find local cat breeders. The judges talk to the audience as they examine each cat, sharing information about the breed and pointing out the good qualities in the cat they are judging. Breeders are usually happy to talk to the public, so if you see a breed you're interested in, don't be shy to approach the breeder and ask for some information. They love their work, and no one knows more about their cats.

This might seem like a lot of work, but it will be worth it. Otherwise do what I do and go for the domestic shorthair, which are in plentiful supply at your local shelter. Although not as exotic as the hairless sphynx, domestic shorthairs come in a variety of colors and temperaments and, as we all know, every cat is unique.

CAT REGISTRIES

In North America, three major organizations register pedigreed cats: the Canadian Cat Association, the Cat Fanciers' Association (CFA), and The International Cat Association (TICA). These groups offer public education programs and sanction cat conformation shows, where judges examine the cats to determine their breeding suitability. CFA also puts on cat agility shows (yes, this is a real thing!). Cat shows are open to the public and are a great way to meet many cats of various breeds.

BREEDERS

Even though I run an animal shelter, it doesn't mean I believe that people should only go to a shelter to get a new dog or cat, or bunny or iguana for that matter. I know that people sometimes want a specific purebred that we might not have in a shelter or have in limited supply. Many shelters often have purebreds, but depending on where you live and which breed you're looking for, it could take a long time to find what you

HYBRID CAT BREEDS

There is something about the wildness of hybrid cats that appeals to people who love cats. You can't have a lion or tiger as a pet, but you can have an Asian leopard cat crossed with a domestic shorthair to create the Bengal cat. The Bengal itself has been crossed with other cats to create additional hybrids like the Serengeti and the toyger. The Savannah was created by crossing an African serval with a domestic shorthair. Hybrid cats can be tricky, though. You don't want the first generation (F1). It takes several generations to have a domesticated cat who is safe and enjoyable to live with. When buying a kitten, look for a generation F3 or higher on the pedigree.

Bengal

want. For instance, let's say you live in Southern California and want a Chihuahua. Great news! Southern California shelters are typically filled with Chihuahuas. But if you're looking for a Havanese puppy or a Persian cat, you're probably not going to find those breeds at a typical animal shelter, at least not right away. Remember that the primary purpose of animal shelters is not to be an adoption store but to protect and save homeless animals. That entirely depends on which animals need protecting and saving at any given time. If you want a purebred and can't find one through a shelter or rescue group, your next option should be a responsible breeder.

A good, responsible breeder cares deeply about his or her breeding stock and their offspring, is up to date on the latest medical and behavioral issues concerning that breed, will responsibly manage and try to elimi-

nate congenital issues, and will stand behind the sale of that animal for its life. Reputable breeders are committed, talented, and caring individuals who are devoted to their breed. A good breeder will help you every step of the way. Of course, there are also some not-so-great breeders and unfortunately, even downright terrible ones. A bit of research will help you weed out the great from the not-so-great.

Havanese puppies

Golden retrievers

Finding a Dog Breeder

So, how do you find a great breeder, and what should you look for? The best way to track down a reputable breeder is to contact the breed's national club. Every breed has a club, whose members are devoted to protecting and maintaining the breed for future generations. Club members are usually dog breeders, dog handlers, and breed judges. Most clubs also have a breeder referral service. Simply call or email, and ask for referrals to member breeders in your area. To find the national club for your breed, do an internet search for the breed name and "club" or "association." For instance, searching "Golden Retriever Club" will bring you

Boxer

to the Golden Retriever Club of America and "Boxer Club" will get you the American Boxer Club. In addition, the American Kennel Club publishes a list of breed clubs and breeder referral contacts on its website.

If you go the breeder route, go local if possible. Get to really know your breeder through interviews and visits, and ask to see the dam (mom) and the sire (dad). Don't be surprised if the sire is not on the premises because great breeders match their dogs with the best dogs possible; they don't just breed their own two dogs over and over. The ideal male might be owned by another breeder across the country.

You might not be able to find a great breeder in your city or even state, especially if you're looking for a rare breed. What if the breeder is in Oregon and you're in New York? Plan on going to Oregon to pick up that puppy yourself. You want to meet your breeder in person, see where her animals live, and meet the puppy's parents. Get to know where your companion came from and develop a strong relationship with your breeder just in case you need her later. If you need another reason to bring back that puppy or kitten yourself, consider this: Chances are you paid a premium for that animal, but even more important, this trip will be the first one your new pet has ever made. Don't you want to be there? After all, you're not just ordering a tent from a camping store.

During your breeder search, interview potential breeders via Skype or FaceTime or whatever technology you're comfortable with, even if it's just over the phone. Any good breeder will love to talk to you about his or her beloved breed and dogs. And the best ones will keep their puppies until at least eight to 12 weeks so they can learn from each other and even get a jump on basic manners training. Get a gut feeling level of comfort on that first call. If you don't feel good about a particular breeder, you're probably going to have a difficult time communicating a problem after you've purchased that dog.

Make no commitments until you see the papers on the parents to make sure the animals are truly purebred. There are a lot of registries out there, but many of them are junk registries: Documentation from them means nothing other than the breeder paid a fee to get "papers." For most breeds, the only papers with real meaning are from the American Kennel Club (AKC), the United Kennel Club (UKC), or the Canadian Kennel Club (CKC).

At the end of the day, papers hold little meaning if the dogs are not happy, healthy, and well cared for. I'm more concerned about the actual, visible status of the breeding facility and animals. Is it clean and organized? How happy and healthy do the animals look? Are they kept in run-down conditions, or do they live in the home where they're treated like family members? This all comes back to one main point: Find a breeder who shares your standards and values, and when you do, meet her in person. You won't regret this.

WHAT IS THE AMERICAN KENNEL CLUB?

The AKC is a national organization that recognizes and registers purebred dogs. It also sanctions conformation dog shows, during which judges evaluate dogs for their potential breeding value. Not a "purebred-only" organization, the AKC also offers a puppy training certification course (AKC STAR Puppy), a therapy dog program, and a wide variety of sports and activities for both purebred and mixed-breed dogs, including agility, earthdog, which tests the hunting prowess of terriers and dachshunds, field events, herding, lure coursing, obedience, tracking, and more. One thing the AKC is not, however, is a certifying organization for the welfare of animals. That's the role of veterinary or animal welfare organizations. To learn more, visit *akc.org*.

RESPONSIBLE BREEDERS

When searching for a responsible breeder, look for someone who:

- breeds only two or three litters a year;
- owns a reasonable number of animals;
- has a clean home;
- provides pedigrees for her animals;
- can produce veterinary records, including recommended health tests on the parents before breeding;
- offers a health and a return guarantee;
- requires you to spay or neuter your pet if you won't be showing him; and
- shows or enters her animals in other competitions.

A bad breeder is someone who:

- doesn't fit the descriptions opposite;
- has different breeds or "unique" colors or sizes;
- allows you to take home an animal younger than eight weeks old;
- doesn't know the breed well;
- doesn't ask many questions (good breeders care where their animals go);
- doesn't let you visit or tour; and/or
- sells animals over the internet sight unseen.

If you're concerned a breeder is violating animal welfare laws, contact local animal services.

Finding a Cat Breeder

Like good dog breeders, pedigreed cat breeders care about their cats and kittens and want to find the best homes for them. Pedigreed cats will be registered with the Cat Fanciers' Association (CFA), The International Cat Association (TICA), or the Canadian Cat Association (CCA). These organizations offer breeder referrals through their websites, which can be invaluable. You still need to do your research, visit your breeder in person, and go local if you can. There is nothing like meeting a breeder face to face and seeing her home and animals for yourself.

THE FINE PRINT

Once you've decided to buy a purebred puppy or kitten, you might feel as though you're signing as much paperwork as you do for a new home. Don't let this bother you; it's a good thing that protects both you and your breeder. At the very least, a solid contract shows a concern by that breeder for the health and well-being of her animals. On top of that, a contract clearly outlines mutually agreed-on expectations by both the seller and buyer, with the main objective being the health and welfare of the animal.

Good contracts require consent to provide humane care and conditions for the animal, including access to fresh food and water, no chaining or living outside, and never permitting the animal to roam about unattended. Contracts might also require your new pet to be spayed or neutered and microchipped (if this was not already done by the breeder) and will spell out any health guarantees on the part of the breeder.

These are all good things. Responsible breeders want to maintain the standards of their lines and do not want to contribute to pet overpopulation by allowing their puppies or kittens to reproduce. The spay or neutering requirement in the contract ensures that their animals will not be used for breeding purposes. Show-quality animals are another story, but if you wish to show and possibly breed your puppy or kitten, you will have an entirely different contract with your breeder, who will likely be acting as your mentor.

Great breeders will provide a health guarantee for their animals for a certain period of time. Make sure you understand exactly what is (and isn't) covered under your breeder's health guarantee, as well as how the guarantee will be fulfilled if the puppy or kitten develops a covered disease. Some breeders will refund the purchase price but ask you to return the puppy or kitten. Others will give you a refund and allow you to keep your pet. Some will offer a replacement puppy or kitten, either allowing you to keep the sick pet or asking you to return it. Some breeders will even pay for medical treatment for your puppy or kitten. The very best breeders will always want to know how their animal is doing, even after the guarantee period has elapsed.

Return Clauses

Some contracts have clauses that state that you must return the animal to the breeder if you have any issues or concerns that require you to relinquish him. The best breeders care enough for their animals to want them back if you have any problems with them. They don't want the animals they brought into the world to end up on the street or in a shelter. Good breeders will get to know you and will keep in touch for the life of your pet. Some even send holiday and birthday cards. The important thing to know is that these people genuinely care about their breed, enjoy the challenge of continuously improving that breed, and really adore their animals. The best ones feel responsible for the life they literally created, so this offer stands for the lifetime of that pet. If you happen upon a breeder who doesn't do this, find someone else.

A WORD ABOUT PET STORES

I'll make this easy: Don't ever buy a pet from a pet store. Most, if not all, puppies sold in pet stores come from commercial breeding facilities, largely located in Missouri, Pennsylvania, Ohio, and New York. Often referred to as puppy mills, these are horrifying commercial farms where dogs and sometimes cats are bred over and over, never leaving a tiny, filthy cage and with little to no human interaction or even veterinary care. It's time for these institutions to go away. With more than 200 cities, and two states (California and Maryland and more on the way) in North America passing bans against selling puppies and cats (and sometimes rabbits) in pet stores over the past 10 years, that day might be near.

If, despite this advice, you do go to a pet store, ask to see the originating bill of lading on that puppy. If it's from Missouri, Pennsylvania, Ohio, or New York, chances are that pup came from a puppy mill. If you ask where the puppies come from, you often won't get a straight answer. In fact, most pet stores will specifically tell you that their puppies don't come from a puppy mill but instead come from local breeders. Rarely is this true. Local, small-scale, conscientious breeders don't sell their animals through pet stores; they personally find responsible owners for their puppies and kittens.

Pet stores offer few means to assist you with that pet once you've left the store, and most stores inadequately address the health and emotional needs of their animals. Their margins are thin, and therefore the care for those animals is even thinner. Many stores that sell puppies don't provide good or consistent veterinary care and little socialization. Don't even think that your new puppy will be housetrained. Puppies sold in pet stores live in cages. They are used to stepping in and lying in their own urine and feces, so they can be even harder to housetrain than usual.

Ask DR. GARY:

When Can My Pet Come Home?

You shouldn't bring your new puppy or kitten home before eight weeks old, the age of weaning for both species. Earlier than that, and they won't have had time to nurse sufficiently or learn the basics of socialization with their mother and siblings. Consequently, they're at risk for certain diseases, as well as some socialization-related behavior issues that could arise from breaking the bond between mother and baby too early. Some breeders prefer to keep their puppies until they are eight to 12 weeks old (especially for toy breeds), and cat breeders often want to keep kittens until they are 12 to 14 weeks old.

One more note of caution about pet stores. Some "sales" contracts from pet stores are actually "lease" agreements, a detail that many buyers are not fully aware of. This happens when people opt to finance the sale of their pet so they can make monthly payments. This lost detail has caused some buyers to discover that after making all the payments, they don't own their puppy outright and instead owe hundreds or even thousands of dollars to complete the sale. Worse yet, the pet store can actually demand your puppy or dog back if they don't want to do prescribed veterinary treatment for your new family member. Such practices should be illegal, and states increasingly are cracking down on this.

Maybe you fell in love with a puppy in the window and just had to "rescue" it. Don't feel bad. It's not that puppy's fault that he ended up there.

But for the future, remember that every puppy you "save" from a pet store keeps that store in business to continue to sell animals born into cruelty. It's as simple as that. When people stop buying puppies in pet stores, puppy mills will go out of business.

There's good news, though. Progressive pet stores, including Petco and PetSmart, are leading the way with a new humane model of "pet sales." Although such stores might unfortunately still sell pocket pets (hamsters, mice, guinea pigs, and rats), fish, and birds, they have stopped selling dogs and cats and often rabbits. Instead, these stores advocate for adoption by hosting events organized by local rescue groups and animal shelters. Such pet stores are part of the solution to end animal homelessness and should be applauded for their leadership. ■

CHAPTER 4

Bringing Your Pet Home

When I brought home my youngest dog, Betty, 10 years ago, I loaded her and all her supplies into my truck, excitedly drove home, parked, and brought her into the house. I went back to the truck, grabbed her new crate, and carried it back to the house to deposit in the living room. That all went as planned. What didn't go so well was what I stepped in when I went back into the house that second time. It didn't matter. That's a new dog for you, and a puppy at that.

My point is that you need patience to start a new relationship. It might be challenging, or even at times upsetting, sleep depriving, and nerve-racking.

Pets are animals, after all. But what relationship isn't worth a little work and patience? Your new relationship will take time to develop—not just how you react to your pet but how she reacts to you. In fact, chances are that your pet's true personality and behavior won't be evident for weeks or even months. But once you go through that initial gauntlet, it will lead to a long-term, no-comparison, beautiful relationship you'll never have wanted to miss.

HOW TO HELP YOUR NEW PET SETTLE IN

You can take some easy steps to help your new pet get acclimated. Consistency is the single most important thing you can provide your new animal. It's not only the easiest way for new pets to learn, it's the easiest way for you to become comfortable with them. Come up with a schedule for feeding, walks, playtime, and training, and stick to it.

Get the essentials out of the way by having everything up and ready before you bring your new dog or cat into the home (read about all of the supplies you'll need in Chapter 5). Would you invite human guests to stay with you and not stock the fridge with their favorite food or make their bed with fresh linens? Set up a crate and bed for your dog in a quiet, safe space. Find a cozy bed or blanket for your new cat, and place it in a quiet room. Stock up on toys, training treats, food, and bowls.

Be organized from day one, and life will be easier for everyone. Oh, and don't vary the routine. You'll thank me for that when you start housetraining.

INTRODUCING EXISTING PETS TO YOUR NEW PET

Whether you're bringing home a new puppy or kitten, cat or dog, hamster or rabbit, you need to introduce the newcomer to your other animals carefully. If it's another dog, you may have already done this at the shelter (or, better yet, tried it at home). In truth, we're a little wary of doing introductions at the shelter because it's such an abnormal environment for both animals. A better way is to do a first meeting on neutral ground for both

GIVE YOUR PET A SAFE SPACE

The most important thing you can do for your new pet is to give him his own safe space. This can be a quiet room, a corner of the den for a dog bed or open door crate, or a cat tree in the living room, preferably underneath a sunbeam. Remember that your pet is getting used to his new human family as much as you're getting used to your new pet. If all goes well, your pet will never want to be in that quiet space without you nearby.

Ask DR. GARY:

My Old Cat Hates My New Cat. What Should I Do?

I take a deep breath when I hear this question, mostly because there is little we can do to rush this relationship. The cats have to work it out themselves — or not. However, there's a difference between fearful hatred and lingering contempt. We recommend waiting at least two months before throwing in the towel as long as the animals aren't in danger. Do everything you can to mediate, starting with giving them treats every time they're together and feeding them near each other when they're ready (but not too close!). If necessary, step back to the safe room approach and swap the two cats every couple of days. Then build up to feeding in sight of each other. Give it time, and provide both cats a safe place to retreat. They might never become best friends, but they might learn not to be mortal enemies!

dogs somewhere other than your home or the shelter. Regardless, there are a few basics to keep in mind. First, go slow. For a new puppy or dog, be sure to keep both animals safe. That means a leash for both dogs, or at least for your current dog if you bring home a puppy who doesn't know about leashes yet. Be cautious until the animals get a good look at each other; then allow a little more contact until they're both safely playing happily together.

For cats, we recommend a different approach because the feline social structure is much more complicated and takes more time. One much repeated scenario is to slowly introduce the two cats to each other over the course of about a week by keeping them secluded in separate areas of the house. But this doesn't really work! Cats aren't easily fooled, and they full well know there's another cat behind door number one.

Instead, I recommend a hybrid approach. Don't just plop your new cat into the living room with the current queen of the house. Use that spare room to get the new feline used to her new home and make sure she has a safe place to retreat to. Then let her come into the rest of the house when she feels comfortable. It's far better for the two cats to see each other than it is for them to speculate about the interloper behind the closed door. Next, you can reverse the scenario and have the home team use the spare room for a few days to allow your new cat to get the gist of the land (and the scent!). Finally, shoot for positive associations between the two cats. Try feeding a particularly coveted treat like wet food to both cats on opposite sides of a door or baby gate. It's hard to hate the newcomer if she reminds you of tuna!

That first meeting might not go as well as you had hoped, but don't be discouraged. Feline

relationships take time. One last tip, it's not a bad idea to plug in a Feliway diffuser before even bringing your new feline friend home. It releases synthetic feline pheromones that are reported to calm cats. I'm a fan of at least trying this. When it comes to cats, we need all the help we can get.

What about mixing species in a household? Not impossible. Certainly, be aware of the instinctual limitations between species, but even then, all might not be lost. Cats can live with birds and fish, dogs with rabbits, and even terriers with rats. The number one injunction on this, however, is to know your animals and keep them safe. Cats and birds might be able to hang out in the same room, but make sure birds are safely out of reach. The same goes for cats and rodents.

CHILDREN AND PETS

Before bringing home your new family member, lay a little groundwork with your children to prepare them for pet ownership. Depending on the age of your children, they will be able to interact with your new pet in different ways. Safety is the most important consideration—the safety of both your child and your pet.

Pet Safety With Babies or Toddlers

Most shelters and breeders recommend waiting until a child is five years old to get a pet, and for good reason. Children under the age of five have a hard time listening and following rules, and many simply lack the impulse control needed to interact with pets in a safe way. An overly rough toddler or child can unintentionally injure or even kill a small pet; sadly, it happens more than you think. This is especially true for very young kittens and puppies, toy breeds like Chihuahuas and Yorkshire terriers, hamsters, rabbits, and reptiles. On the flip side, dogs and even cats can injure a child, sometimes with disastrous outcomes. Whenever an animal or child gets hurt, most times it's a case of an adult not supervising closely enough and something tragic happening in an instant.

Not everyone waits until their youngest child is five years old to bring home a new pet, and babies are often born into households that already have pets. Diligent supervision and creating some ground rules can create an environment where all family members—kids and pets—are safe and happy.

Toddlers and dogs present the biggest challenge. Be on high alert, always making sure your dog feels comfortable and your child is safe. If you can't supervise, separate! Use baby gates or crates, or put the dog in another room or outside if you're distracted while cooking or talking on the phone. Finally, never leave dogs alone with young kids, especially with babies and toddlers. Being proactive will keep your kids and your dog safe, ensuring everyone will enjoy their special bond with the family dog. If you're planning to start early with pets, a great resource for families with babies and toddlers is Family Paws (*family paws.com)* or Colleen Pelar's book *Living With Kids and Dogs.*

With cats, kittens, puppies, and other smaller pets, allow your young child to play with and pet the animal only when you are right there to ensure both the pet and your child are safe. Don't let kids play with your rabbit in the living room while you cook dinner in the kitchen. Keep everyone in your eyesight at all times. Teach your children safe and gentle handling, and separate the pet and child if your child can't follow the rules. Cats usually head for higher ground if they're afraid or annoyed. Make sure your cat always has a safe place to escape for some quiet time.

Preventing Dog Bites

More than 4.5 million people in the United States are bitten by dogs every year, and about 800,000 of these cases are serious enough to require medical attention. Kids are the most likely to suffer severe injuries from dog bites. But why?

Children engage in certain behaviors that make them targets for dog bites. They scream, run around wildly, and make strange, jerky motions with their bodies. Imagine if you saw an adult acting the way a typical four-year-old acts; you'd probably be on high alert, concerned that the person might be under the influence or dangerous in some way. If you see a kid acting that way, you dismiss it as normal, but dogs don't always differentiate between kids and adults. Some dogs don't know what to make of such behavior and react with wariness and fear. A dog who is afraid is a dog who could potentially bite, even if he is a good dog. Other dogs treat kids like puppies, and "correct" them for annoying behavior the way they would correct a puppy—with a growl or a bite.

Kids engage in other dangerous behavior around dogs, whether it's their own dog or strange dogs. I'm sure you've seen it: kids bear-hugging dogs around the neck, kids lying on top of dogs, dogs and kids wrestling on the ground, toddlers "riding" a dog or chasing him around the house, tugging on his ears or tail. These types of behaviors are never okay, even if you have a great dog who doesn't seem to mind. They create unstable conditions that could lead to a bite under the right circumstances.

Most dogs do not like hugging. Hugging is a human behavior. (Think about it: Do dogs hug each other?) Some dogs put up with it (and, yes, there are some dogs who do enjoy it), but most dogs do not like hugs, especially from kids. Pulling a dog's ears or tail can hurt, and wrestling or riding on a dog is a really bad idea. Chasing a dog or erratically running around a dog invites trips and falls. A dog who is startled or injured might bite if an unsteady child steps on his tail or falls on top of him. Allowing such behaviors sets your dog up for that one day, that *one time* when they are accidentally hurt or scared or just tired of being chased or hit. That one time, a dog could bite—even a "good" dog. One bad bite to a child's face could be a death sentence for a dog, even if up to that point he was friendly and nonaggressive.

But this doesn't mean your kids and your dog can't play together. Just do your part to make sure their relationship is built on safety and mutual respect. Dogs and kids are the best combination

KID SAFETY WITH STRANGE DOGS

Teach your kids to calmly walk over to a strange dog (no running!) and ask the dog's owner for permission to pet the dog before approaching him. Also teach them to wait for an affirmative response from the owner before actually touching the dog. Kids often ask, "Can I pet your dog?" while simultaneously reaching out to pet the dog. Show your kids how to let dogs sniff their hand and how to gently pet a dog. Most dogs are more comfortable with petting on the shoulder or back as opposed to the face or top of the head.

when vigilant parents set and enforce clear rules. Remember these important guidelines:

No kids' faces in dogs' faces. A bite can happen in an instant.

No hugging, especially around the neck. This type of behavior makes many dogs feel threatened or uncomfortable. It also places the child's face near the dog's face, which you're trying to avoid.

Respect the dog's space. If your dog is trying to escape, make sure your child doesn't back him into a corner or block his exit. Most bites happen from stress and fear; you don't want your dog to feel trapped.

No chasing, especially while screaming. Your dog can get scared or get so excited he bites in play. It can also trigger a prey-drive response, leading to chase-catch-bite behavior. If you have a herding dog, you might also need to work on not letting the dog chase the kids. It's tempting for these breeds to herd the kids, nipping at their ankles and legs, but this behavior can become problematic.

No wrestling, lying on the dog, or riding him. Many dogs find these activities stressful, and such situations can quickly escalate into something dangerous. However, some dogs do seek out cuddling with kids and even seem to enjoy it when their kids lie on top of them. At the end of the day, you know your dog best. However, if you have a dog like this, make sure to teach your kids they may engage in such behaviors only with their own dog and not with any other dogs.

Pet Chores by Age

Pets provide a wonderful opportunity to teach your children empathy and responsibility for other creatures. When your kids are more involved in your pet's daily care, they become more bonded. Kids can assist with many pet duties (although a parent should always oversee all of these activities). Some younger kids who are more mature might be able to handle more advanced pet chores, and others might not be ready for some of the chores on this list, despite their older age. You know your child best, so use your good judgment and always supervise.

2 to 4 years old

- Feed pets (parent fills the bowl, child places the food on the floor, parent restrains the pet until the bowl is down and the child is out of the way).
- Fill water bowl (give your toddler some help, and take the same precautions listed for feeding).
- Toss treats.
- Throw a toy for dog to retrieve.
- Play with cat using a feather wand.

5 to 9 years old

Everything toddlers can do, plus:

- Brush dogs, cats, or rabbits.
- Clean small animal cages (hamsters, rabbits, reptiles).

10 years old and up

Everything younger kids can do, plus:

- Walk dogs (only if the child is physically capable of restraining the dog).
- Clean litter boxes or pick up poop (they should always wash their hands after).
- Attend training classes with a parent, then practice at home.
- Assist parents with brushing the dog's or cat's teeth.
- Assist parents with bathing dogs or cats.

WAYS TO BOND WITH YOUR NEW PET

I have a confession. I didn't fall madly in love with my pit bull, Betty, right away. In fact, I didn't fall in love with her for almost a year. That's hard to believe given how I feel about her now. I hear this all the time, and every time I know how guilty the person confessing this feels. For me, Betty was new and was "replacing" my recently lost dog Lucy, something I simply wouldn't let her get away with. Relationships are complicated. For me, this was guilt protection (I didn't want to get hurt again by falling in love and losing another pet) and, well, Betty wasn't a perfect fit yet to say the least. She is now, at least in my eyes.

I think we all feel this way. Sometimes you do fall in love at first sight. I did with my German shepherd, Jake; I don't know why. If I hadn't, I probably never would have because Jake is a difficult character. Sometimes the relationship takes time. The best way to make sure it happens, and ensure it stays that way, is to give it time. Rome wasn't built in a day, and neither are strong, head-over-heels relationships. You will fall in love, believe me. And once that bond develops, it will never fail you.

So how do you develop that bond and give yourself and your pet more confidence? It's simple: Give it some time and just do things together. Training is a wonderful way to develop a close bond with your pet. With puppies, start off with a puppy kindergarten class. If your newly adopted pet is an adult, enroll in a beginning obedience class or even a trick training class. (See Chapter 17 for more about training.) Grooming your new pet, whether it's a bath or gentle brushing session, helps you both learn about each other. Take your new dog for long walks or for car rides, or even just sit together on the patio of your favorite coffee shop. Read the paper with your new cat on your lap, or teach him how to give a high-five—yes, you can train a cat! Many veterinary clinics and shelters also offer kitten kindergarten classes to help your kitten start off on the right paw (see "Socialization and Training" in Chapter 19). Pretty much anything you can do together will bring you closer. It will pay off in ways you can't even imagine. ■

CHAPTER 5

Pet Supplies

Remember those old game shows where contestants got a pile of cash and a timer to race against while they did a massive shopping spree? That's how I feel every time I go into a pet store to purchase supplies for my pets. And it's never more exciting than when you've decided on your new pet and you go to buy supplies for the first time to set up his whole new world at home. It's kind of like painting a new nursery: You're full of hope, nerves, and joy at the prospect of taking care of a new life.

Most of us don't skimp at this point. Maybe it feels like if we buy all the right equipment, food, and toys, we'll have all the right ingredients to raise the perfect pet. Maybe it's true. If possible, schedule that first shopping trip a week or more before you bring your new pet home, and plan on a high tab. I can't guarantee you'll raise the perfect pet, but follow these guidelines below and at least you'll have a blast trying.

BUDGETING FOR YOUR PET

Pets, our lifelong companions, certainly have an initial cost, anywhere from free to thousands of dollars. And then there's the maintenance. One simple estimate is that a dog will cost on average $158 a month for food, medicine, and supplies. For cats, costs may be a bit lower since there are fewer outdoor supplies in general. Rabbits and some exotics may have a higher cost than cats because of their special requirements, not the least of which includes fresh fruit and vegetables. Add on the unanticipated costs of routine and emergency vet visits, special diets, trainers, groomers, carpet cleaners, fencing, and other unexpected supplies, and those monthly costs could double or triple. Don't be discouraged; it's just something to consider when planning on the needs of your new family member. It's no different from buying a new car, and pets are much more fun.

We all budget for groceries, utilities, and entertainment, and it's a good idea to budget for pet supply costs as well. Depending on where you live, those costs can vary. Recognizing that, the ASPCA has a few general guidelines to help you determine what the financial future looks like for you and your new pet (visit *aspca.org* and search "pet care costs").

PET SUPPLIES: WHERE AND WHY TO SHOP

Today, we've got the whole world at our disposal when shopping for our pets. In the United States alone, pet supplies are now nearly an $85 billion industry. That's a lot of kibble. You can purchase supplies any place that's comfortable for you. Go into a brick-and-mortar pet store or big box store, or order online. Some large shelters sell pet supplies (with the proceeds helping homeless pets). At the San Diego Humane Society, we even have a Petco store right in the lobby. You might also consider gently used supplies, which are great for big-ticket items like crates and exercise pens. Look for used supplies in good condition on resale websites like Craigslist and virtual, or actual, garage sales.

PUPPY AND DOG SUPPLIES

Once you've committed emotionally and financially, there's no question that puppies and dogs need a lot to get started on a good life. Don't be discouraged; it's easier than it seems. Puppies need some different supplies than adult dogs do, and sometimes there are differences depending on the breed. But would you expect otherwise? You wouldn't buy the same bed for

HEALTHY TREATS

Did you know you can feed your pets foods as healthy as those you'd feed your children? Most dogs and puppies love fruit and vegetables. There are a few to avoid (see "Toxic Foods" in Chapter 21). For weight reduction and mainte-nance, there's no better treat than apple slices and green beans. For a healthy coat, I love pears and melon. I've never seen this myself, but I've been told that some dogs will even eat lettuce. Dogs love to chew, so crunchy celery and carrots are great low-calorie options. Another healthy snack is a few table-spoons of plain yogurt, peanut butter, or plain cottage cheese. Just check the ingredients for these three to be sure they are low in sugar and free from artificial sweeteners.

an adult human as you would for a child or expect a child to eat what an adult would order at a restaurant. The same philosophy applies to your new puppy or adult dog. So, get out a pen and paper, and let's go shopping.

Food

When it comes to food, there is a world of choices, but it's pretty easy since most pet foods specify an age range. Start by buying a small bag of the brand of food your new pet was eating before you brought him home (ask the shelter, rescue group, or breeder for the name). Often your shelter will send you home with a starter bag. If you want to switch foods, do it gradually. Mix 25 percent new food into 75 percent old food for the first week, then use a 50:50 mix for a week, then 75 percent new food and 25 percent old food for the last week of the transition. Some pet food companies even list specific breeds on their bags (for an in-depth discussion about food, turn to Chapter 10).

Treats

Treats are great for training and rewarding good behavior (although you'd be surprised how much some dogs will do for some petting and praise). You don't want to overdo it with treats. Tiny treats, whether crunchy or chewy, allow you to reward your dog many times without too many calories. Look for treats made with healthy, natural ingredients. I always recommend that new puppy or dog owners buy a box of simple biscuits—the smallest size for puppies and medium for large dogs, just to start. You can get fancy later, but these are a tried-and-true treat, and usually easily digested by all dogs. Initially, avoid elaborate treats like dried sweet potato, twists, jerky chews, and unusual combinations. And avoid any treats made in China because the pet foods and treats made there are subject to health concerns. We've just seen too many negative issues with pet food and treats made in China.

Bowls

I attend national pet supply expos regularly, and the variety of pet food bowls and stands available is stunning. I'm a big fan of ceramic bowls. They have a nice feel, are easy to wash, and are nonreactive to pets' skin. They're also generally microwaveable if you want to heat up refrigerated canned food or other cold items. Stainless steel bowls are also terrific; they are sanitary and easy to clean. Look for a heavier-weight bowl or one with a nonskid rubber grip at the base so they stay in place. One word of caution: Avoid plastic and anything hand painted. Some of these bowls contain toxic ingredients and should never be microwaved or placed in the dishwasher. Because plastic bowls are also porous, they can harbor bacteria and be hard to sanitize.

I'm also a huge fan of food bowl stands for medium and large dogs. An elevated bowl is more anatomically forgiving for your dog's neck and back and keeps the bowl where it's supposed to be and not in the far corner of the living room after your puppy plays air hockey with it for 15 minutes.

For animals who gobble their food too quickly (cats included), slow-feed pet bowls are designed to slow down the excitement with ridges, rings, and barriers that cause the pet to slow down and work harder to eat the food, giving those overly enthusiastic animals a chance to breathe between bites.

Collars, Leashes, Harnesses, Tags

Here's an important category, with lots of options. Think of it like your pet's clothing, ID, and safety gear all in one. Go into any pet supply store, big box store, or boutique, and you'll be astonished by the variety of types and styles of collars and leashes you can find. Go online, and you might be paralyzed into indecision.

We all want our dogs to listen to us and walk calmly by our side when we're out and about. But let's get something out of the way: Don't use prong collars, pinch collars, choke chains, or electric shock collars. Just don't. If you have to do any of these things, you have not trained your dog. In certain extreme circumstances, a tension collar might be appropriate as a last resort, but that is exactly

what it is—never your first option. For prong collars, there is a bit of debate: Some trainers do advocate these when other means of control fail. Still, they're among my least favorite tools to train dogs. Dogs, like people, are motivated by reward. They seriously want to please us. Neither of those characteristics deserves nor is responsive to punishment, which, no two ways about it, is exactly what these collars are. For that reason, I'd much rather you use positive training and a no-pull harness than any kind of pinch collar.

Now that we know what you shouldn't use, let's go over what you should. First, buy an appropriately sized nylon or leather collar from which to hang your dog's identification tag (be sure to include a contact number for you and your family in case your dog gets loose), license, and vaccine tags. (Read more about ID tags in Chapter 6.) Second, if your dog pulls on the leash, consider a no-pull harness, which is what you'll use to train and protect your dog. I personally love the SENSE-ation Harness from Softouch Concepts and the Freedom No-Pull Harness, but there are many other options. No-pull harnesses cut down on pulling because of the sensation your dog feels against his chest as you walk him. These training tools allow you to have full control over your dog in a positive manner. And you'll be safer too by not getting pulled into the street every time your pup sees a squirrel.

Now that you have a collar for your dog's tags and a harness to train and walk your pup, you just need a "steering wheel," otherwise known as the leash. Happy news: This one is all up to you. Leashes come in nylon or leather (I've also seen chain leashes but these are heavy and can hurt your hands and your pup). Choose a four- or six-foot leash, which allows you to easily keep your dog by your side when you're out walking.

I'm not a fan of retractable leashes. You'll never have full control with a retractable leash because it allows your dog to range far ahead of you. Your dog can step out in front of a car, trip up a jogger or biker, or easily swipe that doughnut from a toddler, all as you fruitlessly try to reel him back in like a trout. Retractable leashes can also encourage pulling due to the tension of the leash. To safely give your dog the freedom to roam, go to a space like a large, fenced-in backyard (preferably your own), a safe open field, or a dog park.

Crates, Beds, and Bedding

Your new dog or puppy will love a soft place to rest and sleep at night. Consider a plush dog bed or a crate with a fluffy crate pad. Crates are made of wire, plastic, or canvas. Wire crates provide a lot of ventilation (you can cover them with a blanket at night). Plastic and canvas crates provide more privacy. Many canvas crates fold flat for easy transport. But if you have a chewer or escape artist, you might want to skip the plastic or canvas.

Toys

This one is easy. The single best all-purpose toy you can give your dog is a Kong. Other manufacturers make similar types of toy, but Kong is the leader. This heavy-duty rubber cone is versatile,

CRATE CONSIDERATIONS

Crates are great housetraining tools for puppies because dogs naturally want to avoid soiling where they sleep. To work best, the crate should be just big enough for the puppy to comfortably stand up, lie down, and turn around. Any bigger, and he will be able to go potty at one end, then curl up nice and snug at the other end. As your puppy grows, he will need a larger crate. This is where a "gently used" crate can come in handy. Some crates come with a divider so you can buy a larger crate, then section off space to suit your puppy's size. (Read about crate-training your puppy in Chapter 16).

comes in plenty of sizes and shapes, and is pretty much indestructible. You can use it as a treat, as a distraction, and even to feed a bored dog. You need at least two so you can freeze one with treats or food inside (sealed with peanut butter or plain yogurt). This combo toy-treat is the perfect way to occupy your dog when you have to leave him

in his crate for a few hours or in the living room with a promise he won't be a bad doggie before you come home.

Other great toy options include a medium-size soft ball to throw (it must be bigger than the diameter of your dog's throat to prevent choking), a few inexpensive, plush squeaky toys (be sure your dog doesn't chew out the squeaker and swallow it), a flying disc to fetch (unless your pup is smaller than a Frisbee), and a good tug-of-war toy like a durable nylon rope. You can augment this list as you get to know your pup's preferences and aptitudes (a Frisbee is no good if your dog thinks fetching is a bore).

Kong classic toy

Grooming Supplies

All dogs need to be bathed. How often your dog will need a bath depends on a number of factors, including how dirty he gets and what type of coat he has. Let's start with shampoo. Choose a gentle, moisturizing shampoo, preferably one made with natural ingredients. I love oatmeal-based shampoos. There is no need for flea shampoo because your dog's monthly flea preventive will take care of those intruders for you. (Read more about flea and tick preventives in Chapter 13.)

All dogs need nail trimmers. It's important to trim your dog's nails regularly to prevent overlong nails that can snag on something and tear. Nails can also grow all the way around and end up embedded, painfully, in your dog's paw pads. Get your pup used to your placing his paws in your hand as a first lesson in the fun of the pedicure. Do this by touching his paw and giving him a tasty treat as a reward. Trim your pup's nails about every other week to once a month to keep them short and comfortable. Pick up some styptic powder as well, which you can apply to the nail with pressure to stop bleeding if you accidentally nick the "quick" (the vein in the nail). If you're dealing with black nails, be very conservative and take off only the tips of the nails or let your veterinary technician or groomer do the nail trim for you.

The types of brushes or combs you'll need depend on your dog's coat. Smooth-coated dogs need nothing more than a soft bristle brush. For medium-coated dogs, look for a soft slicker brush (test it on your arm to make sure it's not too sharp or rough). Long-coated dogs need more tools, typically a slicker brush, pin brush, and metal wide-toothed comb. The FURminator is a wonderful invention that removes loose hair from your dog's coat (before it ends up all over the floor and your couch). It removes the undercoat, so it is intended for use on double-coated dogs (those with both an undercoat and an outercoat).

Cleaning Supplies

Dogs create mess. That's just an accepted fact (especially those rambunctious puppies), but lots of products help keep everything under control. Definitely pick up a big supply of poop bags; these come in many varieties from basic plastic to flushable and biodegradable. A pet vacuum has special attachments to help control hair, and a small handheld carpet cleaner comes in handy to clean up accidents. Finally, numerous enzymatic pet cleaner products will erase all evidence of accidents so pets don't return to the scene of the crime again.

CAT AND KITTEN SUPPLIES

Believe it or not, cats are emotional creatures who like and need us. Don't decide to get a cat because you don't have time for a dog. Cats need as much enrichment as dogs do. There are special toys to help them stay healthy and stimulated, which is important since most of them spend their lives indoors on a windowsill soaking up sun instead of prowling on the big hunt outdoors.

For cats and kittens, there is no better toy than one that simulates the hunt. It is, in fact, the single best way to keep your cat mentally healthy (and not spraying on the dining room cabinet). The best toys for cats allow them to exercise their most important instincts: Cats have to climb, jump, chase, and hide to be happy. Keep those four items in mind with your toy purchases, and you'll have a happy camper at home.

The best cat toys are usually the cheapest. It never fails that the more money you spend on a toy for Fluffy, the more likely she'll prefer the paper bag it came in. Your cat needs more than toys, of course. Here are the basics to get you started.

Food

All kittens and cats need food that is unique for them. If possible, buy a small bag of the brand of food your new pet was eating before you brought her home. Ask the shelter, rescue group, or breeder for the name of the food. As for dogs, most shelters will give you a starter bag of the food they were feeding. If you want to switch foods, do it gradually. Mix 25 percent new food into 75 percent old food for the first week, then use a 50/50 mix for a week, then 75 percent new food and 25 percent old food for the last week of the transition. (For an in-depth discussion about food, turn to Chapter 10.)

Treats

Cats love treats. Many cats also have weight issues—especially middle-aged and older cats. Keep treat portions small, and try not to go overboard. Look for treats made with healthy, natural ingredients (read the ingredients list). Avoid any treats made in China due to recent health concerns. It might take a bit of trial and error to determine what treats your cat likes (they're cats, after all), but it will be very clear once you present a smorgasbord for them to select their favorites. Remember: everything in moderation. Avoid too much real tuna, which can cause health issues (see Chapter 33).

Bowls

As for dogs, for your cat's bowls, choose real ceramic or stainless steel, which are sanitary and easy to clean. Stay away from plastic, which can harbor bacteria and might contribute to "kitty acne," a condition that affects a cat's chin. A stand

CAT GRASS AND CATNIP

I'm a huge fan of live cat grass, catnip, and edible safe plants. You can buy a kit and plant the seeds yourself or purchase grass already sprouted in containers. Limit the catnip to no more than a few times a week. Cats don't really eat catnip; they smell it and bite into the leaves to release a compound called nepetalactone. There's no documented harm from it, but too much can cause stomach issues. Other cat-safe plants and grasses are fine to give as much as your cat prefers. Cats want to be outdoors prowling for food, but we want cats to be indoors staying safe, so bring some of the real world in to them (see what plants and flowers to avoid in Chapter 21).

for food is a great way to keep the bowls in one place, but that's up to you. One thing that's a bit different for cats than dogs is their insistence on drinking clean, cold, running water. Dogs love clean, cool water too, but cats are particularly fussy about their drinking water. Commit to refreshing that bowl throughout the day or consider purchasing a cat water fountain. Yes, these really exist. We vets love to hear that cats are drinking enough water (they tend not to), so anything that encourages them to do this is a good thing.

Collars, Tags, Harnesses, Leashes

Indoor cats, which I hope your cat will be (your cat may feel differently), should always wear a collar with an identification tag. Of course, you should microchip your cat, but just in case your little one sneaks outside, a collar signifies that she is an owned cat. It only takes a moment for your cat to escape, and if she does, you want to give her the best chance at being found. Your cat's collar should always be a breakaway style, which might save her life if she ever gets her collar caught on anything, whether in or out of the house. Such collars might be labeled "safety collars" or "quick-release collars."

If you do have an outdoor cat, be sure to put a bell on her collar to warn the birds that a master hunter is on the prowl. Also, be sure that your collar is inexpensive because you're going to need a lot of them if you have an outdoor cat. She will probably come home without her collar a few dozen times.

You might consider taking your cat out for a walk with a leash and harness. It will take time to acclimate her to the gear, but it's worth it. When I lived in Washington, D.C., one of my neighbors

took her two beautiful tabbies out for a walk every single day. It was a gorgeous sight, and those two proud felines thought they owned the world.

Litter Boxes and Litter

Cats can be extremely picky about their bathroom accommodations. (Can you blame them?) Set yourself up for success by purchasing at least one litter box per cat in the house, and make sure these are at least one and a half times the length of your cat.

Litter boxes can be as simple as a low-sided, plastic tub or as fancy as a box that automatically scoops itself every time your cat uses it. You'll find covered and uncovered boxes. Some cats prefer the privacy of a covered box, but others can't abide the smells that get trapped inside. In fact, in multicat households, a covered box can create anxiety about being pounced on by another cat. If you want to get fancy, consider an automatic

LITTER CONSIDERATIONS

You have a plethora of choices in litter, from basic clumping clay litter to litter made from silica crystal, wheat, pine, corn, and recycled newspaper. In general, most cats like a soft, fine clumping litter, so starting there is a safe bet. Although humans like perfumed scented litters, most cats have a highly sensitive sense of smell and find them overpowering, even offensive. And the last place you want to offend your cat is the litter box. (Cat behavior issues are addressed in Chapter 19.)

litter box that regularly runs a rake through the box to self-scoop the litter clean. This is a terrific concept, but in my experience most cats aren't impressed with it and take some training to use it properly or at all. Stick with what works, and keep it simple, at least initially.

Scratchers and Cat Trees

For your own sanity and your cat's health, get your cat a large cat tree and scratching post. Without these, you don't have a cat—you have a frustrated

SCRATCHER VARIETY

Some cats like scratching vertically (like the side of your couch, unfortunately) and others prefer scratching horizontally (your beautiful new rug). Take note of your cat's scratching style, and provide a scratcher that meets her needs (and saves your furniture). Cats also like different scratching surfaces, so consider trying a variety: carpet, sisal, and even cardboard.

decoration in your home. Cats need to climb, jump, play, and scratch. If you don't want them doing that on your new sofa, get them what they want: safe things to climb and scratch their claws on. You should never declaw your cat (we'll get to that in Chapter 12). In the meantime, give your cat a scratcher and the ability to climb and survey her kingdom from above. Just accept it. This will put her in exactly the place she believes is appropriate: superior to everything below.

Beds and Bedding

Cats love to sleep! In fact, adult cats sleep as much as 15 to 20 hours per day. Give your cat one or more cozy places to stretch out with one of the many styles of beds, pads, and even kitty tents, which act as both a bed and snuggly hideaway. Some cats also love to snuggle up to a stuffed animal in their bed. It's pretty endearing.

Toys

Like dogs, cats love to play. The best toy you can ever get your kitten is another kitten to play with. But once your kitten has grown up, she'll be a little more independent. And you might only have one cat from there on out. Cat play is different from dog or human play (at least most dogs and humans) in that cats love to play only one game: master hunter. Everything they like is all about the hunt: the initial ear perk, the prowl, the stalk, the jump. I love cat reel rods and feather wands to start the chase, as well as toy mice and bell balls. They're all safe and a great way to interact with your cat. I'm not crazy about laser rods to get your cat to play unless you're very coordinated (never shine the light in your cat's eyes). If you use a laser, make sure you give your cat a real toy or a treat every time she "catches" the red dot, or you'll just end up frustrating her. It always makes me smile to hear about the elaborate toys people buy their cats only to find the cat inside the shopping bag the expensive toy came from instead of playing with the toy. Cats also love hiding in boxes and bags (try to stick with the paper ones for play).

Grooming Supplies

Most cats benefit from brushing, which removes loose hair before it ends up on your furniture or, worse, in your cat's stomach (Hello, hairballs!). Whether brushing is a daily or weekly occurrence depends on the type of coat. Cats with long, plush coats like a Persian, need daily brushing to prevent mats. Short- and medium-hair cats can often get away with weekly brushing, although many cats love being brushed, so do it as often as your cat likes! Look for a soft-bristled slicker brush (test it against your forearm before buying to make sure it won't scratch your cat's delicate skin).

Although most domestic cats hate water (oddly enough, their wild ancestors swim quite happily), the occasional bath will remove dust, saliva, and dander, leaving the coat shiny and soft. Choose a gentle moisturizing shampoo made specifically for cats. Forget about flea shampoos. With new flea monthly preventives, these aren't necessary. Also pick up nail trimmers so you can trim your cat's claws monthly. After some negotiation, of course.

Cleaning Supplies

Cats are generally very clean creatures (isn't that one of the reasons we love them?), but they do shed. Some cats shed only moderately, but others are veritable fur tornadoes. Pet vacuums come with special attachments to help control hair, and a small handheld carpet cleaner will come in handy to clean up the evidence of hairballs hacked up on the rug. Some cats mark or spray when they are upset or sick; enzymatic pet cleaners can help remove the stain and smell. ■

CHAPTER 6

How Not to Get Lost

One of the biggest nightmares I grapple with is the thought of physically losing a pet. One of the worst things in the world must be the uncertainty of not having any idea what happened to your pet or not knowing where she is. Luckily, technology has come to the rescue and now we have many options beyond the traditional lost pet poster to ensure this doesn't happen. From implantable microchips and tracking collars to facial recognition registries and digital license tags, there are numerous ways to make sure we never lose touch with our pets, even when we can't find them.

COLLARS AND TAGS

Let's start with the tag. A good ID tag contains three critical pieces of information: (1) your pet's name, (2) your name and address, and (3) your cell phone number (for text or calling). Nothing is more important than that last piece of information. Of course, I love microchips (see below), but your pet should also wear a tag since your distant neighbors, who might end up with your dog in their garage, probably don't have a microchip reader handy. Would you ever go out without your driver's license? Not usually. Don't ever let your pets go out without theirs. In this case, that license is their identification tag. Having a tag could mean the difference between getting your pet home in an hour or staying up all night worrying about where your best buddy is. That said, tags can and do fall off, which leads us to another important topic: microchips.

MICROCHIPS

One of the most critical inventions in the battle against pet homelessness is the microchip. Since the implantable pet microchip came on the scene in the 1980s, many thousands of pets have been returned to their owners, some after unbelievable lengths of time—weeks, months, even years—to the astonished euphoria of families who had grieved and given up hope of ever seeing their pets again. Yet here they are with tales to tell, if only they could.

Let me make this easy. If you have a pet, you MUST have a microchip. It's as simple as that. But a microchip doesn't act like a GPS device; it emits no signal and can't tell you where your pet is. In order to work, an implanted microchip has to be read by a scanner. There are many microchip manufacturers and all are different. Fortunately, most shelters and veterinarians now use universal scanners, which means they can read many different microchips.

Scanning an animal for a chip is still highly dependent on the skill and patience of the human using the scanner. Microchips are not foolproof. You might scan an animal and not read the chip and think the animal doesn't have one. That can happen because of improper scanning technique, a chip that moved, or a scanner that can't detect that particular chip. Newer technology is making that issue less of a problem now.

Microchips are injected under the skin between the shoulder blades. In theory, they are

MICROCHIP ODDS

A microchip could mean the difference between your lost pet returning home or not. According to the American Veterinary Medical Association, a study looked at the outcomes for more than 7,700 stray dogs and cats who ended up in animal shelters. According to the study, dogs without microchips were returned to their owners 21.9 percent of the time; dogs with microchips were reunited with their owners 52.2 percent of the time. The outcomes for cats were even more dramatic. Cats without microchips were returned to their owners only 1.8 percent of the time; chipped cats were reunited with their owners a whopping 38.5 percent of the time. You can't argue with those odds.

no more painful than a simple injection, although the needles are much larger. Still, pets don't require anesthesia to be microchipped, and when the procedure is done by an experienced professional, the injection is much the same as a simple vaccine. If your pet is already going under anesthesia for a spay or neuter surgery, this is a great time to also implant a microchip.

Placement is critical. The microchip is a small electronic chip enclosed in a tiny glass cylinder about the size of a grain of rice. When placed normally, it should sit for eternity between the shoulder blades. However, the microchip can end up in a very different spot in a dog or cat from where it originally started out. This is caused by anatomic migration, which can sometimes occur because of changes in skin density, fat deposits, and other physiological changes. When scanning for a chip, good technicians move the scanner up and down the shoulder area to find the chip. Very occasionally, microchips can migrate and move down the sides of an animal toward the sternum. Newer chip designs help keep them in place.

Your pet might come to you already microchipped (if you adopt from a shelter). If not, your veterinarian can place the chip. Once your pet is

Microchip sizes compared with a penny

chipped, the shelter or vet will provide information about registering the chip. Microchips don't work if you don't register them. Call, email, or visit the website of the microchip manufacturer to register your pet's chip with your contact information: home address, phone number, and email. Always keep your microchip information up to date. If you move or change your phone number, you must contact the microchip company to update your information, just like you would your billing address for your credit cards. That way, the company can contact you if someone finds your missing pet and scans his chip. There is a fee to register your pet but believe me, it's worth it. In some cases, one fee provides a lifetime of coverage for your pet.

After all this cheerleading for microchips, you might ask why on earth you need to have old-fashioned tags on the collar. If every lost pet were to end up in a veterinary hospital or shelter, a simple microchip alone would be fine because these facilities routinely scan stray animals for microchips. Where trouble arises is the lost dog wandering into your yard with no tags. Most pet owners don't have microchip scanners just lying around. For this reason, I always recommend both a microchip and a collar and tag with information that's up to date. Sometimes it's good to play it simple. Having both a chip and a tag will increase the odds that your pet finds his way home if he ever gets lost. No insurance in the world is worth more than that.

PET TATTOOS

It used to be that the only dog you'd ever see with an identification tattoo was a racing greyhound or a purebred breeding dog. Not anymore. Although it might seem anachronistic, the veterinary community went back to tattooing animals about a decade ago to identify them as spayed or neutered. This happened for a number of reasons, not the least of which to ensure that female dogs never had an unnecessary spay surgery (it can be difficult to determine if a stray female dog was previously spayed). It's pretty easy to tell if a male dog is neutered (just take a look at his undercarriage).

There are other reasons someone might elect to tattoo a pet with an identification number. A tag can fall off or be lost, and a microchip might not be readable, but a tattooed identification number is permanent, though it can fade over time (and need a touch-up). It can also be a visible deterrent to someone attempting to keep a lost or stolen pet.

The other great thing about tattooing is that you can put your phone number right there on the tattoo. That would be enough incentive for me to never change my number! The only downside to this permanent identification is that it must be done under anesthesia or a good sedative. Some companies argue that tattooing can be done without anesthesia, but it can't. The usual places for tattoos are where the fur doesn't grow (for instance, on the abdomen). The best time to do this is when your pet is already under sedation for his or her spay or neuter.

The only other issue with tattoos, as well as microchips, is that the finder must know to look for these. A veterinary clinic or shelter will do that automatically, but some animals never make it to

WHAT TO DO IF YOU FIND A LOST PET

If you find a lost pet and you don't recognize him and aren't able to return him to his home, secure him in a quiet, safe place in your house or garage. Put out a small amount of pet food if you have it and a bowl of water. Take a picture of the animal and call your local animal shelter. If it's after hours, hang onto the pet until the next morning and bring him to the shelter or your veterinarian so they can scan him for a microchip. If the animal is hurt, call animal control or the police and ask to have them contact animal services to help you as an emergency. Often, if you provide the information and photo to the shelter, you can keep the animal at your home and help the shelter find the pet's owner by posting Found Pet flyers in your neighborhood.

a shelter or vet. If you do tattoo your pet, consider registering him with Tattoo-A-Pet (*tattoo-a-pet .com*), AKC Reunite (*akcreunite.org*), or the National Dog Registry (*dog-register.co.uk*). Whatever form of identification you choose, tag, microchip, or tattoo, always use redundancies. When it comes to a lost pet, you can never give too much information.

PET GPS TRACKERS

Pet trackers are new technology and illustrate beautifully the direction we're going in pet location and identification technology. Trackers have a collar monitor that sends out a signal to your smartphone, but someday we might be talking about an implant that does the same thing. Regardless, pet trackers do for dogs what LoJack did for cars in the late 1980s. These are really amazing. The drawback is that they're only good if they stay on your pet, which doesn't always happen. I recall a time the GPS monitor fell off my German shepherd's collar at the beach. Miles and miles of beach. Once I got home and realized I lost about $90 worth of technology, I picked up my phone and got the signal back. I returned to the beach and found the tracker, about the size of a half dollar, lying on the sand in the middle of about 600 feet of surf line. Amazing.

Pet trackers, which can run $70 to $250, work through either GPS or radio frequency technology.

FIVE TIPS FOR AN EFFECTIVE LOST PET POSTER

The Missing Pet Partnership (MPP) recommends a highly effective method for creating lost pet signs. According to the theory, you have only five seconds and five words to get the attention of walkers or drivers passing your sign. Use these tips from the MPP to grab people's attention so they can help you find your missing pet:

1. Make signs huge.
2. Choose fluorescent poster board.
3. Post signs at major intersections near where your pet was lost.
4. Keep wording brief, using huge capital letters: HELP FIND LOST DOG! BEAGLE! RED COLLAR!
5. Tape a smaller flyer with a photo and your phone number to the center of the poster, with the large capital lettering above and below it.

To learn more, visit *missingpetpartnership.org.*

They can help you locate your cat or dog with technology linked directly to your cell phone or computer. Some do other things, like track your dog's activity, sleep, and rest. Before buying a GPS tracker for your pet, do some research to compare the various models and choose the one that will best suit your pet's needs. One I like is the Whistle 3, which sends text and email notifications with maps to help you find your pet. Whistle GPS trackers have a monthly fee. It's more than worth it if your pet isn't always under your trusty gaze. And who's is?

LOST PET RESOURCES

Losing your pet is a terrifying feeling, but there are many steps you can take to bring her back home. Try to remain calm, and work your way through your options to track down your missing family member. Above all, never lose hope. A friend lost her beloved Siamese who was missing for nearly three months. But my friend kept going out to the field she thought he escaped to armed with a lawn chair and his favorite food. Quiet and patience eventually paid off when she got the best gift in the world: her long-lost boy tentatively peeking out from the shrubs at the edge of the clearing.

What to Do If Your Pet Is Lost

You just bathed your boxer and let him run around the house, rolling on the carpet to dry himself. It's a sight to behold—until he runs out the door without his collar, which is still where you put it before you hauled all 93 pounds of him into the tub. You run out after him but all you hear is the wind blowing the gate back and forth in your front yard. Panic sets in. You have to get your dog back. Here's what to do in 10 steps:

1. Canvass the neighborhood on foot.
2. Canvass the neighborhood by car.
3. Talk to your neighbors and let them know your pet got out.
4. Call or visit all local animal shelters, and let them know your pet is missing. Email a good-quality photo or bring a printout you can leave with the front desk.
5. Call your microchip company, and let them know your pet is missing.
6. Alert all local veterinary hospitals that your pet ran away.
7. If your dog is registered with Finding Rover, alert the company that your pet ran out the door. (See opposite.)
8. Make outdoor "Lost Pet" signs and post them all over your neighborhood. Always include a good photo (see sidebar page 81).

LOST CAT TIPS

If your indoor-only cat gets out, some basic knowledge about cat behavior can help you find her. First, cats are territorial. This means they don't like to stray far from their home. Second, if a cat feels scared or threatened or is injured, her first instinct is to hide. Lost cats are frequently found in and around their homes, silently hiding. This could be under a porch or deck, in a woodpile, in a crawlspace, or any other good hiding spot. A lost cat usually will not come out of hiding when you call her name, so investigate all possible locations on your property, as well as your neighbors within a five-house radius of your home. For more tips, visit your local shelter's website or *missingpetpartnership.org*.

9. Put your pet's favorite food and bed outside (if he's nearby and just scared, that could lure him back).
10. Check your local shelters (all of them) daily in person to look for your pet.

Pet Detectives

If you saw the zany 1994 movie *Ace Ventura, Pet Detective* starring Jim Carrey, you might think that "pet detective" is a made-up profession, but pet detectives are real, and they can help track down your lost pet.

Pet detectives (also called "missing animal response technicians") are often a last-resort option since hiring one can be pricey, but they can and do find

lost pets, including pets who have been lost for long periods of time. Most pet detectives use tracking dogs specially trained to sniff out missing pets, as well as their own expert knowledge on lost pet behavior.

Whether you lost a dog, cat, turtle, or snake, a pet detective might be able to reunite you with your pet. It's best to contact a pet detective as soon as possible. Time is of the essence when trying to locate a missing pet. To find a pet detective in your area, check out the Missing Pet Partnership's online directory at *missingpetpartnership.org*.

Facial Recognition

This is the latest in new technologies coming out to save lives and return animals home again. One company developing this amazing technology is Finding Rover, and it's brilliant. Finding Rover has developed facial recognition for dogs and is working on fine-tuning the technology for cats (it's much more difficult due to a cat's more flattened facial countenance). What happens is stunning. You register your dog at *findingrover.com*, provide your contact information, and upload a current photo of your dog. If your dog becomes lost, anyone who finds your pet (individuals who have the Finding Rover app on their phones, as well as shelters and vet offices) can check the app, click on your pet, and contact you.

The reverse is true as well. If you find a dog, you can aim your phone at his face; if that dog is registered in the database, you will get his owner's contact information. It's extremely cutting edge and really brings animal welfare into this century. The only thing we need for this to work well is to enroll as many people and pets as possible. Shelters are the perfect vehicles to launch this registry. Once these databases become more robust—imagine if they contained every dog or cat in the country—we'll have the promise to make life much easier in changing lost to found. Fortunately, this database is steadily growing as most shelters in the United States now know about Finding Rover. ■

CHAPTER 7

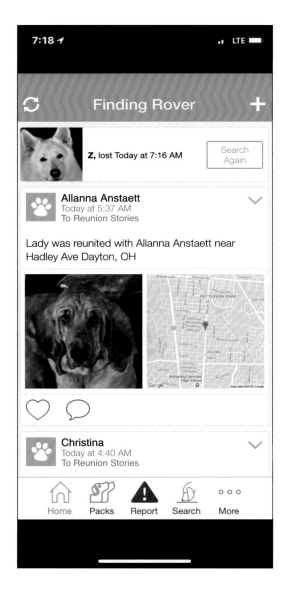

Animal Happiness

Animal happiness is a relatively modern concept. Consequently, animal *un*happiness is an equally modern concept. All animals deserve humane care, enrichment, love, and compassion. If you didn't believe that, you probably wouldn't be reading this book. It's not complicated. At the most basic level, animals, like humans, need a few rudimentary things to be happy.

Progressive animal sheltering is modeled on the Five Freedoms, developed in the 1960s in the United Kingdom to ensure the humane treatment of livestock (see Appendix A). Today, the Five Freedoms have been adopted by many shelters, rescues, and veterinarians. At the San Diego Humane Society, we have them emblazoned on our lobby wall. All animals have these rights:

1. Freedom from pain, injury, or disease
2. Freedom to express normal behaviors
3. Freedom from discomfort
4. Freedom from hunger or thirst
5. Freedom from fear

The Five Freedoms apply to all animals everywhere, including the 78 million dogs and 85 million cats living in households across the United States. The Five Freedoms embody the minimum promise we should make to all animals. They're essential, but they're just the start. True animal happiness also requires enrichment, love, and compassion. It's no surprise that this is the formula for both animal and human happiness since we all basically require the same things. We can add other "spices" to the basic recipe, but nothing happens without these simple ingredients. Enrichment ensures that animals have a chance to express normal behaviors and be stimulated and challenged as they would in nature. Love is essential not only when we're talking about our pets; it also defines the respect and gratitude we should feel for those animals who give their lives so we can eat, ride, and learn from them. Finally, there is compassion. None of the above would be possible without a human compassion that motivates us to do what's right, for each other, for our planet, and for our animals. ■

Ask DR. GARY:

How Do I Know If My Pet Is Happy?

How can we know if our animals are happy? How can we be certain they are fulfilled, comfortable, and their lives are enriched? It's easier than you'd think. Start with these three ingredients to be sure your pet of any species is happy:

1. Provide access to good and clean food and water and a comfortable place to sleep (animals do a lot of that).
2. Allow him to express as many normal behaviors as you can (this includes giving him fellow animals for companionship if you can).
3. Spend time with him as often as you can. Remember, you're replacing the company of his own species.

This last part is important. Bring whatever pet you get into your home because you truly plan to spend time with that animal. Nine times out of 10, enrichment for pets, pretty much by definition, is truly defined by being with you.

PART 2

Everyday Pet Health and Nutrition

Once you find your perfect pet, make it your mission to ensure your new friend is as healthy and happy as he can be. Overall health and wellness has many facets, including adequate exercise and enrichment, proper nutrition, preventive veterinary care, and grooming.

CHAPTER 8

How Do You Know Your Pet Is Healthy?

Animals can't tell us how they're feeling, but there are other ways to know if your pet is healthy. Start with posture, the look of his eyes, the tilt of his ears, the bearing of his shoulders, and the position of his tail. People often tell me, "It must be so hard to treat animals since they can't tell you what's bothering them." It can be difficult, which is why veterinarians go to school for so long. But when you love animals, you're in tune with them. You know when they're not feeling well or when their eyes aren't quite right. They can't speak, but that doesn't mean they don't say a lot. You just need to know how to listen.

TOP FIVE VISUAL SIGNS OF HEALTH

The most important piece of information any vet can obtain from a pet owner is his or her own assessment of how the pet feels. No one knows your pet better than you. We'll go through the clues all animals give us. Often, they're less subtle than you'd expect.

Energy

Your pet's energy level is an excellent clue to how your pet is feeling, and it's one of the easiest things to assess. It's no different from energy levels for humans. Is your cat having a hard time getting up in the morning? When you ask your dog if he wants to go for a walk, does the question get its usual enthusiastic response? It's all about what's normal for your pet and you are the best one to tell us that.

Skin and Coat Quality

The skin is the body's largest organ. It's composed of proteins, lipids, and fatty acids. When the skin isn't getting the nutrition and circulation it needs, health issues become visibly evident. For instance, Cushing's disease, an imbalance in adrenal hormones, can manifest early with chronic skin rashes, a pot-bellied appearance, and hair loss. Zinc deficiency can cause dermatitis in huskies and malamutes, and protein deficiency can lead to slow hair growth and brittle fur. Dry, flaking skin (dandruff) or, conversely, overly

oily coats can indicate anything from skin maladies to metabolic or genetic disorders.

Certain behaviors affect the coat and are their own indication that something might be wrong. Is your dog's coat shiny or dull? Thick or thin? Is it falling out or changing color? The coat can be affected if your pet is chewing, biting, scratching, or rubbing the skin or coat. Such itchiness can indicate anything from allergies or fleas to metabolic or nutritional deficiencies.

Keep in mind that the coat goes through normal cycles, from regular growth patterns to heavy shedding periods. Such variations could be part of regular cyclical patterns, but compared against your pet's normal, it tells a story.

Nail Strength

Nail strength is related to coat quality in that it can be an indication of good or poor health. As with coat, nails that are dry, broken, or flaking can indicate metabolic, nutritional, or overall health issues. Overgrown nails can be caused by lack of grooming or lack of exercise and energy.

Eye Brightness

This might seem more cartoon-like than medical, but it's real. That gleam in the eye, the spark of excitement our pets normally exhibit is something

we usually take for granted—until it's not there. Dullness, sagging eyelids, and gaze avoidance are all indicators that your pet is not feeling his normal, happy self.

Nose "Luster"

The canine nose is self-lubricating with thousands of mucus-producing cells. A dog can lick his nose hundreds of times a day. One reason is that they want to moisten it or it itches. Dogs also lick their noses when they're nervous, a behavioral communication known as an appeasement gesture. The nose can also indicate how healthy an animal is. Normally the nose is smooth, shiny, and relatively dry. However, the oft-mentioned warm nose syndrome that many pet owners call their vets about means very little. As long as your pet is acting normal, don't worry too much if his nose is warm. Fever can sometimes be the cause, but most often, it just means your pet is warm. More frequently, a dull, overly dry, or rough nose can indicate that your dog isn't feeling well: Either the normal self-moisturizing function of the nose is slacking off or he's not feeling well enough to lick it. Usually, though, a dry nose is just due to a hot or dry day and is nothing to worry about.

ASSESS YOUR PET

How do you know when you need to bring your pet to the vet? One way is to do a quick at-home assessment of your pet's health. Start by checking out the top five visuals we just covered: energy, coat and skin quality, nail strength, eye brightness, and nose luster. This is your pet's overall presentation, meaning how your animal appears to you or your vet at this point. Veterinarians call

HOW TO TAKE YOUR PET'S TEMPERATURE

There are no special pet thermometers. Just use a basic human digital thermometer. (You might want to write your pet's name on it—you don't want to put this one in your mouth!) Coat the tip with petroleum jelly and insert it about one inch into the rectum. Leave it in for one to two minutes. It helps if someone can help you to comfort and hold your pet, especially if you're trying this on a cat. A normal temperature for dogs and cats is 100°F to 103°F. Ear thermometers are still pretty inaccurate in animals, so stick to the old-fashioned kind.

this "signalment" and include notes of your pet's age, breed, gender, and, of course, demeanor.

Next, begin your at-home physical. Start with the head, and work your way back. Look at the eyes, ears, nose, mouth, and teeth. Are the eyes dull? Are the ears swollen or red? The eyes and ears should look the same on both sides. Feel around the neck for bumps and swellings, and run your hand down the back to the end of the tail. Reach around and feel the belly (cautiously with cats: They don't appreciate this!). Check your pet's breathing rate by counting his breaths for 15 seconds and multiplying by four to get a rate per minute. A normal respiratory rate should be around 60 to 78 breaths per minute for most cats and dogs (for other respiratory rates, see Chapter 31). You can also simply note whether your pet is breathing faster than normal or seems to be having any trouble breathing. Again, no one knows your pet better than you do.

Body Condition Score

Animals come in all shapes and sizes, so the number on the scale isn't the best way to judge if a pet is overweight or underweight. Veterinarians use a body condition score to assess if an animal is a healthy weight, assigning a score of 1 to 5 (or 1 to 9 depending on the system), with 1 being emaciated and 5 or 9 being obese. To check your pet's weight, touch his ribs and spine. You should be able to feel them but not see them. If you see them, he's too thin; if you can't feel them, he's too fat. Look at your pet from both the side and above. Pets should have a "waist" when viewed from above; in profile, the belly should not be saggy.

10 Key Health Indexes

The following key points are absolutely critical to helping vets (and you) "speak" for your pet. If you're wondering if you need to make that vet appointment, first do this homework to look for critical clues:

1 Appetite and weight are a good place to start. Most pets love to eat. At the very least, consistency in appetite is important. You know whether your pet is eating the way he normally does. If you think something might be amiss, identifying any weight loss or weight gain is invaluable. Weight loss in particular is important to note and is a good reason to book that vet appointment. In general, most animals eat better in colder months of the year when they're naturally programmed to store more weight.

2 Drinking quantity is a critical indicator of health and should be discussed with your vet if your pet is drinking more or less water than usual. To get a general sense of how much your pet drinks normally, note how often you fill the water bowl. If you really want to get serious, measure how much water the bowl holds and write down how much he normally drinks during a typical day. Are you filling it twice as often? Is your dog hovering over the bowl much of the day? Diseases like diabetes, liver disease, Cushing's disease, or hyperthyroidism can cause your pet to drink more. Few disorders cause a decrease in water intake unless your pet is very weak and too ill to drink. If that happens, go immediately to your vet or emergency hospital.

3 Urination habits are noteworthy. What goes in should come out. If your pet is having accidents in the house, is urinating frequently, or if his urine is dark or tinged with red, it might indicate a urinary tract infection or other kidney or bladder disorder. Much as you might not want to, look at the color and note the smell of your pet's urine. Healthy urine should not have much of a smell. An infection can give urine a very pungent ammonia-like smell. It's especially important to watch for lack of urine output in male cats. If you see a drastic reduction in the amount of urine in your cat's litter box, call your vet immediately. In both dogs and cats, very little urination and even no urination is a true medical emergency (see Chapter 20).

4 Stool quality is a big tip-off to certain health problems. Tell your vet if your pet is having normal stools, diarrhea, or constipation.

HOW TO CATCH A URINE SAMPLE

This is not as difficult as it sounds. For dogs, find a clean plastic container with a lid, wait until he starts to go, then sneak the container under the stream. You only need to collect about five tablespoons. For smaller dogs, I like using a paper cup on the end of a straightened-out wire hanger. For cats, unless you can pick some of it up from an accident on the floor, leave the sample collection to your vet. If you can't get a sample from your dog, don't worry too much. Your vet can usually collect a sample with a needle.

This information is like gold to your vet if he or she is worried there might be a foreign-body obstruction or infection in the gastrointestinal tract. Constipation is an indicator of other issues, such as dehydration or diet problems and, especially for cats, tells a lot about their overall health. If possible, bring in a fresh stool sample when you visit your vet; it reveals a great deal. Color and consistency are important indicators of diet and fat content. Blood, while alarming to see, can be present during any inflammatory event, such as acute colitis or irritable bowel syndrome (see Chapter 28), or even something as innocuous as feeding a different pet food. It's important to let your vet know you saw blood in the stool, but don't panic about it.

5   Vomiting is impossible to ignore. Note what you see in it, but don't feel the need to bring any of it to the veterinary hospital unless you find a foreign object that you want to show us. Much to the disappointment of many of my clients, it really doesn't give me any more insight. Your pet vomited. Enough said.

6   Gait refers to the way your pet walks. Note whether your pet is limping, and try to observe which leg is causing trouble. This will save everyone about an hour in the exam room. For hard to pin down front legs, note when the head drops—that's usually the side that is causing discomfort. Limping frequently "disappears" at the hospital because your pet's adrenalin kicks in and masks the pain. Cats almost never show signs of limping because they won't move

HOW TO COLLECT A STOOL SAMPLE

This one is simple. Invert a plastic poop bag in your hand and pick up the sample. Tie it off at the top and bring it in to your vet as soon as you can. If you have to delay, put it in a plastic container in your refrigerator. In the case of very loose stools, you can just scrape a little into a plastic container. Your vet just needs a good tablespoon or so for tests.

on the exam table. Try to take a video with your phone of your pet limping at home. A picture says more than a thousand words.

7   Energy is something you can assess in several ways. Excessive sleep might seem like an unusual thing to assess in creatures that snooze at least 12 hours a day (some cats sleep up to 20 hours a day!). But too much sleeping

or sluggishness is called lethargy in medical parlance. Lethargy is the opposite of energy, and it can indicate many things. For instance, if your Labrador retriever is sluggish and gaining weight, hypothyroidism might be the culprit. On the other end of the energy spectrum is high energy. An overly stimulated middle-aged cat might have hyperthyroidism (see Chapter 27).

8 Coughing is never normal. See your vet if your pet's cough lasts more than a day.

9 Sneezing can be common and is nothing to be overly concerned about unless it's persistent or accompanied by teary eyes, blood, or a leaking nose. Animals sneeze for the same reasons that we do: a tickle, an irritation, or an infection like a cold. Unlike us, some can also sneeze because something is stuck in the nose like a foxtail or piece of grass. Continuous sneezing means a trip to your vet is necessary.

10 Excessive chewing or scratching is a behavior to note. An itchy rash might be due to fleas, skin allergies, or infection, but a non-itchy rash could be due to a metabolic disorder. Skin disorders can be quite tricky to diagnose. Dermatologists, the greatest medical sleuths in veterinary medicine, will tell you that specifics about your pet's rash are absolutely critical to deciphering the cause. It gets complicated, but the more information you can provide, the better your veterinarian can make the correct diagnosis.

HEALTH CARE FOR SMALL PETS

When it comes to small pets, or exotics as we sometimes call them, health care is very specialized. Whether it's guinea pigs, who must have an external source of vitamin C, or chinchillas, who need dust baths to keep their coats and skin healthy, these small pets have specific requirements to stay healthy and happy.

Chinchillas

There's almost nothing cuter than the chinchilla. That luxurious fur coupled with oversize ears and a little nose make for a starring role in a Disney film. But as cute as they are, chinchillas require special care and should never be brought home on an impulse. Chinchillas are nocturnal; they spend most of the day sleeping and play at night. Chinchillas require dust baths at least twice a week. This is natural for chinchillas, who are from the desert environment of the high Andes mountains where water is available only in ice form. Rolling around in a pile of fine dust keeps their skin and coat healthy by absorbing dirt and oils, similar to the process of using a dry shampoo in humans. Chinchillas are always chewing, so don't put their cage close to door frames! They require special chews to help wear down their teeth and also need multitiered habitats with a solid bottom (not wire). Finally, handle with care. Chinchillas are extremely fragile, especially their rib cage.

Guinea Pigs

Guinea pigs are sweet little pets. They're extremely social so it's best to adopt two guinea pigs rather than one (choose two girls or two boys, or you will soon be knee-deep in piglets). Guinea pigs need adequate vitamin C (ascorbic acid) in their diets to prevent scurvy (that sailor's disease you learned about in school). Feed them a diet fortified with vitamin C, offer fresh vegetables high in vitamin C (like kale, spinach, and broccoli), and consider a supplement if your vet agrees. Give vitamin C supplements directly to your guinea pig rather than adding them to its water. Otherwise, you'll never be sure how much vitamin C your guinea pig is ingesting, and the vitamin C degrades when exposed to light. Provide your guinea pigs the largest habitat possible, and make sure they get daily play time outside their cage. Do this right and you'll be rewarded with the happiest squealing sounds in the animal kingdom!

Rabbits

Rabbits are wonderful pets. They are affectionate, intelligent, clean animals who thrive with human attention. They're also surprisingly easy to house-train. They require high-fiber, low-protein diets; plenty of fresh hay; and lots of appropriate chew items. Even with these, rabbit teeth grow continually and often unevenly, and will cause damage to their mouths if the incisors and cheek teeth aren't worn down appropriately. Rabbits are social and love living in pairs, but some bunnies get along better than others. Be careful housing male bunnies with other males, and avoid opposite-sex pairings unless one or both bunnies are fixed. Regardless, it's important to spay female bunnies due to their high incidence of uterine cancer. ■

Ask **DR. GARY:**

How Often Should I Clean My Pet's Cage?

Whether you have a hamster, rat, mouse, rabbit, guinea pig, or other small pet, a clean habitat is important for overall health. Spot-clean the cage, and wash the food and water containers daily. Do a complete cage cleaning at least once or twice a week (how often depends on the number of animals you have in that cage). First, remove your pet and confine him to a safe place. Next, dump all the old bedding, wash the cage with dish soap and water or a pet-safe disinfectant (look for this in pet supply stores), dry thoroughly, and replenish the bedding. Your little friend will squeak with delight when you return him to his fresh, clean home.

CHAPTER 9

Exercise and Enrichment

Ask yourself this question: "What makes my pet happy?" Running, swimming, perching, stalking, and sniffing are all normal behaviors for our animal companions. Ensure your furry friend gets to do these as often as possible, and he will live a healthier and happier life. Dogs and cats who are bored and underexercised often find ways to provide their own enrichment, and these ways are usually not what you want (digging, destructive scratching and chewing, barking, and other undesirable behaviors). Because dogs and cats are very different animals, and because we recommend that cats live primarily indoors, enrichment and exercise look different for each species, but the concept remains the same: More is always better.

ENRICHMENT FOR DOGS

If dogs were still living in the wild, they would live much as wolves do now: hunting and foraging for food almost constantly, testing each other for dominance by playing and fighting, mating, and sleeping together in a big, furry pile of lupine grandeur. In the wild, environmental enrichment just comes naturally. Because dogs do live with us and not a pack, and because we'd prefer they not roam the neighborhood looking for food and trouble, we must find ways to keep them engaged.

Getting Out of the House

Think about how often you get out of the house every day. You go to work or school, visit friends, do the grocery shopping, and the list goes on. Imagine how it would feel to be stuck in the house all day. You probably wouldn't like it much. Neither do our dogs. For a species derived from ancestors who ranged many miles every day in search of food, staying cooped up in a small house is not natural. Go for daily walks, visit local parks, have a date at your favorite coffee house, and bring your dog with you while you watch your kids play baseball. Your pup will love every minute.

Socializing With Other Dogs

It's critical that we give dogs time and opportunity to socialize with their own kind. If you think about it, how odd is it for humans to be the only

companions to another species? This is the main reason I like dog parks. Dogs need to be with their own species. They need to sniff hind ends, see other tails wagging, and play instinctual games only they understand. To do that successfully and safely, socialization needs to start when they are young. I love starting this at puppy kindergarten, which is the main reason these early classes are offered (see "Socialization" in Chapter 16).

Regardless, try to let your dog have experiences with other dogs. The best dog families are multidog families. For some dogs, this doesn't work, either because genetically they aren't social or because the dog didn't get the early socialization he needed. If you are a one-pup family but your dog likes the company of other dogs, set up dog playdates with friends, relatives, and neighbors who have friendly, healthy dogs.

Off-leash dog parks can be great places for dogs to run, play, and socialize with members of

CAN DOGS TELL TIME?

We used to think that dogs had no concept of time and didn't really know how long we were gone, but researchers at Barnard College's Dog Cognition Lab recently postulated that dogs can in fact *smell* time. According to noted animal behaviorist Alexandra Horowitz, each part of a day "wears a different smell" to dogs. For humans, the world is primarily visual, but dogs "see" their world in smells. If you think your dog doesn't know when it's time for you to come home, think again. He can smell it all over you.

Ask DR. GARY:

Why Do Dogs Sniff Butts?

What on earth is that embarrassing ritual of sniffing other dogs' back ends all about? It's frankly perplexing to us humans, and maybe a little disgusting. But it's completely natural and serves a purpose. Dogs sniff butts (and other places) to learn what they can about the other dog's life: his gender, disposition, and diet. Amazingly, they can get all that from a quick sniff! Thank heaven we can't.

their own species, but not every dog in a dog park should be there. All too often, well-meaning owners take their unsocialized or unfriendly dogs to dog parks. Dog fights can and do happen, sometimes with tragic results. Stay alert every time you visit a dog park, and watch for bullying or aggressive behavior from other dogs. If you or your dog is uncomfortable with the "vibe" for any reason, leave and come back another day.

Using Problem-Solving Skills

Pet toys are getting more sophisticated as we realize that dogs need more than a tennis ball to stay engaged and enriched. The best toys replicate natural behaviors. Enrichment toys and play are essentially substitutes for the survival skills dogs were born to develop. Lots of interactive toys are designed to entice your dog to put his nose or paws to work to release treats, replicating foraging and hunting skills, and use his brain to problem-solve. Interactive pet feeders challenge dogs to figure out patterns to get a food reward. The simplest interactive toy is a rubber KONG—stuff one with your dog's food so he must work for his meal. Such devices obliterate boredom, sometimes obesity, and even anxiety in dogs.

EXERCISE FOR DOGS

You can't have a healthy dog without enrichment, and there's no such thing as enrichment without exercise. Exercise is critical to physical and mental health, helping with mobility, weight maintenance, and overall fitness. According to the Association for Pet Obesity Prevention, nearly 60 percent of cats and 54 percent of dogs in the United States are overweight or even obese. They, like us, need to hit the gym to stay healthy and happy.

Everyday Exercise

Dogs should be outside exercising every single day. The best exercise of all is off-leash playing and running in a safe environment, whether that's a dog park, a ball field, or your backyard. If you don't have an easily accessible place to let your

DOGS WITH JOBS

All breeds were originally developed to do specialized jobs, like retrieving birds for hunters, herding livestock, or pulling carts to market (dogs at one time delivered milk in Belgium and the Netherlands). Many of today's working dogs have high-tech careers, sniffing out drugs and bombs, and even bedbugs or cancer. Some dogs work in conservation, using their keen sense of smell to track whales by following the smell of what they leave behind. Others guard African farmers' livestock, deterring hungry cheetahs, which stops farmers from killing the big cats to protect their livelihood. Many dogs work side by side with humans, acting as service dogs for people with autism, seizure disorders, diabetes, and more. When you think about all the things dogs do for humans, it's truly incredible.

dog safely off leash, there are many other great options for both you and your dog.

I'm a fan of long walks with a dog or with a human. Just do it. Get your dog out as often as possible. A tired dog is a good, happy, and healthy dog. As a routine, plan on a "business" walk at least twice a day; longer walks and hikes are great, but most of us can't count on those until the weekend. Hiking through wooded trails was my favorite activity when I lived in the heart of Washington, D.C. We'd drive over to Rock Creek Park and hit miles of trails through mature oaks and birches along Rock Creek. I loved it and my dogs loved it (and we all weighed about 15 pounds less thanks to our weekend hikes). How far you go depends on your dog's energy level, age, breed, and physical fitness.

Now that I live in San Diego, you can't throw a stone without hitting a beach. To my thrill, these beaches aren't just for people: Six separate off-leash dog beaches are officially open to the public and their canine charges. If you're lucky

enough to live close to a dog-friendly beach, give your dog the opportunity to run in the sand and frolic in the surf.

I actually don't love taking dogs on runs. Most dogs are sprinters, not long-distance runners like us. That means many of them are running to keep

up with us, not because they love to run three to five miles a day. When I say I don't love this, it's because I know it's really not comfortable for some dogs to do this, but I also know that some really energetic dogs do benefit from limited runs. Be mindful, and watch how your dog reacts to being your running partner. If running isn't his thing, run alone; then take your dog to the park for some short-distance sprinting sessions after a tennis ball.

If you know you want a canine running partner, certain breeds were developed to cover long distances, like huskies and other sled dogs. Dalmatians were originally bred to "coach," running in front of horse-drawn wagons, clearing the path for the horses. Other athletic breeds, like sporting and herding dogs, were bred to hunt in the field all day and might be able to handle running distances. Brachycephalic dogs (short-nosed breeds such as bulldogs, pugs, and Pekingese) should not be jogging partners. They can have difficulty breathing and staying cool due to their short muzzles.

The long and short of it is that some dogs love to run, but others don't. Whatever breed you have, ensure

BREEDS WITH HIGH ENRICHMENT NEEDS

Some breeds retain their original working instincts so strongly that they need lots of enrichment, exercise, and mental stimulation if they're going to be kept as pets. Alaskan malamutes, Australian cattle dogs, Belgian malinois, border collies, Catahoula leopard dogs, Dutch shepherds, kelpies, and Siberian huskies are just some of the breeds that need experienced owners and real jobs or huge amounts of enrichment, including tons of exercise, lots of training, brain games, and competing in dog sports or activities. Leave one of these dogs alone too long without stimulation, and you might come home to destruction.

that your dog enjoys the run and is healthy and fit enough for vigorous exercise. Don't force it if your dog doesn't like it.

Another activity to be careful with is biking with your dog. Even dogs who can tolerate a long-distance run may not be able to keep up as you make like a Tour de France yellow jersey holder and barrel down a hill in the imaginary final stage of the race. Be reasonable and ensure that your dog likes running alongside you on your bike. If he's panting heavily with his tongue hanging out behind you, choose another form of exercise. If you do bike with your dog, don't overdo it. Remember that you're seated, but your dog is at a full canter. My last caution is about keeping yourself and your dog safe while biking. Make sure he isn't hurt by the bike or obstacles on the road, and make sure neither of you gets hurt by getting tangled up in the leash. If you're dead set on doing this, use a bike attachment that prevents your dog from crossing in front of you (find one by searching for "dog bike attachment" online).

Exercise Games

I wish I were more of a game player. If I were, my dogs would know how to catch a ball and run after a Frisbee. Sadly, they more resemble the YouTube videos of dogs getting hit in the head with a Nerf ball instead of catching it.

Nonetheless, playing fetch, tug-of-war, or ultimate Frisbee are all terrific exercise routines for your dog. You can even find special toys that help you throw farther, faster, and longer. The Chuckit! by Petmate is a simple contraption that helps you fling a tennis ball to the far reaches of the dog park without blowing out your rotator cuff. And automatic ball launchers keep the game going long after your throwing arm has had enough—your dog can even play fetch in the house while you catch up on your DVR list.

Sports and Activities

Dogs bring out the game player in all of us. Regardless, to really have fun while giving your dog the exercise and enrichment he craves, check out one of the many different dog sports and activities. Most of these sports are designed to let dogs use their innate skills and instincts.

Agility is a sport in which a handler directs a dog through an elaborate obstacle course. It's amazing to watch, not only for the athleticism of the dogs but also the transfixed joy it brings to your pet. Training for agility stimulates your dog's

Ask DR. GARY:

Is It Okay to Play Tug With My Dog?

Tug is a great game for most dogs and terrific exercise, but follow a few simple rules to make sure it doesn't get out of hand. This is especially important to ensure that a reactive dog plays by the rules and doesn't overreact to you or others, especially in other real-life situations. First, make sure you are always the one to initiate the game. Second, teach your dog to release the toy on your command. Finally, teeth should never go beyond the boundaries of the toy. Don't let children play tug-of-war with your dog; this is an adults-only game. When tugging, pull only side to side, not up and down (which is a nonanatomic motion for dogs).

physical abilities as well as his mental ones. Agility is fantastic for intelligent dogs with energy to spare. No doubt, competing in agility is a commitment. You'll want to sign up for sessions with

Ask DR. GARY:

When Can My Puppy Start Agility?

You can start training for agility with your puppy around four to six months, but skip jumping and repetitive running while your puppy's joints are still developing. All other agility obstacles are fine, including A-frame, dogwalk, table (a great way to practice the stay command), teeter-totter, tunnels, and weave poles. Hold off on real endurance work and jumping until your pup is at least one year old (18 months to two years for giant breeds).

a skilled trainer at an approved agility course. Some trainers also offer "fun" agility classes for people who want to try it out but might not be looking to compete.

Disc dog competitions are incredible to watch. You might have seen YouTube videos of these exciting events, where dogs run, jump, and seem to fly as they race to catch that elusive Frisbee. Fast, athletic dogs, like herding breeds and retrievers, excel at flying disc events. It takes a lot of skill on your part too as you learn to throw the discs with accuracy. You don't have to compete to have fun with this sport; simply buy a few discs (they sell special soft ones for dogs) and start tossing! To learn more, check out *skyhoundz.com*.

A great activity for water-loving dogs is dock jumping (also called dock diving), an easy yet exciting sport. Dogs run down a short ramp and leap into the water to retrieve a floating toy tossed by their handler. Competitive dock jumping includes both distance events and high jumps. All you need for training is a body of water (pool, pond, or lake), something to jump off, and a dog who knows how to swim. Great for summer exercise, dock jumping is a fun, family-friendly sport. To learn more, visit *dockdogs.com*.

If you have a small terrier or dachshund, the sport of earthdog just might be his version of heaven on earth. Earthdog is a simulated hunt. The dogs run through underground tunnels, using their noses to sniff out a rat (safely caged at the end of the tunnel). The tunnel systems are elaborate, and the dogs sometimes must dig through false walls and climb over or under tree roots to reach their quarry. Earthdog gives your terrier or dachshund the opportunity to use his natural instinct to chase and dig in an approved environment (rather than your flower bed!). Just in case you were wondering, no rats are harmed during earthdog events. Everything is safe and fun! Learn more at *akc.org/events/earth-dog*.

If your dog is obsessed with tennis balls and loves to run and jump, flyball might be the sport for him. Flyball is a team event. Each team is made up of four dogs. During a race, two teams compete against each other on side-by-side courses. One dog per team runs down a straight course, jumping over hurdles. After the last jump, the dog comes to a box, where he must jump on a lever. The box ejects a tennis ball, which the dog must catch in his mouth before returning back over the hurdles. As soon as he crosses the finish line, the next is released to race over the hurdles. The team that finishes first wins. Flyball is fast and exciting. To learn more, visit *flyball.org*.

Freestyle, also called dancing with dogs, is a type of obedience competition in which you and your dog perform a choreographed routine set to music. It's truly magical to see the incredible teamwork between dog and handler. Anyone and almost any dog can train for freestyle events or just do it for fun at home. To learn more, check out *canine-freestyle.org*.

If you have a herding breed, it can be fascinating to watch him put his instincts to work. Herding trials are competitive events that evaluate a dog's and handler's herding skills. In such events, dogs herd ducks, sheep, or cattle. Many groups also offer herding instinct tests, during which your dog is simply exposed to the livestock and evaluated for his natural instincts and trainability. It's a great way to dip your toe in the water to see if you might like to train for herding trials. To learn more, see *akc.org/events/herding*.

There's no doubt that some dogs were just born to chase furry little creatures. Lure coursing puts

Flyball event

that instinct to chase (called "prey drive") to work in a safe and contained environment. No actual animals are chased in lure coursing events; a lure (usually a white plastic bag) stands in for the "bunny." Sighthounds, which include the subset of hound breeds that were originally developed

Ask DR. GARY:

Can I Jog With My New Puppy?

Please don't take your puppy with you for your daily or weekly run. Between two and 12 months of age, puppies go through an enormous growth spurt—equivalent to a human's zero to 18-year growth spurt. You can only imagine what that does to their bones, ligaments, joints, and tendons. Their anatomy is simply trying to survive this growth assault, so you should limit any additional stress to the system— and that includes jogging. Wait until your puppy is at least 12 months old to start (18 months to two years for giant breeds).

to hunt using their excellent eyesight, are eligible for competitive lure coursing trials, but any breed or mix may participate in the noncompetitive coursing ability test offered by the American Kennel Club. To learn more, see *akc.org/events/ lure-coursing*.

Inspired by working detection dogs, nose work is a fun search and scenting event. Think of it like an Easter egg hunt for dogs, only instead of using their eyes to find an egg, they are using their noses to find a scent. Dogs search in different environments, including indoors, outdoors, and in vehicles. Any dog can participate in nose work activities, and it's an absolute blast for dogs who love to hunt for that treat. Find out more at *k9nosework.com*.

Formal obedience trials are an extension of the basics (sit, lie down, stay, heel, and come). Training for competitive obedience will exercise your dog's body and mind while deepening your bond. Higher levels include jumps, retrieving, and scent-discrimination exercises. Learn more at *akc.org/events/obedience*.

A more relaxed obedience competition, rally includes many of the same exercises as obedience but at a slower pace. Handler and dog heel along a course, stopping at a series of stations, where a sign prompts them to execute a specific exercise, such as sit or down. Find out more at *akc.org/ events/rally*.

Often described as urban herding, treibball is a simulated herding event in which dogs "herd" large balls around a course. The sport originated in Germany, and the word *treibball* means "push ball" in German. Herding dogs often excel at treibball, but any breed or mix may participate. To learn more, visit *americantreibballassociation.org*.

Dogs "see" their world in scent, and tracking events put their powerful noses to work. During a trial, dogs are on leash as they follow a prelaid scent trail across fields and in urban environments. Find out more at *akc.org/events/tracking.*

Dogs love to pull, and not just sled dogs. You don't want your dog pulling on the leash and dragging you down the street, but weight pull events allow dogs to pull in an acceptable way. Dogs wear special harnesses and pull weighted carts or sleds short distances. Large, muscular dogs excel at weight pull events, but any dog can play. Learn more at *ukcdogs.com/weight-pull.*

ENRICHMENT FOR CATS

Behavioral stimulation is just as important for cats as it is for dogs—maybe even more so since many cats only have you and the world you create for them inside your home. Take your roles as "kitty theme park superintendent" seriously. Create a world inside your home that allows your cat to do what cats want to do: stalk, pounce, hunt, climb, and scratch.

When we talk about cats, it's always about instinct. A species that has been domesticated to live with us for about 9,000 years (less than half as long as dogs have been domesticated), cats bridge that amazing gulf between domestication and wild. That's a big part of why we love them. It's also something to keep in mind regarding what stimulates them. For cats, everything good is based on the hunt. Cats must stalk, pounce, grab, and bite their prey, whether it's a real mouse (hopefully not, for the mouse's sake) or a toy mouse.

Toys and Play

Without toys and play, a cat has no freedom to express normal behavior. It might seem that all they want to do is lie around in the sun, but if that's all they have to do, you'll have an unhappy cat. An unhappy cat leads to a very unhappy owner, so don't skimp on cat toys. Some of my favorite toys for cats are boxes to disappear into, feather wands to chase, paper bags to hide in (choose one without handles, which can be a strangulation hazard), and even laser pointers (as long as you give her a real reward on a successful pounce and don't shine the beam in her eyes). Playing fetch, by the way, isn't just for dogs. You can also play this game with your cat, using a toy mouse, jingle-bell ball, or even a ball of paper. She might not always bring it back, but she'll have a great time chasing after it!

Using Problem-Solving Skills

Like dogs, cats benefit from mental stimulation. Some newer toys and games for cats acknowledge this, allowing cats to exercise their own survival-based problem-solving skills. Puzzle toys and interactive games are a great way to keep cats entertained while you're away from home, helping them stay physically and mentally stimulated and active.

Food-dispensing toys are plentiful for cats, as are puzzle boxes with holes and compartments to hide toys and treats for your cat to find. Also look for treat mazes, massage centers, and electronic rotating laser toys. I only wish these interactive toys could be lease-to-own. You don't know which of them will appeal to your cat more than the box they came in.

Climbing and Perching

It's critical to allow your cat to have a vertical playground in your home. Cats need to climb to feel safe (it helps her see potential danger), and they need to perch to survey their kingdom. Again, this all goes back to your cat's wild instincts.

Check out the numerous cat climbing trees, shelves, and perches to find some that work well in your home. You can also do what some very committed cat owners do and build wall-mounted shelves and pathways for your cat. Either way, your cat will be thrilled.

Scratching

Scratching is an absolute necessity for cats for behavioral and anatomical reasons. This is what cats do. When they're prevented from doing it, for instance, by declawing, frustration and even aggression can develop. (Please do not declaw your cat. The number of vets who will do this today are a fraction of what they were a decade ago as we're professionally acknowledging what a barbaric thing this is to do.) To protect your sofa, provide the right substitutes for your cat to scratch. Cat scratchers come in dozens of sizes and types, materials and substrates, ranging from cardboard ramps the size of a shoe box, to floor-to-ceiling posts, and full scratching and perching cat trees.

Exercise

When it comes to exercise, we usually think of dogs, but cats need exercise too. You can encourage your cat to get more exercise indoors by providing lots of places to climb (cat trees, towers, and shelves) and setting aside 10 or 15 minutes a few times a day to entice your cat to chase a feather wand, run after a toy mouse, or play with a special interactive toy. Of course, I won't stop you if you want to get creative and teach your cats to walk on a harness the way you would a dog. Some cats love going for walks, and as a bonus, it gets them safely out of the house.

Experiencing the Outdoors Safely

I once attended a cat behavior workshop held by my friend, Nicholas Dodman, BVMS, a world-renowned veterinary behaviorist who knows cats and dogs like no one's business. One of the things I remember him saying is that cats allowed to roam outdoors have the best lives but the shortest. That is so true. Be it cars, predators, other aggressive cats, or viruses and parasites, living outdoors has its dangers. On average, a feral cat will live five years versus the 15-plus we hope for with our indoor cats. Dr. Dodman wasn't necessarily advocating for cats to be allowed outside, but acknowledged that keeping cats confined to a house limits their ability to express normal behaviors. We've made their lives safe but, sadly, often inadequate.

Keeping your cat indoors is certainly the wisest choice, but you can still let her spend some time outdoors. You can buy or build a special cat enclosure that allows your cat to bask in the sun, roll in the grass, and watch the birds in your yard. A very simple option is simply purchasing a large wire dog crate and putting your cat inside it in the backyard or on your patio or balcony. Don't leave your cat outside in inclement weather, and make sure she has water and access to shade on sunny days. Also check on your cat frequently in case a predator happens by or your cat seems ready to come back inside.

EXERCISE AND ENRICHMENT FOR SMALL PETS

Just like for dogs and cats, exercise and enrichment are vital to the health and well-being of

---

ROOM TO THRIVE

Make sure you provide an adequately sized enclosure for your small pet. Unfortunately, many animals are housed in cages and habitats that are far too small. Most cages found in pet stores average 2.5 to 5 square feet in size. Guinea pigs, for instance, require at least 7.5 square feet of living space, and rabbits need a minimum of 12 square feet. When buying a habitat for your pet, bigger is always better and there is no such thing as too big. Also, skip any cage with a wire bottom. This is bad and painful for your little pet's feet.

---

small pets like birds, rabbits, guinea pigs, hamsters, rats, and mice. One of the best ways to provide social enrichment to small pets is keeping more than one at a time. Rabbits, guinea pigs, hamsters, and other small critters are social beings and enjoy the company of their own kind (this doesn't always work with birds). Just make sure you have two girls or two boys, or you might end up with more than you bargained for (spaying or neutering is also an option for many small pets). But remember, not all pairs of animals get along any more than all humans get along. Have plenty of safe hiding areas when needed.

Time to Roam and Play

Imagine if you lived in your bedroom: eating, drinking, and using the bathroom all in one room, never coming out. You would go crazy from boredom. It's no different for your bird or small animal. A life in a cage 24/7 is not a fun life, so make sure your small pet gets daily time to roam, explore, and play with you outside his enclosure. Always supervise your pet while he's out roaming to make sure he stays safe.

Exercise and Toys

Exercise balls and running wheels are great for mice, gerbils, and hamsters, but these aren't recommended for rabbits, guinea pigs, or rats because they can cause spinal issues. Instead, consider acrylic balls which they can roll around the house for exercise and exploration. Most small pets enjoy playing with toys. You'll find many types of toys for pets of all species, including tubes, tunnels, and ramps to climb; wooden chew toys; and balls to push around. Also consider hides—little houses and huts for your pet to turn

into a luxurious nest filled with shredded tissue and bedding. For birds, the array of toys is endless. Rotate your bird's toys periodically to keep them interesting. Check all bird toys for safety. Many birds have strong beaks and can break off pieces and ingest them, leading to intestinal foreign bodies and even toxicities.

HELP AT HOME

It takes a village to help raise a happy pet. For times you are away from home, enlist the help of a qualified professional. And you'll want help during the "terrible twos," which is the time span between two months and two years. Most dogs, and some cats, look full grown and physically

APPS FOR PET LOVERS

We live in a digital age so why not enlist some of that technology to help you with your pet? Apps like DogVacay, Rover, Trottr, and Wag can connect you to pet sitters and dog walkers, sometimes within just a few hours. Each app is slightly different, but you can contact your dog walker, see where she walked your dog, what time she arrived and returned your pet, and when she securely locked your house. Another app, Bring-Fido, locates pet-friendly hotels, restaurants, parks, beaches, and more. Dog Park Finder Plus finds local dog parks, and MapMyDogWalk logs your walks with your dog so you can keep track of how far you walk together.

developed by one year old, but that doesn't mean they're mature adults. Much like human teenagers, they're still learning, testing their boundaries, and bumbling through life for the first few years. You'll need all the help you can get to raise a good puppy or kitten to be a great dog or cat.

Dog Walkers

I've got one word for these heaven-sent angels: invaluable. Yes, dog walkers are pricey, but so is your living room furniture. If you want to keep that furniture in good condition, your dog needs to be well exercised and entertained. If you must leave your dog for more than six or seven hours a day, get a dog walker to break up the monotony of the day. Eight to 10 hours a day in the house is simply too long for your pet. He needs to get out to use the bathroom, stretch his legs, and do something interesting. Remember: Boredom equals mischief in the dog world.

If you have a puppy, plan on hiring someone to let your pup out of his crate or puppy-proofed area in your house several times a day. This could get costly if you use a professional, so if possible, ask a kind neighbor or family member for help. Raising a puppy is hard, and it's even harder (or more expensive) when you're working full-time. Like I said, it takes a village. Don't be afraid to ask for a hand.

To find an experienced dog walker in your area, seek out word-of-mouth referrals from friends, neighbors, or your veterinarian. You can also try an app like Rover, Trottr, or Wag. Simply download the app and sign up

to request a walker. These apps are a bit like Uber for pets: The walker comes over and takes your dog for a walk. Walker apps are a big help when you have a last-minute need for an outing for your pet. (Check out page 109 for more pet apps.)

No matter which way you go with a dog walker, reviews are critical for choosing the right one. Look for membership in the International Association of Professional Dog Walkers (IAPDW), which can also come with dog walker certification. Make sure your walker is licensed, insured, and bonded. This is insurance that your walker takes her job seriously, and so do her underwriters.

Pet Sitters

Pet sitters are a great alternative to boarding kennels. I use a team of two pet sitters exclusively for my dogs. These professionals are often certified by the National Association of Professional Pet Sitters. A good pet sitter knows your pets and your home as well as you do. More important, your pet knows his sitter. It's almost like a member of the family staying at home with your pets. Pet sitters might visit your home two or three times a day to walk your dog, feed him, play with him, and simply spend time with him. You can also hire pet sitters who will stay overnight in your home, keeping your pets company. Some pet sitters provide grooming services, and many will bring in your mail and water your plants. As with dog walkers, get reviews and make sure your pet sitter is insured and bonded.

You might wonder if you need a pet sitter for your cats when you're away. The answer is yes. Although cats are more independent than dogs, they can also suffer from boredom during the day and need human companionship. Cat sitters should come by at least once a day (preferably twice a day) to feed and play with your cats and clean the litter box. Cats, being cats, might be a bit standoffish at first, but eventually they'll probably accept their new, occasional visiting "family member." This is definitely a case where familiarity breeds content.

Boarding Facilities

Transparency is key here, even if it's within opaque walls. To find a good, responsible boarding facility, you should expect a warm, welcoming environment and knowledgeable staff with a full willingness to show you around. If you don't experience that, go somewhere else. Boarding kennels can vary from small group boarding environments, which might even be in someone's home, to full-scale runs in large, warehouse-like buildings. Some of the newest ones provide closed-circuit TVs to watch your pet while you're away. The type you pick depends on your dog's preference and your budget. Avoid any boarding facility that is not transparent about how it operates. And skip any that are overly noisy (which can be stressful for pets), don't smell clean, or don't require current vaccinations (especially an up-to-date kennel cough vaccine for dogs). Trust your gut. If you don't have a good feeling about the facility, chances are your dog won't either.

Doggie Day Care

Doggie day care is a nice middle-ground solution, combining the benefits of dog walkers, dog sitters, and even dog parks all in one location by offering group play for dogs in a safe, monitored, and controlled environment. Simply drop your dog off in the morning and pick him up at the end of the day—happily exhausted and fully exercised. Many day cares even offer overnight boarding. Some owners, especially those who work long hours, use doggie day care every day. You can also send your dog off to the occasional day at "camp" to break up the week. Most day cares have cameras so you can watch your dog playing with his best friends all day.

Regarding best friends, if your dog tends to be a wallflower at dog parks or would rather go to the vet than play with other dogs, doggie day care is probably not for him. I brought my sweet Betty to one a few years ago and watched her on the online camera all morning. I then drove as fast as I could back to the facility to pick her up three hours early because all I saw was my sweet dog hunched over on the sidelines shaking. Even though she likes other dogs (in small doses), doggie day care was not for Betty. ■

Ask DR. GARY:

What Should I Look for in a Doggie Day Care?

When searching for a reputable doggie day care facility, look for friendly, patient staff who welcome you with open arms, tours of the facility (never leave your pet anywhere where tours are off-limits), video cameras so you can watch your pet online, and a clean and odor-free building. Day cares should require proof of up-to-date vaccines for all dogs. Of course, day cares must be licensed, insured, and bonded. Check out Yelp reviews, get references from friends, and make sure you feel completely comfortable with your visit. If you have a gut feeling that something isn't right, it probably isn't.

CHAPTER 10

Diet and Nutrition

A healthy diet sets the stage for a healthy lifetime. I'd be a happy camper if I could subsist on chips and peanut butter for the rest of my life, but my life might be significantly abbreviated if I got my wish. The same goes for your pet. Animals have definite nutritional requirements, and sometimes these are unique to species. These are facts you shouldn't ignore when considering what to feed your pet. Remember the Five Freedoms, the most basic care all animals deserve. One of those is "freedom from hunger or thirst," and it goes beyond simply providing food and water—your pet deserves much more than just the basics to survive.

However, pet food choices can be overwhelming. Grain free, high protein, low calorie: All of these subtypes make choosing the right food for your pet a challenge. Let's take a closer look at the ins and outs of pet food so your trip to the pet store is a little easier.

TYPES OF PET FOOD

Commercially available pet food comes in many different forms. Understanding the key types will help you choose the right option for your pet. Each form has its pros and cons, relating to cost, convenience, taste, freshness, and nutrition.

Dry Food

Dry food, or "kibble," is by far the most popular form of pet food. You can't beat the convenience factor (simply open the bag and pour it in a bowl), and it's the most cost-effective type of pet food. Dry food also lasts a long time after you open it—for many weeks when stored properly. Most dogs and cats enjoy the taste of crunchy kibble, and it's ideal for animals who like to graze throughout the day because it won't spoil when left out.

Dry food, however, doesn't stay fresh and edible forever. Keep it cool and dry by storing it in your pantry. Kibble can only be stored for a maximum of one year in an unopened bag. Once you open the bag, you should use it within two weeks to a month. If you've been pouring your pet's food into a plastic container, you might want to reconsider. Those thick bags are specially made to keep the food fresh. Just roll the top of the bag down as far as it goes and secure it with a clip.

Due to the nature of how it's made, kibble tends to contain higher amounts of grains and carbohydrates than meat. Kibble is also highly processed; it's cooked and extruded at high temperatures, which can degrade the quality of nutrients. If you guessed that a food called "dry" doesn't have a lot of moisture content you would be right. However, just stick your hand down into that bag and you'll also see that kibble has a good deal of oil in it. That's what makes it palatable, provides essential fats, and keeps it from spoiling.

Wet Food

Wet food, which may be canned, packaged into pouches or trays, or sealed in plastic like a sausage link, is highly palatable—picky eaters frequently enjoy eating this. Wet food, as you might have guessed, has the highest moisture content of commercially prepared food options. This is ideal for pets who need to consume more water, such as senior pets, those with kidney disease, and all cats (many of whom are chronically underhydrated).

The downside to this high moisture content is you have to feed more of it relative to dry food. Because of this, wet food is more expensive than dry food. Wet food is also highly perishable. Once opened, it must be refrigerated within about an hour and used within a few days from the fridge. In general, wet food is somewhat less processed than dry food, although it's subject to the high temperatures required for cooking and sealing into its packaging.

Semimoist

Semimoist food lands somewhere between dry and wet food. It has a higher moisture content than dry food but not as much as wet food. Semimoist food takes on a pelleted form like kibble, but it's chewy rather than crunchy. Most semimoist foods are not the best for your pet. They typically contain a lot of sugar (which helps them stay moist and chewy) and tend to be expensive.

Commercial Fresh

Some manufacturers offer a form of pet food categorized as "fresh," meaning it's lightly cooked and minimally processed (for a processed food, that is). Some commercial fresh foods are sold via pet stores, supermarkets, and big box stores in special refrigerator cases. Other fresh foods can be purchased online and shipped to you in a

cooler with dry ice. Still other companies operate retail stores and sell small batches of cooked food to local customers. For pet owners who are concerned about feeding highly processed foods, commercial fresh foods are the next best thing to home-cooked meals yet still convenient to buy and serve. There are quite a few meal kit options available online, and they're worth looking into. Some fresh food companies allow you to tell them your pet's statistics, including breed, current weight, and desired weight, then send you a personalized quantity of food per meal. I'd kind of like that for myself.

That convenience comes with a high price tag, however. Commercial fresh foods are among the most expensive pet food options. They are also highly perishable and must be used within a few days of opening or thawing (for food purchased or later frozen). Similar to wet food, fresh food cannot be left out all day for pets who like to graze.

Raw Food

Raw food diets have become increasingly popular over the past two decades. The philosophy is rooted in the idea that in nature, pets would be eating raw food (hunting and eating animals) rather than cooked food. Proponents of raw food say their pets are healthier, with firmer stools, fewer allergies, and cleaner teeth. Commercial raw food may be freeze-dried or frozen. Freeze-dried food is often fed in a similar way as kibble—just pour it in the bowl. Some freeze-dried raw food is designed to be reconstituted with water. Frozen raw food must be thawed before feeding.

From a veterinary perspective, raw food is bad, and there is no scientific basis for the advantages of a raw diet for pets. In fact, the American

---

IS DRY FOOD BETTER FOR MY PET'S TEETH?

I once heard about a veterinary dentist who likened the idea of kibble cleaning a pet's teeth to thinking that cookies will clean our own teeth because they're crunchy. It just doesn't work that way. The only exceptions are diets specifically formulated to help keep teeth clean, like those certified by the Veterinary Oral Health Council (VOHC) for their effectiveness slowing or preventing tartar buildup. The VOHC certifies many different products that keep your pet's teeth clean, including food, treats, chews, gels, rinses, and toothpaste. View them at *vohc.org*.

Veterinary Medical Association specifically cautions against feeding any "animal source protein that has not been subjected to a process to eliminate pathogens." That would include most raw diets (some commercial raw diets are pasteurized with a high-pressure processing technique). I can't say I disagree with the AVMA. Everything I know about physiology screams danger here. Proponents justify the safety of raw diets by touting the fact that pets have higher levels of stomach acid and shorter digestive tracts and are therefore not as susceptible to pathogenic bacteria. The key phrase here is *as susceptible*. Physiologically, this reasoning doesn't make sense since animals don't deactivate toxins any better than we do.

Nevertheless, there are plenty of animals for whom feeding a raw diet seems to work, or at least it doesn't seem to harm them. Strictly anecdotally, I have seen dogs who appear to thrive on these diets, and I appreciate the back-to-nature aspect, as well as the benefits for pets who are especially sensitive to processed foods (for example, every German shepherd I've ever known). If you have no other options, my advice is to feed raw diets with extreme caution and resort to them only when other diets have failed.

Here's where the extreme caution comes in. Raw food is obviously made with raw meat, so there is a risk of salmonella and other bacterial contamination. Although pets may not get sick, there have been dozens of recalled commercial raw diets due to these contaminants, especially salmonella, listeria, and *E. coli* (to be fair, many cooked commercial diets have also been recalled for salmonella). Whether pets will get sick from most raw diets or not, this is a game of Russian roulette I don't want my dogs to play. In addition, humans

feeding these foods are always at risk of becoming sick from bacteria due to cross-contamination while preparing the food (pets can also shed the bacteria in their stool). Take care to thoroughly

WHAT'S BETTER FOR CATS: DRY OR WET?

Any vet will tell you that the best food for a cat is wet food. Cats just don't drink enough water and pay for this with urinary tract issues and, ultimately, kidney disease. Canned foods provide that extra water they need. In addition, dry foods have more carbohydrates and oils and can lead to more obesity in cats. You can supplement with some kibble to give them variety and a good crunch, but try to feed canned food as much as you can. It's more expensive than dry food and a little more work but well worth it.

DECODING THE BACK OF THE BAG

1. **Ingredients:** Just like ingredient lists on your favorite foods, the ingredients are listed in descending order by weight. The best options should have specific protein, like salmon, listed first.

2. **Guaranteed Analysis:** If you want to know exactly what amount of certain nutrients, like protein or carbohydrates, are in foods this is where to look.

3. **Pet Food Formulations:** There are many formulas to choose from and most apply to your pet's life stage. Speak with your vet if you think a special formula, like weight control, is necessary for your pet.

wash your hands, bowls, and countertops after handling, preparing, and serving raw food. Any food not immediately consumed should be refrigerated or thrown away. Similar to commercial fresh foods, commercial raw food diets are typically among the most expensive to feed.

READING LABELS

Most of us like to know what we're eating before we eat it, and you should extend that consideration to your pet. To know if a food is healthy and appropriate for your pet, you're going to have to do a little investigation by reading the label. It might seem confusing, but I'm going to walk you through this. If you're embarking on this for the first time, or considering a change to your pet's regular food, ask your vet for advice.

Ingredients List

The ingredients list is the place to look to figure out what's inside that bag or can. Just like with human food labels, ingredients on a pet food label are listed in descending order by weight. That

means the food contains more volume of the ingredients that appear at the beginning of the list, and less volume of those that appear at the end. Don't panic at the complexity of these lists; we'll decipher it step by step.

WHY IS THERE ASH IN MY PET'S FOOD?

Ash is just the mineral residue in pet food that remains after you burn away the protein, fat, and carbs. In other words, ash is what's left in food if you were to, say, set it on fire (which you should not do). Ash is not a filler. Quite the contrary, it provides the calcium, phosphorus, iron, and zinc essential for dogs and cats. Too little ash can lead to bone and neurological problems; too much might indicate a lower quality protein because it's oversupplied with bony material. Ash content shouldn't exceed 4 percent. We used to think ash affected cats' urinary tracts, but it turns out that ash content doesn't have much effect on cat urinary health at all.

Protein

The main protein source in most pet foods is usually meat. The best pet foods list meat as the first ingredient, and this is what we want. The key things to look for here are the type of protein and the form of the protein. Look for foods that list named meat ingredients—for instance, chicken, beef, or salmon. This is better than "poultry" or "fish," which could be any type of poultry or fish, or even many different types of poultry or fish, and likely not the best parts of them. Least desirable is an ingredient listed as "meat." That could be almost anything. Please don't feed your pet mystery meat!

You might see meat listed in its whole form (for instance, lamb or beef) or as a meal (lamb meal or beef meal). Meat meal is not necessarily a lesser quality ingredient than meat; it's simply meat with its water content removed. In a dry food, a meat meal is a more concentrated form of protein. If you see an ingredient list with whole meat first, then a meat meal farther down the list, it's possible that the food contains more of the meat meal than the whole meat once you account for the water weight.

Carbohydrates

Carbohydrates appear in many forms, including corn, wheat, rice, potatoes, oats, and even more exotic grains like barley, millet, and quinoa. The South Beach diet has done a number on us regarding our perception of carbs, but carbohydrates are important nutrients for pets. In the right proportions in their diets, carbohydrates satiate our pets just like they do us, and they are great sources of energy. Carbohydrates in and of themselves are not essential in a pet food, however, and none are particularly worse than any other.

COUNTING CALORIES

Calories in pet food are listed as kilocalories (kcal) per unit of measure. You can calculate exactly how many calories your pet needs per day, but it's not really necessary since the label states how much to feed (often on the high end):

1. Figure out your pet's ideal weight in pounds.
2. Take that weight and divide by 2.2 = weight in kilograms (BW).
3. For dogs, do this calculation: BW + 70 = resting energy requirement (RER) in kcal/day.
4. For cats, do the same, but multiply your result by 0.8.
5. Adjust this up or down a bit depending on your pet's activity level.

Alternatively, many websites, such as *dogfoodadvisor.com,* will do this for you.

Like us, pets can become obese when fed diets that contain too many carbohydrates, which is where moderation comes in. If your pet becomes a little too heavy, feed less, switch to a light formula, or ask your vet to recommend a food that's lower in carbs. This works well for weight loss, especially in cats.

Fat

Fat is a great source of concentrated energy. High-quality fat sources provide your pet with essential fatty acids and

Salmon

ADDITIVES AND BY-PRODUCTS

Most commercial foods contain additives, and many contain by-products. Unless you feed a homemade diet, you can't avoid additives, and you don't have to; they are necessary in commercial diets, adding required vitamins and minerals and maintaining the food's composition and shelf life. Meat by-products, however, are less desirable. These are the parts of an animal left over after everything humans would eat is removed. By-products are a cheap source of calories and protein used to increase the nutritional value of the food. If you can't find a food that contains no by-products, at least avoid foods that contain unnamed "meat by-products." These can contain things I don't even want to mention here.

contribute to overall health, including skin, coat, and brain health. In addition, many vitamins require fat for absorption. Again, look for named fat sources. "Chicken fat" is better than "poultry fat," and please steer clear of "animal fat," which is anybody's guess. "Flaxseed oil" or "sunflower oil" is better than "vegetable oil." Fish oil is generally a high-quality fat, even if it's not specified by species, but you may sometimes see "salmon oil" or "herring oil" listed, which is a good choice.

Guaranteed Analysis

The guaranteed analysis lists the minimum or maximum guaranteed amounts of certain nutrients, including protein, fat, fiber, and moisture. This is high-level stuff, but if you're interested in finding out exactly how much protein or carbohydrates are found in a particular food, this is the place to look. Note that if you wish to compare the nutrient percentages of two foods, they must be the same type of food (for instance, two dry foods or two canned foods) because the water content is considered.

PET FOOD FORMULATIONS

When buying a pet food, look at the label for the nutritional adequacy statement from the American Association of Feed Control Officials (AAFCO) that states the food is complete and

balanced for the life stage the food is intended (either growth and reproduction, or adult maintenance). Beyond the nutritional adequacy statement, foods come in a variety of formulas, including those intended for weight control, special health conditions, and more. If you really want to get fancy, some foods are even intended for specific breeds, something that I would argue is not entirely necessary.

Adult Maintenance

Adult maintenance meets the nutritional adequacy requirements for feeding adult dogs and cats. Compared to growth formulas, adult maintenance formulas provide fewer calories and less protein (minimum 18 percent), fat (minimum 5 percent), calcium (minimum 0.6 percent), and phosphorus (minimum 0.5 percent).

All Life Stages

A food labeled for all life stages should meet both the nutritional adequacy statements for any animal, from puppies and kittens, to adults and seniors. From a veterinary perspective, it's better to feed your pet a food formulated for his specific life stage—growth, adult, or senior. Growing puppies and kittens need more protein and carbohydrates than adult animals, and seniors need less protein of a higher quality than do adults or puppies. That said, you can feed a food labeled for "all life stages" to a pet of any age. The trick with feeding these foods is to feed the correct amounts for that stage of your pet's life. If this isn't clear on the label, contact the manufacturer to ask how much to feed your pet for his particular life stage. Raw and "fresh" foods are formulated for weight rather than age. This

is somewhat controversial but is probably acceptable for these foods.

Grain Free

A relative newcomer to the sea of pet food options, grain-free food contains no grain (for instance, corn, wheat, rice, and oats). However, grain-free foods are not necessarily carbohydrate free. Dry foods particularly require some kind of starch (like potatoes, sweet potatoes, or peas) to bind the food together. Grain-free foods are fine for pets with known allergies or sensitivities to a particular grain. They do, however, tend to be more expensive. Grains are not an essential element of your pet's diet, but they do provide energy and some needed variety to the diet. Grains also taste good, so don't go out of your way to avoid them, unless your pet doesn't react well to eating grain.

IS CORN BAD FOR MY PET?

Corn has gotten a bad rap over the years. Many people claim it's a filler and a major allergen for pets. It's actually neither of these. Corn is a grain, a whole one at that, and it is not Enemy No. 1 to dogs and cats. It's no better or worse for your pet than wheat, barley, or rice. You don't have to avoid it unless your pet doesn't like it or for some reason doesn't tolerate it. That can be said for every other ingredient you feed your pet, so let's stop vilifying this noble grain. Regardless of the type, however, grain should not be the first ingredient in the bag or can.

Growth

Foods labeled "growth" are intended for puppies or kittens, or pregnant and lactating adult females, who require higher levels of certain nutrients. Compared to adult formulas, growth formulas provide more calories, protein (minimum 22 percent), fat (minimum 8 percent), calcium (minimum 1 percent), and phosphorus (minimum 0.8 percent), as well as higher amounts of certain amino acids.

The age at which you can switch from a growth formula to an adult formula varies for each pet depending on size and how quickly your pet's growth is progressing. Always consult your vet before making the change, but in general, small to medium dogs, as well as cats, can switch to an adult formula at one year old. Large dogs continue their growth phase for much longer and should switch to an adult diet between 14 months and two years. One exception is large dogs who are outgrowing their bone development (see Chapter 29). Your vet might advise moving your large or

CAN MY DOG EAT CAT FOOD?

Dogs love cat food. It's appealing to dogs because it's chock-full of fat, which is what entices cats to eat their dinner (no feeding dog food to your cat; she would probably turn up her nose anyway!). The extra fat is great for cats but not so great for dogs. Dogs who indulge in cat food too often can gain weight and may even develop pancreatitis (see Chapter 27). Something that dogs don't know about cat food is that it contains a whole lot of taurine, an essential amino acid cats need to survive. Taurine won't necessarily hurt your dog, but he doesn't need it in those quantities.

giant breed dog to an adult diet much earlier in these cases.

Large Breed Growth

Large and giant breeds sometimes grow at a rate that outpaces the growth of their bones. These dogs are at a higher risk for developing hip and elbow dysplasia, as well as a painful disorder called panosteitis in puppies. In addition to genetics, rapid growth has been associated with a higher risk of developing these orthopedic disorders. Large breed formulas therefore have slightly lower amounts of calories, fat, calcium, and phosphorus. These diets are specifically designed to support the growth rate of large breed dogs while also ensuring that rate does not exceed the ability of the bones to keep up with the rest of the body. In some cases, your vet may advise a

switch to a lower-protein diet if your big dog is growing faster than his bones can tolerate.

Limited Ingredient

Limited ingredient diets contain fewer ingredients on the whole and are usually limited to one protein source (such as lamb or salmon) and one grain or carbohydrate source (such as rice or potato). They are mainly marketed for pets with food allergies or intolerances. Often prescribed by veterinary dermatologists, the most advanced of these formulas even break the proteins down molecularly for the cleanest, most limited formulation possible. Some are composed of a single, very unusual protein and carbohydrate source such as kangaroo and sweet potato, or whitefish and barley. The idea is to give your pet a food that he has never had and therefore won't have had the opportunity, or misfortune, of developing a skin allergy or gastrointestinal sensitivity to it.

Low-Calorie

Designed for overweight pets, low-calorie diets (also called weight management, lite, reduced calorie, diet, or healthy weight) contain fewer calories but are designed to be filling so your pet doesn't feel overly hungry. I'm not a big fan of low-calorie foods. In general, they don't work very well. Instead, I prefer feeding less of a regular food and augmenting with healthy snacks like fruit and vegetables, or feeding a lower-carbohydrate, veterinary prescription diet for weight loss.

Low-Fat

Exactly how it sounds, low-fat formulas contain less fat than standard adult maintenance foods.

PRESCRIPTION DIETS

It might seem strange to think of food as a medicine, but it can be. Whether dry or canned, prescription diets are commercial foods prescribed by your veterinarian to address everything from weight loss and food allergies to diabetes and cognitive disorders. Hills and Purina have the most prescription diets and a great deal of research has gone into them. They're relatively pricey until you consider that they treat real disorders and often replace medication altogether. Considered that way, these are among the best deals you can ever get in veterinary medicine.

Low-fat diets might be advantageous for pets recovering from a medical illness like pancreatitis, but in general, they're not all that good at lowering weight.

Low-Protein

You won't see many commercial low-protein foods because these are very controversial. It used to be thought that senior animals or those with liver or kidney problems needed less protein in their diets, but that is no longer the recommendation. There are times when a low-protein diet may be advised by a veterinarian, but these cases are rare. Instead, vets advise foods with high-quality, meaning easily digestible, protein sources for senior animals or those with liver or kidney disease.

Senior

Senior formulas are generally lower in calories and fat and higher in fiber. Some senior foods might be lower in protein than adult foods, but some might actually be higher. It's about quality, not quantity. Senior animals need fewer calories, and they might eat less, so you want to feed them high-quality, easily digestible, sources of protein.

Your decision to switch to a senior diet should be made with your vet, but most commercial pet foods label their products for dogs from seven years and older. For cats, it's from 10 years and older. It's important to weigh in other factors before making the switch, like how active your pet is. If your seven-year-old chocolate Lab is a tireless bundle of energy, knocking out three hikes a week, stick to adult food and reevaluate him in another year. If your 10-year-old cat lies around on the windowsill all day, it's probably time to switch to a senior diet.

Small Breed

Small breed formulas generally contain more calories per cup. Some small dogs have faster metabolisms and higher energy requirements than larger breeds. The trick here is to get enough calories into your small dog before he fills up. With dry foods, the kibble size is usually smaller for little mouths.

Vegetarian

Vegetarian and even vegan pet foods are out there, but I don't recommend them. Dogs are real omnivores and cats are obligate carnivores, so feeding them a nonmeat diet is unnatural at best, and harmful at worst. I respect the vegetarian position on meat production, but feeding dogs and cats a vegetarian diet is just a bad idea. If you don't want to feed your pet meat, consider an herbivore pet like a rabbit, guinea pig, or hamster. Some animals, however, do have true food allergies to meat proteins. This is rare but fortunately, the majority can tolerate an egg-based diet.

PET FOOD DEFINITIONS

You might see the words *natural, organic,* or even *human-grade* used on pet food labels, but do these words carry much weight? As it turns out, some terms have official or legal definitions and others do not.

Natural

You've probably seen the word *natural* used on pet food labels, but what does it really mean? AAFCO defines *natural* as "a feed or feed ingredient derived solely from plant, animal or mined sources" and goes on to say that "*natural* is a liberal term that includes more ingredients than it excludes." In a nutshell, foods labeled *natural* cannot contain chemicals or chemically synthesized ingredients. A bonus to choosing a natural pet food is that it won't contain any chemical additives. Keep in mind that many additives are safe and important to keeping the food structurally sound and fresh. These include vitamins, antioxidants, preservatives, emulsifiers, and even some flavors without which the food would not be complete and might be uninteresting to your pets. Keeping additives to a minimum is what you should look for in a pet food.

Organic

Organic is a definition that food officials take seriously. Although pet-food-specific organic regulations are still being developed, the USDA's National Organic Program has stated that for now, organic pet foods must meet the same standards as organic human foods. To be considered organic and display a USDA organic seal, at least 95 percent of the food's ingredients must be organic. Organic foods are those grown without pesticides, genetic modification, artificial fertilizers, radiation, or sewage.

Human Grade

According to AAFCO, there is no official definition for *human grade*. There is, however, a USDA definition for *edible*, which means a product is fit for human consumption. AAFCO states, "Extremely few pet food products could be considered officially human edible or human-grade" and "human-grade does not automatically equal nutritional safety for pets." Personally, I do try to

feed my animals foods that are considered "human-grade" when I can. It's more expensive for sure, but at least I generally recognize the ingredients. My dogs think they're eating my dinner instead of their own (not that this stops them from begging for mine).

HOMEMADE FOOD

Every year, a few clients ask me how to make homemade diets for their pets. I actually love hearing this because it means they're utterly devoted to their pet. What's better than that? It was something that occurred more frequently back when commercial pet foods were very limited. If you had a dog who needed to eat a limited-ingredient diet, for instance, you had no other option but to make it yourself. A special diet is entirely appropriate and even critical for some pets, such as those with liver or kidney disease, urinary-tract issues in cats, and even occasional intestinal upsets. Today, consumers have a dizzying array of commercial pet food options, including customized fresh food that can be purchased online. However, some pet owners still wish to cook at home for their pets, whether for health reasons or simply so they have total control over the ingredients going into their pet's food.

Cooked Homemade Food

If you decide to go this route, be aware that it's not easy. Making homemade food is a commitment. Pet food manufacturers have spent decades researching their food so it provides complete and balanced nutrition. When cooking for your pet, you

HOMEMADE DIET DOS AND DON'TS

If you want to cook for your pet, use fresh ingredients, and store them properly. Follow these simple rules:

- DO follow a complete-and-balanced recipe approved by a board-certified veterinary behaviorist.
- DON'T make major changes to recipes without consulting a vet.
- DO feed whole, unprocessed foods.
- DON'T feed too many carbohydrates. The bulk of your pet's food should be meat.
- DO ensure your pet gets the essential vitamins, minerals, and other nutrients he needs.
- DON'T feed your pet a vegetarian diet. Dogs are omnivores, and cats are carnivores. I applaud you for choosing a human vegetarian diet, but dogs and cats are simply not designed to be vegetarians.
- DON'T give up. Cooking for your pet takes effort, but if you do it right, your pet will certainly benefit.

must provide the correct amounts of four essential ingredients—protein, carbohydrates, fat, and fiber—as well as the right balance of calcium, phosphorus, and other vitamins and minerals. This can be tricky, so follow a recipe that has been approved by a board-certified veterinary nutritionist (find one through the American College of Veterinary Nutritionists at *acvn.org/directory*). This is especially critical for cats, who have very specific nutritional needs (taurine is an important one), and growing puppies and kittens, who have increased protein and energy requirements.

Homemade diets for pets usually contain cooked meat, eggs, vegetables, and grains, or other carbohydrate sources like potatoes. Some recipes also call for fish oil and a vitamin-and-mineral supplement, particularly calcium. Ground eggshells might also be used to provide calcium. Cats require a taurine supplement as well.

If you wish to cook for your pet, don't wing it. Follow a recipe for cats or dogs from your vet, or explore the many recipes online (for instance, *dogaware.com* or *catinfo.org*). A note of caution on this: There are tons of recipes online with absolutely no verification of the credentials of their authors, so always run your recipe by your vet before buying 20 pounds of mackerel.

Raw Homemade Food

If you wish to feed a homemade raw diet, proceed with caution; it requires an even more high-level commitment and attention to detail as a cooked homemade diet. For raw diets, it's imperative that you use fresh food and keep it at a safe temperature. There is no messing around with this choice for your pets—keep raw food refrigerated for up to four days max or frozen until ready to use. Always follow a veterinarian-approved recipe for a balanced raw diet for your pet. One source is

Dr. Becker's Real Food for Healthy Dogs and Cats (Natural Pet Productions, 2011).

Raw food diets are composed of mostly meat—muscle meat and organ meat. So that your pet gets the calcium he needs, most raw diet enthusiasts also advocate feeding raw bones (non-weight-bearing bones like chicken necks and backs) in addition to raw meat. Raw bones are soft and won't splinter the way cooked bones do (never feed your pet cooked bones), but some pet owners choose to grind the raw bones to take away any choking hazard. Others feed whole raw meaty bones. If you don't feed raw bones, raw diets must be supplemented with calcium, using either ground eggshells or a commercial calcium powder. Again, be very careful about feeding raw food, bones or otherwise.

Although you can feed your pet fruits and vegetables, dogs and cats can't digest raw vegetables well. Raw veggies won't hurt your pet, but he won't be able to extract many nutrients from them. Cooking or pureeing raw vegetables in a blender helps your pet digest them easier.

FEEDING

Feeding a pet is one of the true joys of having a pet. I could watch my animals eat all day long (and they'd love to do just that!). But knowing how much to feed and how often can be complicated. Fortunately, if you feed a commercial diet, much of the complication is taken out of the equation for you by the manufacturer.

How Much to Feed

This isn't as easy to answer as it looks. It's difficult to calculate exactly how much you should feed your pet. Food quantity depends on the type of food and your pet's size, metabolic rate, daily exercise amount, appetite, and energy needs.

If you want to try to calculate how much food your pet needs, go for energy level, measured in kilocalories per day. For dogs, this varies from 800 to 1,400 kcal/day. Calculating that number isn't easy. There's an easier way to do this: Read the pet food label. The scientists behind commercial pet

DO I ALWAYS HAVE TO FEED THE SAME FOOD?

Imagine eating the same food every day of your life. Sounds boring, right? And yet we do this to our pets all the time. It's important to change things up occasionally, either by changing the flavor of the food or main meat profile. Some animals readily tolerate switching between different brands or types of food. Just be sure to do it very gradually, mixing the old food with the new over a period of about a week. Some brands of food come in different flavors, which makes it easy to liven the menu while avoiding stomach upset. Cats are a little less receptive to variety, but all you need to do is "ask" them by offering it.

foods have already done the math necessary to determine the approximate amount of food you should feed your pet.

Two caveats to these recommendations. First, these amounts are nearly always way too much food for domestic pets—they could feed Olympian dogs and cats, not the simple mortal pets I usually see in the exam room. So start with slightly less than the amount listed on the label; if your pet loses weight, feed a little more. If he gains weight, feed a little less. Now isn't that easy?

Second, you should also factor in weather. Ever notice how animals eat more in the cold weather? That's not just your imagination. They do so because they need more energy to increase their metabolic rate to stay warm. If your pet seems hungrier in winter, go ahead and feed him more.

How Often to Feed

Most pets should eat at least twice a day. That means feed dogs and cats half the recommended daily amount for breakfast and the other half for dinner. Puppies and kittens less than five months old should have an extra meal around lunch. Vets really don't recommend free feeding your pets as this can lead to obesity. Conversely, feeding only once a day is not ideal because of the size of that one meal. Deciding when to feed may be driven more by your lifestyle than an absolute need to break up the meals, but ideally, twice a day is best for domestic pets.

Breed Considerations

Different breeds might have different dietary requirements. For the most part, however, dogs are dogs, and what one breed eats works for the other. A few years back, some pet food manufacturers started producing diets specifically formulated for

different breeds. With very few exceptions, these diets consider growth rate, energy levels, and geographic origins for the breed. It gets complicated. If you want to try an Akita or great Dane formula, go for it, but it's not necessary. What really matters is if you're feeding a complete and balanced, high-quality dog food and your pet is growing or maintaining a healthy weight.

TABLE SCRAPS

I don't shudder at the thought of table scraps for pets. If you think about it, the reason dogs came to live with us in the first place was to forage for scraps of food. Then our ancestors deliberately

gave dogs scraps so the dogs would hang around, providing early warning of and protection from predators.

Some table scraps are perfectly safe and even healthy to feed your pets, and some should be avoided. You can give your pets limited amounts of what you ate (not true garbage). Just give a taste of what you had, not a plate full of Thanksgiving dinner. Never give foods like fat and grizzle from meat, poultry skin, pure grease, bones, or sharp pieces, and be careful of foods your pet doesn't have a good track record with. Feeding pets fatty food can cause intestinal issues like vomiting, diarrhea, or even pancreatitis, which can be very dangerous. Feeding bones can potentially cause a blockage of the intestinal tract. A word of caution: Don't get your pets too used to eating table scraps, or they might turn their noses at their pet food. Also, it's a good idea to feed scraps in your pet's bowl rather than from the table so he doesn't pick up the bad habit of begging.

TREATS

Think of pet treats like cookies, cake, and candy. They're fun but not necessarily healthy. On the other hand, what is life without treats? We can live without them but do we want to? Pets love treats too. Use them as training rewards or for a special occasion and feed them in moderation.

Healthy Treats

If you're dedicated to an all-natural diet for your pet, don't despair. You can purchase organic and natural treats, which are pretty much everywhere now, even in big box retail stores. Organic might be a little harder to find, but these too are available in high-end pet stores and online. For complete control over the ingredients in your pet's treats,

THE TROUBLE WITH JERKY

Over the past decade, there have been multiple recalls and warnings about dog jerky treats, especially those from China. Such treats have been linked to a syndrome affecting the kidneys in dogs making them very sick; a few have even died. These mostly involve dried chicken tenders or strips, as well as jerky treats made with duck, sweet potato, and other ingredients. I've stopped feeding my dogs jerky treats entirely, mostly because we still don't know exactly what the culprit is (the FDA is still investigating). Some large pet stores have stopped stocking treats from China until we can be assured of the safety of the ingredients and know better what is causing harm to our dogs.

make your own homemade treats. It's easy and fun to bake up biscuits, dehydrate jerky, and make other yummy treats. You can find lots of recipes online and in pet cookbooks. Some books are dedicated entirely to homemade pet treats.

Chews

Dogs love to chew. Chewing is a natural behavior that alleviates boredom and anxiety and helps keep the teeth and gums healthy. If you don't give your dog something acceptable to chew, you might need to buy new shoes sooner than you planned. The trick is to find something that will occupy her need to chew but doesn't upset her digestive tract.

Chews come in a huge variety for dogs. When selecting flavored chews, consider the source of these flavorings. Many are made up of pure chemicals, sugars, colorizers, and, yes, sometimes even real meat flavors. Even the main ingredient, the hide, is a by-product itself, often soaked in hydrogen peroxide followed by an acid or formaldehyde for processing, so what on earth do you suppose the flavoring is composed of? Certainly not organic or natural ingredients.

Rawhide, arguably the oldest type of chew on the market, is a popular choice. But is it safe? The simplest answer is not entirely. Consider plain, unflavored, nonbasted, unstuffed rawhide. It certainly keeps dogs entertained, but it can also cause stomach upset, diarrhea, choking, foreign body blockage, stomach torsion, and even death. That's before we even start talking about the mystery ingredients contained in the basted or stuffed varieties. So why have we fed these to dogs for decades? They love them. If you want to give your dog rawhide, feed nothing smaller than their front

paws, stay away from as many chemicals and flavorings as you can, and avoid any treats or chews made in China. In addition, supervise your dog closely whenever he chews on rawhide. If he tears off a large, gummy chunk and tries to swallow it, he could choke. (Ever wonder why dogs like shoes? Rawhide is the underbelly layer of those leather

Ask DR. GARY:

What Are the Safest Chews?

The best chew depends entirely on your dog. What kind of chewer is he? When you give a chew, always monitor your dog. Avoid giving certain chews if he bites off and swallows large chunks. Also, some chews might cause intestinal upset. Go with the cleanest, least complicated chew possible. If your dog has a hard time digesting a particular type of chew, try something else. If all goes well, you'll find a great chew treat for your dog. Just give them in moderation—no more than one a day.

shoes in your closet—it's what's left over after the rawhide is stripped from the outer layer of hide.)

So what should you look for? Bully sticks, cow ears and hooves, tracheae, tendons, pig ears, hooves, deer antlers—if it's an animal part, you will probably see it offered as a chewing treat at your local pet store. (If you find unicorn horn, let me know.) These options are now pretty mainstream, but don't assume that your dog's gastrointestinal tract will appreciate every offering. Less desirable choices include antlers, hooves, and hollowed out bones, all of which can break teeth. Pig ears are high in fat, have been known to carry salmonella, and can cause stomach upset. What you give your dog depends on a little trial and error (see "What Are the Safest Chews"). Just be sure error doesn't compromise your dog's safety.

SUPPLEMENTS

If you're feeding a balanced, nutritionally appropriate diet, your dog or cat should not need supplements. Convincing a vitamin enthusiast otherwise is a futile effort, but it's simply true. Commercial diets are specifically formulated to contain 100 percent (or more) of a pet's daily nutritional requirements.

Vitamins and Minerals

Healthy pets who eat a complete-and-balanced pet food do not need a vitamin supplement. The exception is if your vet recommends a vitamin supplement for an iron deficiency, B vitamin deficiency, or other abnormality. It's a different story entirely if you're feeding a

homemade diet, in which case, vitamins and minerals are essential. Look for a multivitamin and mineral supplement formulated for pets.

Essential Fatty Acids (EFAs)

The omega-3 fatty acids EPA (eicosapentaenoic acid) and DHA (docosahexaenoic acid) have documented benefits in pets, reducing inflammation, improving skin and coat health, and possibly supporting the immune system, heart, brain, and nervous system. DHA has even been attributed to decreasing the progression of many cancers. EFAs, when used in conjunction with antihistamines, even appear to have a synergistic effect, helping dogs with atopic dermatitis (otherwise known as skin allergies), more than the antihistamines alone.

Recognizing the benefits of omega-3 fatty acids, many manufacturers add them to commercial pet foods. Unfortunately, EFAs degrade quickly when exposed to light, air, and heat, so the amounts found in your pet's food might not be high enough to be beneficial. Luckily, it's easy to supplement with fish oil, which provides EPA and DHA. Some fish oil supplements made for pets come in handy pump bottles so you can simply pump the oil right over your pet's food. You can buy fish oil supplements from your veterinarian or in pet stores.

Probiotics

Probiotics are live organisms, usually "good" bacteria, yeast, or fungi that in recommended amounts might exert certain health benefits when consumed. These are all the rage in the human world. Their use has become increasingly popular as we learn more about the gut and how it influences

Fish oil capsules

our overall health. Although the effect of probiotics in animals is still being researched, probiotic supplements might be beneficial for pets and are unlikely to be harmful. Probiotics may be used daily for overall health or may be given during times of gastrointestinal upset.

Many pet-specific probiotic supplements are available. Some need to be refrigerated, so read the label carefully. Yogurt is also a good source of probiotics for pets. Simply add a tablespoon to your pet's food. Be sure the yogurt contains active cultures of *Lactobacillus acidophilus* or *Bifidobacterium lactis,* is plain (unflavored), and has no artificial sweeteners or nuts. Also, be sure your pet does okay with milk products before feeding it or you'll both regret it.

Nutraceuticals

Nutraceuticals are compounds derived from food and herbs that might be beneficial to health.

A good example is glucosamine and chondroitin sulfate, often used to treat and prevent joint problems and arthritis in pets. The value of nutraceuticals, like many other things in nutrition, has not been irrefutably proved. Although research has been ongoing for decades and continues forward, there is still little definitive proof that these compounds have a real effect. The other issue with nutraceuticals is that they are unregulated, and the amounts needed to produce an effect are unclear. Formulations can vary widely by manufacturer.

Having said all this, I'll confess that I use nutraceuticals for my pets, including glucosamine and chondroitin sulfate to help with joint pain. Many have anecdotal benefits and at the very least don't cause harm. I can't afford to wait out the FDA regulation of these products during my own pets' lifetimes, and I wouldn't expect you to do that either.

NUTRITION FOR NEWBORNS

Most of the time, newborn kittens and puppies get all the nutrition they need from their mother's milk. But when babies are orphaned, humans need to take over. Bottle-feeding kittens or puppies is a challenging endeavor but well worth it if you can save the lives of a litter of helpless young animals.

Bottle-Feeding Kittens

Spring is the season for every shelter's onslaught of kittens. Female cats (called queens) typically have their babies between March and November. To help with "kitten mountain," as many shelters dub it, volunteers help bottle-feed orphaned kittens throughout kitten season. These kittens come to shelters by the thousands through good Samaritans who find abandoned litters of kittens or even single newborns. It's a good idea to check with your vet or local shelter about how to take care of the kittens, but you may wish to care for the kittens yourself, especially if you live in an area where the shelter is unable to care for newborns. With a little training, it's not as difficult as it looks.

Kittens less than four weeks of age must be fed a kitten milk replacement (KMR) using special kitten formula bottles (most pet stores carry KMR and bottles). Warm the formula to 101 degrees Fahrenheit. Feed kittens by placing them stomach down on a soft towel (which simulates mom) and opening their mouths to insert the nipple (first puncture it with a pin). Feed until your kitten has had enough—she'll tell you by stopping eating. Never let a kitten flip on her back while feeding or she might aspirate (inhale) the milk into her lungs, which can be fatal. Kittens must eat every three to four hours. Wake them up if they are asleep at dinner time. They'll forgive you.

After each feeding, wipe the kittens' bottoms with a warm, moist cotton ball to stimulate them to defecate and urinate. Mom would do this if she could. For extra credit, comb their backs with a soft toothbrush after dinner to simulate mom's tongue cleaning them and releasing the bonding hormone oxytocin, and you'll have some very happy growing kittens.

Bottle Feeding Puppies

There isn't a defined "puppy season," but there certainly seem to be more of them in the spring and summer months. They are less frequently in need of bottle feeding than kittens because mother dogs tend to be glued to their litters. In addition, there are simply fewer feral dogs than cats. Nevertheless, some circumstances necessitate bottle-feeding a litter of puppies, including orphan situations, illness, or even death of the mother.

If this happens, it's pretty much the same deal as for the kittens. You can purchase puppy milk replacement (Esbilac and other brands are widely available) from your vet, online, or at pet stores. Feed every three to four hours with a puppy formula bottle. Keep the puppies warm and dry, and use warm, moist cotton to stimulate

FRESH FRUITS AND VEGGIES FOR RABBITS AND OTHER PETS

Most rabbits, birds, guinea pigs, hamsters, rats, mice, and other small pets enjoy fresh fruits and vegetables as nutritious treats. Each species varies slightly when it comes to which fruits and vegetables are safe and which are not. For instance, rabbits should not eat beans, nuts, seeds, rice, potatoes, corn, or avocado. And some pets can eat as much fresh fruits and veggies as they want, while others should enjoy them in moderation. Too much can be as dangerous as too little. Dietary requirements can also change seasonally due to breeding and with age. Always ask your veterinarian for advice regarding your specific pet.

them to urinate and defecate. Grooming daily with a soft toothbrush will help their digestion as will holding them up, belly down, towards your shoulder after a meal to "burp" them. Yep, you're definitely in it now. You can even do this same routine for orphaned rabbits using KMR but adding a teaspoon of whipping cream to it for extra calories.

Weaning Bottle-Fed Kittens and Puppies

You've been a hero and bottle-fed orphaned kittens or puppies every four hours for the past 21 days. How do you know when to regain your nights and start them on the road to eating on their own? At three to four weeks of age, it's time to start babies on solid food, preferably canned kitten or puppy food. Supplement with bottle-feeding for about a week until they're happily gaining weight on the wet food, and you'll soon see the light at the end of the tunnel of no sleep.

NUTRITION FOR RABBITS, BIRDS, REPTILES, AND OTHER SMALL PETS

Nutrition is just as important for rabbits, birds, snakes, and pocket pets as it is for dogs and cats. If you're new to owning a small pet, do your homework and find out what your new friend needs to eat (or not eat) to stay healthy and thrive. Although some pet store employees might be well versed in the care of these pets, others are not as well educated, so be careful who you ask. As with all other topics, there's much misinformation floating around about the proper care and feeding of small pets. To get the best advice, go straight to an expert. When you bring your pet home, take him to a veterinarian who specializes in birds or exotic pets (this is the veterinary term used to describe almost any pet other than dogs and cats). At your pet's first exam, your vet can tell you exactly what and how much to feed your new friend. ■

CHAPTER 11

Obesity

Pet obesity is a big problem in the United States, where an estimated 54 percent of dogs and 60 percent of cats are overweight or obese. As with people, pets who carry excess weight are at higher risk for many diseases and problems, including diabetes, arthritis, high blood pressure, heart disease, kidney disease, and some types of cancer. Too much weight can also exacerbate joint problems and even decrease your pet's life expectancy. We all know that leaner is better. Seemingly from every direction, we're bombarded with messages about losing weight, maintaining a healthy diet, and increasing activity to lose weight. We hear these messages, but our pets do not. It's entirely up to us to help them maintain a healthy weight or, as is the case for my little pit Betty, lose some of their excess mass. Like us, genetics plays a role here. That doesn't mean it can't be overruled by diet and exercise, but some pets are simply predisposed to gain weight.

MEDICAL CAUSES FOR WEIGHT GAIN

Other than the obvious cause of simply taking in too many calories by eating too much and burning too few calories by not exercising enough, certain medical issues can cause weight gain. If your pet is gaining weight despite a good diet and exercise, you should check with your vet to rule out some common, controllable diseases that might be messing up those scale numbers.

Metabolic or endocrine diseases can cause weight gain. In dogs, these include hypothyroidism (low thyroid levels) and hyperadrenocorticism (high cortisol levels), a syndrome that's known as Cushing's disease. In the United States, hypothyroidism is the most common metabolic disease in dogs, with a preponderance of golden retrievers, Labrador retrievers, and spaniels being affected, although it can affect any breed. Cushing's disease affects far fewer dogs but is a common rule-out in dogs with weight gain, potbellies, and skin issues. For both disorders, there are probably many dogs who go undiagnosed. Sometimes medical treatments, such as taking prednisone, can also induce weight gain.

For cats, there are far fewer excuses in the form of metabolic disorders. In fact, most endocrine diseases cause weight loss, not gain, in cats. We'll cover that issue in Chapter 27.

Finally, the queen of all metabolic issues, pregnancy, can certainly cause weight gain in dogs and cats. It will cause a few other things as well, which should become more than obvious. Spaying your pet will certainly avoid this complication.

Spaying and neutering might also cause weight gain. Spayed and neutered pets gain weight because these surgeries significantly decrease the production of the sex hormones estrogen and testosterone, both of which contribute to an increased metabolism in all animals. Without either of these hormones, the body tends to accumulate fat. It happens to us, and it certainly happens to our pets. This is an unfortunate side effect of a very necessary procedure that controls pet overpopulation and provides other benefits for our pets (see Chapter 15).

Although it's important to have your pet checked for a medical cause for weight gain, the majority of our dogs and cats are overweight simply because we feed them too much and exercise them too little. It's as simple as that.

HOW MUCH TO FEED TO AVOID OBESITY

I'm a firm believer that food equals love. I love to feed my pets, I love to watch them eat, and I love to give them treats. What I don't love is what too much food and treats can do: cause weight gain, health complications, and a shortened life span. To enjoy food and avoid the fallout, it's imperative that you feed the right food in the right amounts and give treats in moderation. Use treats to motivate rather than entertain.

The right food is one that's designed for the age and activity level of your pet. Look for a food that contains more protein than carbohydrates, and feed no more than the amount recommended on the label. You may actually find that amount to be surprisingly high. I do too. Talk to your vet about the exact amount you should feed.

Always measure the food you're feeding. You'd be shocked at how off you can be by simply guessing at the amount. When you scoop the food, don't use any old cup—use a measuring cup. Feeding twice a day rather than just once a day helps with weight maintenance too. Grazing is better than feasting. But be careful of free feeding, which just adds more dog or cat to your pet. Keeping the food bowl filled at all times keeps your pet filled at all times. Food is reward number

one, and it's unlikely a full food bowl will remain that way for long.

We have a cat room at the San Diego Humane Society that is set up entirely for our "fat cats." They're on a prescribed weight-reduction diet and get a bit more exercise than the other cats at the shelter. They are losing weight slowly. If this can work for them, it can work for any pet. We even have a video camera broadcasting our fat cats so the world can watch their progress (good thing we don't need consent for this!).

DIET FOODS

If your pet needs to lose weight, the process is simple: Reduce calorie intake and increase exercise. To cut down on calories, you have a choice: Feed less of the same food (and try to ignore those big brown eyes pleading for more) or feed a diet that is lower in calories itself.

First, ask your veterinarian how much weight your pet needs to lose. For minor weight loss of 10 percent or less, I recommend feeding less of

HEALTHY TREATS

If your pet is overweight, treats can add to the problem, and faster than you'd ever think possible. Commercial pet treats, including biscuits, jerky, and chews, can be high in calories and fat (think of these as nutritious as candy bars are for us). Treats are not a necessity; they're treats. Try to limit them to no more than once or twice a day. You can even choose low-calorie treats like fruits and veggies. For dogs, try cooked or raw carrots, sugar snap peas, and green beans, as well as apple slices (no seeds) or blueberries. For cats, try cooked carrots, broccoli, and green beans, or let them nibble on some cat grass.

Sugar snap peas

your pet's regular food. If your pet needs to lose more than 10 percent of his body weight, you might want to switch to a lower-calorie diet. If you go this latter route, you have a couple of choices. If the food you're feeding comes in a lighter variety, give that a shot. If it doesn't, gradually switch to a similar brand with lower calories (the transition should happen over at least a week).

For those of you who missed calculus, there are online optimal weight calculators to give you about the amount of food you should feed to achieve your pet's target weight. Or better yet, use the label recommendations or ask your vet. Just know that the label will probably overestimate the amount to feed and your vet will probably decrease it (we get pretty aggressive about

weight loss!). If your pet isn't under your vet's treatment for weight loss, use the label as a high-end recommendation.

For specialty pet foods (available online or sold through retail stores), you can often calculate your pet's feeding regimen precisely based on his weight and target weight. Most even include an age and activity variable. This is what I'm doing with my dog Betty, using a very cool new, prepackaged online fresh food formulated by a veterinary nutritionist. Betty's food comes in individually sealed fresh packs to feed twice a day. She loves it and has no idea she's on a diet. Now if only I could get her out on that racquetball court.

For cats, the best way to help them lose those extra pounds is to cut the carbs. Sound familiar? The "catkins" diet is prescribed by veterinarians

IMPORTANCE OF EXERCISE

Just like humans, pets' bodies go into conservation mode as soon as they figure out that they're getting fewer calories. This means metabolism drops, energy drops, and boredom rises. Why boredom? We're talking about animals for whom food is happiness, enrichment, and entertainment. Months and years on a calorie- or carb-restricted diet can eliminate one of the true joys for an animal. Hence the boredom. You can counter some of that, and you should, with exercise and other enrichment. Just don't keep your pet on a diet his whole life.

Regular exercise is a necessary component of any pet weight-loss regimen. Diet is good and necessary, but diet without exercise is just slow burn. It doesn't have to be extreme: A simple extra walk on the leash a day, maybe uphill occasionally, will do wonders for weight loss. It's great for you too.

A note of caution. Don't rush full speed ahead into your pet's new exercise routine, especially if your dog isn't used to walking up a hill twice a day or hiking the Pacific Trail. Everything goes better if begun gradually. Don't start jogging with your overweight Labrador until he's mastered a good 45-minute power walk. Starting slowly allows time for building muscles and endurance and protects his joints from injury. The last thing you want is a ruptured cruciate ligament (see Chapter 29).

Exercise is essential for cats too. Despite how sedentary we've made them (and they appear to have taken to it like moths to a light), cats are athletic creatures and do need exercise. Get out her favorite toy for a game of toss, or a feather wand for a game of stalk-and-pounce at least once a day.

for cats who really need to lose weight. You can start with a lighter food of the same type you're currently using, but for more weight loss, you'll need to have your vet prescribe a carefully regulated low-carb diet for her. They're easy to use; just be sure to stop the diet when your cat reaches her target weight. Too often I see pets who are on their weight-reduction diets until seemingly the end of time. These diets are intended for limited use—maybe six months to a year max. Then just watch for that weight creeping back in the future. In multi-pet families, you might luck out and be able to feed the same diet to all your pets, but more likely you'll have to feed your pets separately, possibly in different rooms.

Rabbits and pocket pets also need an outing at least once a day. To give a larger but still enclosed space, use a wire exercise pen or baby gates for bunnies. Pocket pets will benefit from a running wheel and as large a cage as you have room for, with tunnels and ramps to climb. Add to that an acrylic exercise ball and you'll have the best-looking hamster in the neighborhood.

YOUR VET: YOUR PET'S PARTNER IN WEIGHT LOSS

Your vet is your partner in maintaining the health of your pet, and that includes a healthy weight. Many vets offer programs to help you with diet planning and might suggest you bring your pet in for weekly weigh-ins to track your progress. They can consult with you about the diet your pet is eating and might recommend a prescription diet. All diets are safest when preceded by a physical exam; your vet can also rule out any medical reasons for weight gain so you're not putting your pet on a diet when a medication might be indicated. ■

PRESCRIPTION DIETS FOR WEIGHT LOSS

For pets in need of a more serious weight-loss regimen, special weight-loss diets can be prescribed by your vet. Most of these diets are carbohydrate controlled, often with increased levels of fiber and moderate protein. They've also been formulated to increase palatability. You can, but don't need to, purchase these from your vet; many online pharmacies carry them and ship directly to your home. You'll still need a prescription however. Most animals don't need prescription diets for more than six months to a year. Wean your pet onto a regular diet as soon as his weight-loss goals have been met and maintained for six months.

CHAPTER 12

Preventive
Veterinary Care

Your veterinarian is your partner in your pet's health care, even when your pet is not sick. Let me change that: *especially* when your pet is not sick. Visiting your vet for preventive care is just as important as going when your pet is ill or injured. In fact, staying on top of your pet's health when he's well can help spot diseases early so they can be treated fast. An ounce of prevention is worth a pound of cure doesn't apply only to humans. If you're a first-time pet owner, if you haven't owned a pet in a while, or if you have recently moved, you'll have to select a veterinarian for your pet. Asking friends, family, and neighbors for referrals is great. If that's not an option, turn to the internet for help.

HOW TO CHOOSE YOUR VET

Great veterinarians are worth their weight in gold. Instead of choosing one at random, do a little research. First check out online reviews to come up with a short list; then narrow it down based on a few factors, including the clinic's distance from your home, the personal rapport you feel with the vet and staff, and, of course, cost. Location is important. If most consumer behavior is applicable, pet owners will travel to a clinic that is within 20 minutes of their home. That makes sense; it's far more convenient to visit a hospital nearby as opposed to one across town or even in another city. This is particularly true if your pet is ill and needs to see the vet frequently. Some people choose to drive longer distances to patronize a veterinarian they particularly love, but if you can, find a vet close to home. There's nothing more valuable than having a nearby vet when you're dealing with an emergency.

All licensed veterinarians can treat your pet, but each veterinarian is an individual, with different communication skills, bedside manners, beliefs, and styles of practicing veterinary medicine. Some vets are more conservative in their treatment recommendations; others prefer more aggressive treatment and diagnostic plans. Many vets are middle of the road, taking one approach or another depending on the particular case.

Then of course there is the hospital itself. Do you want a state-of-the-art facility that's very clinical and modern? Or are you more comfortable with a family practitioner feeling? Do you like a corporate chain, or would you prefer a one-owner practice? Finally, are you comfortable seeing a different vet each visit, or do you want to establish a relationship with one or maybe two vets?

Ask DR. GARY:

Should I Buy Pet Insurance?

Yes! I strongly recommend pet insurance. Premiums are usually reasonable for puppies, kittens, and younger healthy adults. Plans cover illnesses and injuries, prescriptions as well as routine and preventive care depending on the plan. Read your premium information carefully and even call the insurer to make sure you understand what is covered and what isn't. Alternatively, you can set up a medical fund for your pets, putting aside money every month, but in reality, most people don't follow through with this. Pet insurance provides peace of mind. Someday if you really need it, it might be the smartest thing you've ever done.

You and your pet deserve great service. Finding a clinic with great office staff is just as important as finding a great veterinarian. You will interact with these people the most—every time you call to ask a question, schedule an appointment, or bring your pet in for an exam or procedure. Look for friendly, knowledgeable staff who seem to really care about you and your pet. If you're treated indifferently or the hospital staff members aren't professional and well informed, find another clinic.

Personal Connection

The rapport you feel with a veterinarian is of the utmost importance. Do you feel comfortable asking questions, and do you understand the answers? Do you and the vet see eye-to-eye on topics like vaccine protocols or nutrition? You and your vet don't need to have the exact same opinion on everything, but you should be able to agree to disagree when necessary. For instance, maybe you choose to feed your pet raw food, but your veterinarian isn't a proponent of such a diet. This doesn't have to be a deal breaker as long as your vet supports your choice and as long as you respect that the veterinarian has reasons for not loving raw diets (see Chapter 10).

Most important is the sense of trust you feel with your vet. After all, you're placing the health of your beloved companion in his or her hands. If you don't feel comfortable with a vet for any reason, it will be hard to make the relationship work. Yes, this is a partnership. Working together, you can help your pet stay healthy and happy for a very long time.

Cost Considerations

Don't base your choice solely on cost. Choosing the cheapest vet in town might not be in your pet's best interest. The old adage "you get what you pay for" applies to veterinary care too. On the flip side, you don't want to overpay if you can avoid it. Some veterinarians charge more than others because they offer premium services, pay expensive rent on their clinic space, or offer services demanded by a wealthy client base and that location's overhead. If you're on a budget, check around to see what vet prices average in your area. Sometimes you can save money without compromising your pet's care simply by choosing a clinic on one side of town versus the other.

Let me make one important point. All vets want to help animals and no vet wants to charge

Ask DR. GARY:

Should I Get My Cat Declawed?

Let's make this easy. Don't ever do this. Declawing a cat is not a "deep and permanent nail trim"; it's a toe amputation. Imagine if someone cut off the tips of all 10 of your fingers at the first joint, sewed your fingers up, bandaged them, and sent you on your way. Your hands would never be the same. Don't do this to your cats, even if your vet uses a laser that allegedly shortens the recovery period. More and more vets refuse to do declaws. Instead, trim the nails frequently, provide appropriate scratching surfaces, or use Soft Paws, which are acrylic caps placed over the nails.

TAIL DOCKING, EAR CROPPING, AND DEW CLAW REMOVAL

You know where I'm going on this one: Don't do it. Ear cropping and tail docking procedures are purely cosmetic and are outlawed in most countries other than the United States. In some cases, it might be a good idea to remove dewclaws (they can snag and be torn off), but I'd wait until your puppy is spayed or neutered to do this under a single anesthetic procedure. Other than that, let's leave all the parts on our puppies alone. They're pretty much perfect just as they are.

you more than you can afford. It just doesn't make sense from a medical or a business aspect. It won't help the pet and it won't make you happy. Unhappy clients are the worst advertising in the world. That said, modern veterinary medicine is sophisticated, complicated, and, yes, can be expensive. A good working partnership with your vet can help you both develop the best treatment plan for your pet. That's priceless care.

WELLNESS AND PREVENTION

You might think there's no real need to visit your veterinarian if your pet seems healthy. Nothing could be further from the truth. Annual exams and preventive testing provide valuable information and can catch disease early.

Annual Exams

About a decade ago, the veterinary profession instituted new vaccine protocols changing the frequency of routine vaccinations from yearly to once every three years. There is even discussion now that some vaccines might need to be given only once during the life of an animal. An unintended consequence of this new regimen was a decrease in the number of annual exams pets were getting. People thought that since their pet didn't need vaccines that year, they didn't need to see their vet.

Coming to the vet every year has never been just about vaccinations. The value in examining a pet annually is recording a baseline on which future exams can be compared. In other words, you have to know what's normal before being able to recognize what's not. For instance, you might just think your dog is acting odd but not be able to say exactly why. It's a whole lot better if your vet can identify a physical difference

in your dog based on what was normal the previous year.

As far as how often you should visit your vet, if you consider that one year for you is roughly equivalent to six or seven of your pet's years, the value of the physical exam is even more compelling. So, please, schedule a physical exam once a year, even if vaccines are not due. It will be the most valuable ounce of prevention you'll ever spend on your pet.

What Is a Wellness Plan?

Many veterinarians offer wellness plans. Modeled somewhat on the human health maintenance organization model, these plans cover routine checkups, vaccines, dewormers, and some tests on a set schedule. The beauty of these plans is twofold: Costs are lower overall, and you get an easy-to-follow schedule for checkups. Puppy or kitten packages are the most common wellness plans, but your vet might also offer young adult and senior wellness plans.

Some pet insurance providers also offer wellness insurance, which works like medical insurance, but instead of covering illnesses and injuries, it covers only preventive services, like vaccines, well visits, spaying or neutering, and dental cleanings. Such plans may be purchased individually or as an add-on to your pet's medical insurance.

VACCINES

If it's been a while since you last had a pet, you might be surprised to learn that vaccination protocols for dogs and cats have changed dramatically in the past decade. This is good news. In the past, adult pets went to the vet once a year for their annual vaccines, but today most vaccines are given every three years. Vaccine schedules for puppies and kittens are a bit different so let's get into those.

PREVENTIVE TESTING

Your vet might recommend certain tests, based on the age, species, and condition of your pet. It's best to do them annually, but talk to your vet about every other year if cost is an issue and your pet appears healthy.

Dogs

Puppies	Fecal exam
One to seven years	Heartworm test,* fecal exam
Seven years and older	Heartworm test,* fecal exam, CBC (complete blood count), organ profile, urinalysis (UA), and thyroid level (T4)

Cats

Kittens	Fecal exam
One to seven years	Heartworm test,* fecal exam, feline leukemia test**
Seven years and older	Heartworm test,* fecal exam, CBC, organ profile, UA, and T4

* In endemic areas
** For outdoor cats (indoor cats with a negative feline leukemia test need not retest unless a new cat enters the home)

PHYSICAL EXAMS FOR EXOTIC PETS

Admittedly the preventive physical exam is less common for exotic pets (birds, reptiles, rabbits, guinea pigs, hamsters, and other pocket pets), but it's nonetheless very important. Most vets see these animals only when there is a problem, which is unfortunate. This is simply a matter of practicality and economics. Far fewer vets are experienced with exotics, so they're harder to find. In addition, many pocket pets like rats and hamsters have a cost value many times less than the cost of a physical exam. This doesn't mean that's all they're worth; it's simply perception. If possible, find a vet who has experience with exotic pets, and bring your small pet in for regular annual visits.

Puppy and Kitten Vaccines

Nursing puppies and kittens get maternal antibodies from their mothers that protect them for a short period of time. Once those maternal antibodies wear off, usually by four months of age, they need vaccines in order to be protected from common and deadly diseases. Although puppies and kittens may start their vaccines as early as six weeks of age, most puppies and kittens start their vaccine series at eight weeks.

Puppy and kitten vaccines are given as a series. That means they receive three or four sets of vaccines every three to four weeks. Let's make it easy: Plan on three sets of vaccines given once a month at two, three, and four months of age. It might seem as though pets get a little bit of immunity with each set of vaccines until they have full immunity by the end of the series, but that's not exactly how it works. Multiple vaccines are also given as a series because maternal antibodies can interfere with vaccines, preventing the body from mounting a full immune response.

Basically, vaccines won't be completely effective until the maternal antibodies have waned and that varies among animals. Giving vaccines multiple times over the course of several months

YOUR PET'S AGE IN "HUMAN YEARS"

If you want to know how old your pet is in "human years," just multiply her age by seven, right? Not exactly. Pets mature faster than humans, particular during the first few years of life. Also, large dogs have shorter life spans than small dogs and cats. We consider pets to be "adults" at one year of age, but multiply one by seven and you get seven—not an adult at all. To make it simple, one-year-old dogs and cats are about 15 in human years. By seven, pets are 44 to 50, depending on breed and size. Once a pet reaches 16, she's the equivalent of an 80- to 120-year-old human.

ensures your pet will be protected once the maternal antibodies wear off.

Core Vaccines

Vaccines are categorized as core and noncore. Core vaccines are those that are recommended for all pets. For dogs, the core vaccines are DHPP and rabies. "DHPP" stands for distemper, hepatitis, parainfluenza, and parvovirus. We just refer to it as distemper. For cats, the core vaccines are FVRCP and rabies. "FVRCP" stands for feline rhinotracheitis, calicivirus, and panleukopenia (otherwise known as "distemper" too). Although feline leukemia (FeLV) is considered a noncore vaccine, the American Association of Feline Practitioners recommends initial vaccination for all kittens under one year of age. I disagree since I prefer to minimize vaccinations and avoid the ones our animals won't be exposed to. If you're particularly concerned about FeLV, have that conversation with your veterinarian.

There's one more vaccine available for puppies: coronavirus, an early gastrointestinal virus that can affect puppies until about eight weeks. Responsible breeders might consider it, and you should too if you wind up with a pup between six and eight weeks of age. There's no need for the vaccine after that because your pup is no longer susceptible to coronavirus.

Noncore Vaccines

Noncore vaccines are those that might be recommended for your pet based on several factors, including the area in which you live and your pet's lifestyle. Noncore vaccines available for dogs include *Bordetella bronchiseptica* and canine parainfluenza virus (both associated with kennel cough and prevented with one vaccine), canine influenza (dog flu), *Leptospira* (leptospirosis), *Borrelia burgdorferi* (Lyme disease), and *Crotalus atrox* (rattlesnake vaccine). Talk to your vet about which of these noncore vaccines your puppy needs. Always work to keep the vaccine count to a minimum.

PARVOVIRUS

Parvovirus is highly contagious. Although any dog can get parvo, puppies are the most vulnerable. Parvovirus generally causes vomiting, severe diarrhea, painful cramps, lack of appetite, and weight loss. Untreated parvo can be deadly. Even with treatment, about 10 percent of dogs with parvo die. It is spread through infected fecal matter and can live in the environment for several months. This is why it's very important not to take your unvaccinated puppy to places frequented by other dogs, such as dog parks and pet stores.

there is insufficient evidence that the vaccine provides adequate protection so its use is not generally recommended.

Adult Dog and Cat Vaccines

After the initial puppy or kitten vaccine series, adult dogs and cats should be revaccinated with core vaccines one year later, then every three years after that. Noncore vaccines are generally boosted once every year.

With the lowered frequency of vaccinations today, your vet might recommend your pet have a vaccine titer drawn. This simple blood test will tell you whether your pup needs another vaccine to boost his immunity and, better yet, whether you can skip the next round because he's protected enough. This is a terrific idea because there

Noncore vaccines for cats include feline leukemia virus (FeLV), feline immunodeficiency virus (FIV), *Chlamydophila felis, Bordetella bronchiseptica,* feline infectious peritonitis (FIP), and dermatophyte vaccines. If your cat is going to be an outdoor cat (or if you plan on bringing outdoor cats inside), your veterinarian might recommend the FeLV and possibly the FIV vaccine. It's important to test for FeLV and FIV prior to vaccinating cats for these diseases because the vaccine will not help if your cat already has the virus. As a side note, any cat who tests positive for either of these viruses should not go outside so as not to spread the viruses to other cats.

The vaccine for feline infectious peritonitis has been on the market since the late 1990s, but

VACCINE-ASSOCIATED SARCOMA

An increase in vaccine-associated sarcoma, a malignant tumor, has been identified over the past 25 years. These are highly aggressive cancers linked to certain vaccines in cats. They are rarely seen in dogs and ferrets. Although the overall incidence of vaccine-associated sarcomas is small, they are a real concern for cat owners and their veterinarians. These sarcomas are very difficult to treat and are usually fatal. Of primary concern is the link between these cancers and feline leukemia vaccines, but the rabies vaccine might also be a risk for our cats. It's another reason to minimize unnecessary vaccines in all of our pets, perhaps most of all in cats.

is no other way to truly know how protected your pet is from a particular virus. So far, we don't have great titer measurements for cats, but these may be on the horizon.

Vaccine Risks

Vaccines protect your pet from dangerous diseases, but too many vaccines are not beneficial and could even be harmful. Anything you inject, feed, or apply to your pet's skin, including vaccinations, has the potential to cause a reaction. Some animals are more sensitive than others to vaccines, but this doesn't necessarily mean they're allergic to the vaccine. They might be sensitive to the inactive ingredients in the vaccine. Often these are aluminum compounds, which can be irritating. Incidentally, these inactive ingredients are often what causes the shot itself to hurt.

In rare cases, a pet might have or develop a true allergy to a vaccine and can have an anaphy-

WHAT TO DO IF YOUR PET HAS A VACCINE REACTION

This is a true emergency. Immediately call your veterinarian from the car and let her know you're on your way back to the clinic. If the clinic is closed, head to your nearest emergency clinic. Keep your pet warm and as nonstressed as possible until you can get to the vet.

lactic reaction, a severe, life-threatening allergic reaction that is a true emergency and needs immediate medical treatment. If your pet is having an anaphylactic reaction, you might notice increased respiratory rate, labored breathing, hives, and panting. It can progress to full-blown collapse and even death. That's why we take it so seriously and often recommend that pets wait at the vet clinic for a minimum of 15 minutes after

CANINE INFLUENZA (DOG FLU)

Canine influenza, otherwise known as "dog flu," is highly contagious and spread through coughing, sneezing, and even barking. Most dogs show signs of nasal discharge, lethargy, fever, and cough. Although some fatalities have been reported, most dogs recover, although they remain contagious for up to three weeks. An effective vaccine exists but it must be given in two doses three weeks apart. Depending on the prevalence of flu in your area, your veterinarian may want to add canine influenza to your dog's vaccine schedule. Some cats have

been reported to contract dog flu, although it's rare. There is no vaccine for cats yet. Just in case, keep cats away from infected dogs.

being vaccinated so staff can watch them and be on hand in case an allergic reaction occurs.

It all sounds scary, but allergic reactions to vaccines are not common. Chances are you'll never have a problem, but it's important to keep an eye on your pets after they get their shots. I always watch my pets for several hours after vaccinations. If your pet has an allergic reaction to a vaccination, talk to your vet about what to do to prevent it from hap-

pening again. For dogs, your vet might recommend giving an antihistamine an hour before vaccinating. But antihistamines are strangely ineffective for cats, so if your cat has a reaction, your vet will likely recommend that be the last vaccination she gets.

YOUR PET'S DENTAL HEALTH

Imagine how you would feel if you didn't brush your teeth every day. What if you skipped brushing for a week or even a month? What if you never brushed your teeth for your entire lifetime? Yuck. Not only would your mouth be disgusting, but you would probably not have very many teeth left in your old age.

This is the reality for many pets. Very few pet owners brush their dog's teeth every day but we should! Daily brushing is the best thing you can do for your pet's teeth and gums, but good dental care goes much further than that.

VACCINES FOR EXOTICS

If you have a ferret, he should receive a juvenile series of DHPP just like puppies, followed by the same schedule as dogs. The rest of our pocket companions are safe from vaccine needles because there are no licensed vaccines for rabbits, guinea pigs, birds, reptiles, or other pocket pets in the United States.

Why Dental Health Is So Important

Dental disease is caused when bacteria in the mouth form plaque on the teeth. Plaque then hardens into calculus (also called tartar) above the gum line, where you can see it, and below the gum line, where you can't see it.

Plaque and tartar under the gum line wreak havoc on your dog's or cat's mouth, leading to gum inflammation, bleeding, and tooth loss. Studies have shown that dental disease can even contribute to heart disease, liver disease, and kidney disease. And let's not forget horrible pet breath! It's not normal for your pet's mouth to have a terrible stench; if that's the case, it's time for a dental exam by your vet.

Plaque can be brushed away, but tartar can only be removed by a professional cleaning, much like the biannual cleanings you get from your own dentist. Still, you can space these professional cleanings out by brushing your pet's teeth at home, which will make a huge difference in the health of his teeth and gums. The key is to brush at least every other day, although daily is best. After brushing, plaque starts re-forming within 24 hours. If you don't brush away the plaque, it then hardens into tartar within three to five days. Once tartar forms, you can't brush it away.

Puppy and Kitten Teeth

Like human children, young puppies and kittens have baby teeth that fall out and are replaced by adult teeth. The baby teeth are called deciduous teeth and they fall out between three and six months of age. You might notice a little bleeding when your puppy or kitten loses a tooth, and you might find teeth on the floor or in the food bowl (although puppies and kittens often swallow the teeth when they fall out). Sometimes the deciduous teeth don't fall out before the adult teeth start coming in. If your pet has retained deciduous teeth, your vet might want to pull them out to prevent damage to the adult teeth coming in. The best time to do this is during their spay or neuter.

You might think brushing is not necessary for puppies and kittens. After all, those teeth are just going to fall out any way, right? But don't miss this training opportunity: It's much easier to train puppies and kittens than older dogs and cats to accept tooth brushing. Starting early also ingrains the habit into *your* routine, making it more likely that you will continue to brush your pet's teeth every day.

Introducing the Toothbrush

To get started, you'll need a toothbrush and some pet toothpaste. Pet toothbrushes come in a few styles. Finger brushes are small plastic tubes that fit over your finger with soft bristles on the tip. You can also use a pet toothbrush that looks more like your own, although pet toothbrushes have very soft bristles. Pet toothpaste comes in many flavors designed to entice your pet, including malt, vanilla-mint, and the ever popular poultry flavor (trust me, your pet will love it but don't accidentally put it on your own toothbrush!). Never use human toothpaste; it will make your pet sick.

To warm up, just let your puppy or kitten lick a dab of toothpaste. Next, put a small amount of toothpaste on your finger and gently rub a few teeth. Praise your pet for cooperating. Go slowly, brushing a few teeth at a time and pausing to praise your pet, until the entire mouth is brushed. Graduate up to a soft brush from here and you're on your way to a new world of pet dental hygiene.

Eventually you'll be able to quickly and easily brush your pet's teeth. Brush at least every other day, and more if you can. You can brush your pet's teeth when you brush your own teeth to help you remember.

One other armament in the fight against tartar is a diet designed specifically for dental health. There are several brands to choose from, and all are slightly different, but in general, the kibble pieces are extra hard and composed of a meshwork of fibers that actually clean your pet's teeth as he's eating it. Hills Science Diet makes a terrific one called T/D. The key is eating, not swallowing whole. If that happens, all you've done is find a new delectable calorie source for your pup. I like dental diets as treats, not necessarily as a diet source, even though it's a complete diet. It's just too heavy and full of fat to feed a whole bowl. Save that for something a little less caloric.

Professional Cleanings

Brushing your pet's teeth at home is the best way to keep his mouth healthy, but most pets still

THE TRUTH ABOUT ANESTHESIA-FREE DENTISTRY

You might think no-sedation dentistry is a better way to clean your pet's teeth, but think again. The instruments used to scale the teeth are extremely sharp, which means that it's uncomfortable and an awake pet can become injured from the slightest head movement. Anesthesia-free dentistry also can't clean below the gums, the most important part of a cleaning. What you see above the gum line is just the tip of the iceberg compared to what lurks below. Finally, without anesthesia, your pet can't have dental x-rays to look for disease, broken teeth, and other dental issues. The procedure might even be illegal if prac-

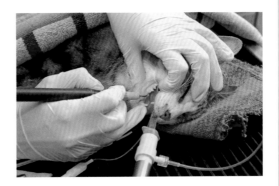

ticed by a non-veterinarian. Do your pets a favor — have their dentals done properly under anesthesia by a veterinarian.

benefit from professional cleanings at least once every other year. Your vet or a trained veterinary technician will use special equipment to clean above and below the gum line. Often this equipment is an ultrasonic cleaner exactly like the one your dentist or hygienist uses on your teeth.

Ask DR. GARY:

Do Pets Get Cavities?

Although dogs and cats can get cavities, it's rare. But pets commonly develop other dental problems like microfractures, erosions, and loose and infected teeth. They can also get fur caught up inside the gum surrounding their teeth, leading to inflammation and infection. Cats especially suffer from something called tooth resorption, which are erosions at the base of the tooth along the gum line. These can be almost impossible to see and can cause a great deal of pain for your cat, who will try to hide her discomfort. It's another reason to schedule regular dental x-rays and cleanings.

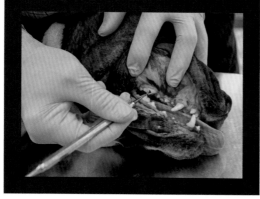

Although the procedure is similar to what we have done at the dentist, pets are put under general anesthesia for dental cleanings. This is because they won't sit there and hold their mouths open while someone scrapes and cleans their teeth for 30 minutes. Although general anesthesia is safe for healthy pets, most vets will recommend preanesthetic blood testing to check your pet's kidney and liver function first. Your vet should also place an IV catheter any time your pet is under general anesthesia.

Let's talk about the elephant in the room. You make that appointment to have your pet's teeth cleaned. As the date nears, you become more and more worried about this "optional" procedure. You wonder what you were thinking. It involves general anesthesia, after all. I'll admit, when my own pets are nearing their date with the dentist, even I get a little nervous, although I know better. Veterinary anesthesia is very advanced now and is safe under the careful eye of your veterinarian, even for senior pets. With good preparation, by which I mean an exam and a preanesthetic blood test to screen for any problems, your pet should be fine having this procedure. Always insist on IV fluids, especially for senior pets. This will flush the kidneys and clear the pre-gas anesthetics more quickly (the lungs will take care of the gas anesthesia).

So why are we so nervous about having a dental procedure done? It has a lot to do with the fact that despite how much your pet benefits from a dental cleaning, it's an elective procedure—or that's what we think. Only a full dental exam and cleaning under anesthesia will reveal fractured teeth, painful erosions, or loose incisors. Animals don't tell us they're in pain until

FELINE GINGIVOSTOMATITIS

This painful, debilitating gum and dental disease causes severe inflammation of the gingiva (gums) and even the mucosa (inside tissues of the mouth). Although we don't know exactly what causes this, it's frequently seen in cats with feline immunodeficiency virus or other viral or bacterial infections. Cats with this disease have extremely inflamed red gums, visible ulcers on the mouth, and difficulty eating. It can be very difficult to treat. Steroids and antibiotics can help, but for very difficult cases, the only treatment is to remove all the teeth. As harsh as this sounds, the disease never recurs after the teeth are removed. The absence of teeth is far better than the presence of pain.

things get really ugly. Just think about what it's like to have tooth pain yourself. Do yourself and your pet a favor and plan on having a full dental procedure done every other year once your pets turn seven. Some pets need dental cleanings more frequently. Yes, I'm talking to you, little Yorkies, toy poodles, shih tzu, and other small breeds. They're adorable but cursed with very high-maintenance dental needs.

The last thing to bring up about the teeth is the advent of the veterinary dental specialist over the past few decades. Veterinary dentists are geniuses with teeth. We've come a long way since the early days of just pulling teeth and cleaning a few of the remaining ones. Veterinary dentists do amazing things with pets' teeth these days. From root canals, to implants, to canine reparative therapy,

no animal needs to be at a loss for oral health any longer. Some general practitioners are also great with teeth, but try to see a specialist if your pet needs an advanced dental procedure.

Dental X-Rays

Humans get dental x-rays regularly. If your pet is going to have a dental exam, make sure your vet has the ability to do x-rays too. Without these, the dentistry is really being done in the dark. X-rays provide valuable information about what's going on beneath the gum line. Your vet will be able to see any hidden root problems or broken teeth, as well as infection.

Dental issues, often lurking below the surface without any symptoms, can be insidious. Pets tend to mask their pain and might not show any outward signs of discomfort, even if they're in pain. Dental x-rays provide a window into the mouth, revealing any problems so they can be remedied. If you're going to go to the trouble of doing a proper dental, make sure your vet has x-rays! ■

CHAPTER 13

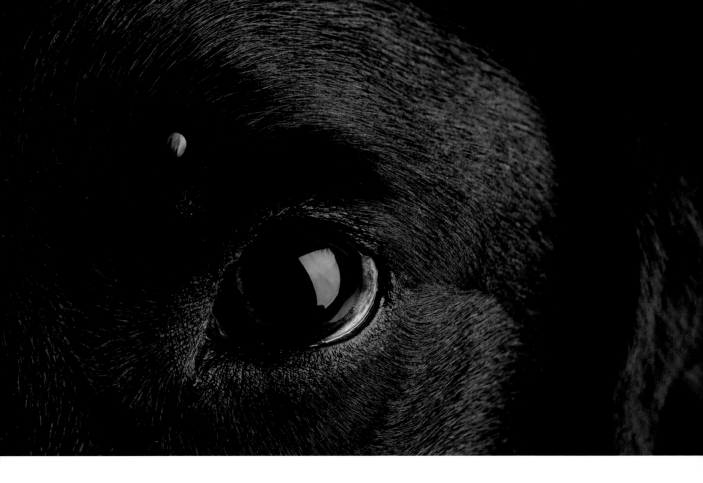

Fleas, Ticks, and Other Parasites

Parasite control is probably not the most appetizing topic, but we do need to cover it for the sake of your pet. Fleas, ticks, heartworms, and intestinal parasites are harmful, prevalent, and just plain a fact of life with animals. Parasites can really hurt your pet, and some can even be transmitted to humans. Fleas and ticks can be seen with the naked eye, but others can silently harm your pet without a sign. Decades ago, parasite control was a struggle, but today we have many preventatives available to keep parasites from harming your pet. The more you know about the various parasites that can affect your pet, the better, so your whole family can stay safe and parasite free.

FLEAS AND TICKS

Fleas and ticks have plagued pets since the beginning of time. Several decades ago, we had to resort to harsh sprays, collars, and dips to keep these bloodthirsty pests off our pets. Luckily, flea and tick control is a lot simpler these days and a lot safer. Many safe and effective monthly topical treatments and even pills destroy ticks and fleas, kill flea eggs, and even prevent internal parasites.

Fleas

To prevent flea infestations in your home, it's helpful to understand the flea life cycle, which has four parts: egg, larva, pupa, and adult. An adult flea will hop onto your pet for a blood meal, then lay eggs in your pet's fur. These eggs fall off throughout your pet's environment, where they wait for optimal conditions to hatch. This can be days or weeks depending on the temperature and humidity.

Flea larvae hatch out of the eggs, and within a few days to weeks they develop cocoons, entering the pupa stage. After another few days or weeks, adult fleas emerge from the cocoons, ready to hop onto your pet and start the life cycle all over again. Flea pupae can lie dormant in their protective cocoons for many months, hatching when conditions are just right. Although fleas are more prevalent in the spring and summer, they can appear anytime temperatures rise above 65°F, no matter the season.

Fleas irritate your pet's skin. Some pets are extremely sensitive to them, developing itching, hair loss, scabbing, and in some cases, secondary bacterial skin infections. Pets can even develop flea allergies and have intense reactions to even a single flea bite. With bad infestations, very young kittens and puppies, and even some adult animals, can develop anemia due to blood loss from fleas.

In the worst cases, you might even see fleas on the human members of your household. Generally, pet fleas don't particularly like human dinners, but if pushed by numbers, they will infest people as well as pets. The white sock test is a good way to check for fleas in the house. Walk around the house in a pair of clean white socks then check the bottoms. If you see little brown or black spots, or even live fleas, you've let things get very out of hand. If this happens to you, treat your whole house (see below) and the animals and we'll never mention this to anyone!

Flea Control

Several options are available to kill fleas on your pet, including topical spot treatments that are applied to your pet's skin once a month, as well as monthly oral treatments available in chewable pill form. Always ask your veterinarian to recommend a flea-control product because some products on the market are ineffective and even dangerous. Stick to the ones your vet advocates, most of which you can now buy online or at pet supply stores. Always use the correct dose for your size dog or cat. And that flea collar you just bought at the store? Go ahead and return it because they just don't work.

Fighting a Flea Infestation

If not dealt with, fleas can reproduce at an alarming rate. One female flea can lay up to 50 eggs a day, and each resulting flea can lay up to 50 eggs a day. You can see where this is going. With that in mind, it's easy to see how fleas can get out of control fast.

To break the flea life cycle and eradicate infestations, you must take a three-pronged approach: killing the fleas and eggs on your pet, in your home, and in your yard. Treat all three of these at the same time.

First, bathe your pet and apply a spot-on flea treatment like imidacloprid or fipronil or give an oral medication prescribed by your vet. In your home, gather up anything your pet lies on and wash it in hot water in the washing machine. This includes pet beds, crate pads, blankets, your own bedding if your pet sleeps on your bed, and any other washable material. If you can't wash something (for instance, the couch), vacuum it thoroughly. Also vacuum all the rugs and carpet in your home. Vacuuming sucks up fleas and flea eggs and even kills adult fleas, which have pretty fragile bodies. Then vacuum up a little bit of natural flea powder,

CAT SAFETY WITH FLEA MEDS

Topical flea preventatives are very safe when used as directed. Where the problem comes in is when people don't read the label carefully. Products labeled for dogs should never be used on cats. This goes for any flea-control product, but cats are especially sensitive to the insecticides pyrethrin and pyrethroid (a synthetic version of pyrethrin). Symptoms of pyrethrin poisoning include vomiting and diarrhea, drooling, muscle tremors, incoordination, and seizures. If you think your cat is having an adverse reaction to a flea-control product, seek veterinary care immediately.

such as diatomaceous earth (DE; see below), to ensure no fleas hatch or escape from your vacuum. Toss the vacuum bag, or dump and wash out the receptacle when you're done.

Now, despite your thorough cleaning, you're not done yet. The easiest way to deal with this is to call a pest-control service to professionally treat your home and yard for fleas. That's also the most expensive way. You can also spray or flea-bomb your home on your own, carefully following the directions outlined on the product. Make sure all living creatures (other than fleas) are out of the house when you do this: people, dogs, cats, and especially small animals like birds, reptiles, pocket pets, and even fish—these small creatures are especially sensitive to pesticides. Don't return until the can or bottle says you can (usually a minimum of two hours). You'll have to repeat all of these steps again in two weeks because that's when the next set of dormant flea eggs will hatch. Now that professional service doesn't look so bad, does it?

Also treat outdoors if your pet spends a lot of time out there. Use specific sprays made for outdoor fumigation. Most of the time, this isn't necessary, especially in more frigid climates, but if you have a particularly nasty flea situation, you may need to address your outdoor environment.

If using pesticides makes you uneasy, DE is a natural option to kill fleas in your home and yard. It might not work as well as the harsher chemicals, but that's the compromise you make when going natural. You'll just have to repeat the treatments more often for it to be as effective. DE is a fine white powder made of pulverized fossils. The jagged edges of these tiny fossils pierce fleas' exoskeletons and they die of dehydration. The best way to use this product is to simply sprinkle the powder in areas where fleas hide. Fleas typically like dark places away from sunlight, so sprinkle DE under couches, chairs, and beds; along baseboards; and in places where your pet lies frequently, like under his crate or bed, and on carpets and rugs. You can also sprinkle DE on your grass, in your garden, and around your yard. DE is nontoxic (be sure to purchase food-grade DE), but you shouldn't breathe it in, so wear a mask when applying it and try not to disturb the powder once it's applied. After some time, you can just vacuum it up (wear a mask). It's available at hardware and garden stores, and even some big box stores.

Ticks

Ticks are opportunistic hitchhiking bloodsuckers. And that's saying it nicely. They cling to tall grass and weeds and wait for an unsuspecting pet (or person) to happen by so they can climb aboard for a blood meal. After a tick bites, it stays attached

Ask DR. GARY:

How Can I Tell If My Pet Has Fleas?

The simplest way to tell if your pet has fleas is with a flea comb—a simple plastic comb with very fine teeth. Use it to comb through your pet's hindquarters, checking for small black specks (called flea dirt). These specks are flea feces filled with digested blood. Wipe the specks on a wet paper towel. If it turns reddish brown, you can be certain it's flea dirt. If your pet is particularly infested, you might see fleas running for safety on your pet's belly where the hair is shorter.

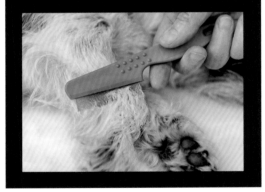

to your pet for several days, slowly savoring its meal. Once it's done, it detaches and drops off your pet, but the damage may already be done. Ticks carry and transmit a number of diseases, including Lyme disease, Rocky Mountain spotted fever, ehrlichiosis, babesia, and anaplasmosis—serious diseases you don't want to mess with. Generally these diseases are bacterial (a specific genus called *Rickettsia*) and can cause fever, rashes, blood count abnormalities, lameness, and joint pain. Your vet will test for them if your pet falls ill with these symptoms. Fortunately, most can be treated successfully with antibiotics.

Dogs and cats who go outdoors are most at risk of getting ticks. Your pet is at risk of picking up ticks on walks and hikes through fields and woods, scrub near beaches, and even in your yard. Always check your pet carefully when you get home from such excursions, parting the fur to the skin to look for ticks and feeling all over the body with your hands. Pay special attention to tick hiding places: between the toes, under the armpits, on the elbows, in the groin area, in and on the ears, and under the tail.

If you do find a tick, remove it immediately (see sidebar below) and watch the area carefully for skin irritation, which will always occur to some degree as it does for any bite. If you see a bull's-eye mark (a red circle of skin around the bite), it's a good idea to visit your vet. Chances are it's just irritation from the tick, but symptoms of tick-borne disease can show up weeks to even months afterward. Your vet might want to draw some blood for a tick titer test to get a baseline for your pet. These are simple tests vets run to gauge the amount of antibody your pet has against certain tick-borne diseases. Many of these tests can be run at the clinic and give a simple yes or no about exposure; more specific quantitative tests must be sent out to a lab. Tick titers can show a baseline immunity level against the disease, as well as show any changes following the bite.

Tick Control

Topical spot-on treatments applied to your pet's skin once a month are the best way to kill ticks. Some are specific for ticks, but most of these products kill both fleas and ticks and even other parasites like mosquitoes and mites. Some even take care of other internal parasites.

HOW TO SAFELY REMOVE A TICK

Forget all the old wives' tales about removing ticks: Whatever you do, please don't burn them off! When removing a tick, you must dislodge the head from the skin. The best way to do this is to scoop the tick right out of your pet's skin using a small plastic "tick spoon" (available online or at pet supply stores). Slide the tiny notched end under the tick's head and gently pull the tick out of the skin. Seal the tick into a baggie with some rubbing alcohol and toss it in the trash. Your pet won't even know you did it, although you may relive the procedure for many nights to come as you're falling asleep.

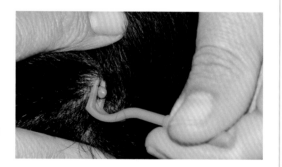

For dogs, several monthly oral preventatives that kill fleas and ticks are available in chewable pill form. Talk to your veterinarian before using a tick-control product on your pet. An older but still somewhat effective preventative is a tick collar. Unlike flea collars, tick collars may actually work. I'm not the biggest fan of these because of the chemical residue on the collar, but if you live in an especially tick-infested area, a tick collar might provide an extra boost of prevention when combined with a topical tick preventative. For most of us, a topical alone will do the job perfectly well.

If you think your pet might be picking up ticks from your yard, call a pest-control company to treat your home and yard for ticks. As with fleas, you can sprinkle DE in your yard to kill ticks (and other pests), focusing on cool, shady places your pet hangs out. You can also make your yard less inviting to ticks by keeping grass short, trimming back or tearing out long brush, removing piles of wood or leaves, and clearing out yard debris.

HEARTWORM

Heartworm is transmitted by mosquitoes. These dangerous parasites live inside your pet's heart, lungs, and the associated blood vessels, where they cause lung disease, heart failure, and damage to other organs as they grow. Pets infected with heartworms can have 30 or more worms in their heart and lungs, and each worm can be 12 inches long. Dogs and cats can harbor heartworms for years before they have any obvious problems with them. Heartworm is more deadly in dogs than cats, who are atypical hosts for heartworms. However, if cats do contract heartworms, they can't go

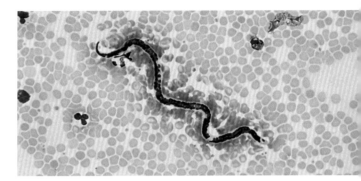

Heartworm

through the same treatment that dogs can because the drug used is not safe for cats.

Heartworm Prevention

Monthly heartworm preventatives come in chewable pill form or as spot-on topical products. These contain the drugs ivermectin, moxidectin, milbemycin, or selamectin and are marketed under numerous trade names. Most chewables also protect against intestinal parasites like roundworms and hookworms, and some spot-on products also protect against intestinal parasites as well as fleas. There is also an injection your vet can give that lasts six months. The monthly preventatives must be given or applied every 30 days. There is some leeway, but if you're late giving your pet's heartworm preventative, he might not be protected. If you have concerns about remembering to give your pet his heartworm preventative, talk to your vet about the twice-yearly injection.

Although mosquitoes are certainly more prevalent in certain parts of the country, cases of heartworm have been found in all states. Year-round heartworm prevention is recommended for all dogs and for cats who go outdoors in heartworm endemic areas.

Treating a Heartworm Infection

Dogs who test positive for heartworms can be treated, but be forewarned that the heartworm treatment is both costly and involved. There are two approved treatments for heartworm; both can be difficult, which is why prevention is so much better than treatment.

Ask **DR. GARY:**

Does My Dog Really Need a Yearly Heartworm Test?

Generally, you should have your dog tested in his first year, then as directed by your vet. In low-prevalence areas, the test can be done once every few years; in other areas like the Deep South, it should be repeated annually. This is because the preventatives, although highly effective, aren't foolproof. Always test for heartworm before starting a heartworm preventative. This is not because it's dangerous to give the drug if your pet has heartworm (as we used to think), but because you want to know if your dog has the parasite before assuming you're in prevention mode.

The original heartworm treatment, using an arsenic-containing compound called Caparsolate (thiacetarsamide sodium), was given intravenously and could cause liver disease and burns at the injection site. It's very rarely used today. A newer drug, Immiticide (melarsomine dihydrochloride), is much safer and highly effective. It's given as a series of intramuscular injections. Your vet will walk you through the procedure, but the full course of treatment from the two injections to cure usually takes about six months, during which time you must keep your dog fairly quiet so the dying worms don't shoot around the body like little lethal projectiles into the lungs and heart.

Sadly, there is no cure for cats once they pick up heartworm. Talk to your vet about how common heartworm disease is in cats in your area to decide whether your cat needs the monthly preventative. In my experience, the preventative is not often used in cats.

INTESTINAL PARASITES

Let's face it: No one wants to talk about worms. Yuck. But it's good to know how to prevent intestinal parasites and what to look for in case your pet gets them.

Tapeworms

Tapeworms are long, flat parasites that live in the intestines of affected animals. Because the body of a tapeworm is segmented, tiny pieces break off, which you might see in your pet's poop (they kind of look like grains of rice). Pets might contract tapeworms from various sources, but the most common way is via fleas: Your pet can become infected if he or she swallows a flea. If your pet has fleas, there's a good chance he also has tapeworms, so get his stool checked.

Tapeworms can cause weight loss and poor skin and coat condition. In very young puppies and kittens, tapeworms can be more serious, causing anemia, failure to thrive, and even possible intestinal blockages. Some pets with tapeworms will scoot their butts on the ground or carpet (the worm segments can be itchy and irritating). If your veterinarian suspects worms, he will perform a test on some of your pet's stool. If you can't get a sample but see tapeworm segments in your pet's stool, just tell your vet. We generally believe you and will prescribe treatment.

Treatment for tapeworms is simple: a deworming pill to kill the worms. Your vet will also talk to you about starting a flea-control regimen to ensure your pet's tapeworms don't make a repeat appearance. Don't panic if you see a whole pile of tapeworm segments in the stool or, worse yet, your pet vomits a big pile of whole tapeworms. This can happen and is nothing to worry about. I know you can't unsee that and, sure, you might need counseling, but it's good motivation to prevent fleas! One positive: Pet tapeworms cannot infect humans.

Roundworms

Although a pet of any age can contract roundworms, they are commonly seen in puppies and kittens. For this reason, your vet will routinely check a young puppy or kitten's stool at every visit and give a prophylactic broad-spectrum dewormer at least twice.

Like tapeworms, roundworms can be seen with the naked eye (they look like long, white strings) when your pet poops them out or throws them up. Puppies and kittens with roundworm infections often develop a pot-bellied appearance. Even if you don't see any roundworms, your vet can look for microscopic roundworm eggs by doing a fecal test and prescribe a medication to kill the worms. These are easily treated by vet-prescribed dewormers. Please don't use over-the-counter medications on your own—they just don't work. Roundworms can also cause infection in people, generally children, for whom they can be very dangerous—another good reason to use heartworm and deworming monthly preventatives and have that stool sample checked by your vet.

Hookworms

More common in dogs than cats, hookworms attach to your pet's small intestines, where they suck out blood, and as a result, you won't see hookworms in the stool. These can cause severe diarrhea and weight loss. As with other intestinal parasites, your vet will check your pet's stool to look for eggs, then prescribe the appropriate dewormer.

Whipworms

These worms are also more commonly seen in dogs than cats. Symptoms include weight loss and mucousy stool. Whipworms can be tricky to diagnose. Although your vet can look for whipworm eggs in a fecal test, this particular parasite doesn't shed a large number of eggs, so multiple

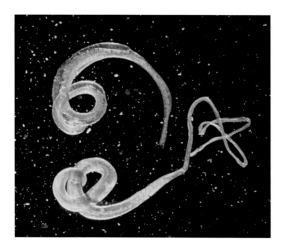

tests over the course of a few days or weeks might be necessary for a definitive diagnosis. Alternatively, if your vet suspects whipworms but can't confirm them, he or she still might just try deworming your pet for whips. If the symptoms go away after treatment, it probably was those darn whipworms causing the problem. Treatment takes a few weeks and usually needs to be repeated.

Giardia

Not a worm like some of the other intestinal parasites, giardia is a one-celled organism called a protozoa. Giardia usually causes diarrhea and vomiting in young animals, but some pets show no symptoms. The parasite is transmitted through contact with the feces of infected animals, often through contaminated water. Your vet can test your pet's stool for giardia and prescribe a medication to treat it. To prevent giardia, don't let your pet drink from puddles, gutters, or other standing water when out and about. Giardia can be transmitted to people, especially young and older humans and those with immune system compromise.

Coccidia

Like giardia, coccidia is another one-celled organism. It causes watery, mucousy diarrhea and is frequently seen in puppies. Coccidia is diagnosed by a fecal test. Treatment is typically a sulfa-type antibiotic.

Intestinal Parasite Prevention

Many monthly heartworm and flea-and-tick preventatives also control common intestinal parasites, including roundworms, hookworms, and whipworms. Yearly fecal tests are also recommended to make sure your pet hasn't contracted one of the parasites for which preventive medication is not available (for instance, tapeworms, giardia, and coccidia).

MITES

Mites are microscopic parasites that live in various places on your pet's body, including the skin and ears. Some types of mites live in low populations on healthy pets' skin, causing no disease, but an overgrowth of these mites can lead to itching, hair loss, and scabby skin, a condition often referred to as mange. Ear mites are extremely itchy. They cause irritation and inflammation in the ear, leading to infection. Ear mites are more common in cats than dogs and are most common in kittens and outdoor cats.

Several species of skin mites cause mange in pets. Some are specific to dogs and some are specific to cats. Some mites can be passed between pets and humans, but others pose no threat to you. The two most common types of mange in dogs are demodectic mange and sarcoptic mange. They are both caused by different mites. The best way to tell the difference is by where they affect your pet. Demodex mites cause hair loss and a rash all over the body; sarcoptes mites (often called "scabies") prefer under the arms, groin, head, and neck. Demodex mites are generally not very itchy, but sarcoptes mites can be intensely itchy for your poor pet. Demodex mites affects puppies and immunocompromised dogs. Some dogs with poor immune systems might deal with demodex their whole lives. Demodex is not contagious, but sarcoptic mange is contagious to other dogs, as well as humans.

Diagnosing and Treating Mites

Veterinarians who suspect skin mites will do a skin scraping, a simple procedure, and look at the cells under a microscope. Once diagnosed, and even if just suspected, several effective treatments containing ivermectin, milbemycin, selamectin, fluralaner, or afoxolaner can be given orally or topically. These are some of the same medications used to prevent fleas and ticks, but check with your vet first because the doses might need to be adjusted. Adult dogs with demodex should always be examined for an underlying cause of the immunosuppression, which opened up the doors to demodex in the first place.

If your vet thinks your pet has ear mites, she will swab the ear and look for mites under a microscope. After performing a good ear cleaning, she will prescribe antibiotic/anti-inflammatory eardrops, and ivermectin eardrops or one of the flea prevention topicals that can also treat ear mites, as well as an ear cleaner that you will need to use once a day until the mites are resolved (see the "How to Clean Your Pet's Ears" sidebar in Chapter 14). After a week or two, the mites should be gone for good.

OTHER PARASITES

There are other parasites that might affect your dog or cat, but these are extremely rare. Fortunately, most can be diagnosed just like intestinal parasites: through a stool sample.

Respiratory

There is really only one lungworm we're particularly concerned about in domestic animals and that is *Aelurostrongylus abstrusus,* which affects cats alone. It's not particularly common, but it can cause a persistent cough and weight loss. Fortunately, it's relatively easy to treat, doesn't affect humans, and is transmitted by snails, which means it's rare. If your cat has a persistent cough, your vet will certainly want to check a stool sample.

Urinary

Dogs and cats can get a small, threadlike worm called *Capillaria* in their bladders, but this is very uncommon. However, once affected, worm eggs will pass out of the body through the urine right into the ground and back into your pet (or others). Diagnosis is made through a urine sample and is easily treated. Fortunately, these worms are not known to affect humans so you can breathe a sigh of relief. ■

CHAPTER 14

Grooming Your Pets

Grooming goes beyond keeping your pet clean. It helps you stay aware of any health concerns like lumps, bumps, cuts, or other problems so you can seek veterinary care early. Frequent brushing and regular bathing can even cut down how much hair ends up all over your house. As the happy owner of a never ending, fur-flying German shepherd, I can sympathize with your problem. Some grooming, like brushing and combing, can be done at home. You can bathe your pet at home too (yes, even cats!), but if the task seems too daunting, a professional groomer can bathe and dry your pet for you. If you own a breed that requires regular haircuts, you will most likely want to enlist the help of a professional groomer, although you can also learn to do this yourself.

INTRODUCING YOUR PUPPY OR KITTEN TO GROOMING

Don't wait until your pet is six months old to introduce the hairbrush or nail trimmers, or you might feel like you're trying to groom a Tasmanian devil instead of a puppy or kitten. The sooner you introduce your pet to the process, the more easily she will accept brushing, bathing, ear cleaning, and nail trimming. Even if your pet has a short coat that doesn't need much brushing, go through the motions so she gets used to it, and bathe her every so often, keeping the process positive.

For brushing and nail trimming, place your puppy or kitten up on a high surface like the top of your washing machine or a bathroom counter. Bring some treats and offer them as you run the brush through your pet's coat. Go slowly, and give lots of praise for good behavior. Clip the nails with the nail trimmers, removing just the very tips (see below). If you're met with too much resistance to nail clipping, go back a step and just try holding the paws for 10 seconds every day. That will get your new pet used to having her paws handled. The more often you brush and trim the nails, the more your pet will come to accept and stand calmly.

Some pets develop deposits of tears, mucus, and minerals at the corners of their eyes. This is more commonly seen in certain breeds like poodles, Maltese, and Persian cats; in dogs with allergies; and even cats with colds. Your pet might never let on that this eye gunk bothers her, but it does. Cleaning the eyes is easy. Wet a soft cotton ball with lukewarm water and simply wipe off the gunk. If any gunk is in the eye itself, rinse it gently with saline solution, then wipe it off the lid with a cotton ball. If the condition worsens or the eyes look red, it's time to see your vet.

How to Trim Your Cat's Nails

Cat nails are very easy to trim as long as your cat cooperates! The best way to get your cat to comply is to trim her nails frequently in kittenhood so she gets used to the routine. To trim a cat's nails, place her on a table or on your lap and gently grasp one paw in your hand. Press lightly in the center of the paw to extend the claws; then use pet nail trimmers to clip the sharp hook off each

one, taking care not to cut the quick (the vein inside each nail). Because cat nails are generally see-through, it's easy to spot the quick—it's the pink area close to the nail bed.

How to Trim Your Dog's Nails

Place your dog on a table if he's small enough so he can't move away. For large dogs, you'll have to do this on the floor. Use pet nail trimmers to clip the tip of each nail where it starts to curve, being careful not to cut the quick (the vein inside the nail). If your dog has white nails, it's easy to see the quick; it's the pink area close to the nail bed. If your dog has black nails, you have to guess. Be conservative, trimming a tiny bit at a time. If you nick the quick, stop the bleeding with styptic powder (available at pet supply stores). You can also use

corn starch. Place a small amount on the nail with your finger and press firmly for a minute.

BATH TIME

All dogs need baths, whether because they get dirty or simply to wash out dust, dander, loose hair, and oily residue from the skin. If you or someone in your family suffers from mild dog allergies, frequent bathing can reduce the amount of dander on the coat and in your home. How often your dog needs a bath depends on breed and coat type, as well as how much he is outside playing in dirt and mud. Although you might have heard that it's bad to bathe dogs too much, the truth is that most dogs do fine with

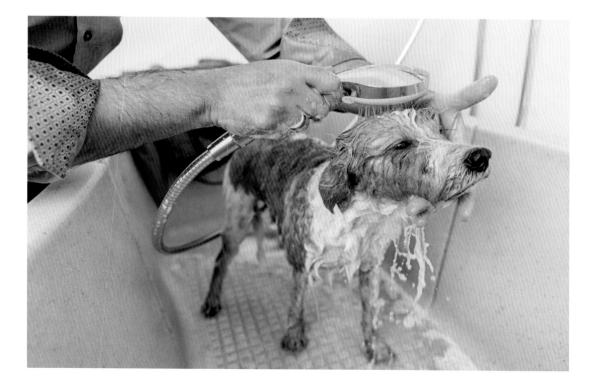

monthly or even weekly baths as long as you use a gentle, moisturizing shampoo and completely rinse all the soap out of the coat. If your dog's skin seems to dry out after bathing, wash him less frequently.

Cats can be bathed much less frequently—twice a year might be sufficient unless she goes outside or becomes dirty. Cats really can learn to tolerate baths, and contrary to everything you've heard about cats hating baths, some even seem to enjoy playing in the water. Just watch ten minutes of lion videos on YouTube. The key is to start regular bathing early, especially with cats, but the same goes for dogs.

Bathing 101

Rule number 1: Always make bath time a good bonding experience. Puppies, kittens, and adult cats are usually small enough to bathe in a sink, but you can also use a bathtub or even a plastic tub in the shower. You can bathe larger dogs in the tub or your shower. It might seem convenient, but please don't bathe your pet outside with the hose unless you have warm water. You wouldn't enjoy a cold outdoor shower, and neither would your pet.

Consider putting a tiny amount of artificial tear ointment in the eyes before the bath. This will prevent soap from irritating your pet's eyes. Your vet or vet tech can show you how to do this, but it's easy. Just put a small dot on your clean fingertip and dab it in the inside lower corner of the eye near the nose. You'll get the hang of it soon enough; your pet will be happy to not have redeye after the bath.

Fill the sink or tub with a few inches of warm water, making sure it's not too hot for their delicate skin. If the bottom is slippery, place a towel

Ask **DR. GARY:**

What Shampoo Is Best for My Pet?

There are a lot of choices for pet shampoos. The best one for your pet is really a personal choice, but I love oatmeal-based shampoos. They're gentle, hypoallergenic, and moisturizing. Stay away from anything with harsh chemicals or too much scent. That includes flea shampoos. These don't work, and they're completely unnecessary given modern treatments for fleas (see Chapter 13). For pets with specific skin issues, your vet might suggest a special shampoo. Consider every new shampoo you use to be an experiment but an easy one. It has visible results.

down so your pet isn't scrambling to gain sure footing (remember rule number 1: the whole experience will be more pleasant if your pet feels comfortable and safe).

Use a moisturizing shampoo made for pets. Don't use human shampoos; most will dry out the skin. Working with a small amount of pet shampoo, lather up your pet, taking care not to get soap in his eyes, ears, or mouth. Take your time, offering praise along the way. Then let the water drain out of the sink and rinse your pet off using a shower spray attachment or plastic cup. Rinse, rinse, and rinse some more; any soap left in the coat will be itchy and make the hair look greasy. Try not to scare your pet by dumping water over his head. If necessary, use a washcloth to gently rinse any soap off his face. Depending on the type of coat, some pets might benefit from a conditioner after shampooing, although it's not necessary. If you use one, be sure to rinse it all out.

After your pet is rinsed off, use some soft towels to gently rub the coat dry. If you have a long-coated breed, you might want to use a pet hair dryer to dry the coat more completely. You can use a human hair dryer, but make sure the setting is on low (warm) and not hot, or you will burn your pet's skin. If you gently brush the coat while using the hair dryer, the hair will be incredibly soft and shiny. It might take some time to introduce the hair dryer. Go slow, and put the dryer away if your pet becomes too stressed by it.

HOW TO CLEAN YOUR PET'S EARS

Pets who get frequent ear infections or a lot of buildup in the ears will benefit from weekly or biweekly ear cleanings. Start out with a big cotton ball (cotton batting is even better). Wet the cotton with the ear cleaner, and use it to swipe out the inside of the ear. A small amount of cleaner will naturally drip down into the ear canal. Gently massage the base of the ear with your fingers. Stand back and let your pet shake his head (drape a towel over his head to minimize the mess). Then use the cotton ball to softly wipe out the ear. Never stick a cotton swab into the ear canal; you can rupture your pet's eardrum.

BRUSHING AND COMBING

Depending on the type of coat your pet has, you might need to brush it or comb it (or both). Generally pets with very long hair need combing to separate the strands so they don't tangle and mat. A wide-toothed metal comb is best. Shorter-coated animals usually just need brushing. Use a wire slicker brush for medium-hair coats and a soft bristle brush for smooth-coated dogs.

HOW TO REMOVE A MAT

Be extremely careful if you decide to do this on your own. But once you learn, you might become a pro. Dog and cat skin is thin. You don't want to make that frantic call to your vet for an emergency appointment for sutures. Slide a comb under the base of the mat and gently lift the mat from the skin so you can safely cut it along the top edge of the comb with a grooming scissors. If this is a frequent occurrence, consider purchasing electric clippers. Always give a treat afterward! Keeping

up with brushing is the best way to ensure your pet won't develop mats.

How often you need to brush your pet depends on her coat. You might think short-haired dogs need less brushing, but many of these dogs shed a lot. Brushing more frequently will cut down on how much hair ends up on your clothes, couch, and visitors. Some dogs with medium hair need brushing just once a week. If your dog or cat has a long, plush coat that's prone to matting, you

might need to brush and comb daily or have a groomer trim the hair short.

TRIMMING AND CLIPPING

Some dog breeds require routine clipping and trimming. Poodles, shih tzu, Yorkshire terriers, Maltese, Portuguese water dogs, as well as many Labradoodles, goldendoodles, and similar breeds should be clipped every four to eight weeks. If you don't have this done, the hair will just keep growing and growing, eventually developing unsightly and painful mats throughout the coat. Neglect grooming appointments, and your groomer might have no choice but to shave your dog down to the skin. No one wants that.

You can find a professional groomer to clip your dog, or you can learn to do it yourself. In fact, grooming your own dog is not terribly difficult if you take the time to research it properly. You need to invest in the right equipment for your breed (clippers, clipper blades, scissors, a grooming table, and a pet dryer), which can be pricey. However, professional grooming is also expensive, so the investment can be worth it. If you got your dog through a breeder, she might be happy to teach you how to groom your pet. Just ask!

There are many great grooming books available, including some for specific breeds. You can also watch some of the many YouTube videos on pet grooming to learn about safety and correct technique. But a word of caution: Grooming scissors are extremely sharp. Be careful that you

AT-HOME GROOMING DOS AND DON'TS

When grooming your pet, safety always comes first. If you aren't entirely comfortable, consult a professional groomer for advice. Some groomers offer lessons for a fee. While grooming:

- DO go slow. If your dog is not cooperating or you find yourself feeling frustrated, take a break and try again later. Remember, this should be a good experience.
- DO use caution when cutting out mats. Slide a comb between the mat and your pet's skin so you don't accidentally cut him. You can also use clippers to shave off mats.
- DON'T neglect your equipment. Clippers, blade, and scissors are expensive. Always clean them after each use, and have them professionally sharpened periodically.

- DON'T get discouraged. Every grooming session is an opportunity to learn. The hair always grows back.

don't accidentally cut your dog's delicate skin, and use caution when working around the face. Clipper blades are also very sharp. It's important to position them flat against the skin when clipping to avoid irritating the skin. Clipper blades also heat up as you use them, becoming hot enough to burn your pet's skin. Place them against your wrist periodically as you work to check their temperature. You can use a clipper spray to keep them cool or alternate between two sets of blades (place the set you're not using on an ice pack covered with a towel to cool off while you use the other set).

HOW TO FIND A GREAT GROOMER

A professional pet groomer is one of your partners in pet care. Groomers not only cut hair but also bathe and dry, trim nails, clean ears, brush teeth, express anal glands, and more. Some grooming salons even offer spa services like doggie facials. (I'll let you decide if that's a good thing or not.)

When looking for a groomer, read online reviews and ask for referrals from friends, neighbors, and your veterinarian. (Some veterinary clinics offer grooming services as well.) Talk to the groomer in person to make sure you feel comfortable with him or her. Ask to see where your pet will stay before and after the grooming. Some grooming shops have glass windows so you can watch your pet being groomed, but if your groomer asks you not to stay while your pet is on the grooming table, don't be offended. Some pets simply act up more when they can see their

Ask DR. GARY:

Should I Shave My Pet for the Summer?

In general, no. Depending on the coat type, shaving dogs doesn't always keep them cool, and it can increase their risk of getting sunburned. Double-coated breeds like Siberian huskies shed their undercoat in summer. The best way to keep them cool is to bathe and brush regularly to remove that loose undercoat. If your dog seems overheated in the summer, get him out of the heat and into the air-conditioning. If your dog pants all summer despite your best cooling efforts, you could try shaving as a last resort. If you do shave down your dog, just one good clipping in June should do. Clip cats down only if they get particularly matted (daily brushing will prevent this).

owner (perhaps thinking you might swoop in and rescue them from the indignity of a bath or haircut). Many pets magically turn into angels when their owner isn't around (this is true at the vet office too). ■

CHAPTER 15

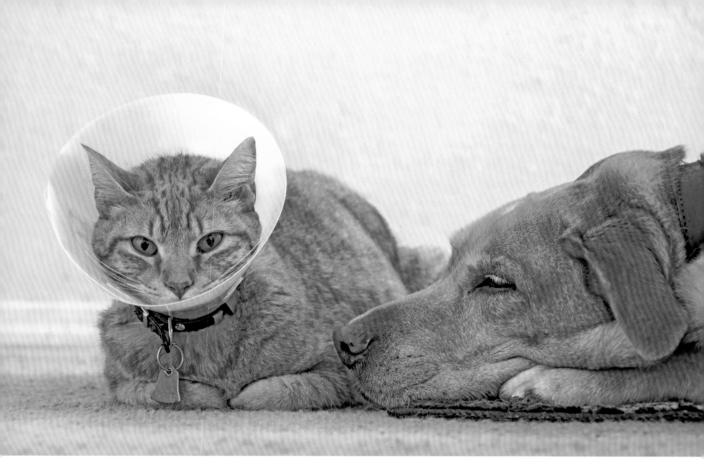

Spaying and Neutering

Spaying and neutering your pet (sometimes called "altering" or "fixing") is a means of permanent birth control, ensuring your pet will never accidentally contribute to the pet overpopulation problem. Spaying and neutering also have some health benefits (including a decrease in certain cancers) and behavioral benefits for pets who live in a human world. We used to think there were no real downsides to spaying and neutering, even when the procedures were done at a very young age, but this topic is no longer black and white. A number of studies have come out in recent years linking spaying and neutering, and particularly pediatric spaying and neutering, with certain health disorders. This has yet to be proven. Some research has also linked spaying and neutering with an increase in behavioral problems.

Although we still have much to learn about how removing our pets' reproductive organs affects their overall health and well-being, many experts still believe the benefits outweigh the risks. However, it's more important than ever to take an individual approach to spaying and neutering whenever possible. If you adopt your pet from a shelter or rescue, it's likely he or she will already be spayed or neutered. If not, talk to your veterinarian about the best time to spay or neuter your pet, taking into consideration breed and other factors.

TIMING OF SPAYING AND NEUTERING

Most pets are spayed after eight weeks but before six months of age for two reasons: This is the age after weaning and the period before a female's first heat. It's also the age at which most puppies and kittens are adopted (and most shelters must spay or neuter their animals before release). If you have a pet from a breeder, your breeder might require you to spay your pet so it isn't used for breeding.

The best age for spaying your pet is under some discussion these days. For nearly two decades, veterinarians have recommended the best age to be between five and six months, before the first heat, in order to prevent mammary cancer later in that animal. However, this theory has been recently challenged by researchers (see "Spaying and Neutering Research"). Most vets agree, however, that later spaying might allow the urinary tract to fully mature and thereby prevent possible incontinence later for your pet.

For now, I still recommend spaying between five and six months of age, but ideally not before that. Until we know more about the link between a female going into heat and the risk of devastating mammary cancers, we still recommend doing this by six months. Most shelters don't have the option to wait until six months because of state or local mandates to spay before placement. And of course, the fact that many people simply won't come back to get their pets spayed. Expect this debate to continue for the foreseeable future.

Like the discussion about timing for spay surgery, there is also some debate about the timing of neutering surgery. Specifically, some research suggests that males should not be neutered before they are fully mature, around one year. Males don't go into heat, so I recommend neutering your pet between nine months and one year of age. Again, most shelters don't have this option because pets must be neutered before placement. Breeders will often require their puppies and kittens to be neutered by a certain date; however, many breeders are comfortable with a later age for neuter (and some prefer it).

In summary, if you can, spay your female dog or cat by six months and neuter your male dog or cat by one year.

WHAT IS SPAYING?

Spaying (ovariohysterectomy) is the surgical removal of a

female animal's reproductive organs (the uterus, ovaries, and fallopian tubes). It is an abdominal surgery performed under general anesthesia, meaning your pet is completely asleep during the procedure.

Your vet might suggest preoperative blood work for your pet. This is generally not necessary in a healthy puppy or kitten, but that's a discussion you should have with your vet because it might be indicated in certain instances. The procedure is straightforward but always requires general anesthesia.

Here's what happens: Your pet is given a pre-medication like Valium for sedation and often an injectable nonsteroidal anti-inflammatory drug for dogs or a morphine-type pain medication for cats. Most female pets should have an IV catheter placed to provide fluids for support during surgery and to keep an access point handy just in case of any irregularities. This is also the route for anesthesia to begin (we call this "induction").

Induction agents include intravenous Valium-like compounds, ketamine, or propofol. These smoothly drift your pet into a pain-free state of unconsciousness.

Once your pet is asleep, an endotracheal tube is placed in her throat to provide oxygen and anesthetic gas. Today's anesthetic gases (isoflurane and sevoflurane) are the state of the art in anesthesia safety and have very little residual sedative effects. These short-acting gases are sensitive to adjustment during surgery and are therefore much safer to administer. Once your pet is stable under gas anesthesia, the abdomen is shaved and disinfected, and surgery can begin.

Although spaying is the most routine of all veterinary surgeries, don't underestimate it. This is a major procedure to remove all of the female reproductive organs. It requires an incision down the midline of the abdomen to visualize the ovaries and uterus. Think about the reproductive tract as a mirror-image three-part organ made up of two ovaries, two uterine horns (fallopian tubes), and one uterine body. In an ovariohysterectomy, the ovaries are clamped so they won't bleed, ligated (tied off) with dissolvable suture, and removed from the abdominal cavity. The uterus is clamped at the base, ligated, and removed along with the ovaries. Most veterinary surgeons are very proficient at this and can do the surgery in less than a half hour. The surgical site is closed in two layers: the first at the abdominal muscle wall and the second for the skin using dissolvable sutures or glue so that no suture removal is required. On occasion, your vet may wish to add a few regular sutures, which must be removed within 10 to 14 days.

Once out of surgery, your pet will be gently awakened on a heating pad or under a heat

HOW TO USE AN E-COLLAR

Elizabethan collars, also called E-collars (the dreaded "cone of shame"), prevent pets from licking a surgical site or other wound. Your pet doesn't necessarily have to wear the collar every waking hour. If you can watch your pet closely, take it off for feeding and walking. Some pets don't even need the collar. But it's better to have it and not need it than the other way around. Traditional E-collars are made of hard plastic. New collars include soft collars, neckbands, and donuts, which keep your pet's head from turning too far. Some of these don't work as well as traditional collars. Use trial and error to find the right one for your pet.

blanket. Anesthesia drops the core temperature of the surgical patient, so these devices bring that temperature back up gently and comfortably. Most animals can go home that evening.

Vets do everything they can to make your pet as comfortable as possible after a spay, but this is a serious surgery. Expect to have a groggy, even slightly disoriented pet for the first night at home. Feed a small amount of her regular food and follow the directions for pain medications you've been given. Keep your girl quiet, comfortable, and calm for the first week after surgery. Keep her from licking at the surgery site (you may need an Elizabethan collar to help with this; see sidebar above). It will take about 10 days for the incision to fully heal. Your biggest challenge will be holding your pet back from running and jumping around. Do your best, and she'll be fine.

The Future of Spay and Neuter

The veterinary field is evolving with changes to make spaying more comfortable for pets by using lasers that cut and cauterize (heat seal), making the procedure faster and quicker to heal. Other improvements include laparoscopic spays, which are far less invasive but are not commonly performed yet. I love this technique because it requires only two very small incisions; the surgery is guided by a fiber-optic scope inserted into the abdomen. This technique requires extensive training, but I hope eventually this will become the standard of care for veterinary spay surgeries, just as it is in human medicine.

Another advanced technique is an ovariectomy, in which the ovaries are removed, leaving the uterus intact. Leaving the uterus makes it a less invasive surgery, but veterinarians are still weighing possible disadvantages of ovariectomy, such as a potential uterine infection (called a pyometra), which can occur in the years following the surgery.

Finally, there is some discussion about tubal ligation, which leaves all the reproductive parts intact but ties off the fallopian tubes so the ovaries

cannot be fertilized. One advantage to a tubal ligation is the animal maintains normal female hormone production, which can have positive and negative effects on behavior: positive because these are normal hormones, which can have a calming effect on the animal; negative because of possible mammary cancers, and the pet will still

go into heat with bleeding, which makes this less than appealing for most owners.

WHAT IS NEUTERING?

Neutering (or castration) is the surgical removal of a male animal's testicles and is performed under general anesthesia. Castration is under some discussion these days as well. The advantages of epididymectomy, or ligation (tying off) of the spermatic duct, are being considered as an alternative to full castration in pets for whom testosterone production is preferred for behavioral reasons.

As with spaying surgery, your vet might suggest preoperative blood work for your pet. Again, this is usually not necessary in a healthy puppy or kitten, but that is a discussion you should have with your vet. The prep for procedure is much like

WHAT TO EXPECT IF YOU DECIDE NOT TO SPAY OR NEUTER YOUR PET

If you decide against neutering, make sure you're responsible with your pet. We've got enough "extra" dogs and cats out there. There may be some benefits to not altering your pet, which may include lower anxiety and fewer musculoskeletal injuries, among others. Here's what to expect if your pet isn't spayed or neutered:

Females

1. Heat cycles with behavior changes and discharge
2. Increased risk of mammary cancer
3. Risk of ovarian and uterine cancers
4. Increased risk of pyometra
5. Risk of unwanted pregnancy

Males

1. Increased spraying (cats) or marking (dogs)
2. Increased tendency to stray or roam
3. Possible increased aggression
4. Increased risk of testicular or prostate cancer

the spaying surgery prep already described, with the same sedatives and pain medication, gas anesthesia, and surgical site clipping and disinfecting. The only difference is that the procedure does not usually require full general anesthesia for male cats for whom an endotracheal tube is not placed, and IV fluids are usually not indicated. That's not because male cats aren't as special as our other pets; it's just that a cat castration is so quick that it would take longer to place a tube and an IV catheter than it takes to do the whole surgery.

Castration in all animals is the same. Only the techniques differ, and that's true whether we're talking cats, dogs, rabbits, guinea pigs, or horses. A routine castration involves a small incision just between the start of the penis and the scrotal sac through which each testicle is pushed through the skin. Ligaments are broken down; the spermatic cord and blood vessels are tied off with sutures,

and the testicles are cut with a scalpel and removed. It sounds awful, but it's all pretty quick, and most animals recover rapidly from this surgery. It's even quicker in cats. We do a procedure called an autoligation in which each cord is tied into a knot with itself and the testicles are excised (cut out). No sutures needed!

For dogs, the surgical site is closed with dissolving sutures or glue; no suture removal is required. For cats, the site is either left to close on its own, or tissue glue is placed to close the wound. As with spaying surgery, your pet will be gently awakened on a heating pad or blanket and will go home that evening.

It's imperative to keep your pet quiet and comfortable after his neuter surgery. This is almost more important for males than females because heavy activity can lead to hemorrhage within the surgical site, causing pain and a serious and

WHY DID YOU TATTOO MY PET?

In the past decade, veterinarians have started tattooing dogs and cats after they have been spayed or neutered. The reason is simple: We don't want to accidentally attempt to spay or neuter them again. For neuters, it's a bit of a head scratcher since it's generally obvious they've been neutered (although it is not so easy to tell in cats), but for spays, it's essen-tial to be able to know if a pet has been spayed. Don't expect anything special like a ship or unicorn tattoo – the standard post-spay tattoo is a single orange or black line slightly right of the midline on your pet's abdomen. You might never even notice, but we vets will if anyone ever brings that animal back for a spay.

painful swelling of the scrotum. Be sure to continue any prescribed anti-inflammatory medication, and your pet will be on the way to a full recovery within 10 days. As with the girls, you might need an E-collar to prevent traumatic licking of the surgical site.

EFFECTS ON HEALTH AND BEHAVIOR

Spaying and neutering has its benefits, but for some animals, altering is not an ideal solution. Working dogs, athletes, and show dogs should not be neutered if they are expected to perform at their ideal standard for their breed. But for most pets, spaying or neutering is necessary to prevent them from going into heat (females) and reproducing (both males and females). Recent research has suggested that spaying and neutering may be linked to behavioral issues (anxiety), and even joint and other orthopedic problems. It's still the best way we know to decrease animal overpopulation but you should discuss this fully with your vet.

Health Benefits of Spaying and Neutering

Altering has some very specific health benefits, including:

1   Eliminated risk of pyometra, a uterine infection that can be life threatening (see Chapter 20)

2 Eliminated or reduced chances of certain types of cancer, such as mammary or ovarian cancer, and even lymphoma and hemangiosarcoma according to recent studies

3 No unwanted pregnancies

4 No heat cycles or associated bleeding and attention from stray males

5 Decrease in hormonal fluctuations, which can lead to metabolic disorders such as diabetes

Health Risks of Spaying and Neutering

We've touched on some of the risks of spaying and neutering. These include:

1 Surgical risk and complications (these are very rare)

2 Restricted or abnormal growth (if done too early)

3 Increased risk of obesity

4 Increased incidence of urinary incontinence (spayed females)

5 Increased risk of certain joint disorders in some breeds

Behavior Benefits of Spaying and Neutering

Spaying or neutering has no effect on your pet's personality. However, the presence or absence of testosterone or estrogen can affect extremes. Males might be a bit more passive, and females might be a bit more aggressive or bossy. But you generally won't notice any of this in their everyday personality. It's all very subtle, but we have to consider this whenever we alter the normal physiology of animals.

Ask DR. GARY:

Is My Bird a Boy or a Girl?

If you want to know if your bird is a male or female, don't look at its hind end. You'll never figure it out that way. Some birds are easy: they're color-coded. Parakeets have a colored area over their beak called a cere, which is blue in males and beige in females. Many birds are monomorphic, meaning there's no external difference between males and females. If you don't want to wait to see if your bird lays eggs (a dead giveaway), a commercial DNA kit can give you an answer. These require blood, feathers, or eggshell (when sexing a chick) and give results within two weeks.

The behavior benefits of spaying or neutering are primarily alterations in male behaviors, such as marking, mounting, roaming, and fighting. It's still to be determined whether neutering really affects most of these behaviors. In my experience, I have not seen any decrease in aggression in neutered males compared with their intact counterparts. For males, neutering usually eliminates some negative behaviors like everyone's favorite

SPAYING AND NEUTERING SMALL MAMMALS

Dogs and cats aren't the only animals we recommend spaying or neutering. Rabbits and ferrets should be fixed. Rabbits, after all, breed like rabbits, and intact male ferrets, called "hobs," smell very musky. In this case, you and your neighbors will be the real beneficiaries of a neutered ferret. Guinea pigs and rats may also be spayed and neutered if two can't be separated and might reproduce. There are some medical benefits to spaying all these species. Rabbits, rats, and ferrets suffer from a higher-than-average incidence of uterine, mammary, and ovarian cancers, respectively. Spaying will allay these concerns in these pets.

of humping other dogs and people (although that can't be guaranteed in either males or females!).

In cats, neutering is almost essential in that it stops the less-than-enjoyable odor of intact male cats and cuts way down on urine spraying in the home. From a behavioral vantage point, "desexing" can significantly affect pets. Most of these observations are so far anecdotal. Still, it's worth noting that spayed females might be more aggressive and neutered males might be more passive and anxious than their counterparts. A recent study also noted an increased prevalence of cognitive changes in older spayed and neutered animals. Whether that will be proven true is currently under consideration.

SPAYING AND NEUTERING RESEARCH

For the past decade, we've been evaluating the health advantages and disadvantages of spaying and neutering pets. This includes surgery timing, as well as general and specific effects on certain dog breeds. It's no small feat to decipher the data coming out on this subject, and, unfortunately, there's little agreement on what we've learned so far. On top of that, some studies have led to more questions than they've answered. In the next few years, we can expect more definitive recommendations for spaying and neutering best practices.

Here's what we know: Spaying will lower or even stop the production of the female hormones estrogen, progesterone, and oxytocin. Neutering significantly cuts down on the production of testosterone. The absence of these hormones stops the development of secondary reproductive effects, such as mammary gland development, and elimi-

nates the heat cycle in females. In males, neutering significantly decreases the incidence of prostate disease and entirely eliminates the possibility of testicular cancer (for obvious reasons). Similarly, spayed females can never get ovarian cancer.

Recent studies have illuminated some of the medical disadvantages of spaying and neutering, which have come as a bit of a surprise. In a 2014 study, Dr. Benjamin Hart and his colleagues at UC Davis School of Veterinary Medicine identified a link between early spay surgery and cancers like hemangiosarcoma, lymphosarcoma, mast cell tumors, and lymphoma. Their work includes a retrospective cohort of 90,000 spayed or neutered dogs and identified a statistically significant increase in these cancers along with orthopedic issues like cranial cruciate tears, which were three times more prevalent in neutered than non-neutered pets. Some breeds like German shepherds, golden retrievers, and Labradors had an

increased risk according to these studies. One possible confounder is that the study only looked at animals under nine years of age which excludes pets at exactly the ages in which cancer is most common. More recently, Dr. Michael Kent and his colleagues at the same institution have questioned these findings by including older animals and identified a significant decrease in cancer in spayed or neutered dogs. Completely confused now? You're in good company.

Then there are the behavioral changes, such as increased anxiety in neutered male dogs. This isn't conclusive, with much debate over the group of dogs studied since the majority were patients in a teaching hospital and might not represent the norm. However, this work has opened our eyes to how complicated animal physiology is and how sensitive the equilibrium is within the body's systems. Stay tuned. Much more information is clearly on its way. ◼

PART 3

Pet Behavior and Training

Understanding natural pet behavior
is the key to a happy relationship.
Whether you're training your new puppy
or kitten or managing behavior issues,
you'll find everything you need
to know in this chapter.

CHAPTER 16

Puppies

Ahhhh puppies! What could be more adorable? (Okay; we'll get to kittens later.) It's a good thing puppies are so cute because it helps us (and them) get through the many challenges of raising a puppy. You've probably heard it all before, but it bears repeating: Puppies are a lot of work. They need near-constant supervision to keep them safe and your belongings intact. They require consistent training to teach them how to behave in a human world. They need daily exercise and play so they can develop strong muscles and have tired brains so they don't destroy your life. Puppies need intensive socialization both inside and outside your home so they can develop into confident, well-adjusted dogs. With the right approach, you can survive puppyhood and reap the reward: life with a well-behaved dog. If there is only one thing you take away from this chapter, it's the importance of consistency and patience. Puppies thrive on routines and learn the rules when you set them up for success.

WHAT TO EXPECT

Part of getting through puppyhood is having realistic expectations. The more you can recognize normal puppy behavior, the better you can set up your puppy for success. Puppies have accidents in the house. They chew on things. They jump up, bark, bite, dig, track mud through the house, create messes, and make you want to tear your hair out. They also snuggle, give kisses, and make you laugh. They absolutely adore you and have a type of breath that's so good it bears their name.

Every time your puppy does something that drives you crazy, try to remember that he's just a baby. A 16-week-old puppy is a lot like a one-year-old human. Both are still learning what you want from them and exploring their world though play. A one-year-old baby might draw on the walls with crayons. Your 12-week-old puppy might chew up your favorite shoes. In both cases, a lack of supervision allows for that particular incident. When my pup Betty was around six months, she ate holes in the center of my new living room rug. When your puppy makes a mistake, ask yourself if there's something you could have done to prevent it. A lot of puppy mischief can be prevented with supervision (and my rug could have been saved). If that doesn't do it, just breathe. This too shall pass, and it's vitally important puppies learn during puppyhood much of what they'll need to become "good dogs."

When you bring home your puppy, know that this journey from puppyhood to adulthood might last until your puppy is 18 months to two years old. Puppies learn a lot in the first six months, but then the teenage period hits. Many people find canine adolescence to be even more challenging than the early puppy months. During this time, many dogs will regress in their training, testing their boundaries and conveniently "forgetting" everything they've learned. It's much like the teenage years in humans, where well-behaved children suddenly turn moody and distracted. For dogs, this period lasts anywhere from about six to 18 months. If there's any consolation, while they may steal your keys, few dogs learn to drive.

There's a reason so many dogs in shelters are nine months to 18 months old. Lots of people give up on their dogs during the adolescent period, thinking their sweet puppy has grown up into a bad dog and there's nothing they can do about it. The teenage months are tough, but if you're prepared, there are lots of ways to work through this time and come out on the other end with an amazing dog who will be your best friend for life.

WHAT NOT TO EXPECT

Unrealistic puppy expectations can set you up for a lot of frustration. When you bring your puppy home, he'll start learning and doing what you ask in a somewhat linear fashion, but don't expect that he will never regress in his housetraining or behavior. In fact, it might be many months (even a year or more) before your puppy is reliably housetrained and able to roam free in all areas of your home without chewing something up. All dogs are different in this regard. Some might never be able to be in the house without supervision but that's rare. As far as energy levels go, some puppies become more laid-back dogs earlier, but many puppies need lots of exercise and extra training until they are 18 months to two years of age, at which time they start to settle down. Don't expect your puppy to behave like your neighbor's puppy or your previous puppy, even if they're the same breed. All puppies are individuals, especially when it comes to learning and maturation.

HOUSE RULES

Your puppy will learn faster if you have clear and consistent household rules from day 1. If you're inconsistent in what you allow and don't allow, your puppy won't know what you expect of him. For instance, if you usually don't let him on the couch but make an exception once in a while (because you can't resist those pleading brown eyes), how will he know when he's allowed on the couch or not? If he's never allowed on the couch, he'll learn to accept the rule and is less likely to try to hop up. He's not judging or lamenting this; it's just reality.

It helps to make your list of house rules before you bring your puppy home. Will he be allowed on the couch? The bed? How do you feel about feeding him from the table? Talk with everyone in your family to create and agree on the house rules. If you really don't want your puppy begging at the table

WHAT COULD HAPPEN?

Puppies get into everything because they don't know what's okay and what's not okay to chew or play with. The best course of action is to never leave anything within your puppy's reach, including shoes, purses, phones, cords, kids' toys, and basically anything chewable. Some things are especially dangerous for puppies. Keep these deadly items far out of your puppy's reach:

Antifreeze

Batteries (especially tiny button batteries)

Coins (especially pennies)

Contents of trash cans (use lids or stow cans under cabinets)

Disposable razors

Human medications

Household cleaners

Paints and solvents

Rodent poison

Slug and snail bait

but some family members insist on sneaking food to him at mealtime, you're going to have an issue. You have to train your family before trying to train your pup, or it won't work.

ROUTINES

Puppies thrive on routines. Creating and following a puppy schedule helps tremendously with housetraining and general puppy management. If your puppy eats at the same time every day, he'll likely poop on a somewhat consistent schedule: a very important first lesson. Taking your puppy for regular walks around his usual bathroom time can also do wonders for housetraining since walking generally helps things "move along" in that regard.

Your puppy will feel more content when he knows what to expect—and so will you. Routines help him learn the rules and how your household works ("this is how we do things here"). This is especially important because dogs don't inherently know how to live in a human world. The easier you can make it for him to figure out how humans live, the better he'll be able to adapt.

Create a simple schedule for your puppy (you can print it out and hang it on your refrigerator to remind yourself), including meals, bathroom (potty) breaks, walks, naps (or quiet time), and bedtime. Make it fun by using a dry erase board with spaces to note the day's activities (this is great for kids, but it's still good even if you don't have young ones to fill in the board). For an eight-week-old puppy, it might look something like this:

Note: Provide potty breaks every one to two hours when your puppy is awake.

6:00 a.m.	Wake and potty
8:00	Breakfast
8:30	Walk
9:00	Nap/quiet time
12:00	Lunch
12:30	Walk
1:00	Nap/quiet time
2:00	Training session (5 minutes) followed by a potty session if needed
4:00	Nap/quiet time
6:00	Dinner
6:30	Walk
9:00-10:00	Last potty and bedtime
2:00 a.m.	Middle-of-the-night potty (if he wakes; hopefully this one is temporary!)

Older puppies (over four months) eventually drop the lunch meal. Younger puppies can sleep 18 to 20 hours a day, but their sleep needs gradually drop as they get older, resulting in less daytime sleep. Many puppies need to get up at least once in the middle of the night to go to the bathroom, but if yours doesn't wake up and whine, count your blessings. When your puppy gets older and masters housetraining, your schedule might become a bit more fluid, but it's good to keep mealtimes and walks regular if possible.

HOUSETRAINING

Puppies aren't born knowing that we humans want them to go to the bathroom outside, so it's up to you to clearly communicate that rule. Every time your puppy goes to the bathroom outdoors, it reinforces the idea that outside is the place for doing his business. On the flip side, every accident your puppy has inside the house sets him back. Your goal is to anticipate his needs so he has lots of opportunities to go to the bathroom outside and fewer chances to go in the house.

Some people think you need to start out with puppy pads or newspaper for housetraining, but that's not a great idea because it teaches your puppy that it's okay to go inside the house. If you ultimately want your puppy to eliminate outside, skip the puppy pads and bring him directly outdoors to go to the bathroom. If you live in an apartment or don't have a yard, you might want to teach your puppy to eliminate using a dog potty. These are for you skyscraper dwellers. They range from litter boxes similar to those used for cats, to artificial grass, to boxes intended to be used with sod. Such boxes can be used on a patio or balcony, or indoors. They require regular maintenance and cleaning to keep them sanitary.

Housetraining Basics

The first step is to choose a designated bathroom spot in your yard, preferably a small section of grass in a quiet place like your backyard. Bring your puppy to this spot on a leash every time he needs to go. A leash is important because it keeps your puppy in that spot and focused on the task at hand. Otherwise, he might just run around sniffing and playing instead of going to the bathroom, and then have an accident once you bring him back into the house. You might have to stand out there a long time before he actually goes, especially in the beginning when he's learning.

Once he goes to the bathroom, praise him effusively. You can offer a treat too, which is particularly important if your pup just isn't getting it. Then let him off leash to explore and play. Eventually you won't need the leash at all—assuming your yard is safe and contained, of course.

HOUSETRAINING DOS AND DON'TS

When teaching your puppy where to go to the bathroom, remember these key points:

- DON'T use puppy pads or newspaper in the house unless you primarily want your dog to go potty in the house permanently (for instance, if you live in a high-rise apartment building).
- DO go outside with your puppy every time so you know if he went potty.
- DON'T scold your puppy for having an accident, and never rub his nose in the mess.
- DO anticipate your puppy's needs, and take him out frequently throughout the day.
- DON'T get discouraged. Housetraining takes time. Your puppy really will get it eventually.

Very young puppies need to go out at least once every one to two hours, sometimes more frequently. In general, take your puppy out first thing in the morning, after meals, when he wakes up from a nap, after playing, and right before bed. Yes, it's exhausting. Remember how this chapter started? Take him out more frequently if he drinks a lot of water, especially after play sessions or on a hot day. Some older puppies can go two to three hours between bathroom breaks, although some puppies do better with more frequent opportunities.

The more times your puppy goes outside to the bathroom spot, the more quickly he'll understand that this is where he should always go. But he hasn't graduated from housetraining school yet. If he has an accident in the house, handle it calmly. If you catch him in the middle of going, simply say, "Let's go outside," and gently and quietly scoop him up and carry him to the outdoor bathroom spot and say, "Go potty," or whatever embarrassing instruction comes naturally. I won't tell you what I say to my dogs, but I'll deny I said it if anyone overhears me. If he goes again outside, praise him calmly and give him a treat if you have one. If he doesn't go, repeat the words "go potty" and offer praise anyway.

Go back inside, calmly clean up the mess, and vow to watch him better next time. Never yell, hit, or punish your puppy for having an accident. And please don't rub his nose in the mess. This ridiculous and outdated advice won't teach him to go outside, but it will teach him to be afraid of you and to sneak off to hide when he does go to the bathroom in the house. When training any animal, whether a baby or a grown adult, a gentle approach is not only the most humane method but the most effective one. Animals respond quickly and eagerly when training is positive and fun.

Prevent accidents by taking your puppy out very frequently and watching him like a hawk for signs he's about to go: sniffing the ground intently, circling, or stopping play and freezing in place. Never forget that your puppy is just a baby. Not only does he need time to learn the rules, but his bladder needs time to develop so he can hold it while inside. Even when he understands that going to the bathroom should happen outside, he can hold it only so long before an accident happens. If you can't supervise your puppy while he's doing his business, use a crate or exercise pen to prevent accidents.

Housetraining Troubleshooting

Sometimes frequent accidents in the house can be caused by a medical issue like a urinary tract infection or intestinal parasites, so it's a good idea to make an appointment with your vet to rule out any of these issues. If your puppy gets a clean bill of health and just doesn't seem to be "getting it," ask yourself some questions:

- Are you taking your puppy out frequently enough?

    Some puppies just need to go more often than others, especially smaller ones. If you've been taking him out every two hours, try every hour or even more frequently. You won't have to do this forever, but every time he goes in the house, it reinforces that the house might be an okay place to go, so be sure to set him up for success. Think of it as a substitute teacher coming in and giving your class the opposite instruction you've

Ask DR. GARY:

Why Does My Puppy Eat His "You Know What"?

Many puppies, and even adult dogs will eat their poop — or worse yet, another dog's. Although repulsive, this is normal and is called coprophagy. It is simply the normal dog love of smelly things and not a dietary nutrient issue. Remember that dogs are scavengers by nature, and dog mothers stimulate puppies to urinate by licking their hind ends. Say no more, right? It usually won't hurt your dog, but it will give you pause when he tries to lick you in the face. Some dogs need to be specifically trained not to do this. Ironically, making a big deal about house accidents can sometimes itself be a cause. Fortunately, most dogs grow out of it.

been giving. Cutting down on how many opportunities he has to make a mistake will greatly help your housetraining efforts.

- Are you taking him to the bathroom spot on a leash to make sure he goes before playing in the yard?

    Lots of puppies are so excited to be outside that they get distracted and might not remember that they have to go. Your puppy could be out in the yard for 20 minutes chasing leaves and having a blast but forget to go to the bathroom. Once you bring him inside, he relaxes

TEACH YOUR PUPPY TO RING A BELL

Some puppies learn to bark or whine at the door to be let out, but others don't. One way to solve this problem is to teach him to ring a bell to go outside.

Hang a bell on a ribbon or string from the handle of the door that leads to the yard. Every time you take your puppy out to the bathroom spot, ring the bell, then open the door. Eventually your puppy might investigate the bell with his nose. If he does this, open the door immediately. Most dogs quickly pick up on the fact that nosing or pawing the bell makes the door magically open.

a bit and realizes, "Hey! I have to pee!" and goes right on the carpet. This scenario happens more often than you might think. Many people think their puppy is being obstinate or vindictive. That's not true. Taking him out on a leash and waiting for him to go will help. If he won't go, come back inside for five minutes, watch him like a hawk, and then go back outside to the bathroom spot. Do this until he goes to the bathroom; then praise him and let him off leash to play.

■ Are you feeding him too much?

What goes in must come out. Too much food can lead to too much poop. If your puppy has been eating three meals a day, but he's not cleaning the bowl every time, it might be time to switch him to two meals a day. Also watch the volume of food you're feeding him.

■ Are you feeding him on a schedule?

Predictable meals and treat times can lead to a predictable pooping schedule, which can help you anticipate his needs.

■ Are you giving him too much freedom in the house?

Puppies who are still housetraining should not be allowed to roam all over your house without supervision. It's too tempting to sneak off to the far reaches of your home to go potty in secret. Limit your puppy to certain areas by using baby gates, closing doors, and using a pen or crate when you can't watch him like a hawk. You can also try tethering him to your waist with a six-foot leash so he stays in your eyesight.

■ Are you cleaning up accidents thoroughly?

If your puppy can still smell where he had a previous accident, he might revisit the scene of the crime to go there again. Clean up accidents as quickly as possible using an enzymatic cleaner designed for pet messes. They work wonders.

CRATE TRAINING

If you're new to crate training, confining your dog to a small cage might seem like a cruel practice, but when used appropriately, crate training is far from cruel. Crate training taps into a dog's natural instincts because it creates a safe, secure place for your pup to rest, like a den. It's debatable whether dogs used these in the wild, but there's no arguing that dens are warm, cozy, safe places where dogs can rest without having to worry about a predator sneaking up behind them.

When crates are introduced correctly, most dogs love them. Think of a crate like your dog's private bedroom. It's a comfortable place to sleep and relax. It's also a safe place to put your puppy when you leave for short periods of time. When he's snuggled in his crate, your puppy can't tear apart your house or get himself into trouble. Because dogs naturally don't want to go to the bathroom where they sleep, it's also a great tool for housetraining.

As a general rule, you can leave a puppy in a crate for one hour per month of age. A three-month-old puppy could, in theory, be in her crate for up to three hours, although it's safer to give her more frequent opportunities to go to the bathroom. Daytime hours spent in a crate should not exceed four hours, no matter your dog's age. The exception to this rule is overnight: Your puppy can sleep in his crate all night, but keep the crate in your bedroom so you can hear him rustling or whining if he needs a potty break in the middle of the night.

Keep in mind that crates are a training tool, but they should not be abused. Crating is not the right solution for all-day confinement. Never leave a puppy (or adult dog) in a crate for eight-plus hours a day while you're at work. If you must leave your puppy at home all day, find another safe place to confine her, such as a puppy-proofed room, a safe and comfortable garage space, or a secure and shaded yard with a doghouse or other protection from the elements. Better yet, get a dog walker.

Crate training is not just for puppies. If you adopt an adult dog who isn't housetrained, you can use a crate as a training tool while he learns the ropes. Introduce it just as you would for a puppy (the same goes for housetraining). Some adult dogs with anxiety issues might feel more comfortable in a crate overnight or for a few hours during the day rather than being loose in the house because a crate mimics a safe, den-like environment.

Choosing a Crate

The key considerations in choosing a crate are style and size. Style will be personal preference—yours and your dog's—but the crate's size is critical for training success.

Crates come in many different styles. Plastic crates are usually the least expensive. They are

sturdy, easy to clean, and provide privacy. Larger plastic crates might be hard to transport since they don't usually fold up. Wire crates fold flat for easy transport. They are durable and stay cool in summer, but since they are very open, they provide more of a cage-like experience than a den experience. Draping a wire crate with a towel, sheet, or blanket can help. Nylon crates are a nice retreat for your dog and often travel well. Some dogs can scratch or chew through the nylon, so these aren't the best choice for determined escape artists, or veteran chewers.

The size of your crate is absolutely critical if you are using it for housetraining. The point of using the crate is to take advantage of your puppy's instinct to avoid eliminating in his bed. If the crate is too big, your puppy will be able to go to the bathroom at one end, then curl up and sleep at the other end.

The crate is supposed to be small (picture that cozy den), but your puppy should have enough space to stand up, turn around, and lie down. Since your pup will grow rapidly in the coming months, you might have to buy more than one crate. Some crates come with dividers. This allows you to buy one crate that will be large enough for your puppy when he reaches his adult size and adjust the space inside as your puppy grows. You can also buy a larger crate and use a box or other item inside the crate to block off space and make it smaller. You might consider getting a second-hand crate since your puppy might quickly outgrow the first one you buy.

Location of the Crate

Place the crate in a quiet area that isn't isolated, such as a corner of the living room or kitchen. Your puppy wants to be part of the family, not

CRATE-TRAINING DOS AND DON'TS

- DO make the crate a comfortable and cozy space to relax.
- DON'T use the crate to punish your dog.
- DO give your dog special chews, treats, and toys inside the crate.
- DON'T leave your puppy in the crate too long, or he might be forced to eliminate in the crate, which defeats the purpose.
- DON'T let anyone bother your dog when he's in his crate. This is his safe space.
- DO give it time when introducing the crate. Most dogs come to tolerate and even enjoy being in their crates.

stuck in a back room somewhere by himself. One exception to this rule is if your household is extremely chaotic and loud. In that case, your pup might appreciate a quieter place to snooze. At night, place the crate in your room, beside your bed, so your puppy can hear and smell you and so you can hear your puppy if he wakes up and needs to go out.

Introducing the Crate

Make the crate inviting for your puppy. You can buy a fluffy crate pad or line the bottom with soft blankets or towels. Some puppies take to crates immediately without a peep: They just curl up and go right to sleep. Others need a bit more acclimation.

The first few times you use the crate, stuff a Kong with kibble and peanut butter and put it inside. Open the crate door and encourage your puppy to go inside. Gently place him in the crate if he doesn't enter on his own. Close the door and stay nearby while your puppy enjoys the Kong treat. As soon as he's done, open the door. Repeat this process, using smaller treats and toys, always opening the crate before your puppy tries to get out. Leave the puppy in for longer and longer amounts of time until he is comfortable in his crate.

You can pair a voice cue ("crate") by saying the word every time your puppy enters the crate. If you make the crate experience rewarding enough, eventually your pup might dash into the crate every time you say the cue. When my dog Betty was growing up, we'd just say, "Betty, go in your box," and she'd dutifully and happily run right in.

Crate-Training Troubleshooting

If your puppy whines or cries in his crate, ignore him. Wait until he's quiet to let him out, or you'll be teaching him to cry longer and louder. This will be hard initially, but be strong. If he cries at

night, he probably has to go out. Silently remove him from his crate and carry him outside to the bathroom spot. Don't play, talk, or engage him during this time, or he'll think 2 a.m. is the perfect play time. Wait for him to do his business; then silently return him to his crate. If he cries, gently say, "good night," toss a blanket over the crate, and wait for him to quiet down. But don't fall for it and take him out. It might take a few nights for him to get the idea that nighttime is for sleeping, but most puppies figure it out quickly.

SOCIALIZATION

Socialization is the process of exposing your puppy to the world: sights, sounds, smells, people, places, animals, and experiences. That exposure should be a positive experience. Socialization is a critical part of puppyhood. Dogs who don't get proper socialization at the right age can grow up to be fearful of people, places, and other animals. Some unsocialized dogs develop more serious issues like anxiety and aggression.

When you bring your puppy home, don't delay in starting the socialization process. The key time frame for socializing your dog is very short: from four to about 14 weeks of age. During this brief window, a puppy is naturally open to investigating new things without much fear, so it's an ideal time to teach him all about the world.

During this time, expose your puppy to as many different people, animals, places, and things as you can. Brings lots of treats with you

---

SOCIALIZATION CHALLENGE: 100 THINGS IN 100 DAYS

Make it a goal to try to introduce your puppy to 100 different people, places, sights, and sounds in the first 100 days you have him. Start with this list, and add to it as you go along:

- Men (sorry guys but we're scary)
- Men with beards
- Men with hats
- Doorbells
- People in wheelchairs
- Kids playing sports
- People in hats or hoodies
- Skateboards
- Bikes
- Motorcycles
- Garbage trucks
- Vacuums
- Lawnmowers
- Cats
- Other dogs
- Coffee shops
- Restaurant patios
- Ocean or lake
- Hiking trail
- Farmers markets
- Music festivals
- Parades

everywhere you go so you can reward your puppy whenever he investigates something new. This way, your puppy will associate yummy treats with the new experiences. Go slowly, never pushing your puppy past his comfort zone.

If he seems nervous about a particular situation (for instance, he refuses to move forward or hides behind your legs), take a few steps back until he relaxes, then give him treats and talk to him in a calm, upbeat voice. Stand tall and keep your body still. Don't bend over your puppy or pick him up. If your puppy thinks you're worried about something, he'll worry about it too. When he seems relaxed, try to approach the "scary" new thing slowly, and let him explore it on his own terms. If your puppy seems overwhelmed and doesn't want to approach something, don't force it. Simply remove him from the situation and try another day.

Around 16 to 24 weeks of age, many puppies enter one of several brief fear periods (called fear imprint stages). This is normal and eventually passes; however, during this time, even well-socialized puppies might react to new things with fear or become afraid of things they are familiar with.

It's harder to start socializing an older puppy or adult dog, but it's still possible. Simply go very slow when your dog seems afraid or cautious. Let your dog dictate the pace at which you approach new things. Use extradelicious treats, and give a lot of them. Depending on his personality, it might take longer for an older puppy or an adult dog to accept new experiences or he might naturally be curious and bold.

Socializing With People

Invite your friends, family, and neighbors over to meet your puppy. Let them give your puppy treats, hold him, pet him, and play with him. If you don't have kids, ask your friends and neighbors with

BONDING WITH A SHY RABBIT

Rabbits are naturally shy. In the wild, where they are prey animals, it pays to be alert to potential danger. But there are ways to develop your bond and earn your bunny's trust. Hold a carrot or apple slice and sit on the floor in the same room as your bunny. Be still and quiet, and let the bunny come to you when she's ready. Let her nibble the treat while you hold it, but don't pet her or pick her up. Repeat this daily until your bunny sees you as a nonthreat-ening friend. When your bunny is more comfortable, work up to petting and holding her. In time, she will hop right up to you for some love, and probably a carrot.

calm, well-behaved kids to come play with your puppy and give him treats. Always supervise kids and puppies together to make sure no one gets hurt accidentally.

When you go out for walks, carry a stash of treats in your pocket. This is a good time to discover the wearable treat pouch. When strangers approach and want to pet your adorable puppy, ask if they will give your puppy a treat. Your puppy will associate strangers with delicious rewards, and no self-respecting dog forgets that. But don't force it: Your puppy may feel better if you hand him the treat, and he'll still form positive associations with the new person.

Socializing With Other Dogs

I've talked with many new puppy parents who are afraid to introduce any other dogs to their pup. Don't be. If your puppy is an only dog, let him play with vaccinated, healthy, well-behaved dogs you know. Don't take him to a dog park until he's com-

pleted his vaccine series, but by all means, go for walks or have controlled healthy dog playdates. Once your pup has finished his vaccine series, he still may not be ready for a dog park. These places can get rowdy and be overwhelming to puppies (and sometimes to adult dogs!). Better yet, socialize your puppy in an off-leash puppy socialization class or play group. If you can't find one of these and your pup is making friends with bigger dogs, make sure you watch your puppy for signs that he's uncomfortable and remove him if the play is too rough.

Socializing With Other Animals

If possible, introduce your puppy to other animals during the prime socialization window. If you live in an area that's home to livestock, let him check out horses, cows, goats, pigs, and chickens. If you have other pets at home, you can allow them to interact as long as you are right there with them, using caution to make sure no one gets hurt. Many puppies can learn to get along famously with cats, rabbits, reptiles, birds, and even small pets like hamsters and rats. Regardless of your pup's previous experience, make sure you're always there to supervise that the smaller animals remain safe.

Socializing Puppies Before Vaccines Are Complete

The optimal time for socialization happens to coincide with the period of time that your puppy will be getting his vaccinations. In the past, we used to recommend that puppies stay inside and away from other dogs until they completed their vaccination series. Today, we know that keeping your puppy in quarantine is detrimental to his mental and emotional development. Vaccines might not be complete until 12 to 14 weeks of age, at which time the prime window for socialization is closing. Proper socialization is just as important as protecting him against disease. So how do you balance the two?

Once your puppy has received his first set of vaccines around eight weeks of age, you can take him out in public and even attend puppy kindergarten classes since all the puppies in the class will also have had their first set of vaccines. However, until the vaccination series is complete, avoid places where many dogs congregate: dog parks, pet stores, doggie day cares, animal shelters (except for puppy classes!), and any other place that has strange dogs of unknown health status. Letting your puppy socialize with animals of other species is safe because there is little to no risk of contracting a serious disease. There are still lots of places you can take your puppy for socialization, including many coffee shops, restaurants, hardware stores, public parks, hiking trails, and beaches.

BASIC TRAINING

Puppies don't naturally learn how to behave simply by growing up. Some people neglect to start training early in puppyhood, then wonder why their one-year-old dog still jumps up, pulls on the leash, or runs away. It's up to you to teach your puppy how to behave. It's much easier to teach puppies the correct way to do things than to fix ingrained problem behaviors.

One training technique that works well with young puppies is based on having your puppy "earn" the things he wants in life by doing certain behaviors. Known as Say Please, Learn to Earn, or Nothing in Life Is Free, such training methods entail asking your puppy to sit or lie down before he can have the things he desires. For example, at mealtime, ask your puppy to sit before you put down the bowl. If he wants a toy, ask him to sit before giving it to him. Before heading out for a walk, ask your puppy to sit before he can go out the door. This method gives your puppy a way to ask for something he wants by doing something you want (sit) rather than something you don't want (jumping up, barking, shoving his way out the door). As your puppy gets older, turn the behavior into a sit-stay, asking him to wait longer and longer before giving her the reward.

When to Start Training Your Puppy

You can start teaching your puppy to sit, lie down, stay, and walk on a loose leash at eight weeks old or as soon as you bring him home. At this young age, keep training sessions short—five minutes or less. That's all the attention span he has. At 12 to 16 weeks, you can lengthen training sessions to 10 to 15 minutes. Always end training on a high note when your puppy got something right and before your puppy becomes frustrated or distracted. (See below for more tips.)

Puppy Kindergarten

Puppy kindergarten classes are a fantastic way to introduce your puppy to basic training while also providing excellent socialization. In these group classes, dog owners usually learn how to teach their puppies how to sit, lie down, stay, come, and walk on a loose leash. The trainer might also offer tips and advice for common puppy issues like biting, jumping up, housetraining, and more. The classes usually last about one hour, which is about as long as a puppy's attention can be held.

Puppy kindergarten classes are typically designed for puppies who are eight weeks to about six months old. To participate, puppies need to have had at least their first set of vaccines. The classes are offered through private trainers, pet supply stores, and, of course, many shelters. To find one near you, ask your veterinarian, someone at the shelter, or your breeder, or search the internet for "puppy kindergarten" in your city or county.

Getting Through the "Teenage Years"

For dogs, the teenage years are really only months (lucky for us), but those months can be quite challenging. All dogs mature at different rates, but in general, canine adolescence runs from about 9 to 18 months of age. Some breeds peak a little earlier (six months) and some remain teenagers a bit longer (up to two years). During this time, many dogs start defying rules and pushing boundaries. When you ask a young puppy to sit, he does it immediately because he likes practicing new skills, he wants that yummy treat, and he wants to please you. When you ask an adolescent dog to sit, he's thinking, "Hmmmm . . . do I really HAVE to?" Couple that type of boundary pushing with a dog who is now large and is at the height of his energy levels and endurance and you have a recipe for an out-of-control dog.

The best way to have success with your teenage dog is by going back to the basics. Puppies thrive on consistency, but adolescent dogs demand it. For instance, if your formerly "housetrained" dog is having accidents in the house, go back to the beginning and treat him as if he was never housetrained. This means taking him out on a leash at regular intervals and not letting him have free roam of the house. Don't be frustrated with him; he's just looking for clarity. Remember, dogs want to please us. If your teenage dog ignores you when you ask him to sit or stay, go back to a Say Please or Nothing in Life Is Free strategy by making him sit and stay before he gets anything he wants, including meals, play, walks, and attention from you. Finally, consider enrolling in obedience classes with an experienced trainer who can help you get over the hump of the teenage months. Your hard work will be rewarded when your dog settles down at about 18 months to two years of age. ■

CHAPTER 17

Training and Trainers

Puppies don't learn how to be good dogs on their own. They need guidance from us. Although puppies do need a lot of training initially, training your dog is a lifelong process. It's kind of like playing golf: You have to keep practicing to stay proficient. The same goes for dogs, especially dogs who never received adequate training in puppyhood. During your puppy's first year, focus on the basics like sit, lie down, stay, come, walking nicely on a leash, and good manners (no jumping up or biting on hands or clothing). Once he has a good foundation, you can explore trick training or some of the many dog sports and activities explored in this section.

THE EVOLUTION OF DOG TRAINING

Decades ago, it was thought that the only way to teach a dog was to force him into compliance. That was wrong. If you haven't trained a dog in a long time, you'll be happy to know that modern training methods are much gentler—and more effective too. Gone are the days of yanking on choke chains and trying to dominate your dog. Positive training uses praise and food rewards to encourage your dog to behave as you'd like him to. Because dogs get rewarded for doing certain behaviors, they're motivated to keep doing whatever it takes to get that treat.

Sadly, there are still people using old school "force" methods of training. When researching trainers, ask the trainer what methods she uses and try to observe a class. Avoid any trainer who recommends using choke chains or prong collars as standard training equipment or who throws around the word *dominance* a lot. Your dog does not feel the need to dominate you, much as some people proclaim. It's true dogs look to their humans as their leaders, but your golden retriever is not constantly jockeying for a higher position in your household. Conversely, there is no need to dominate your dog—and, frankly, you can't. Dogs have two basic switches: fear and no fear. A dog can learn anything to avoid pain, but he won't learn it for the right reasons, and using force and fear to train a dog destroys your bond. Fear is the last thing you want to add to your dog's teaching regimen. Remember the Five Freedoms? They include freedom from pain, discomfort, and fear.

That said, some persistent behavior issues (let's call these "stubbornness" instead of "dominance")

can come into play with expert-level breeds like Akitas, German shepherds, and chow chows. These breeds require more advanced training from people who have lots of experience with the breed.

POSITIVE REINFORCEMENT TRAINING

The first rule of dog training is the easiest to learn: bribery. To be accurate, it's really reinforcement, which is the key to canine behavior. In the training world, we talk about reinforcement and punishment. I'm not a fan of punishment, especially when reward works so well. Dogs are incredibly motivated by reward, and food is at the top of that list! But for some dogs, playing with a special toy that comes out only during training can also be very rewarding. This is all positive reinforcement.

Some trainers, like those we employ at the San Diego Humane Society, focus on positive reinforcement. But these trainers might actually use a mix of positive and negative reinforcement. Don't confuse negative reinforcement with punishment. Negative reinforcement is taking something away to stop an unwanted behavior. An example is putting a toy away if your dog keeps barking for it. This isn't really punishment, although your dog may think it is.

Another example of negative reinforcement is turning away from your dog and ignoring him when he's jumping up. Taking away your attention is the motivator. If your dog stops jumping up, you turn back to face him and give him praise (the reward). On the flip side, jerking on a choke chain is just plain punishment, which is not something you should ever do (and, again, avoid trainers who use such methods).

SHOCK COLLARS

I'll make this easy—never use an electric collar or "shock collars." Pain has absolutely no place in dog training. Believe me, it's a painful shock (if you have any doubt, check out some of the videos online of humans testing the collars on themselves). In most cases, shock collars cause more training harm than good, especially if used to try to overcome cases of anxiety, stress, and fear. A terrified dog isn't thinking about the training; he's just trying to avoid the shock. There are far better ways to train your best friend.

Punishment has no place in training animals. Equipment like choke chains, pinch collars, and electric shock collars do not belong in training. Neither does the proverbial can of pennies or air horns, both of which use fear to stop a dog's behavior. Even gentler methods like citronella sprays on a bark collar or gentle water sprays are in fact punishment. Even though these are better alternatives than, say, using a shock collar, they are still not good ones. Remember the Five Freedoms: You never need to cause pain or fear; dogs want to please us and do what we want them to do; they just need to understand what that is. No idea sticks better than those implanted with a food reward.

In fact, there is nothing more bonding than using rewards to train your pup. Dogs get to do the three best things in the world: be with you, learn a behavior, and eat all at the same time. Plan on enrolling in a beginner or basic training class. Not only will you learn how to speak to your pup, he'll learn basic manners and skills, and you'll both get the inestimable benefits of a room full of fellow dog lovers and their dogs. The value of socialization (for canine and human) cannot be understated. You only need two pieces of equipment for this to work: a treat bag (one worn around the waist is greatly convenient) and the treats. Some of the best treats for training are cut up hot dogs (small pieces) or string cheese.

That's all elementary. After the initial class, you can sign up for more group training on specifics such as reactive dogs, marvelous manners, shy dog classes, and even graduate school for your dog for skills, such as rapid recall, agility, and even Canine Good Citizen certification—the college degree of dog training.

TYPES OF TRAINERS

As much as we love our pets, no pet is perfect. At some point, many pets can develop an unwelcome behavior or two, whether it's excessive barking or pulling on the leash. If your efforts to solve the issue yourself at home have failed, you have many options for help. Great professional trainers or animal behaviorists are worth their weight in gold, especially when it comes to resolving behavior problems and even for just teaching the basics. Before choosing one, it helps to understand a little bit about the different types of trainers.

Certified Dog Trainers

Dog trainers are not required by law to be licensed or certified. This means that anyone can create a website and call himself a dog trainer. But you don't want just anyone teaching you and your dog. A great dog trainer teaches you how to teach your dog so you can continue your training throughout your dog's lifetime.

Find a dog trainer who has been certified by an independent training organization, such as the Certification Council for Professional Dog Trainers. These trainers adhere to a code of ethics and training and have the designation "certified professional dog trainer" (CPDT-KA; the KA stands for "knowledge assessed"). Keep in mind that certification does not guarantee that a trainer uses positive reinforcement or humane methods and is skilled in the art of dog training and behavior. However, it does show that the person has put forth the effort to learn modern training methods and theories, and these certifications require continuing education to remain current.

WHEN ENOUGH IS ENOUGH: ADDRESSING CHALLENGES

How do you know when it's time to seek higher-level help for your pet's behavior problems? For issues like barking, jumping up, and pulling on the leash, you can try to work with a certified dog trainer. If you try this without success, consider reaching out to an applied animal behaviorist or veterinary behaviorist. Often such specialists will work hand in hand with your trainer. If your pet's issue is severe (separation anxiety, resource guarding, fear, reactivity, aggression) or if you have a cat who is peeing outside the litter box, skip the trainer and go straight to one of these higher-level professionals. (Read more about severe behavioral issues in Chapter 18.)

Certified dog trainers are your best option for puppy training, basic obedience training, trick training, performance sport training (like agility), and resolving common behavior problems like excessive barking, jumping up, pulling on the leash, and running away. You can choose from group classes or private sessions, and some trainers even come to your home.

Animal Behaviorists

Animal behaviorists are the psychologists of the pet world. These professionals hold either a master's degree or Ph.D. in animal behavior and postgraduate training, plus certification from the Animal Behavior Society. Certified individuals holding master's degrees are called associate certified applied animal behaviorists. Those with doctoral degrees are called certified applied animal behaviorists (CAABs). Some are also veterinarians, but that's generally the exception in this field.

Animal behaviorists are experts in normal and abnormal animal behavior. Most can work with both dogs and cats, as well as other animal species, such as birds, horses, and even zoo animals.

Applied animal behaviorists are experts in behavior modification, so they are a good option for resolving difficult behavior problems in dogs and cats, such as aggression, reactivity, fear, and litter box aversion. Training and counseling are all conducted one-on-one and tailored specifically to your pet's needs. CAABs can't treat medical issues but they can recommend behavior-modification drugs for your vet to prescribe.

Veterinary Behaviorists

If certified applied animal behaviorists are the psychologists of the pet world, veterinary behaviorists are the psychiatrists. These are veterinarians who have undergone specialized training to become board-certified in animal behavior. You will see the title Dipl. ACVB (diplomate of the American College of Veterinary Behaviorists) following the veterinarian's DVM (doctor of veterinary medicine) title. To become board-certified, veterinarians must complete a residency in behavior and pass a qualifying exam.

Much like applied animal behaviorists, board-certified veterinary behaviorists can help you resolve challenging behavior problems like aggression, separation anxiety, resource guarding, and litter box issues. The main difference between these two professionals is that a veterinary behaviorist can prescribe medications and can also treat any physical problems with your animal in addition to addressing the behavioral concerns. This is ideal when the behavior problems are rooted in medical issues, but veterinary behaviorists are also masters at resolving behavior alone.

CHOOSING THE RIGHT CLASS

You will find classes for every stage of your puppy or dog's development, from beginning lessons to trick training, and even advanced performance sport training. Don't just stop at one or two. Your training journey can go as long as you and your dog want, and there is nothing more bonding than learning together.

Basic Training (Obedience)

These common puppy and dog training classes are what we offer at the San Diego Humane Society, as do many other shelters, pet stores, and private trainers. They might have different names in different communities, but the basics will be the same.

Puppy preschool: This is first-time training primarily focused on socialization for pups typically eight to 16 weeks of age. These invaluable classes expose your puppy to new people, dogs, environments, and experiences.

Puppy kindergarten: Similar to puppy preschool, these classes are designed to meet the training and socialization needs of puppies

typically between eight and 24 weeks of age. It's possibly the best step in your puppy's lifelong journey to be a "good dog."

Basic obedience: These introductory training classes are for puppies older than six months and adult dogs. They teach you and your dog the basics like sit, down, stay, and loose leash walking using positive-reinforcement training techniques. Every dog should take at least one obedience class.

Advanced obedience: This class builds on the skills of your dog's first obedience class. Hand signals are often added to verbal cues, and you and your dog will practice difficult skills like come and longer stays.

WHAT IS CANINE GOOD CITIZEN CERTIFICATION?

Developed by the American Kennel Club in 1989, the Canine Good Citizen (CGC) program is the baccalaureate degree that celebrates responsible ownership and a well-mannered dog. To earn a CGC, a dog must pass 10 tests:

1. Accepting a friendly stranger
2. Sitting politely for petting
3. Allowing basic grooming
4. Walking on a loose lead
5. Walking through a crowd
6. Sitting and lying down on command, and staying in place
7. Coming when called
8. Reacting appropriately to another dog
9. Reacting appropriately to distractions
10. Calmly enduring supervised separation from the owner

Advanced Training (Performance)

If your dog is at the top of his obedience class, a great big world of dog training awaits him. Specialty classes like trick training will make your pup the envy of your neighborhood. There's also a whole world of dog workshops to explore like agility training, crate training, and dog park etiquette. These often depend on your dog breed's aptitude (see Part 1), your free time, and of course your wallet. Done well, these are positive investments in your pet you'll never regret.

Resolving Behavior Issues

Some trainers offer group classes for basic training challenges like leash pulling or mild dog reactivity. If you can't find a class that fits your needs, most trainers can work with you individually to resolve barking, digging, chewing, jumping up, and pulling on the leash.

TEACHING THE BASICS

Enrolling your dog in training classes is always a good idea, but you can also teach your dog some things at home. The basics of dog training are relatively simple. Notice I said "relatively." The number 1 rule is to be patient and have fun. Everyone wants a dog with manners, but the most important benefit of training is bonding time with your dog.

Clicker Training

Clicker training is sheer brilliance. With this method, you mark the exact moment your dog does a desired behavior with a sound (a click from a small handheld plastic noisemaker), pairing the click with a reward (a treat or toy). This is good old cause-and-effect operant conditioning. The real reward is the treat and not the click. You can't give your dog a treat the very instant he does the right thing, so the click just tells him that a treat is on the way. Timing is everything here so be sure you

Ask DR. GARY:

Is My Dog an Alpha?

The thought that dogs are always trying to be the "alpha" over us is one of the biggest misconceptions of dog behavior. Known as "dominance theory," the idea was based on a study of captive zoo wolves in the 1930s that claimed that wolves fight to gain dominance. In a natural, wild pack, they don't do this once the mating pair is established. Besides, dogs are not wolves; in fact, recent theory suggests they may never have been. Instead dogs and wolves came from a common ancestor before they split lineages. Dominance-based training, which is often punishment based, is not the answer. Your dog doesn't want to dominate you; you're the provider and his whole world.

time these two actions within one or two seconds, or your pet may not make the connection. It's a way to clearly communicate to your dog that he just did the correct thing, a dog-friendly way of saying, "Yes! That thing you JUST did when your bottom touched the floor! That's the thing I want!" Certainly, you could use just a word or other signal to mark the desired behavior, but a click is a distinct, consistent sound and never confusing to your dog.

There are many clicker training workshops, from the Karen Pryor Academy, which specializes in this, to routine training classes, which can incorporate clicker training into the course work. It takes some practice on the human side to time the click to the exact moment of the behavior and give the reward immediately after. Once you and your dog get the hang of it, however, clicker training can open up a great big world of training fun. There's something magical about seeing your dog "get" the game of clicker training. Dogs frequently start offering up behaviors they think will earn them a click and a treat.

Using the Clicker to Teach the Basics

To try clicker training at home, buy a clicker (available online and at most pet supply stores) and arm yourself with some very tasty treats. Some dogs work for anything (including kibble). If that's the case with your dog, fantastic. But for most dogs, true motivation comes from high-value treats. Think cooked chicken, cheese, hot dogs, meat-based treats, or the most coveted of dog motivators: sardines! Just make sure each treat is very tiny (the size of a pea). You'll need to reward your dog many times in each training session, and you don't want him to get full or he'll lose interest. Use a treat

pouch or small plastic baggie to hold your treats.

Before getting started, you must do what's called charging or priming the clicker. Stand next to your dog and grab a handful of treats. Click and quickly give him a treat. He doesn't have to do anything to earn the treat yet. You simply want him to associate the click sound with a treat. Repeat this click-treat process five or 10 times; then click the clicker and don't give a treat. If your dog looks at you or your treat hand in anticipation of a treat, the clicker is charged. In the beginning, it's helpful to start each clicker training session with a brief charging session until you know your dog is fully aware of the game.

Clicker

When clicker training, keep sessions short (start off with five to 10 minutes) so your dog doesn't become bored or frustrated. Always end on a positive note (when your dog does something right and is rewarded for it). If he's struggling to learn a new skill, end the session by asking him to do something he already knows how to do, like sit.

SIX BASIC COMMANDS FOR DOGS

You can teach these simple commands at home or in a class setting. These basics set the foundation for a lifetime of good behavior.

Sit. To teach your dog to sit, use a treat to lure him into position. Hold the treat above his nose and very slowly move it up and back between his

CLICKER TRAINING OTHER ANIMALS

You can clicker train almost any animal, including cats, horses, fish, and even chickens. (Search "chicken clicker training" online if you really want to see something fun.) Clicker training is a fun way to connect and communicate with small pets, including rabbits, guinea pigs, hamsters, rats, mice, ferrets, and chinchillas. Animal trainer and clicker expert Karen Pryor offers easy tips for training small critters on her website. Visit *clickertraining .com* and click on the Library tab to find articles for every species.

eyes and over his head. Most dogs will look up to follow the treat's motion, and as they do, their haunches naturally sink down. Be ready to click the moment your dog's butt touches the floor; then reward him with a treat. If your dog doesn't immediately sit, you can click and treat for slight movements in the right direction. Eventually withhold the click and treat until he goes deeper into the sit. After a while, remove the treat lure and just make a similar motion with your hand.

Say "sit" after you motion with your hand. Eventually you can stop motioning with your hand and simply say "sit," although feel free to keep a hand signal too, such as pointing. Many dogs respond better to hand signals than voice commands.

Lie down. To teach lie down, first ask your dog to sit. Next, hold a treat in front of your dog's nose and very slowly move it down under his chin and to his chest. The key here is to move it extremely slowly to entice your dog to follow it with his nose without standing up. Slowly move the lure down to the ground between his feet. Most dogs will ease into a down position. Click and give him a treat. If your dog won't go all the way down, click and treat for any downward motion, then withhold clicks until he moves farther down. As with sit, eventually fade out the treat and just make the motion with your empty hand; then say "down." You can transition to a hand signal (lowering your hand, palm down) or simply use a voice command.

Stay. To teach stay, ask your dog to sit; then delay the click and treat for a moment. If he stays in position, click and treat. Pause longer and longer between asking him for the behavior ("sit") and clicking and treating. Eventually, pair a voice command and hand signal (hand up with palm facing forward). Ask your dog to sit, say "stay," wait a moment, then click and give a treat. If your dog stands up, ask him to sit and stay again, but wait a little less time before clicking and giving him a treat. Work your way up to longer stays slowly. Over time, your dog should be able to stay in place for up to five minutes or more.

Loose-leash walking. Clicker training is a great way to teach loose-leash walking. Take your clicker and treat bag with you on your walk. Hold the leash so there is little slack and your dog is by your left side. Take a step forward and click and treat your dog for walking that step with you. Keep clicking and treating as your dog walks by your side, then stop, say "sit" and click and treat when your dog sits. Start walking again, clicking and treating every five steps or so, increasing gradually as your dog catches on, then stop, ask for a sit, and click and treat. Eventually click and treat only if your dog is right by your side as you walk. If he falls behind, keep walking, but withhold the treat until he catches up. If he pulls ahead, stop and ask for a sit, then start again. Alternatively, if your dog pulls, turn on a dime and head in the opposite direction, clicking and treating if your dog turns with you. If he starts pulling again, turn again and walk in the opposite direction. This exercise will teach your dog to walk with you and pay attention to you while walking so he can anticipate your next move.

Drop it. This is a handy behavior for getting your dog to relinquish something he shouldn't have (it's also great when you're playing a game of fetch so you don't have to wrestle a slobbery tennis ball out of his mouth). Start with a toy. Entice your dog to pick it up in his mouth; then say "drop it" and offer him a treat. Most dogs will open their mouth to let the toy fall out so they can take the treat. Then pick up the toy, hand it back to your dog, say "drop it," and offer another treat. Over time, your dog will see that the game doesn't necessarily involve losing the item he has in his mouth, so he will be more willing to give it up. The key is not to use a favorite toy to start out with or one that is too exciting for your dog. Eventually you can practice "drop it" with high-value toys and other items, but in the beginning, choose something your dog cares less about than eating a treat.

Leave it. This command could save your dog's life. If you see him moving toward something dangerous dropped on the ground, you can tell him to "leave it." To start, place a treat on the floor, say "Leave it," and cover it with your hand. Your dog will sniff your hand and attempt to get the treat. As soon as he stops trying to get the treat, click and offer him a treat from your other hand (not the treat on the floor). Do this several times. Eventually, he'll realize that the treat on the floor is not the one he is getting and will stop trying and instead look to you for the reward. Once that happens, put a treat on the floor and say, "Leave it." Don't cover it with your hand, but be ready to do so if your dog tries to take it. If your dog doesn't immediately go for the floor treat, click and treat from your hand several times in succession. Gradually lengthen the time your dog has to leave the treat alone before rewarding him from your hand. Then you can practice with other things, like toys. ■

CHAPTER 18

Adult Dog Behavior

As much as we think of our dogs as family, they're not human and not necessarily motivated by the same things that we are. To a dog, your home is kind of like a spaceship and you're the aliens who captured and raised him. Your dog sees a few of his own species, but he's surrounded by another species whose language, and motivations, he can't understand (we humans aren't all about food astonishingly). From your dog's point of view, the aliens seem friendly. They feed and shelter him and even shower him with affection. He wants to please them. But first he must understand them. That's where we come in.

Most dogs, having evolved with us for 20,000 years, are masters at reading us. We, on the other hand, are terrible about reading them. To communicate better, we need to hone our dog (and cat) face, tail, and ear reading skills. In spite of this, dogs fit into our world very well; sometimes, of course, they miss the mark. We'll cover the most common "missed marks," or the basics of dog imperfection if you like, in this section.

HOW TO SPEAK DOG

Humans and dogs are two very different species with very different ways of communicating. Humans' main method of communication is language, spoken or written. We also use body language to communicate to some degree, but verbal language is the most important. Dogs are just the opposite: They communicate with body language. Vocalization comes into play too (growling, whining, barking, and howling), but most communication happens through body language and visual cues.

Dogs don't speak our language, but because they're masters of interpreting the subtleties of body language, they're pretty good at interpreting our habits and moods. They also pick up on the various tones and inflections of our voices. Dogs know when we're happy and sad. They know when we're excited and when we're angry. Whether you're aware of it or not, your dog is always watching your every move and anticipating what you might do next.

On the flip side, most humans aren't so skilled at speaking dog. It's not that we don't want to understand this beautiful species; it's just that

we're not as well versed in reading body language. We rely so much on spoken and written language that we simply don't practice our body language reading skills much. (That goes for our interactions with other humans too.)

Dog trainers, animal behaviorists, and, yes, veterinarians practice reading animal body language every day (it's a good thing or we might get bitten a heck of a lot more than we do). By understanding a little about natural dog behavior and body language, you too can become an expert at speaking dog.

Typical Dog Behavior

Dogs do most of the things that they do because it's a natural behavior for them for survival or social reasons. Unfortunately, a lot of these natural dog behaviors are not compatible with coexisting peacefully with humans. Barking to sound the alarm about a possible intruder serves a good purpose when a dog is living outdoors with a pack of fellow canines or even if you and your dog live

alone in a rural area. However, barking at every sound in an apartment building is going to drive you (and your neighbors) crazy. Digging to capture a gopher to eat is natural and beneficial for a wild dog, but digging up your entire yard and garden is never going to go over well—and worse yet if it's your neighbor's yard.

When your dog is doing something you don't love, think about what could be driving the behavior. When a dog is bored or has a lot of pent-up energy, he'll often resort to a natural behavior to alleviate that boredom or restlessness. Barking, digging, and chewing are all normal dog behaviors that can be channeled into more appropriate outlets. A lot of so-called behavior problems can be easily addressed by adding more exercise and enrichment to your dog's daily routine. (Read more about enrichment in Chapter 9.) Training is also usually needed to overcome ingrained behaviors. Combining exercise, enrichment, and training is often the trifecta solution to that problem.

Reading Dog Body Language

Dog body language is sometimes obvious (growling and baring teeth is a clear sign to stand back), but more often, speaking dog requires specific knowledge about very subtle communication. It takes dog professionals years, if not a lifetime, to master the art of dog communication. But knowing a few key "words" of dog language can help you understand how your dog is feeling. Some basics that are good to know include:

Signs of stress/nervousness
   Licking lips
   Panting
   Drooling
   Yawning
   Turning head or body away
   Averting eyes

Signs of fear
   Shaking
   Cowering (body held low to the ground)
   Tail tucked between legs
   Tail held low and wagging slowly
   Hackles up
   Head held low
   Whining

Signs of happiness or calm
   Ears forward
   Head cocked
   Eyes half closed or squinting
   Wagging tail fast (side to side or helicopter motion)
   Wagging whole rear end
   Lowering front end and raising butt in the air (play bow)

Mouth open, tongue out and relaxed

Whining or groaning

Signs of arousal or aggression

Mouth closed

Wagging tail stiffly

Body stiff

Staring eyes

Hackles up

Growling

Showing teeth

Snapping

COMMON PROBLEM BEHAVIORS

What if you've done all the prep, training, socialization, and bonding, and you still have a less-than-perfect dog? This can happen to anyone. I'm a veterinarian who runs an animal shelter and writes books on dog behavior, and my two dogs are far from perfect. Most dogs want to please us, but they don't always know how. We can help them with consistency, patience, understanding, and a lot of good communication.

Barking

Let's face it: dogs bark. We're generally happy they do this considering they evolved with humans as sentinels of approaching adversaries, including other people and dangerous animals. We continue to use them, formally or incidentally, as security. Who can blame them for not necessarily knowing which "enemy" they should alert us to? The cat burglar at night or the package delivery man during the day? It's all the same to them.

Dogs have many different types of barks. Rapid barking is an urgent notification that something is wrong. Some dogs have been known to bark more than 90 times in a minute. You wouldn't want to live next door to that dog. "Stutter barks" have two parts: The second part is louder than the first. These kinds of barks usually signify a happy dog and are less irritating than the slow, seemingly never-ending barking of a bored, alone dog. That bark is a cry for attention and, frankly, it breaks my heart. Finally, there is howling and baying. Depending on the breed—hounds especially— these are normal sounds and can signify excitement, or just rounding up the pack. If barking is not your thing, consider a basenji. These dogs don't bark, but some can actually yodel!

So what do you do if your dog is a more vocal sentinel than you'd like—or, worse yet, he barks so much when you leave that your neighbors are complaining? Let me start by saying this is a hard one because what you want to lessen or even extinguish is a completely natural behavior (I have a German shepherd, so I get it). However, there are some things you can do to reduce excessive barking:

1. Avoid leaving your dog alone for longer than you have to. If you work, get a dog walker to break up the boredom of the day or consider doggie day care.

2. Never leave your dog alone in the backyard. This will only antagonize your neighbors.

3. Tire your dog out as much as possible with lots of daily exercise and play. The key to decreasing excessive barking is to eliminate boredom. That happens with plenty of bonding time, frequent walks and other exercise, and mind puzzles for your dog.

4. Remove stimuli that can provoke barking.

WHY DEBARKING YOUR DOG IS CRUEL

Debarking surgery cuts a dog's vocal cords while he is under general anesthesia. Most veterinarians won't even perform this surgery. It's horribly invasive, alters your pet in an extremely unnatural way, and doesn't work. Debarked dogs still bark. Their bark is just hoarse and lower. It's damaging and can lead to anxiety because you've extinguished the most natural of behaviors in your dog: his voice. It's the dog equivalent of declawing your cat. Neither procedure has any place in a progressive society.

Close your windows, draw the shades, and even play music. These measures might not completely stop the barking, but at least you won't be adding fuel to the fire.

5 When you leave your dog, give him a frozen peanut butter–stuffed Kong to give him something to do. Be consistent, and make this part of your everyday routine.

6 Add independence training to your dog's curriculum. In other words, train your dog to entertain himself sometimes, even when you're around. Pure reliance on you will make your dog very susceptible to anxiety when you're not around.

7 Never yell at your dog for barking. To a dog, it sounds like you're barking right along with him. Remember, barking is a normal behavior. Acknowledging the "intruder" and thanking your dog for letting you know can sometimes work wonders.

8 Don't resort to a bark collar, which uses negative stimuli to startle your dog into not barking. The shock types are cruel, but even the citronella versions can lead to anxiety issues for your pup.

9 Get a second dog (this could go either way; sometimes the second dog just joins the chorus). Living together is a learned skill for any species, but try out any new dog with your current dog to see how well they get along.

10 If all else fails, consult with a certified professional dog trainer for additional management and solutions.

Chewing

Chewing is another normal dog behavior that can sometimes get out of hand. Excessive chewing is in the eye of the beholder. For your dog, there is no such thing. Dogs have teeth like wolves. They're designed to catch prey, rip it apart, and even demolish the bones. We can't eliminate their urge to chew, but we can ensure that they chew the right things.

If you want your dog to stay away from those shoes you just splurged on, you must give him plenty of appropriate and safe alternatives, like durable chew toys. Be sure to pick them up when they're not in use. When toys are left out, they become part of the scenery and less interesting. Also, do your part by keeping valuables out of reach. Pick up your shoes, put purses and phones up high, and teach your kids not to leave their toys lying around. The less access your dog has to these things, the less opportunity he has to give in to that urge to chew. If your dog has taken a liking to your furniture or walls, try Grannick's Bitter Apple, a nontoxic spray made up of bitter extracts mixed with alcohol that deters most dogs. And again, keeping boredom to a minimum can help. For dogs, boredom is the kindling to the bonfire of bad behavior. Easy solution? Keep your dog active and tired with exercise and play, minimize his alone time, and offer plenty of safe alternatives to chew on.

Jumping Up

All dogs want to be up near our heads. If you think about it, it's common for dogs to play with other dogs by lunging and mouthing around the head and face. They learn this as puppies and carry it through to adulthood. If you watch two puppies playing, they're constantly jumping and biting at each other's heads. But we don't want dogs jumping up at our faces all the time. I love their enthusiasm, but this behavior is annoying and can even be dangerous. It's not a great way to introduce your new pup to your great aunt Mavis.

So how do you stop it? First, fight the instinct to yell at your dog. Ironically, that can backfire by overstimulating him. Yelling can even be rewarding for your dog since he got an excited reaction out of you. The best way to discourage your dog from jumping up on you is to simply fold your arms across your chest, look away, and freeze. That isn't the reaction your dog is expecting. It's not fun at all! If you prefer, you can also simply turn around and walk away. I find that harder since it takes more faith that the dog won't hit you in the back. As soon as your pup stops jumping up, reward him for being calm. This is a great time to use your newly learned "sit" command.

The key to all of this is to teach your dog to play nicely—not just with you, but with every person and every dog he sees. The best way to do this is to reward him for quiet activity like sitting, lying down, or rolling over. Whenever your pup gets too excited, turn the reward off by withholding your attention. Give him attention and praise when all is quiet on the doggie front. He'll get the message sooner than you'd think. Dogs do what works and stop doing what doesn't. Understanding that will serve you well no matter what behavior issue you're tackling.

Destructiveness

We've all seen the pictures. Some of us have even seen it in real life. I remember bringing my very first dog home from the shelter. Bonehead that I was, I left her alone with free run of the living room while I went out for a short time. When I came home, the house was in tatters: Window blinds were bent, carpeting was torn up, and books and papers were everywhere. It was a hard lesson but one I'll always remember. I had forgotten that this was my dog's first visit to the "spaceship" that was my life and we hadn't done any training yet. After about a year of working on her separation anxiety, Sophie, my retired racetrack greyhound, turned out to be a wonderful dog.

If you have a dog who is really destructive and can't be left alone, try to determine why. No treatment works if you don't start with a diagnosis. In the majority of cases, it's either fear or boredom. Both will take some work on your part, but the latter is much easier to deal with. In rare cases, it's real separation anxiety (see "Separation Anxiety").

Let's start with the easy one: boredom. This is the best-case scenario for you because it's the easiest to solve. Don't leave your dog alone and he won't be bored. I admit, that's not practical, but there are some solutions. If you have to leave your dog alone for even a few hours, make his "alone space" as entertaining as possible. Fill his space with toys and stimuli so that he can do as many of his favorite things as possible while he waits. Give him food-stuffed Kongs, puzzle toys, and chews. Use a dog walker or consider doggie day care for more than four hours of alone time. A walker breaks up the day and gives him a much needed bathroom break, and doggie day care is an entire day of play and exercise. A full day home alone can be hard for many dogs.

Your other best friend is the crate which we covered in Part 2. You can also use a baby gate to create a safe area for your dog in the kitchen or another place where there's nothing overt to destroy. Put his bed, toys, water bowls, and even long-lasting

treats in the room. Start leaving the house for very short periods; initially return after about 30 minutes, then extend it to an hour, and then two hours. When you come home, don't make a huge deal about it. Greet your dog and tussle his head, but don't go insane with praise or hugs. That will only ramp him up in anticipation for the next time.

If none of these suggestions do the trick, it's time for professional help with a certified, positive-reinforcement trainer. Remember that punishment has no place in correcting destructive behavior. It will only make things much worse. In some cases, your trainer may suggest you try another dog. I don't mean replace the one you're working with (much as that might occur to you). As an absolute last resort, adding another dog to the mix might help. You might worry that you're setting up a scenario for a veritable gang of canine vandals in your home, but in some cases, two dogs together can help by keeping each other company. Start with a good trainer first.

EXTREME BEHAVIOR CHALLENGES

Some behavioral issues are harder to resolve. Separation anxiety, reactivity, resource guarding, and aggression are stressful for dogs and pet owners alike. However, with help from your vet and often a qualified trainer, it's possible to manage these difficult cases.

Separation Anxiety

Two words that anyone with a dog, and certainly anyone trying to adopt out a dog, dreads hearing are *separation anxiety*. Separation-related behaviors (the better term for a generalized group of behaviors that might include separation anxiety) are among the most difficult to turn around. In an animal shelter, we treat and rehabilitate almost any behavioral issue, but true separation anxiety is a tough one. Other related behaviors include owner hyperattachment (that dog who would follow you into the bathroom if he could), departure cue anx-

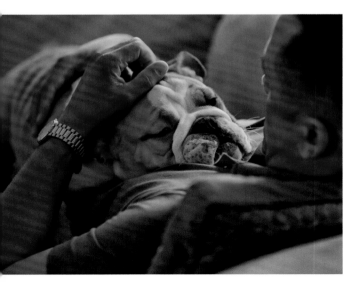

iety (the dog who gets upset when he realizes you're about to leave), and excessive greeting. Separation anxiety can lead to destructive behaviors, self-harm, barking, house soiling, and general mayhem. Basically, separation anxiety is like winning the behavior problem lottery—it can cause nearly all of the behavior disorders you'd rather avoid.

Unfortunately, separation anxiety is common. According to veterinary behaviorists Nicholas Dodman and Gerrard Flannigan, separation anxiety is highly associated with hyperattachment to the owner. It's not necessarily genetic, nor is it due to early detachment from the mother. It's all about us, and it's not easy to fix. Separation anxiety is about insecurity, and the cure is independence training. Increased bonding and demonstrations of affection are a natural response by humans toward dogs who exhibit a real need for us, but in truth, these displays can make separation anxiety worse because they make it even more difficult for an insecure dog to be away from his family. Therefore, it's necessary to detach a bit, hard as that is to do.

Don't go cold on your dog (you couldn't anyway); just tone down the exuberance. Make sure your home is primed for your departure just like you would for a destructive dog (put the dog in a safe place and provide lots of toys and long-lasting chews). Calmly exit your house. Ironically, don't say anything to your dog, not even, "Be a good boy," or you may cue the anxiety you're trying to avoid. Exit the house for just 30 to 60 seconds to start. Come home and quietly greet your dog with a soft pat on the head. Don't fawn all over him; just keep your body language and voice very matter of fact. If your dog reacts with extreme excitement, ignore him for a bit until he calms

HOLISTIC REMEDIES FOR ANXIETY

For dogs who suffer from a milder form of anxiety than the separation variety, there are a number of safe do-it-yourself remedies that can actually help alleviate some of the symptoms. Lavender spray is a safe and pleasant start (use essential oils with caution if you have cats, who are very sensitive to them). I'm also a big fan of products containing dog pheromones (Adaptil by Ceva Pharmaceuticals), which can naturally calm dogs. For dogs who are afraid of riding in cars, a "calming cap" can be a real help. It's no fashion statement, but this soft, over-the-eyes headgear can keep dogs relaxed in the car. Pressure wraps, like ThunderShirts, and vests can also be a real help for anxious dogs, like swaddling

helps a newborn calm down and fall asleep. You just can't leave it on longterm, much as you might be tempted.

down. Repeat this process about a hundred times, slowly increasing the alone interval by 10 minutes after two successful time trials in a row. It may feel overwhelming, but think of it as school for your dog and meditation for you.

If that doesn't work, you really need a trained professional—either a veterinary behaviorist or a positive trainer who works with separation anxiety. In many cases, you might also need some pharmaceutical help. The most commonly prescribed medication for separation anxiety is fluoxetine (Prozac). Veterinary behaviorist Barbara Simpson, and her colleagues evaluated the effects of fluoxetine on separation anxiety and found this drug to be highly effective when used in conjunction with a behavior management plan. But remember that medication alone won't do the trick; you always have to use it in conjunction with behavior work.

Reactivity

Have you ever gone on a walk feeling like you're about to be pounced on by a lion? That's what it's like to live with a reactive dog, who is constantly on the alert for the next canine "intruder" to lunge and bark at. Coincidentally, that's also how your dog feels. It's not a pretty sight, and it's not safe. This is a real liability.

Dog reactivity refers to an emotional state of anxiety or hyperexcitability. Most of the time, it's another dog, but dogs can be reactive toward any animal, person, object, or even a location like a car. Owners of dog-reactive dogs can be desperate. Their dogs are often angels alone, but when another dog crosses their path, they become uncontrollable maniacs. The core of dog reactivity is stress, anxiety, and fear according to trainer and certified behaviorist Jennifer Cattet, who says that

contributing factors may include genetics, poor socialization, hormones, neurophysiological makeup, and experience. Cattet adds that happy little puppies can become monster adolescents, much to the dismay of their owners.

What can you do if your Dr. Jekyll turns into a Mr. Hyde in the presence of other dogs? First, don't panic. Resist the temptation to yank on the leash, yell, or loudly say, "No!" This will backfire by escalating the situation for your dog. The next time he sees another dog, he'll be more anxious than ever before. Taking a reactive dog class with a professional trainer can be a gigantic help. Here are some other tips to help with a reactive dog:

1 Avoid experiences you know will be dog packed, people heavy, or rich with the object of anxiety. These include indoor situations if the reactivity happens in the home. Close the blinds if your dog reacts to the mail carrier. Go to the park when you know it will be quiet.

2 Equip yourself appropriately. Gentle leaders, no-pull harnesses, and other accessories will ensure you have control over your dog. Long leashes, and especially retractable leashes, are the wrong equipment for reactive dogs.

3 Train your dog so that you're the object of his attention (and affection). He should be watching you intently on every walk. Carry lots of treats to reward your dog for concentrating on you. If he can't focus on you and is not interested in what you have, try a new treat and start a new session another day.

When you're ready to not just manage but actually treat your dog's reactivity, find a professional positive trainer. This person can help you work with your dog to break the reactivity cycle. Using cues and treats (here's where clicker training is perfect), stand far enough away from the trigger (for instance, another dog) when your dog isn't reacting, and watch him closely. The moment he sees the trigger and does not react, click and give him a treat. Continue to click and give him a treat any time he looks at the trigger but doesn't react. Eventually your dog will start to look at you when he sees the trigger because you'll become more interesting than the trigger (you have the treats). There's no quick fix for reactive dogs, but you can do this with a good trainer to help you along the way.

Resource Guarding

"Resource guarding" refers to dog aggression (growling, staring, snapping) directed at other dogs or humans to get them to stay away from a particular high-value object. That object might be food, a treat, or a toy, but it can also be a favorite piece of furniture, specific rooms, and even certain people.

Even though this is clearly a potentially dangerous situation, resource guarding is completely normal behavior for a dog, although taken to the extreme. Remember, dogs are scavengers by nature and completely opportunistic about food. They also have a series of progressive behaviors that let other dogs know that something is "theirs," starting with a simple freeze or lip curl and escalating to stiffening, growling, and snapping. For some dogs, the progression of these demonstrations speeds up to the point of unmanageability.

So what can you do if you have a resource-guarding dog? Let's use the food bowl as an example. Your pup growls every time you approach his food bowl (a

scary situation if you have kids). According to the ASPCA's Emily Weiss, a certified applied animal behaviorist, at least one type of resource guarding, food guarding, might be treatable. According to Weiss you should follow these steps, starting with never making feeding time into a big event:

1. Have your dog sit and wait quietly for you to bring him his bowl.
2. Pour small amounts of food into the bowl. As your dog finishes, add more in small amounts.
3. Feed half of your dog's meal in a food-dispensing toy like a Kong.

If you feel confident your dog won't bite you, you can try for an exchange of a high-value food like a piece of cheese or cooked chicken while your dog is eating his regular food. Say your dog's name. If he lifts his head, praise him and drop the higher-value item like cheese, but don't take his regular food away; just let him go back to eating. Eventually you can work up to the next step of trading him for any food or item, even a lower value item like a toy he's not that interested in. But don't take the lower-value food away from him until he's well trained to allow this.

Resource guarding can become dangerous if it gets out of hand. Caution is definitely advised. Working on resource guarding is a whole lot easier (and safer) with a professional trainer by your side. With professional help, it can often be managed.

MANAGING BIRD BEHAVIOR PROBLEMS

Many birds, especially psittacines (parrots), are extremely social. Being left alone for long periods can lead to serious behavior problems, including excessive screaming, feather picking, and biting. Common reasons birds develop behavior problems include cages that are too small, cages that are isolated from the rest of the house (or, alternatively, placed in areas that are too stimulating), boredom, and lack of sleep. If your bird is exhibiting a behavior problem, seek help from a veterinary behaviorist or a veterinarian who is experienced with birds. Early diagnosis and treatment can make a world of difference.

Dog Aggression

Much as we like to believe our dogs are enlightened beings, there are times when their primal nature emerges in full. Dog aggression is dog reactivity on a logarithmic scale. Aggression encompasses behaviors ranging from a dog becoming rigid and still to growling, showing teeth, and lunging. The ultimate act of aggression is biting. Aggression is one of the most difficult things to modify, and in some cases, you're stuck with management rather than extinguishing the behavior completely.

The reason dogs behave this way shouldn't surprise us; after all, this is all about socialization. According to positive dog behaviorist and trainer Victoria Stilwell, dog aggression might occur when a dog receives little or no socialization during the optimum time in puppyhood (about four to 14 weeks of age) or when a dog has had a traumatic experience with another dog. Some genetic factors can predispose a dog to be more aggressive overall than another dog. Breed can be a factor, with chow chows, Doberman pinschers, and German shepherds often leading lists of seemingly aggressive dogs. Also on that list are Chihuahuas, Jack Russell terriers, and even the fireman's favorite, Dalmatians. Nonneutered males are generally more aggressive than females. Ultimately any dog can be aggressive toward humans, and any dog can be dog aggressive. It's also possible for a dog to be aggressive toward other dogs but completely nonaggressive with humans.

So what do you do? First, be realistic. This is not a condition you can cure, but it can often be managed. Success depends on acceptance: yours. Your dog is never going to want to be surrounded by other dogs. Avoid dog parks and situations that you know will be triggers for your dog. No need to bring someone on a diet into an ice cream shop. Next, make sure you never punish your dog for being aggressive. If you remember just one thing about dog training and behavior, it's that punishment only makes things worse.

Treatment must include gentle interactions with other dogs, but do this only under the guidance of a behaviorist and trainer experienced with dog aggression. Start slowly. It takes time, but with patience, protection, and positive rewards, you can often manage this potentially dangerous situation.

Aggression Toward Humans

Aggression directed at humans is the scariest and most dangerous type of aggression in dogs. Unfortunately, it's also the hardest behavior to change. It's one that must be managed forever, even if you succeed in teaching your dog to respond differently. The problem arises when aggression becomes the most common way for a dog to express his needs or when it happens unexpectedly.

As with dog-directed aggression, there are genetic, breed, and gender predilections in human-directed aggression. Some dogs are more aggressive than others, but it might not be the breeds that you think.

According to psychologist and behaviorist Deborah Duffy and her colleagues at the University of Pennsylvania, breed is a poor predictor of aggression, but geographic location plays a role. For instance, the constant noise and activity of a city can push otherwise nonaggressive dogs to a constant state of vigilance and even aggression. Location influences may supersede breed for some dogs. With room to run and more relative tranquility, some dogs will thrive peacefully in a country setting, while their city breed mates are more stressed.

There is a big difference between a significant bite causing enough harm to send someone to the hospital, and a little nip, which might not be reported. According to a 2014 AVMA review, German shepherds, pit bulls, Rottweilers, Doberman pinschers, Jack Russell terriers, chow chows, spaniels, collies, Saint Bernards, and Labrador retrievers are the top biting breeds. Among the most aggressive to humans are collies, toy breeds, Chihuahuas, and spaniels (surprising, right?). Even lhasa apsos, Pekingese, and papillons make the top 10 list according to the website *Canine Journal*. Although pit bull attacks have given a very black eye to this group of dogs, pit bulls aren't in fact a breed but a collection of similar breeds, which may also inflate their biting numbers. These breeds include American pit bull terriers, American Staffordshire terriers, Staffordshire bull terriers, and other bully types, including mixes of these breeds. There is no evidence to support that these dogs are particularly aggressive. Where does this leave us? All dogs can bite. It's up to us to ensure that they are properly trained, prevented from being exposed to people or situations that make them uneasy, and are given what they need to thrive as our best friends.

Determining which type of aggression applies to your pup is critical to understanding and modifying that aggression. According to Weiss, these range from territorial aggression (biting the postal worker who comes into the yard, for example—please don't let that happen) to protective aggression where dogs take defense to a fictional level where no threats exist.

The protocol for addressing human-directed aggression in dogs has just one step: Call a professional CPDT-certified trainer and/or board-certified veterinary behaviorist. Find someone who uses only positive approaches. Aggression is the worst time of all to use punishment. Training consists of unlimited patience, gradual exposure to stimuli, and rewards. This is behavior modification on a macroscale and should be done only by a trained professional.

The Many Faces of Aggression in Dogs

Most dogs are not aggressive just for the sake of being aggressive. There are reasons for them to act this way. Sometimes it's because they haven't had a stable home, care, and food. Other causes are lack of experience with people or different kinds (and sizes) of people. Unquestionably, lack of socialization is the most common reason dogs learn aggression. Incidentally, aggression is never about dominance, which, as we've discussed, doesn't exist in dogs. In some cases though, aggression can be genetic, but fortunately, those cases are rare. Here are a few specific types of aggression in dogs:

1. **Possession aggression** is aggression directed toward humans or other pets who approach when a dog has something that is highly desirable, such as a favorite chew

toy, food, or treat. This is also known as resource guarding.

2 **Fear aggression** results from a fearful or unknown stimulus.

3 **Barrier aggression** occurs when a dog is stressed by being restricted behind fences, gates, windows, screens, or walls, resulting in incessant barking or aggression. Leashes can also act as barriers, which is why some dogs act more aggressively toward others when on leash.

4 **Pain-induced aggression** occurs when a dog is in pain and stressed, which is why your vet might have to muzzle your dog when examining him in the clinic.

5 **Sexual aggression** is aggression caused by frustration or competition during mating.

6 **Redirected aggression** occurs as a response to high arousal and frustration regarding something unrelated to the object of his aggression. For example, many dog bites occur when dogs redirect their aggression to the human holding them back on the leash.

7 **Predatory aggression** can occur when a dog hunts for prey such as a retriever running after a squirrel or a greyhound running toward a rabbit. This type of aggression can be provoked by high-pitched noises.

8 **Territorial aggression** comes from a need to defend or protect his territory.

Aggression can't be extinguished completely because it comes from a natural emotional state, whether that is fear or defense or competition. However, some types of aggression can be reduced or even seemingly eliminated. Because the results of aggression are so unacceptable, we generally recommend that formerly aggressive dogs always be considered potentially aggressive. Never let your guard down and assume your dog is "cured." That's not realistic, as much as you love him. It takes only one setback to regret something for the rest of your life. We don't want that.

In some cases, medications are necessary to help control aggression. Prozac, also used for resource guarding, is an often prescribed medication for these dogs. But as in all the behaviors we've discussed, no medication will work without behavior modification. Sadly, some cases of aggression might not respond to either medication or behavior modification. In those cases, a very difficult decision about euthanasia might be necessary. This is beyond tragic for both the dog and his owner. Thankfully, these cases are rare.

BEHAVIOR DRUGS

In some cases, combining behavior-modification training with medication can lead to better results. Working with a veterinary behaviorist is a good idea as they can develop a behavior program for you and your pet and also prescribe medication to help you with that program. Most of the time, these medications do not need to be given for life. They can be used to augment behavior modification and then be tapered down and even eliminated once the behavior improves. One of the most common medications is Prozac (fluoxetine). For a complete list of the behavior-modification drugs available for your pet (see Appendix C). ■

Prozac tablet

CHAPTER 19

Cats and Kittens

Although it's true that cats and kittens are a bit less work than dogs and puppies, they still need lots of attention, socialization, and some basic training. For the most part, feline behavior problems are natural cat behaviors that humans find unpleasant like scratching on the furniture or urinating outside the litter box. Some simple tips can help address these and make life with your feline companion sublime. One of the best ways to avoid behavioral issues is to give your cat lots of attention and provide stimulation and exercise in the form of environmental enrichment. We recommend that cats live indoors for safety reasons, but home life can get a little boring. Environmental enrichment should include plenty of places to perch and scratch (like cat trees, kitty condos, and a variety of scratching surfaces), lots of toys to play with (including interactive toys so you can play with your cat), and opportunities for safe outdoor enjoyment, such as building an enclosed "catio" in the backyard (a large wire dog crate also works for this purpose) or placing a perch near a window so your cat can watch the birds and squirrels outside.

WHAT TO EXPECT

Kittens are as cute as can be and overflowing with energy. When you first bring your kitten home and watch her scale the living room curtains like they're Mount Everest, you might wonder what you've gotten yourself into! Cats are supposed to be laid-back, right? Chances are that your kitten will settle down when she's fully grown at around one year of age, but until that time, expect lots of activity and antics.

Young kittens (eight weeks to about 14 weeks) basically have two settings: high octane and sleeping. When your kitten is awake, expect nonstop playing and exploring until she crashes for a power nap. Any cat owner will tell you that there's nothing quite as amusing as sitting back and watching a young kitten scamper about. Kittens will turn anything into a toy, from a ball of paper to a milk cap, but they enjoy batting around toy mice too. Expect the play-sleep cycle to gradually evolve into longer stretches of awake time as your kitten grows older. This play-sleep cycle doesn't shut down at night. Quite the opposite. You might have visions of blissfully cuddling your purring kitten all night while you sleep, but don't be surprised if your kitten pounces on your head in a middle-of-the-night ambush attack. A word of advice: Don't engage with your kitten at night unless you want to encourage more midnight play sessions.

That leads us into the next topic. Some of a kitten's antics are not as adorable as others. Until you've had a kitten claw her way up your bare leg, you can't fully appreciate how sharp those talons really are. And kitten teeth are like needles. The first time your kitten clamps down on your hand and bunny kicks you with those razor claws, you might start rethinking this whole cat ownership thing. Never fear. This is normal kitten behavior (albeit the bad kind). Your kitten is just playing and exploring, not trying to hurt you. You can teach your kitten not to attack humans by yelping whenever claws or teeth touch your skin and stopping play until your kitten calms down. Then give her something she's allowed to bite and kick, like a large stuffed animal or other toy.

But there's good news. The crazy kitten stage doesn't last too long. Before long you'll find

yourself looking at your lazybones cat and reminiscing about the adorable things she did as a kitten (and you'll probably conveniently forget about any of the annoying parts!).

Raising a kitten might be an easier job than raising a puppy, but kittens still need plenty of attention and play from you. Try to spend a lot of time with your new kitten so you can bond. This socialization period is absolutely critical to having a well-adjusted adult cat, so invite your human friends to interact with your kitten as much as possible, too. That window is short—get as much socialization in between eight weeks and four months as you possibly can. (Read more about kitten socialization below.)

PREPARING FOR YOUR KITTEN

No matter the size, your home will feel like an enormous palace to a tiny kitten. To help your kitten adjust to her new environment, start her out in just one room, like a bedroom. Put toys, food and water bowls, and a litter box in the room. You can add a cozy bed and a scratching post or even a kitty condo or cat tree. For the first few days, spend a lot of time with your new kitten in that room. Next, leave the door open so she can begin to explore the rest of your home at her own pace. Eventually she will have full range of the house. Once she's spending much of her time outside the room, move her food and water bowls to their permanent spot (the kitchen, for instance) and place the litter box (or boxes) where they will stay. Don't forget to show your kittens where to find the litter boxes and food dishes. (For tips about bringing home an adult cat, see Chapter 4.)

Kitten-Proofing

Kittens can get into more trouble than you could ever imagine. Before bringing your kitten home, walk around the house and look for anything your

TOP KITTEN DANGERS

When you have a kitten in the house, keep an eye out for these dangers:

String (including dental floss, tinsel, thread, and ribbon). If swallowed, string can cause a bowel obstruction. Be especially careful of threaded needles!

Toilets. Kittens can drown in toilet bowls if they fall in and can't climb out.

Houseplants. Lilies are especially toxic to cats. (Read more in Chapter 21.)

Human medications. Pick up dropped pills immediately.

Dog flea preventatives. Never use a topical preventative labeled for dogs on a cat. If you treat your dog, separate your cat until the liquid dries.

Window cords. These are a strangulation hazard.

Batteries, especially button batteries. These are deadly if ingested.

Plastic bags. Kittens love bags but can become entangled and suffocate.

Dental floss

kitten might knock over, swallow, or become entangled in. Remove potpourri and scented candles. Block access to electrical cords, tie up window blind cords so they're out of reach, and move or secure anything that could tip over and fall on a curious kitten, like a flat screen TV. Since kittens will eventually find their way up on your counters, now is a good time to remove anything hazardous, like knives and glasses. Keep toilet lids down to prevent drowning, and don't use automatic toilet bowl cleaners in case your kitten tries to drink the water. (All of these things will happen!) Finally, block access to the outdoors. This might mean fixing holes in screens or doors that don't close. One of the biggest threats to your kitten is getting lost outside, and you do not want that to happen.

THE LITTER BOX

Cats instinctively like to go to the bathroom on a sand-like substrate, so potty training a kitten is often as simple as setting up the box and showing the kitten where it is. However, litter box issues are among the most common challenges for pet owners to overcome, and sadly, going outside the litter box is one reason cats are given up to animal shelters. If using a litter box is instinctual, why do so many cats struggle? The answer is us. If your cat or kitten is not using the litter box reliably, take a close look at your litter box setup. Here are some things to review.

Types of Litter Boxes

There are many different types of litter boxes to choose from. The most basic options are covered or uncovered. I like uncovered. Some cats like the privacy of a covered box, but most cats are afraid of sneak attacks by other cats. Besides, who would enjoy the smells that get trapped inside? Yes, cats are particular that way, and who can blame them? Covered boxes are nice for us humans because less litter ends up on the floor and odors are somewhat contained. If your cat likes a covered box, count yourself lucky; I have found this to be rare. Uncovered boxes are a bit messier since litter gets flung around, but they are also easier to scoop since you don't have to mess with a lid.

In addition to those basic options are more elaborate offerings. Automatic litter boxes are nifty inventions. These robot-boxes scoop themselves every time your cat uses them. Some automatic boxes use artificial litter and not only scoop themselves, but also clean themselves with water and flush the waste away (these hook up to a water line). Talk about fancy. Automatic boxes have sensors with timers that delay the scooping cycle for a number of minutes after your cat uses the box so they don't go off with your cat still inside. Even so, the sound and movement of this type of litter box startles some cats too much and they refuse to use them. On the flip side, you don't even have to use an actual litter box if you want to go low tech and inexpensive. Some people get creative, using inexpensive low-sided plastic storage bins.

Choose a box that is at least one and a half times the length of your cat; otherwise choose whatever litter box appeals to you most and cross your fingers. If your cat likes it, great. If your cat doesn't seem to enjoy your choice, consider trying a different type of box. The height of the litter box sides can be a climbing challenge for older cats or just a personal preference for others, so plan on some trial and error. It'll pay you back in droves.

Number of Litter Boxes

Cats are territorial and skittish animals by nature. In a multicat home, some cats fight over "control" of the litter box. It's sort of like *West Side Story*, but with cats instead of teenagers and not as melodic. Cats can ambush other cats while they are using the box, causing the ambushed cat to resort to going to the bathroom outside the box where she can see who's coming. Providing at least one box per cat and placing them in different parts of the house can help with this issue. Even better is one box per cat plus one, just so there are enough options. Even in a one-cat household, two boxes are always better than one, especially if you live in a multilevel home.

Location of the Litter Box

It's as true for litter boxes as it is for real estate: It's all about location, location, location. Think about it: Most people put litter boxes out of sight—after all, who wants to look at a litter box? But doing this can make the litter boxes far away from the areas your cat generally hangs out—namely, with you. And some cats are simply lazy. They don't want to make the long trek upstairs to the box when they can just go behind that large potted plant in the living room. Sometimes the out-of-the-way location is a laundry room. If the dryer's cycle-complete buzzer goes off while your cat is mid-squat, she might get freaked out enough to not want to go in that room again when nature calls. Choose convenient and quiet locations for your cat's litter boxes. She will thank you by using the boxes instead of the floor, your clean laundry, your shoes, or your bed linens!

Types of Litter

There was a time when people had one choice in cat litter—a coarse, granulated clay litter, the same stuff you use to soak up a grease spill in the garage. It got the job done but was somewhat messy (it's still available today but more often used to help cars get traction on icy roads).

LITTER BOX TRAINING YOUR RABBIT

Cats aren't the only pets who can be trained to use a litter box. Rabbits can quickly learn this skill. A litter-box-trained rabbit can have more freedom to explore without you stressing about poop balls or urine all over the house. To get started, search "rabbit litter training" online for articles and video tutorials. Because rabbits, like cats, naturally prefer to go to the bathroom in one spot, it's easier than you think.

Today, the cat litter industry is booming. You'll find everything from simple clumping clay litter to silica crystals, and litter made from corn, wheat, pine, and recycled newspaper.

Although some cats will go to the bathroom on anything, others are more particular about the feel of the litter on their feet. Your best bet is to choose a soft, clumping clay litter. Most cats like this type of litter. Whatever you do, avoid scented litters; these are for people, not for cats. You might find the perfume pleasant, but many cats find scented litters overpowering. Your cat's sense of smell is much more powerful than yours, and their noses are much closer to the litter. If you've ever developed a headache after riding in an elevator with someone who was wearing way too much perfume or cologne, you can understand how most cats feel about scented litter. Skip these!

Cleaning the Litter Box

When you open the stall door to a public restroom and see the previous person didn't flush, what do you do? Your first reaction is probably to move on to the next stall. Cats are no different, and in fact, they might be even pickier than you when it comes to bathroom cleanliness. Do your cat a favor, and scoop the box two times a day at a minimum. If you really love your cat, scoop it every time she goes. Top off the litter every day or so to keep the level acceptable. Once a week, dump all the litter out, wash the box with soap and warm water, dry it out, and replace all the litter. Always have a spare clean and dry litter box waiting for its turn in the rotation.

SOCIALIZATION AND TRAINING

Like puppies, kittens also need socialization and training so they can grow up to be well-adjusted pets. Socialization means getting your kitten used to all kinds of humans and other animals, as well as the normal goings-on of your household and trips to your vet. Training mainly consists of discouraging the behaviors you don't like and rewarding those you do. You can also teach your cat to do fun tricks, clicker training, or even cat agility (yes, this is a real thing!).

Kitten Socialization 101

The prime window for socializing a kitten is from two to seven weeks of age. However, most people don't get their kittens until they are at least eight weeks old, and many breeders don't let their kittens go until about 12 weeks of age. Let's hope your kitten's early caregivers started socializing your kitten before you got her, but you can continue socialization once your kitten comes home.

Socialization is simply the process of exposing your kitten to the human world in a positive way so she learns to enjoy the company of people and not to fear everyday things we take for granted. For instance, the vacuum can be terrifying to a tiny kitten, and a group of loud kids can be strange to a cat who is not used to them.

The key to socialization is positive experiences. Always let your kitten approach new things on her own terms, and never force her to do something that scares her (except for mandatory outings like vet visits, and even those can be positive). Around the house, let your kitten explore, and expose her to normal household appliances like the sound of the washing machine, dishwasher, blender, vacuum, and TV. Invite friends and family over, and ask them to sit on the floor and play with your kitten (that shouldn't be a hard sell). If you don't have kids but know some well-behaved ones, invite them over too. Just don't let them hold the kitten while they're standing (so the kitten doesn't fall and get hurt). Ask them to sit on the floor with your kitten instead.

This is the ideal time to get your kitten used to the cat carrier, the safest way to transport your kitten to and from the vet and the groomer (if necessary) or when you travel. Help make the carrier more inviting by lining it with a fluffy pad or soft towel. Leave it lying around in the open so your kitten is used to seeing it. If your kitten goes over to sniff the carrier, toss her some treats. If she goes inside on her own, give more treats. The more positive you can make the carrier experience, the better your kitten will accept it.

This is also the time to get your kitten used to brushing, bathing, nail trimming, and teeth brushing. Trying to convince an adult cat that she needs her teeth brushed is a lot less effective than starting a kitten out from day one. Even if your kitten's coat doesn't need much brushing yet, go through the motions so she gets used to it. Trim her nails weekly and bathe occasionally, even if she doesn't "need it." It's much easier to introduce baths in kittenhood than after your kitten is grown.

Yes, You Can Train Your Cat

They might not be as compliant as dogs—cats usually do things only if they feel like it—but food-motivated cats can be trained. The key is to train a cat like a cat and not like a dog. Lots of dogs are happy to practice behaviors over and over, but repetition is not in a cat's nature. Keep sessions short (five to 10 minutes) so your cat doesn't get bored or annoyed. Dogs will work for any old treat, but cats have more discerning tastes. When training cats, use high-value, smelly treats like tiny pieces of cooked chicken breast or tuna, anchovies, or even dabs of meat-based baby food.

Some fun tricks to teach your cat include sit, down, stay, come, and high-five. You can also teach your cat to "target" (touch the end of a stick with her nose). Targeting allows you to direct your cat to move from place to place, for instance, hopping from the floor to the couch or even jumping though a hoop.

Clicker Training for Cats

Clicker training is an effective method for training cats. Really. Like the training we covered for dogs, clicker training involves using a click sound from a small noisemaker to mark a desired behavior. The sound indicates to the cat that she has just done something to earn a reward. As with dogs, you first have to prime the clicker. While your cat does nothing, simply click and give a treat, click and give a treat. After a few repetitions, your cat will likely expect a treat when she hears the click sound.

Next, you can start using the clicker to teach your cat a behavior, like sit. Move a treat next to your cat's nose, moving it up toward her forehead. This is called "luring." Many cats will naturally sit down as they try to follow the food. The exact moment your cat's butt hits the ground, click and give a treat. Repeat several times, saying "sit." Eventually you can try luring your cat into a sit position without holding a treat (click and treat

when she sits), then fade the lure and just say "sit" (or use a hand signal like pointing).

Not all cats take to clicker training or, truth be told, any kind of training. Remember, these things have to be on the cat's terms. Cats who don't care much about food might just not have the right motivation, and some cats will simply stare at you instead of trying to earn clicks and treats. But lots of cats can learn at least a trick or two. Showing off your cat's tricks to visitors is always a hit. And just as it is for dogs, this is a great bonding experience for you both.

Cat Agility

Some cats really take to training. If you have one of these unique felines, you might try your hand (and her paw) at cat agility. Similar to dog agility, cat agility is an indoor cat obstacle course that you and your cat navigate together. Cats jump through hoops, run through tunnels, weave around a line of poles, and scale A-frames. It's quite amazing to watch and fun to do. Learn more at *catagility.com*.

ADDRESSING BEHAVIOR CHALLENGES

Remember our discussion of the Five Freedoms? Number three, freedom to express "normal behaviors" really comes into play when trying to assess cat behavior problems. Noted veterinary behaviorist and personal friend Nicholas Dodman, BVMS, used to say that an outdoor cat is a happy cat but with a much shorter life span. Very true. Ideally, we want our cats to live happy lives for as long as possible while staying safely indoors. So how do we reconcile these two often conflicting pressures?

Not getting to express normal behaviors a cat would experience outdoors (hiding, stalking, pouncing, hunting) can lead to stress, the leading cause of feline behavior issues. Cat behavior challenges can be tricky to figure out. Identifying the source of this stress can lead to successful management, sometimes with the help of your vet or a veterinary behaviorist.

Litter Box Issues

The number 1 feline behavioral issue is going to the bathroom outside the litter box. Many cats are turned in to shelters for this troubling problem. Nine times out of 10 it's behavioral when your cat is going outside her litter box, but the first step you must take is to see your vet to rule out a health problem. When cats are sick, often the first sign that something is amiss is that they start going outside the box. Diabetes, kidney disease, and arthritis can cause this behavior, so get your cat checked out before you do anything else.

If your cat gets a clean bill of health from your vet, it's time to explore common behavioral reasons for going outside the box; the number one reason for this is anxiety.

Number of boxes. Give your cats enough litter boxes so they don't have to fight over them or use a dirty box. One per cat plus one is a good rule to follow, but you can never have too many litter boxes. It might seem excessive to you, but, it's a small price to pay to keep the rest of your house clean and dry.

Box type. Your cat might not like the litter box you've chosen. If you have an older cat or tiny kitten, make sure the sides of the box are low enough for the cat to easily navigate. A flat cement-mixing tray from your local hardware store can be a lifesaver in these cases. Some boxes have ramps that help with entry, but then you might have another scary obstacle for your cat to surmount. For long or large cats, make sure that the box is at least one and a half times their body length.

Litter issues. If you're using a scented litter, switch to an unscented one. Try a soft, clumping litter if you're not using that already (most cats like the feel of that type of litter). You can also experiment with several boxes using different litter types to see what your cat prefers. Some cats like a lot of litter in the box, but be careful of sinkholes, with sopping-wet areas under and in the litter. If this happens it means you need to change that litter much more often. Others prefer the bare minimum in terms of litter, so also experiment with depth of litter in the box. The crystal litters made from silica are very clean and new age, and some cats love these.

Cleanliness of the box. Scoop the box as frequently as you can (at least twice a day, but more is even better). Make sure you wash it thoroughly with soap and water at least once a week.

Box location. If you suspect your cat is having trouble making it to the box in time (or is simply too lazy to walk a far distance), try moving the box closer to the places she likes to hang out. If the box is in a laundry room, bathroom, or garage, consider moving it into a larger or quieter space to see if that helps. Make sure the box is far away from her food and water bowls. Cats do not like to go to the bathroom where they eat (and who could blame them?).

Triggering event. Your cat might have developed a negative association with the litter box. Never yell or otherwise punish a cat for going outside the box. She might connect your anger with the box itself and avoid it even more. In multi-cat households, one cat might launch a sneak attack on another cat trying to enter the box, which can cause that cat to avoid it. (This is why it's good to have a lot of boxes for multiple cats.)

If your cat has been going to the bathroom in a random part of the house, thoroughly clean it up using an enzymatic pet cleaner; then put a litter box right in that same spot. It's okay if you don't want to keep the box there forever; this is a temporary solution to get the cat going inside the box again. Once she's using the box regularly, move it very slowly over the course of many weeks to your preferred location (and make sure your cat is okay with that location).

If you feel that you've tried everything and gotten nowhere, you have one more option: contacting a board-certified veterinary behaviorist. In extreme cases, your vet might even want to try an antianxiety drug, not forever, but just to get your girl over this hurdle.

Aggression Toward People

Being stalked and ambushed by your small house cat is surprisingly terrifying. If your formerly docile cat has become increasingly aggressive toward you or another human member of your household, the first thing to do is have her checked out by your vet. Although rare, some medical conditions can cause aggression, especially if your cat is in pain, so make sure your cat is healthy before deciding it's a behavioral problem.

Feline aggression can have many different causes, and the solutions vary depending on what's causing your cat's aggression. The most common categories of aggression in cats are fear aggression (the cat is afraid of something and can't get away so she attacks), territorial aggression (protecting her home and/or people), petting-induced or play-induced aggression (the cat becomes overly aroused and suddenly attacks), and redirected aggression (the cat becomes frustrated or aggressive toward a stray cat outside or another animal or person she can't get to and redirects her feelings onto another person or animal within reach).

Ask **DR. GARY:**

Why Is My Cat Biting Me?

That cats are not dogs is easier said than understood. Petting a cat is always on her terms, not ours. Too much petting, lifting, hugging, cuddling, or scratching can overstimulate a cat, leading to a knockout swat or bite to the offending human. Then there are those cats who will just bite for no real reason. It's about tolerance, which is specific to each cat. Word of advice? Know your cat and recognize how much touch she'll tolerate. Cats need us, but they want us to perform according to their wishes. By the way, never rub your cat's belly. Most cats hate this and you'll never do it a second time!

Feline aggression is not easy to resolve. Your best bet is to contact a feline-comfortable trainer or a board-certified veterinary behaviorist who has experience with cat aggression. You can ask your regular vet for a referral or visit the American College of Veterinary Behaviorists website (*dacvb.org*). As with all behavior issues, sometimes medication is necessary along with the behavior work.

Fighting Among Household Cats

Here's a tough one I deal with all the time. How many cats is the limit? Hard truth—there's no easy answer. That's because cats often come to us, not vice versa, and our compassion can lead to overflowing cat households. In my experience, three cats is the upper limit for most households. Owning more than three is challenging, and serious behavior issues can result.

Fighting is sometimes a problem in multicat households. Cats can be very particular about who they like and who they don't. Kittens raised together often get along great. This is one of the many reasons it's a good idea to adopt two kittens at the same time. As a matter of fact, always adopt two kittens at the same time. Introducing adult cats is usually tougher, but many cats learn to like each other or at least to get along. Sometimes, though, cats just squabble for whatever reason. One cat might start bullying another cat, or two or more cats might gang up on one cat. Things can get rather heated and lead to other issues, like not using the litter box.

Cats living in multicat households establish their own hierarchies, with one or more cats at the top of the totem pole and others at the bottom. These hierarchies might stay the same for years or might change over time. Certain things can affect this delicate dance, including anything that causes the cats stress, such as moving, rearranging the furniture, new pets, extended vacations, a new baby or a new adult joining the household, or even illness of one of the cats or humans.

If your cats are fighting, you can take a few steps to try to defuse the situation. First, try not to become upset, or at least don't show it. They will sense your distress, and that will add fuel to the fire. Second, make sure all the cats can escape to a private safe zone where they can't be bothered. This is the key. You might have to enforce this by blocking another cat from accessing the space when one cat is using it. Make sure you have enough litter boxes to prevent territorial fighting over the bathroom. Finally, if your cats start to get into it, try distracting them with fun toys, catnip, and other play.

If, despite your best efforts, you can't resolve the WWF-style cat fighting in your home, call a veterinary behaviorist for help. They are worth their weight in gold. Get a referral from your regular vet or visit *dacvb.org* to find a licensed behaviorist in your area.

Destructive Scratching

Cats scratch—there's no getting around it. Coming home and finding your beautiful new couch shredded to ribbons is depressing to say the least.

The key is getting your cat to scratch the right things and leave your furniture and carpet alone.

Don't give up—you can still have nice things. Take two steps to protect your valuables. First, provide your cat with ample "allowed" scratching places. The more things you have that the cat can scratch, the better. When choosing scratchers, one thing to consider is the orientation of the item. Some cats like to scratch vertically (like the arm of a chair). Scratching posts and cat trees are good for that. Other cats like to scratch horizontally (like on your carpet). Scratching pads that are designed to lie on the floor work great for horizontal scratching. Some cats like to scratch both ways, so providing more than one type of scratcher is a good idea for those cats.

Cats also have scratching surface preferences. Different scratchers are made of carpet, sisal, cardboard, wood, and other materials. Try a few different types to see what your cat prefers. This might seem like a lot of work, but remember that you don't have to take your cat on walks three times a day.

The second step to scratch-proof your home is to implement deterrents to keep your cat's claws off the couch, rugs, and other furniture. Attaching plastic, double-sided tape, or aluminum foil to the arms of the couch (or anywhere else the cat scratches) makes that location unappealing. If your cat scratches the carpet, invest in a plastic office chair mat and lay it over your carpet. You usually only have to leave deterrents up for a few weeks or months. Eventually your cat will just "scratch" that spot off his list of preferred scratching spots, especially if you provide appropriate scratchers and encourage their use.

While we're on the topic of scratching, there's something that bears repeating: Declawing your cat is not the solution to destructive scratching. We can hope that this barbaric procedure will soon be a thing of the past. Declawing is an amputation of the tips of all a cat's toes. It is painful and disfiguring and can cause permanent issues with the way a cat moves and walks (imagine how different your life would be if you lost the tips of all your fingers). Some declawed cats even develop subsequent behavioral issues like aggression and litter box aversion. Don't tempt fate and don't subject your cat to this.

Anxiety and Obsessive-Compulsive Disorder

Some cats suffer from anxiety or obsessive-compulsive disorder (OCD). Similar to OCD in humans, cats with OCD engage in repetitive behaviors like pacing, excessive vocalizing, over-grooming (resulting in hair loss), and excessive sucking (on fabrics or people). Some breeds like Siamese might be more predisposed to obsessive behaviors. Anything that a cat finds stressful, such as changes in environment and routine can lead to the development of anxiety and obsessive behaviors. Boredom or lack of exercise might also be a contributing factor.

If you suspect your cat is engaging in repetitive behaviors, schedule a visit with your veterinarian for a diagnosis. You can do a lot at home to ease your cat's stress or boredom. Stick to a familiar routine every day, with scheduled meals, playtime, and litter box cleaning. Avoid rearranging your furniture or moving your cat's bowls or litter boxes. You can also try using a plug-in feline pheromone dispenser to naturally soothe your cat. These can

work wonders. In severe cases, your vet might recommend prescribing a medication to help your cat stop the OCD behavior. Remember, though, you need to eliminate the source of stress along with any medication for the treatment to work. ■

FELINE BEHAVIOR MEDICATIONS

Like dogs, cats are benefiting from a richer world of feline behavior therapy thanks to effective pharmaceuticals that treat anxiety, obsessive-compulsive behavior, urine marking, and aggression. By far the most common medication prescribed for cats is fluoxetine (Prozac), but there are many others. For a complete list of the behavior-modification drugs available for your pet, see Appendix C.

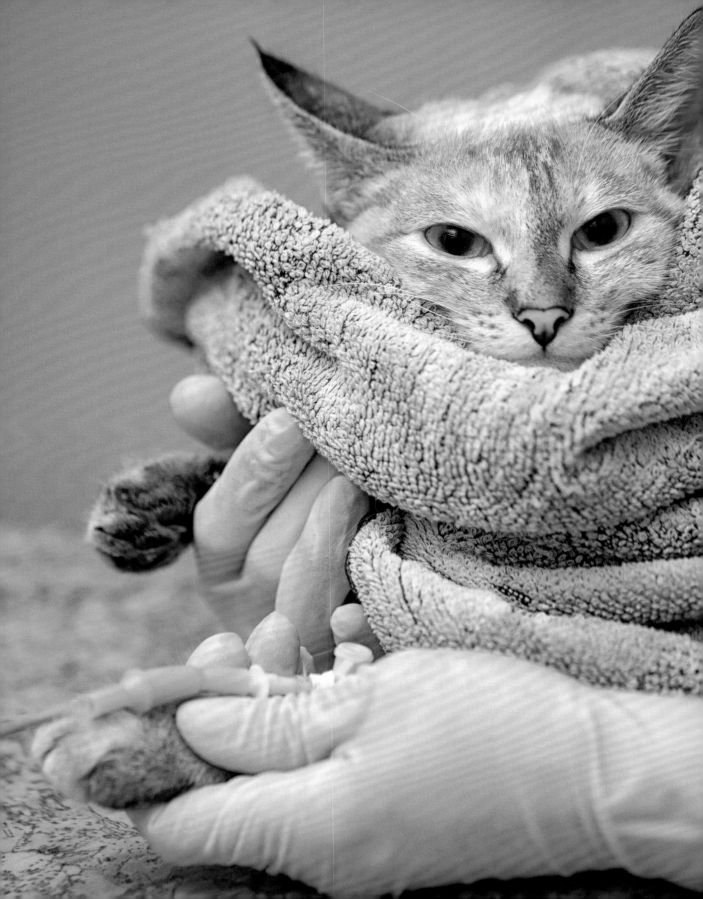

PART 4

Emergencies and Disaster Preparedness

When your pet is sick or injured, it can be scary. Find out what to do in the event of an emergency, and learn how to recognize signs of common illnesses and injuries so your pet can be treated as soon as possible.

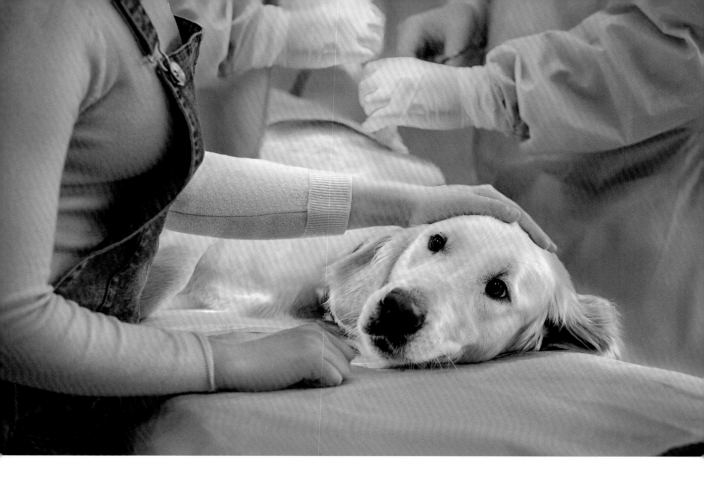

CHAPTER 20

Emergencies

It's 2 a.m. early Saturday morning, and your dog just vomited out in the hallway. How do you know if it's just an upset stomach or a true emergency requiring a middle-of-the-night trip to the hospital? Anything that threatens life or limb is considered an emergency. The trick is to know what can wait and what absolutely cannot. Since many regular veterinary clinics are closed at night, on weekends, and on holidays, it's vital to figure out ahead of time where you can take your pet if he becomes ill or is injured after normal business hours. The last thing you want is to be frantically searching the internet in your pajamas with a sick pet by your side.

EMERGENCY CLINIC BASICS

It's best to know where to go and how to get to the emergency clinic before an emergency strikes. As soon as you bring your new pet home, locate the closest emergency hospital. Time is always of the essence during an emergency. Ask your vet for his recommendation. Do some internet research, check out reviews, talk to neighbors, and look at the emergency clinic's website. It's even a good idea to stop in to meet the front desk personnel and pick up its refrigerator magnet for easy phone access. That surveillance visit will tell you a lot before you ever need to use the clinic.

An emergency clinic works differently than a regular veterinary clinic does. First, many emergency clinics are open only at night and on weekends, basically whenever your own vet is not available. There might only be one emergency vet on duty, so you won't necessarily get a choice in who you see. However, that vet will likely take superb care of your pet, even if you're meeting him or her for the first time. These vets specialize in emergency medicine. They sacrifice a lot, turn their lives inside out to work the night shift, and are very committed to getting your pet back on her feet.

If you have time, call first to let them know you're coming. That gives the clinic time to prepare for you and plan their schedule with other patients. Clinic staff can help carry your pet into the clinic. Bring a book because chances are you'll be there a while. The medical staff isn't trying to torture you, they're just triaging multiple patients at the same time.

Many emergency clinics are part of a specialty hospital. This is optimal because these hospitals are expertly staffed and provide care around the clock. They'll also notify your regular vet and get vital information to help with your pet's care. If the emergency clinic isn't part of a specialty hospital, you'll probably have to transport your pet to your regular vet in the morning because the clinic will close during the day. If it's a weekend, though, you'll have until Monday morning to relocate your pet. Nearly all emergency hospitals require you to be the ambulance, although in rare cases, a special service might be used for very critical patients. Bring someone with you to help transport your animal to your regular vet. You'll likely want the company as well as the help.

COMMON EMERGENCIES

Recognizing a medical emergency might save your pet's life. Animals are susceptible to a lot of the same common emergencies as you and your family. Whether your pet is stung by a bee or cut on his paw, understanding the situation is paramount to making sure he gets the necessary care he needs.

Allergic Reactions (Anaphylaxis)

Typical allergic reactions in pets vary by species. The most common reactions occur from insect bites and stings and can range from mild to severe, just like in people. Most allergic reactions aren't life threatening (termed "anaphylaxis") but they always have the potential to be. Allergic reactions typically cause swelling, rash or hives, itching, and even vomiting. The biggest risks are rapid or difficult breathing, cardiovascular collapse, and even death. If your pet is having any facial swelling or trouble breathing, go straight to your vet or an emergency clinic. Treatment may include fluids along with a cortisone injection and an antihistamine. Life-threatening allergic reactions may require epinephrine, just like in humans.

Neurological Disorders

Neurological disorders can be true emergencies where a timely response might be the difference between walking or not walking again, or even life and death. Others might resolve on their own without treatment. One example of that is something called ataxia, which is a loss of control of bodily movements in the head, limbs, or other parts of the body. It's commonly caused by diseases of the vestibular system in the brain—the area that controls movement and balance. Ataxia can be mild or severe. It's a scary thing to see; it can look a lot like your pet had a stroke. It's impossible to know whether neurological disorders are truly life threatening, so it's best to err on the side of caution and get your pet to your vet or an emergency clinic quickly when he displays neurological signs that came on suddenly: seizures, difficulty walking, head tilt, or paralysis.

Bleeding

Whether from a wound or other reason, uncontrolled bleeding is always an emergency. Common injuries that lead to bleeding include broken nails and cuts to ears, tails, and pads, which bleed surprisingly heavily. Bleeding from the nose or mouth can be especially scary (calming yourself and your pet is a good first step). Bleeding from the nose can be caused by foreign bodies like foxtails (if you live on the West Coast) or fungal

FIVE REASONS TO GO TO THE EMERGENCY CLINIC

If your pet is experiencing any of the following, it's an emergency. This list isn't exhaustive, but these are clues that your pet needs treatment immediately, even if it's the middle of the night. You might lose some sleep (and some cash), but hopefully you won't lose your pet. Always err on the side of caution.

1. Pain. Signs of pain include crying or whimpering, licking, limping, and panting.
2. Difficulty breathing. Breathing heavily or rapidly, open-mouth breathing, panting for a prolonged period when it's not hot out, or blue gums.
3. Uncontrolled bleeding.
4. Collapse, can't walk or stand.
5. Interaction with or ingestion of toxins.

infections (in the Southwest and some other parts of North America). Often there is sneezing along with the bleeding just to make things even more exciting. Tumors, foreign bodies, and broken teeth can also cause obstinate bleeding.

If you can, apply pressure with a bandage so your pet doesn't lose excessive amounts of blood (see Chapter 22). In the case of bleeding from the nose or mouth, use a cloth to catch the blood and quickly get to a vet or an emergency clinic.

Breathing Difficulty

Difficulty breathing (dyspnea) or rapid breathing (tachypnea) can be caused by allergic reactions, asthma, lung or airway diseases, trauma to the thorax (chest wounds), metabolic diseases like diabetes, or heart disease. If your pet is having difficulty breathing or rapid breathing, comfort him and immediately head to your vet or an emergency clinic.

Dystocias

Dystocia refers to difficulty during the birth process. Sometimes it's caused by an abnormal position of a fetus in the birth canal. A condition known as uterine inertia can lead to exhaustion by the mother causing a lack of contractions. This occurs when labor goes on longer than normal.

It's important not to interrupt the birth process with a needless visit to the vet, but true dystocia requires intervention. In dogs and cats, each fetus should be delivered between 20 and 60 minutes of each other. Going longer than two hours between puppies or kittens indicates dystocia. If your pet has active contractions for more than 30 minutes without producing a puppy or kitten, your vet needs to intervene with a manual delivery or a C-section.

COMMON INDICATORS OF DYSTOCIA

1. Contractions lasting longer than 30 minutes without a birth between deliveries after labor has begun
2. No delivery of first puppy or kitten within four hours of contractions
3. No births within two hours of each other
4. Obvious pain or crying from the mother
5. Bloody discharge from the mother

Eye Emergencies

Nearly every eye injury has the potential for catastrophic results up to and including blindness. You never want a little corneal scratch to become a vision-threatening problem.

Corneal Injuries. Corneal injuries are the most common eye emergencies we see in pets and may include superficial abrasions, ulcers, or lacerations. Ulcers are deep abrasions. Lacerations are complete tears through the cornea. Corneal injuries are often caused by trauma from foreign objects like sticks, grass, a cat claw, or chronic issues in the eyes like dry eye. Signs of an ulcer or laceration include red eyes, discharge that is either watery or mucousy, and squinting. The squinting means it's painful. Get to a veterinary hospital immediately so the vet can repair this damage and save the eye.

Proptosis. "Proptosis" means protrusion of the entire eye. Horrifying. The breeds we're most concerned about are those with large eyes and short muzzles, like Boston terriers, French bulldogs, Pekingese, pugs, and shih tzu. Proptosis occurs

when trauma to the head causes the eye to bulge out of its socket. The sooner you get to the hospital, the better the chances are of saving the vision. If this ever happens to your pet, pour an eye saline, like contact lens solution, on the eye and cover it with an inverted paper cup if you can. Then go directly to your vet hospital or emergency clinic.

Lens Luxation. Lens luxation is displacement of the lens from its normal position in the eye. The lens is held in the front center of the eye by ligaments, just behind the iris, the colored part of the eye. Normal pressure in the eye keeps the lens in place by fluid on both sides of the lens. All sorts of things can lead to lens luxation, including trauma and glaucoma (see below). In some cases, you can actually see that the lens has shifted. You'll also see a reddened eye and a blue or gray color to the pupil, and the eye will be painful. Lens luxation itself can also cause other problems like retinal injury and glaucoma. Getting to your vet

or emergency hospital right away is the best way to save the eye and your pet's sight.

Glaucoma. Glaucoma is caused by an increase in pressure of the fluid within the eye. It's extremely painful and can lead to blindness. Many people never know their dog has glaucoma until it is very advanced. (Cats rarely, if ever, get this.) All you'll see is a reddened eye, squinting, a dilated pupil, and possibly a bulging eye. These signs are telling you that your dog is in pain and his vision is at stake, so get to your vet or the emergency clinic right away.

Fractured Bones

Being hit by a car is the number one reason animals break bones. Fractures can also result from falls (especially for cats), pets being accidentally stepped on, and during fights between dogs. Broken bones require an immediate trip to the hospital. If you suspect your pet might have a fracture, secure him in a crate or gently hold him, taking care not to move the limb and get him to your vet or the emergency clinic. Never assume that a fracture will heal on its own. Fractured bones always need treatment, which might mean surgery, followed by rest, and pain medication.

The trouble with fractures is you might not know if something is broken. Sometimes it's obvious by displacement of the limb or, worse, visible bone. But thanks to our pets' fur coat, angled limbs, and stoicism, fractures are not always easily identified. The only way to be sure of a fracture and its extent is through x-rays.

There are two categories of fractures: closed and open. Closed fractures are cracked bones beneath unbroken skin. Open fractures, also known as compound fractures, are far more dangerous. These occur when bone fragments protrude through the skin. They are a true surgical emergency due to risk of life-threatening infection and shock.

Gastric Dilatation and Volvulus

If you've seen the movie *Marley and Me,* you know that gastric dilatation and volvulus (GDV) is the tragic ending for our tail wagging protagonist. Otherwise known as bloat, GDV is a true emergency. Dilatation refers to the stomach filling with fluid or gas. Volvulus is a life-threatening twisting of the stomach. This can trap blood vessels, causing severe damage to the stomach and adjacent organs like the spleen, liver, and pancreas. It can also lead to toxin release, causing heart damage and even death.

GDV can affect all dogs, although it's especially common in deep-chested breeds like German shepherds, standard poodles, and Rottweilers. Other than breed predisposition, we don't really know what causes bloat, but research has suggested genetics and rapid eating. I always recommend feeding dogs smaller meals twice a day rather than one large meal once. Raise the food bowl for large-breed dogs and avoid exercise immediately after eating. We're not entirely sure if avoiding exercise really helps but it can't hurt.

Ask DR. GARY:

Why See a Veterinary Orthopedist?

Your own vet might be comfortable doing a fracture repair, and that's fine, but the gold standard is to use an orthopedic surgeon. These specialists are board certified by the American College of Veterinary Surgeons (ACVS) and are the best surgeons to fix broken bones. They're trained in state-of-the-art techniques, have the best equipment, and are proficient in postoperative care. Using an orthopedic surgeon is also, no surprise, the most expensive route to take. But for greater healing and the comfort of your pet, they're worth every penny. Your vet can give you a referral.

GDV is enormously serious, but it can be difficult to recognize when it starts. Dogs become uncomfortable; they might stand, stretch, pant, gag, or make unsuccessful attempts to vomit. The abdomen might look bloated, but that's not always easy to recognize. If you even suspect your dog might be bloating, see a veterinarian immediately. Emergency surgery is necessary to deflate and return the stomach to its original position, after which it's sutured in place against the abdominal wall in a procedure called a gastropexy. This will ensure that if your dog bloats again, the stomach can't twist.

Veterinarians are pretty proficient at this surgery, so mortality has dropped from a hefty 50 percent to now less than 10 percent. Some people consider a preventive approach by doing gastropexies on predisposed breeds early on in life, often during spay surgery. If you have a breed that falls into one of the highly predisposed categories, talk to your vet about whether this would be a good idea for your dog.

Hit by Car

This is one of the most emergent situations your pet might face. Should tragedy strike, get out your first-aid kit (see Chapter 22) and try to stop any bleeding (see "Bleeding" page 246), wrap your pet in blankets or towels to keep him warm, and head to your nearest vet or emergency clinic. Be extremely careful touching and moving your pet. Any animal in pain might bite, even your own beloved pet.

Some dogs and cats can survive getting hit by a car completely unscathed, something that never ceases to astonish me. Even if your pet seems okay, see the vet immediately to be sure there is no organ damage (this might not be apparent to you but can be life threatening). If everything checks out okay, your vet will want to monitor your pet for at least another 24 hours (this can sometimes be done at home) to be sure there's no damage to the heart muscle, which can show up within a day of chest trauma.

Hypothermia

Hypothermia can occur if your pet is outdoors for prolonged periods during temperatures at or below freezing. Hypothermia is defined as a body temperature below about 99°F (37°C) in dogs and cats. Symptoms include shivering, weakness, shallow breathing, stupor, and frostbite on the tips of ears, paws, and tail.

Always bring your pet indoors when it's cold outside. If a lost pet or a stray is found after being exposed to the elements, act fast to warm him up. If the pet is alert, wrap him in a warm blanket or towel and offer warm but not hot liquids to drink. Keep him dry and calm. Continue warming efforts until his temperature is in the normal range of 101°F to 102.5°F. Once stabilized, head to your vet for an exam to make sure everything is okay. Severe signs of hypothermia include nonresponsiveness and a stupor-like state, shallow breathing, dilated pupils, and even coma. If these are evident, wrap your pet in a warm blanket and rush directly to the emergency hospital. There, doctors will be able to safely warm your pet and support him with fluids and steroids to counteract the effects of the hypothermia.

Poison

In the case of poison, a timely trip to the vet can be the difference between life and death. If you witness or suspect that your dog just ate something toxic, call your veterinarian, emergency clinic, or a poison control hotline immediately (see Chapter 21). Depending on the toxin ingested, the veterinarian might instruct you to induce vomiting at home before coming to the clinic. Then head immediately to the hospital so the vet can assess your pet for damage, perform some tests, and provide supportive care if necessary. Never induce vomiting without direct instructions to do so from a veterinarian. With some poisons, inducing vomiting can cause more harm than good.

Pyometra

Pyometra is an infection of the uterus and can be a life-threatening condition. Because bacteria trapped inside the uterus have nowhere to go, the uterus becomes inflamed, enlarged, and infected. Pyometra occurs in sexually intact middle-aged and older dogs and cats, although it's rare in cats.

Pyometra typically occurs between two weeks and two months after a pet has gone out of heat when hormones are rampant. Signs include weakness, fever, vomiting, diarrhea, and a painful, distended abdomen. It must be treated quickly. Treatment is straightforward: Stabilize the dog, support her with fluids and antibiotics, and perform a spay as soon as possible. Most dogs

INDUCING VOMITING IN DOGS

If your vet instructs you to induce vomiting at home, give your dog 1 teaspoon (5 mL) of 3 percent hydrogen peroxide by mouth per 10 pounds of body weight. You can repeat this dose if needed, but do not give more than nine teaspoons to any dog, no matter his weight. Then take him for a walk outside or someplace where cleanup will be easy. The peroxide should take effect within 10 to 20 minutes. Your dog will probably stop walking and get a really bad look on his face. That's called "nausea." He should then vomit up whatever it was he ate. This is one time it would be good to scoop up a bit of what came out, so the toxin can be identified. This remedy doesn't work for cats and should not be used unless you never want them to come within an inch of you again!

recover pretty quickly. Prevention is even easier: Spay your pet!

Seizures

Seizures are convulsions and are arguably the most common neurological problem in animals and the scariest to witness. They can be short-lived or go on for long periods. Even those that stop after a few seconds are still emergencies if your pet has never experienced them before. Seizures that continue without stopping are called *status epilepticus* and are a true emergency. Only an intravenous injection of diazepam (Valium) will stop these seizures, and the longer they go on, the more damage they'll cause. Most seizures in pets are due to epilepsy but they can also be caused by toxins like snail bait (metaldehyde) and rat bait, the newest of which contain bromethalin, which is a neurotoxin. Other causes include damage to organs like the liver and kidneys and organic brain disease like encephalitis and brain tumors. All of them require an immediate trip to your vet or emergency clinic.

If your pet has a seizure and is not epileptic, remove any nearby objects that might fall on or injure him, darken the room, hold and calm him if you can do this safely, and wait for the seizure to subside. Your pet will be confused and disoriented. He might startle easily and could bite you. Once the seizure stops, help him into the car, using a blanket to pick him up and hold him, and head off to the vet or emergency clinic for a diagnosis and medication if needed. If an animal is stable and no further seizures occur, vets often hold off on starting home medications until the seizures appear to be recurrent. That's a conservative approach rather than sentencing you (and your pet) to a lifetime of medication in the case of epilepsy.

Snakebite

Most common in the southwestern part of the United States, snakebites can be a common danger for your pets. If you suspect that your pet has been bitten, remain calm and keep your pet calm. You might not have even seen the bite or the snake, but you may hear a yelp and see a rapidly swelling and very painful leg or face. If you don't see puncture wounds, that doesn't mean your pet didn't get bitten; we often don't find these even when the dog's been shaved. Keep your pet warm, and head immediately to your vet or emergency clinic for treatment. Do not use a tourniquet, and do not cut an X in the wound to suck out the venom. That's only for old spaghetti Westerns. If you have Benadryl (diphenhydramine), give 1 milligram per pound of weight orally if you can safely open your dog's mouth (don't use over-the-counter antihistamines for cats or other animals). The liquid works almost as quickly as an injection. Remember, your dog may be in pain and even in shock. Always be careful when handling an injured, frightened animal so you don't become injured as well. Above all else, seek professional veterinary treatment as quickly as you can. Your

RATTLESNAKE VACCINE

If you live in an area populated by rattlesnakes and you hike, run, or play with your dog in those areas, you might want to speak to your vet about the rattlesnake vaccine. Although there's no hard evidence to prove it actually works, some vets think it decreases symptoms. On top of that, it's limited to the western diamondback at best. The vaccine lasts only six months and has to be boosted and repeated annually. It doesn't make your dog immune to the bite however; it just lessens symptoms so treatment is still necessary. The best prevention is to leash your dog in rattlesnake areas and avoid hiking during the sunniest part of the day when snakes are out.

pet will need hospitalization, pain medication, fluids, and antivenom.

Urinary Blockage

A true emergency, urinary blockages are rare in dogs and female cats but extremely common in male cats. If you have a male cat, you should know how to prevent them. Long-term blockages can lead to kidney failure and death, but even short-term blockages can cause damage to the kidneys, the bladder wall, and even the urethra. The worst cases can lead to bladder rupture, which is life threatening. Blockages are also extremely painful.

Urinary blockages are most often due to accumulation of mucus, crystals, or even stones (called calculi) that block the urethra, the pathway from the bladder out of the body. Some blockages are simply caused by inflammation of the urinary tract. Regardless, prevention is the key. Canned foods, which contain more water, are preferred for cats.

Common signs include urinating small amounts frequently, straining to urinate (producing drips instead of a stream), taking a long time to urinate, blood in the urine, and urinating in inappropriate places. Cats will stop eating and drinking and will lick at their urethral opening. If your pet, especially a male cat, hasn't urinated in more than eight hours, bring him to your vet or an emergency clinic right away. Within 12 hours, this is a life-threatening situation.

Urinary obstruction is easily diagnosed (your vet will feel a large bladder that is unable to empty). Treatment consists of anesthetizing the cat, putting in an IV for fluids, and manually catheterizing the penis to relieve the obstruction and allow the urine to drain. The catheter is temporarily sutured in place, and antibiotics and pain medications begin.

Most cats recover right away but are usually hospitalized for at least 48 hours. At home, you'll need to watch to be sure there's no relapse and possibly change the food to one recommended by your vet to prevent a recurrence. ∎

PERINEAL URETHROSTOMY

A perineal urethrostomy is a surgical treatment for male cats with recurrent urinary obstructions. The majority of blockages involve obstructions in the urethra, so the surgery permanently opens this pathway for urine to freely move out of the bladder while retaining normal bladder control. Unfortunately, that involves removing the penis entirely. Recovery is not fun, but we keep patients well managed with pain medication and anti-inflammatories. This sounds severe, but you wouldn't believe how much better your cat will feel without ever having the spasmodic pain of a urinary tract blockage again.

CHAPTER 21

Toxins

Pets are always eating things they shouldn't. It's important to know the deadliest toxins to prevent a tragedy. Some substances are dangerous for all living creatures. Others are safe for humans but deadly to pets. Still others are safe for dogs but lethal to cats, or vice versa. Lock chemicals and medications away in cabinets, remove dangerous plants and flowers from your home and yard, keep trash cans secured with lids or stowed under cabinets, don't leave household or automobile fluids lying around, and avoid feeding foods that are toxic to pets. Toxins can act fast. Don't delay seeking veterinary treatment if you think your pet has ingested something poisonous. Timely treatment might be the difference between life and death.

ALCOHOL

Alcohol can poison a pet by ethanol toxicity. The problem with ethanol toxicity is that varying amounts of a poison might cause problems in different pets. Anything that contains ethanol is toxic to pets, including rum cake, mouthwash, cough medicine, unbaked bread dough (due to the fermenting yeast), and even rotten apples. Play it safe and keep all "over 21" beverages out of your pet's reach. Signs of poisoning include weakness and lethargy, lack of coordination, and drowsiness leading to unconsciousness. Left untreated, the toxicity can lead to heart attack and death. With quick treatment, most animals recover within about a day.

ANTIFREEZE

Ethylene glycol poisoning, which occurs when pets ingest antifreeze or hydraulic fluid, is sadly quite common. Pets frequently encounter antifreeze when it leaks from a car onto the garage floor. This bright green liquid has a sweet taste. Pets might take a lick to investigate or might walk through the antifreeze, then lick it off their paws. Just a few licks can do irreversible damage to the kidneys.

Immediate symptoms of antifreeze poisoning are very much like alcohol toxicity. They include drooling and vomiting, uncoordinated or wobbly movement (seems "drunk"), head tremors, increased drinking and urination, muscle twitching, and depression. As time passes, symptoms progress to include decreased drinking but increased urination, low body temperature, extreme lethargy or coma, and seizures.

Untreated ethylene glycol poisoning, even in very small amounts, is fatal in dogs. If you even suspect your dog might have ingested this, seek medical care immediately. When caught early enough (within about five hours of ingestion), most dogs will recover uneventfully within a few days of intensive care in the hospital. In cases of delayed treatment, the kidneys might fail and

IF YOU THINK YOUR PET ATE SOMETHING TOXIC

If you know or suspect your pet ate something dangerous, do not wait: Call your veterinarian, an emergency veterinary hospital, or a pet poison hotline immediately. Some toxins require urgent treatment. If your vet or emergency clinic is not open, the ASPCA Animal Poison Control Center is open 24 hours a day, 365 days a year. Call 888-426-4435 to speak to a professional. You'll be charged a fee but it'll be the best money you've ever spent.

stop producing urine. If that happens, all we can do is support the patient and hope that kidney function is reestablished. In these cases, recovery can take weeks in the hospital, and some pets won't survive.

BATTERIES

Pets might chew or swallow batteries, especially if they chew up something that contains batteries, like a remote control or a child's toy. Button batteries like those found in musical greeting cards and small toys are particularly dangerous because they're so small. Batteries contain alkaline and acidic material that causes severe necrotizing burns. Lithium batteries are the most dangerous and can cause perforations of the esophagus or stomach within 15 to 30 minutes of ingestion. If you find a battery that's been punctured or even a small battery-operated toy that's been chewed on, go immediately to your vet or emergency hospital.

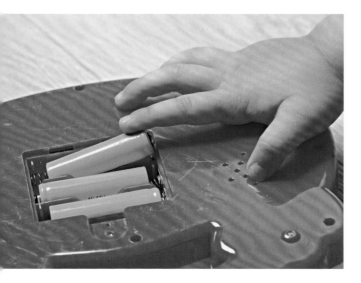

Treatment includes thorough flushing of the mouth with lukewarm water and endoscopy or surgery to quickly remove the batteries from the stomach. We never induce vomiting because leaked material can get a second chance to burn the esophagus and mouth. Time is of the essence. If ingestion is caught early, animals will recover uneventfully.

FLEA AND TICK MEDICATIONS

Although most flea and tick medications are safe when used as directed, pets can have adverse reactions. Some topical flea and tick products contain pyrethrin, a natural insecticide derived from the chrysanthemum flower. Similar chemicals are labeled as pyrethroid or permethrin. Never give more than the recommended dose, double up on applications, or treat cats with products labeled only for dogs. Cats are extremely sensitive to pyrethrins. It's critical to use only approved doses and products made especially for cats. Kittens should never be treated with pyrethrin-containing flea products.

Signs of an adverse reaction in cats and dogs include drooling, vomiting, diarrhea, weakness, incoordination, muscle tremors, seizures, and even death. If you suspect that your pet is having a reaction to an applied pyrethrin medication, immediately shampoo the topical off and go to your vet or emergency clinic. If your pet is already acting very ill, skip the bath and head straight to the vet. With proper care, most animals recover uneventfully. Again, always check labels to be sure the product you're using is appropriate for your pet.

INSECTICIDE TOXICITY

Use caution when treating your home or yard for spiders, ants, fleas, cockroaches, and other insects. Read the product label of the insecticide carefully and follow all instructions, including removing pets from the home if necessary. Animals spend a lot of time on the floor and lick their paws and fur, so the fewer insecticides you use inside your home, the better. You should also keep your pets off recently treated lawns and away from insect spray. Those warning flags and labels are there for a reason.

Signs of toxicity include vomiting, diarrhea, muscle tremors, ataxia, drooling, increased heart rate, seizures, constricted pupils, respiratory failure, and eventually death. If you suspect insecticide toxicity, call poison control immediately and then go to your vet or emergency clinic. Bring the bag or box with the product with you. With quick treatment and supportive care, most animals can recover completely.

MARIJUANA

Veterinarians in the United States are seeing more cases of marijuana poisoning in pets as more states legalize or decriminalize the drug. Pets can become intoxicated by inhaling secondhand smoke or eating marijuana—either the plant itself or food items containing the drug. Symptoms include incoordination, disorientation, hyperactivity, unusual or increased vocalization, drooling, uncontrolled urination, muscle tremors, seizures, and even coma. In rare cases, pets have died after ingesting large amounts of the

WHAT GOES IN MUST COME OUT

When a pet ingests a toxin, the vet will frequently induce vomiting and administer activated charcoal to absorb toxins. It's critical to do this as quickly as possible, so get to the hospital immediately if you think your pet ate something potentially toxic. Vomiting can be induced with a drug called apomorphine or with hydrogen peroxide by mouth. After the pet vomits (usually within 15 minutes or so), your vet will administer a messy drink of activated charcoal, which is essentially a black slurry of charcoal in water. The charcoal absorbs toxins before they hit the bloodstream, so it's well worth it.

psychoactive ingredient in marijuana, tetrahydrocannabinol (THC).

With less toxic potential, cannabidiol (CBD) is the other half of the marijuana equation. CBD is currently marketed without veterinary approval with claims that it can treat everything from joint pain to anxiety and even cancer in dogs. We don't know everything about its potential in dogs, and solid research is needed before veterinary approval to use it in our animals.

Diagnosis is heavily reliant on self-reporting, and many pet owners are reluctant to self-report. We can test for THC levels in the urine, but these tests take too long and are impractical, so an honest history of exposure is critical. Once that's established, vets can make an effective treatment plan. Fortunately, most symptoms are short-lived and resolve quickly in pets.

OVER-THE-COUNTER MEDICATIONS

Some drugs that are safe for use in humans are not safe for pets. Overdose can occur if a pet ingests a large amount of any medication, even one that's safe for use in pets. Refer to Appendix B to read which over the counter (OTC) drugs may be safe and those you should stay far away from.

Never give acetaminophen (Tylenol) to any pet, especially cats for whom it's lethal even in small doses. Acetaminophen causes irreversible liver damage. If you even suspect your pet has ingested acetaminophen, get her to the vet immediately. Symptoms include depression, weakness, labored breathing, vomiting, diarrhea, swelling of the face and limbs, and color change in the gums ranging from yellow due to liver disease to blue or even brown because of disruption in oxygen-carrying ability by red blood cells, which are affected in severe cases. Once the liver begins to fail, jaundice and coma can ensue. If treatment is given quickly, there's a good chance your pet will survive.

In a pinch at 2 a.m., it's okay to give your dog one dose of aspirin to relieve pain—say, from a leg sprain, but never give aspirin to cats. While most dogs can tolerate aspirin, it can be toxic in both cats and dogs. Bleeding can occur, especially in the gastrointestinal tract. Typical signs include poor appetite, vomiting and diarrhea, and even evidence of blood in the stool or vomit.

If bleeding is severe, it can also lead to neurological signs like weakness and ataxia, coma, and untreated, it can even cause death. Most dogs recover well with treatment.

Pseudoephedrine and its milder compound phenylephrine, found in nasal decongestants, is toxic to pets. Symptoms include restlessness, increased heart rate, hyperactivity, panting, and tearing. In high enough doses, pseudoephedrine toxicity can cause shock and even death. But animals generally recover with prompt treatment.

Never give any pet ibuprofen or naproxen, which can be toxic to pets in very low doses. You might see symptoms immediately, or they might take a few days to appear. Signs are similar to aspirin toxicity. In severe cases, blood transfusions might be required. If caught early enough, most animals will recover, but this depends on the amount of medication ingested. Best bet, keep your pets away from these.

MUSHROOMS

Mushrooms are among the most poisonous of organics. Signs of mushroom toxicity vary depending on the type and amount of mushroom ingested. Some cause simple gastrointestinal distress, others affect the nervous system, and still others can lead to liver or kidney failure. The most common symptoms are weakness, vomiting and diarrhea, jaundice, drooling, and abdominal pain. Seizures and coma can also occur.

If you even suspect your dog ate an unsafe mushroom, go immediately to your vet or emergency clinic, and bring a sample of the mush-

room. The mushroom can be submitted for identification, but treatment should not be delayed waiting for this information. With treatment, prognosis is usually good, although particularly toxic mushrooms have a more difficult prognosis dependent entirely on how quickly you can get your pet to the vet.

PRESCRIPTION MEDICATIONS

You can pretty much assume that anything prescribed for you would be bad for your pet so keep those pills, capsules, and tonics safely away from your animals. Some common dangerous prescription medications include:

- Amphetamines (like drugs for attention deficit hyperactivity disorder)
- Antidepressants
- Benzodiazepines and sleep aids
- Birth control pills
- Blood pressure medications
- Diabetes drugs
- Hormone replacement creams, sprays, or gels
- Pain medications
- All narcotics

RODENT POISON

Rodenticides are among the most common and most lethal of pet hazards. Pets might consume the poison itself or eat a mouse or rat that ate the poison. "Rat bait" is appetizing to pets due to flavoring used to attract rodents. Anticoagulants, which cause bleeding and death, used to be the main ingredient in rodenticides. The ingredients used in these types of rodenticides are warfarin derivatives, most commonly brodifacoum, bromadiolone, diphacinone, and difenacoum. Because of the risk of secondary exposure to humans and other nontargeted species in addition to outright rodent resistance to these products, they are much less available today. That's the good news. The bad news is that newer rodenticides, which contain the ingredient bromethalin, cause fluid to build up in the brain (cerebral edema). Another newer type of rat poison is cholecalciferol, which causes irreversible kidney damage. Both of these are far more difficult to treat than the earlier anticoagulant rodenticides. Not a good experience for anyone— dog, cat, or mouse. If you have to eradicate rodents in your home, better to use a quick and lethal spring trap or, better yet, humane traps where you can release the invaders to another area (just not your next-door neighbor's yard). Don't use glue traps—few things are more cruel.

If you suspect your dog or cat has eaten a rodenticide, bring the bag or box to your vet. This is critical for treating the toxicity because different compounds last different lengths of time and have different effects on the body. Signs of rodenticide ingestion might occur up to a week after exposure. Pets might show weakness, loss of appetite, excessive drinking and urination, and neurological signs. Unfortunately, veterinarians have no antidote to these newer types of rat poisons. If the ingestion is not caught early enough to treat by inducing vomiting and supportive care, many pets will die.

SLUG AND SNAIL BAIT

Whether pellets, powders, granules, or liquids, slug and snail bait is one garden product you should never use at home. It's flavored with beef to attract snails, and as a result it also attracts pets. The active ingredient is metaldehyde, and hallmark signs of metaldehyde toxicity are muscle tremors and seizures. Other signs are anxiety, vomiting, diarrhea, multiple organ failure, and, if not treated, death. Signs usually develop within minutes, although that depends on the quantity ingested and can take up to a few hours. It's critical to bring in any products you suspect your pet has ingested. Once animals are on treatment that includes supportive care with fluids and Valium as needed for seizures, the prognosis is good, but it can take a few days to completely rid the body of the poison. Bottom line: Don't use these poisons. Snails are an attractive part of gardens.

TOBACCO PRODUCTS

Pets can become ill by inhaling secondhand smoke, but they can become very ill after ingesting nicotine-containing products: cigarettes, cigars, chewing tobacco, or stop-smoking aids like nicotine patches or gums. Pets might show signs of toxicity within an hour of ingestion. Some tobacco products also contain xylitol (see page 263), compounding the poison risk for your pets.

Signs of nicotine poisoning include vomiting and diarrhea, followed by neurological signs, cardiac collapse, and even death. Initially your dog might just act a little hyperactive and nervous, but if he's ingested enough nicotine to cause symptoms, this is a life-threatening emergency. Successful treatment is dependent on how much nicotine has been ingested and how long your dog has gone before treatment. Treatment within four hours of ingestion might lead to full recovery. In lethal doses with delayed treatment, there is sadly nothing we can do.

TOXIC FOODS

Some foods are not safe for pets because of their metabolic and physiological differences from us. Some can cause organ inflammation or even failure. Don't feed your pet:

- Alcohol
- Apple seeds
- Avocado
- Chocolate (dark chocolate especially)
- Coffee
- Garlic (okay only in small amounts)
- Grapes and raisins
- Macadamia nuts
- Moldy foods
- Onions
- Potato (raw)
- Rhubarb
- Stone fruit pits
- Tea
- Tomato leaves
- Walnuts
- Yeast dough

If your pet eats a large quantity of any food on this list, it's critical that you take him to your vet or emergency clinic. With prompt treatment and supportive care, often with IV fluids and observation, most pets will recover.

Ask DR. GARY:

What's a Toxic Dose of Chocolate?

Two components in chocolate — theobromine and caffeine — are toxic to dogs, but if your dog eats very small amounts, he'll probably be okay. As a general rule of thumb, dogs can ingest up to 45 milligrams of theobromine per pound of weight. You can't calculate it based on pound of chocolate because every type of chocolate varies in theobromine concentration. For instance, unsweetened baker's chocolate contains about 390 milligrams per ounce, whereas milk chocolate has only 44 milligrams, and white chocolate contains none. PetMD has a great online toxicity meter to give you an idea of how worried to be. The best advice: Keep chocolate away from your four-legged friends!

THE POINSETTIA MYTH

Despite what you might have heard, this Christmas plant (*Euphorbia pulcherrima*) is not deadly to pets. At worst, it's a mild toxin that can cause drooling, diarrhea, and vomiting. The sap can also cause mild skin irritation. No treatment is usually necessary, but if you have a particularly voracious plant-loving cat who can't take her mind off those red leaves, it may be time for artificial decorations.

TOXIC PLANTS

Many plants and flowers are toxic to pets. Given their propensity for chewing on plants, cats are at the most risk for plant toxicity. It's critical to keep any toxic plants away from your pets. When you go to your vet, bring the plant sample along with you. Many plants are irritants, meaning they'll cause vomiting, inappetence, and diarrhea. Some also cause inflammation of the mouth, leading to itchiness and swelling. Certain others affect particular organs and might cause difficulty breathing, drooling, irregular heartbeat, or excessive drinking and urinating. The following are common dangerous plants and flowers. For a complete list, visit *aspca.org* and search "toxic plants."

- Autumn crocus
- Azaleas
- Cyclamen
- Daffodils
- Dieffenbachia
- Dracaena
- Hyacinths
- Kalanchoe (mother-in-law plant)
- Lilies (tiger, day, Asiatic, Easter, and Japanese show lilies)
- Lily of the valley
- Oleander
- Philodendron
- Sago palm
- Tulips

ZINC TOXICITY

Zinc toxicosis can be deadly. Zinc is found in coins, diaper creams, sunscreen, cold remedies, and

CATS AND LILIES

Some lilies are very poisonous; others are not toxic at all. Some lilies, like calla, peace, and Peruvian lilies, contain oxalate crystals, which can cause irritation to the mouth, tongue, and esophagus. Others are more dangerous, especially to cats. These include Easter lilies, Japanese show lilies, and tiger, Asiatic, and day lilies. Even small amounts like a few leaves or flowers might lead to kidney failure in cats.

vitamins, as well as metal items like zippers, board game pieces, jewelry, and children's toys. Pennies, specifically pennies minted after 1982, are the coins we really worry about pets swallowing.

Zinc toxicity causes lethargy, depression, vomiting, diarrhea, and jaundice if the liver is badly damaged. Successful treatment is predicated on removing any zinc objects from the gastrointestinal tract via endoscopy or surgery. If the source can be removed and supportive care instituted, the prognosis is very good.

XYLITOL

Xylitol is used as a sugar substitute in many human products and found in everything from gum to diet food products, including some peanut butter, ice cream, and yogurt. Dogs who consume products containing xylitol can develop hypoglycemia (low blood sugar) and seizures. Xylitol can cause liver failure and even death in higher doses. If your dog eats anything containing xylitol, your first move should be to call pet poison control. Xylitol might also cause problems in cats.

Signs of xylitol poisoning start within 30 minutes of ingestion. They include vomiting, weakness, tremors, and even seizures. Severe cases lead to coma, liver failure, and death. With treatment, the prognosis is good for dogs who have not developed symptoms of hypoglycemia, but if liver failure develops, the prognosis is very poor. ▪

CHAPTER 22

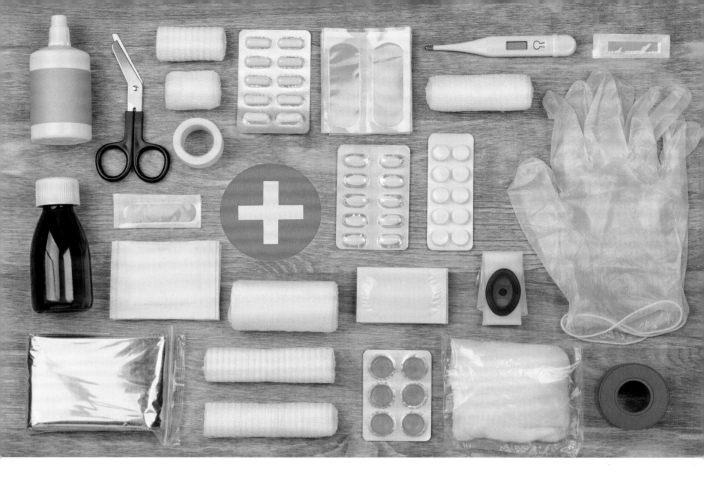

Pet First Aid

When I was a surgical intern, I treated a Labrador retriever who had punctured his jugular vein after jumping through a window. His quick-thinking owner took a pillow from the sofa and pressed it against the hemorrhaging wound, wrapping it in place with a sheet, careful not to hinder the dog's breathing. He headed straight to the hospital, where we rushed the dog into surgery. Without this first aid, the dog would probably not have survived.

First aid comes in handy when your pet has a minor injury that can likely be treated at home. In the case of severe injuries, first aid can even save your pet's life. A quick note of caution: First aid is never a substitute for veterinary treatment. First aid is to be followed by a visit to your vet in *every* case. Giving first aid, however, will increase the odds that your pet will make it until you get to a vet for medical treatment.

FIRST-AID BASICS

Knowing how to handle an emergency can save your pet's life. The first key is to remain calm. If you panic, your pet will panic too. Read on to learn more about common pet emergencies and what to do.

Create a Pet First-Aid Kit

No pet home should be without a first-aid kit. You can buy everything separately, or purchase a starter kit from most pet stores or online. Keep your kit in an easily accessible place in your home, and consider a second kit for the car if you travel, camp, or hike with your pet. Here's what should be in a good kit:

- Self-adhesive bandage (such as Vetrap)
- Nonstick bandages
- Gauze squares
- Cotton balls
- Tweezers
- Scissors
- Nail trimmers
- Digital thermometer
- Petroleum jelly (for the thermometer)
- Saline eye solution
- Styptic powder
- Ear cleaner
- Triple antibiotic ointment
- Diphenhydramine
- Bismuth subsalicylate tablets
- Chlorhexidine solution
- Hydrogen peroxide (3 percent)
- Artificial tear ointment
- Small flashlight
- Two cans of prescription gastrointestinal diet (to use in cases of stomach upset)

THE HEIMLICH MANEUVER FOR PETS

For large and medium dogs, put your arms around the belly and join your hands. Make a fist and push up on your dog's chest just behind the rib cage. Don't pick up your dog. If your dog is lying down, place one hand on his back for support and push the abdomen upward toward the head with your other hand. Lie small dogs and cats on their sides with one hand on the back and the other just below the rib cage, and push firmly upward. Remove any objects from the mouth or throat when you safely can. Don't pull string out of your cat's mouth if it extends down the throat — it could be caught in the intestines.

Choking

One of the worst choking cases I can remember was a dog rushed into my clinic because he swallowed an entire smooth rubber ball while playing fetch with his owner. His family couldn't get the ball out of his throat, so they rushed him to the clinic, where I sedated him and pulled the ball out with forceps. Another five minutes and the dog might not have survived. (This story is a good reminder not to allow your pet to play with any ball made of smooth rubber; these can slip into the airway and are nearly impossible to grasp with your fingers.)

Choking is not always obvious. Your pet might become quiet, panicked, and have difficulty breathing. Be careful because he might bite if desperate for air. If you can, open your pet's mouth to look for an object. If you see something and you can safely pull it out, do so, but be careful that you don't push it farther in. If you see something lodged in the airway but you can't pull it out, place both hands on either side of your pet's rib cage and apply firm pressure quickly three to four times to use air in the lungs to try to expel the object. You can also try the Heimlich maneuver (see "The Heimlich Maneuver for Pets" page 265). If this doesn't work, wrap your pet in a blanket and rush to the nearest vet. When your pet is choking, time is of the essence. Try these first-aid techniques, but quickly. If you aren't making headway within a minute or two, get to your vet immediately.

CPR

Performing CPR on pets is not easy, and unfortunately, it's also not very effective. But if your pet stops breathing or has no heartbeat, you're his last chance. If your pet isn't breathing, open his airway by carefully grabbing the tongue and pulling it forward (use a piece of cloth if the tongue is too slippery to grasp). Look for any foreign objects that might be blocking the airway. If nothing is seen, start rescue breathing by closing your pet's mouth and breathing directly into his nose until you see the chest expand. Continue this with one breath every four or five seconds.

If there's no heartbeat, do the same airway check, and begin rescue breathing. Next, lay your pet on his right side with one hand on the lower chest side and one hand on the upper chest side, just behind the left elbow. Begin chest compressions about one inch deep for medium-size dogs—more for larger dogs and less for smaller dogs. For cats or toy dogs, use your dominant hand to apply pressure to the chest in the same area using your thumb and

---

SIGNS OF SHOCK IN ANIMALS

Shock occurs when the body has been traumatized by sudden injury or severe disease, causing a massive decrease in blood pressure. This leads to a reduction in blood flow to the major organs — specifically, the brain, heart, lungs, and kidneys. Untreated, it will be fatal. If you think your pet is in shock, wrap him in a warm blanket (but don't apply heat), keep his head elevated, and go immediately to your nearest veterinary hospital. Signs of shock may include:

1. Weakness and collapse
2. Possible loss of consciousness
3. Cold extremities and skin
4. Weak pulse
5. Pale gums and lips
6. Dilated pupils and dull or unresponsive eyes

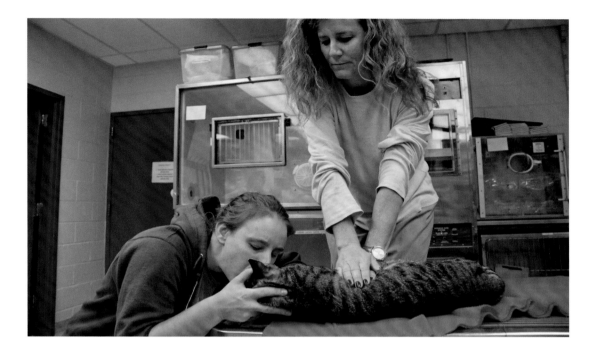

forefinger. Do about 100 compressions a minute for both dogs and cats (fewer for larger animals, more for smaller ones). If you're alone, alternate rescue breaths with chest compressions, with a breath about once every five seconds. If you have help, have your helper do the breaths while you do chest compressions. Once your pet is breathing on his own, head directly to the nearest animal hospital.

Spinal Injuries

Spinal injuries are more difficult to diagnose in animals than they are in people. Animals can't tell us they can't walk, and if they're hurt, they might not even try. Signs of a spinal injury might include unsuccessful attempts to walk, pain on movement, and incoordination. If you have a pet with a suspected spinal injury, the first rule is immobilization to avoid further injury to the spinal cord. Place your pet on his side on a blanket and wrap him up in the blanket so he can't move. Then gently carry him to your car and go to your vet or an emergency hospital right away.

HOW TO MUZZLE AN INJURED PET

Pain and stress might cause your faithful friend to bite or scratch. You might need to muzzle your pet so you can get her to the vet. If you have a muzzle, use it. If you don't, use a soft piece of cloth or a roll of gauze to gently but firmly tie the mouth closed, making sure your pet can breathe freely. Only attempt this if it's safe for you to do it. For cats or dogs with pushed-in faces, scoop them up in a big towel or blanket and transport them to your vet.

SPECIFIC FIRST AID

Use these techniques at home as a stop-gap measure until you can get your pet to a veterinarian for further evaluation and treatment.

Bleeding

Some areas on animals tend to bleed like the dickens: the ears, paw pads, tail, and nails. Fortunately, in spite of the mess, trauma to these areas is not usually life threatening. Bleeding from other types of wounds can be severe, however. In that case, quick action on your part can save your pet's life.

If your pet is bleeding externally, press a thick gauze pad or soft towel over the injury and apply gentle pressure. If you can, wrap the wound with soft gauze and self-adhesive bandage (Vetrap). This stuff is a godsend and every pet owner should have a roll. Keep the wounded area elevated to slow the bleeding. Bleeding usually slows and might even stop after three to four minutes, but you might need to continue applying pressure. If bright red blood is gushing, continue to hold pressure on the wound until you can get to your vet or nearest emergency hospital.

A tourniquet will cause damage so should only be used on the legs or tail if you think your pet's life is in jeopardy due to uncontrolled bleeding. Apply the tourniquet above the wound using a belt or some cloth with a pen to twist into the knot. Write down the time you did this, and get to your vet right away. Release the knot for 30 seconds every 20 minutes.

Pale gums are a sign that your pet is bleeding internally. Right now, when your pet is healthy, look at his gums so you know his normal color. Normal gums should be pink to red. If your pet's gums are dark pigmented, which occurs in many breeds, look

HOW TO TREAT A BIRD'S BROKEN BLOOD FEATHER

Blood feathers, otherwise known as pinfeathers, are newly growing feathers. Pinfeathers turn up during molting. If these feathers break, they bleed like crazy. Here's what to do if that happens:

1. Apply pressure to the broken feather with gauze.
2. Apply styptic powder or cornstarch to the end of the feather shaft with a cotton swap.
3. Keep your bird from pecking at the feather with gentle restraint.
4. If bleeding continues, continue to apply pressure, and go to your vet as soon as possible.

Broken blood feathers might need to be removed. Even if you've stopped the bleeding, see your vet within the next day or two to have the feather checked out. Your vet can show you how to remove blood feathers if this becomes a recurrent problem.

at the tissue surrounding the gums. If the gums are ever pale, something is wrong, and you need to see your vet immediately. Other indications of internal bleeding are cold extremities and weakness.

Whether your dog has broken a nail or you've cut too close to the quick, nails bleed like you wouldn't believe. Despite the mess, however, it can usually wait until morning. If your pet seems otherwise fine, wrap the paw with gauze and Vetrap until you can get to your vet.

If you just cut the nail too short during a nail trim, press some styptic powder (or cornstarch if you don't have the former) against the nail with your finger, and hold it there for a minute to stop the bleeding. Once you've stopped the bleeding, bandage the nail, or it will start up again when your dog licks at it.

Burns

Heat burns or chemical burns can be caused by many things—household cleaners, heaters, or electric shocks, for example. Once your pet is safely removed from the source of the burn, rinse the area for 10 or more minutes with tepid—*not cold*—water. The more quickly you can decrease the temperature of the skin, the less severe the burn will be. After cooling, wrap the burned area with a cold, wrung-out washcloth compress or a frozen bag of peas wrapped in a soft dish towel. Get your animal to a vet as soon as you can. For chemical burns, follow the same protocol; just be sure the contaminant doesn't transfer to another area when you rinse it.

Deskunking

If your pet gets sprayed by a skunk, don't reach for the tomato juice—it does nothing

SKUNK REMOVER RECIPE

The smell and residue of skunk oil can linger up to a year if you don't remove it quickly. Disclaimer: Do NOT make this ahead of time. It can explode if stored.

1 quart 3 percent hydrogen peroxide
¼ cup baking soda
1 teaspoon dishwashing soap

Wearing rubber gloves, mix the ingredients. Wet your dog's entire body to the skin with the solution (do not wet him first with plain water), then thoroughly lather in the solution, avoiding the eyes. Leave it on for 15 minutes (no more or your black Lab will become a blonde); then rinse completely with warm water. Wash your dog again using pet shampoo and rinse thoroughly. You can repeat the entire process several times if necessary.

to neutralize the oil! Instead, use a commercial skunk odor remover or make your own (see sidebar above). Check to be sure your dog hasn't gotten sprayed in the eyes. If his eyes are red and tearing, rinse them with warm water or saline solution, and then head for the bath.

Heatstroke

Heatstroke, or hyperthermia, occurs when the normal bodily protection mechanisms fail to cool the body in a safe range. Moderate heatstroke in dogs (body temperature between 104°F and 106°F) can be resolved within an hour. Severe heatstroke (over 106°F) is an extreme emergency that often has deadly consequences.

Avoidance of heatstroke is the best treatment. A dog's normal core temperature runs hotter than a human's—between 100°F and 103°F (about 38°C to 39.5°C)—and because most dogs wear permanent fur coats, they can quickly overheat even on days when you feel okay. Never take your dog jogging, hiking, or even for long walks when temperatures approach 80°F, especially if humidity is high, because dogs cannot effectively cool themselves through panting in humid weather. Keep pets inside, preferably in air-conditioning, when temperatures reach 90°F, and limit exercise to early morning and late evening. Never leave pets in the car when temperatures exceed 70°F, not even for a few minutes. Temperatures can quickly soar to dangerous levels inside a car, even on only moderately warm days.

Signs of heatstroke include panting, bright red tongue, thick saliva, weakness, dizziness, vomiting, and diarrhea. For moderate heatstroke (you might see your dog slow his pace and pant with his tongue out), move him to a cool place. Slowly lower his temperature by pointing a fan at him and pouring some rubbing alcohol on the outsides of his ears and his back. The alcohol slowly lowers the core body temperature as it evaporates. If you don't have alcohol, cool water is fine, but avoid ice or very cold water because these can lower the temperature too quickly and lead to shock. Check your dog's temperature with a rectal thermometer (see Chapter 8), and stop cooling efforts once it drops to 103°F. Then keep him dry and turn off the fan so he doesn't get too cool. Keep plenty of water at easy access if he wants to drink and call your vet if your dog doesn't bounce back to his happy self within an hour or so.

Severe heatstroke is evidenced by a body temperature over 106°F or severe depression. If your dog is not responsive, it's an emergency. Pour rubbing alcohol on your dog's back and cool your dog as quickly as you can in the car on the way to the emergency clinic (turn on the air-conditioning and aim the vents at your dog). Time is of the essence. Your vet will initiate cooling efforts and give your dog fluids to counteract the toxic effects of hyperthermia, then monitor him for organ damage. In many cases, rapid treatment can avoid a needless tragedy.

Insect Bite or Sting

Remove any trace of a stinger by scraping a credit card against the bite. Then gently clean the area with some mild soapy water or chlorhexidine solution. Apply a small amount of neomycin (e.g., Neosporin), and watch your pet to make sure he doesn't have an allergic reaction to the sting or bite. If you see any facial swelling or difficulty breathing, get to the vet as quickly as you can.

Wounds and Bandaging

Wounds can be mild or severe, acute or chronic. If a wound is relatively small and your pet is feeling otherwise fine, you might be able to treat it at home. This means minor scrapes or cuts, including small abrasions, shallow lacerations, and minor bite wounds. The key is to treat promptly, before infection can set in. One important proviso for any at-home treatment is to be sure your pet, and you, are both safe. If you think your pet might bite or scratch you or if you think your pet is in pain, let your vet treat the wound.

Here's what you need to treat a wound:

1. A water-based lubricant like KY jelly
2. Electric hair clippers
3. Antiseptic solution
4. Antibiotic ointment (like bacitracin, neomycin, polymyxin B)
5. Gauze squares
6. Telfa pad or other nonstick pad (like the middle of an adhesive bandage)
7. Self-adhesive bandage (Vetrap)

First, settle your pet in a comfortable place on a fluffy towel. Lubricate the area with KY jelly to keep the hair out of it and clip the fur from around the wound. Wash the area with warm water. If you can, rinse the wound with a 1-to-10 solution of the antiseptic (my favorite is chlorhexidine solution, which you can buy at any drugstore). *Do not use hydrogen peroxide or rubbing alcohol. These will hurt your pet and inhibit healing.* Pat dry with a soft towel, and finish by applying the antibiotic ointment. If the wound is large, you might need to bandage it.

Place the nonstick pad over the wound and place a few squares of gauze on top of that. Pull out a length of Vetrap, allow it to spring back into its nonstretched position, and then wrap it around the wounded area. As you unroll more bandage, always let it bounce back to its nonstretched state before laying it down. Do not wrap too tightly, or you can cut off your pet's circulation, causing the paw to swell and become painful. After wrapping the wounded area, continue lightly wrapping the limb until you've gone past the first joint above the injury. This will keep the wrap from rolling down and off. Once you've covered the wounded area, tear the bandage off the roll and stick it to itself. Always follow up any bandaging with a visit to your vet so he or she can recheck your work. ■

CHAPTER 23

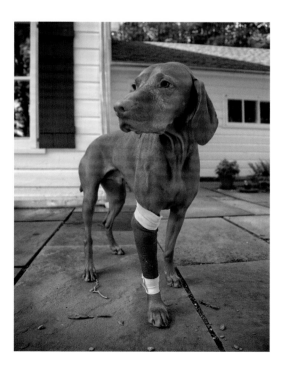

Disaster Preparedness

We hear it all the time: Knowing what to do when disaster hits can make the difference between life and death. That applies to humans facing imminent danger, as well as our pets. But it's very easy to postpone. Planning for the worst means acknowledging it can happen. Whether you live in the hurricane prone Gulf, the Midwest's tornado alley, along tectonic borders, a city sky-scraper, or even a volcanic island in the middle of the Pacific, disasters are part of life these days. The trick is to be prepared. More than just your life depends on it.

HOW FAR WE'VE COME

When Hurricane Katrina devastated the Gulf Coast in 2005, it was shattering for humans, but it was also tragic for the pets who had to be left behind because disaster shelters were not set up to take in pets. This tragedy changed the way people treat animals during natural disasters, eventually making it second nature that when you flee from a disaster, you take your whole family, including your animals, with you.

More recent disasters show how far we've come. Our pets are members of our families. Many of us would no more leave them at home when forced to evacuate than we would a child or a grandparent. Fortunately, federal and local agencies now provide resources for people to do the right thing and bring their animals with them. Doing any less can even lead to prosecution today, which is nothing more than reasonable in a society that values our furred, scaled, finned, and feathered pets.

EMERGENCY PLAN

Hurricanes, floods, fires, tornadoes, earthquakes. The thing about natural disasters is you don't always know when they're going to hit. Sometimes you get some notice, like when a hurricane is headed your way, but disasters can happen without warning. You might be home when a disaster hits, but you might also be at work. Taking the time to create a disaster plan for your family—pets included—will make it easier to deal with everything that's thrown at you in the event of an emergency. Consider the following when crafting your plan.

Many evacuation centers set up for humans will not accept pets, so know where you can take your pet if you must evacuate. This could be the home of a friend or family member who lives some distance away from you, a boarding facility in a neighboring city, or a pet-friendly hotel or motel. If you're hoping to evacuate with your pet to a pet-friendly hotel, do so sooner rather than later; if you wait too long, you might find all the pet-friendly hotels on your list are booked.

Evacuating with large animals is more complicated. Your local animal shelter might have a livestock evacuation plan in place to help you move large animals to safety. If you have a trailer for horses, make sure you keep it maintained and ready for when you might need it.

RESCUE ALERT STICKERS SAVE LIVES

Window decals alert first responders that pets are in the home. You can buy these at pet supply stores or get them free from some animal welfare organizations like the ASPCA. Use a black permanent marker to indicate how many of each type of pet are inside your home, and post the decal somewhere prominent near your door, such as the front window or on the door itself. If you are evacuating with your pets, take the sticker down before you leave or write "evacuated" across it so emergency personnel know the pets are gone.

If you do need to evacuate, never leave your pets behind! This applies to all pets: dogs, cats, rabbits, birds, hamsters, reptiles, horses, and any other pet. If it's not safe for you to stay in your home, it isn't safe for your pets. You don't know when you will be able to return to your home; your pet could be in harm's way and stuck without food or water for weeks. Your pet could also become injured or, worse, escape your home and become lost or stolen. Don't wait until the last minute to evacuate. Gather and pack up your belongings and all your pets' supplies early so you can quickly hop in the car with your pets and leave.

WHAT TO DO IF THE EMERGENCY SHELTER TURNS AWAY YOUR PETS

Today, many emergency shelters allow you to bring your pets with you. This is good news, but it's not universal. If a shelter doesn't allow pets, it might set up a separate area at the evacuation site for pets; often, animal shelter personnel care for animals on site. You'll be encouraged to visit, feed, and walk your pets. In other cases, emergency workers might refer you to an animal shelter where you can safely keep your pets out of harm's way. If no pet accommodations are made, you must make other arrangements, such as staying at a hotel or with friends and family safely away from the disaster area. Prepare a disaster plan well ahead of any real-life emergencies.

Resources now exist to help you during an evacuation, but that's not to say it's easy. Many evacuation sites are in schools and health facilities, which can't take in animals. Although animal shelters aren't always able to accept pets, they might coordinate with other groups to arrange care for animals. At the San Diego Humane Society, we partner with American Red Cross shelters to house and care for animals of families who are in emergency shelters. Most often, we do this at sites adjacent to the evacuation centers so people can continue to care for and see their pets.

If you choose to stay home during a natural disaster, keep your pets inside the house and stay in one room together so you can quickly grab your pets and go if necessary. Especially for cats, close doors to bedrooms so cats don't sneak off to hide. You might even put your cats and small dogs into their carriers so they are close by and safe. Even if your pets have microchips (which they should), make sure all pets are wearing their collars with ID tags. For cats and small dogs, also write your name and contact information on the carrier in case you become separated from your pet after you evacuate. If you think your dog might try to escape, keep him on a leash. Keep your emergency supplies at hand in case you need them.

Once the disaster is over, keep your pets inside or on a leash if you take them outside. Assess any damage to your home to make sure your pet cannot get hurt or escape. Stay away from high water, downed power lines, and debris.

If you're at work when a disaster strikes, you might not be able to get to your pet. Make arrangements ahead of time with a few neighbors to check in on your pet and help if you are unable to get

HOW TO PREPARE YOUR HORSE FOR DISASTER

Set up a buddy system ahead of time with your neighbors so you can mobilize to help each other out when you need to evacuate. In addition to your horse, transport a week's worth of hay and grain in another trailer, veterinary records, and a good photo record of you with your horse. If you don't have a plan to emergency stable your horse, work with your humane society to find the nearest safe space. Well in advance of an emergency, try to train your horse not to be spooked by trailers, emergency responders, and firefighting gear. This is especially helpful if someone other than you has to evacuate your horse.

home (if they also have pets, you can do the same for them). Program your neighbors' contact information (phone number and email address) into your phone so you can quickly contact them when disaster strikes.

Knowing where emergency clinics are located outside your immediate neighborhood is especially important because you may have to leave your local area during an emergency.

You should also know where to look for lost animals. The nearest shelter will be the best place to start, along with local veterinarians and even evacuation centers.

Your Pet's Disaster Kit

Each of your pets needs at least one week's worth of food, water, and other provisions. Store your pet's kit with your human family's disaster kit in an easily accessible place close to an exit. Rotate out and replace food before the expiration date and water every two months. Your pet disaster kit should contain the following:

- Food (dry and/or canned; small cans so you don't have to store leftovers)
- Bottled water (one gallon per day per pet)
- Food and water bowls
- Pictures of you with your pets (to prove ownership or if you're separated)
- Medications (rotate out before they expire)
- Proof of vaccinations
- Can opener
- Towels or blankets
- Crate or pet carrier
- Extra leash, collar, and/or harness
- Cat litter and disposable litter boxes and litter
- Poop bags (for dogs) and plastic trash bags (to dispose of kitty litter)
- Dish soap and sponge
- Disinfecting skin wipes
- Pillowcase (this can be a makeshift carrier for a cat)
- Flashlight

PART 5

Common Health Issues

Fortunately, not every medical issue is an emergency. However, that doesn't mean something is not serious, and letting health issues slide can backfire on you. Any time you suspect your pet is experiencing a health problem, make the next available appointment to see your vet.

CHAPTER 24

Allergies

Allergies are one of the most frustrating conditions for pets and their owners. They can be tricky to diagnose and treat; usually it's more about management rather than curing allergies completely. Depending on the type, allergies can manifest with a host of symptoms, including inflamed, moist, itchy skin; itchy paws; itchy, infected ears; sneezing; runny eyes; diarrhea; and vomiting. The key to resolving allergies is figuring out what's causing them so your vet can implement the appropriate treatment. Often pinpointing the cause of allergies is part guessing game and part process of elimination. If you and your vet can identify the things your pet is NOT allergic to, you are left with a narrower list of culprits to consider.

FOOD ALLERGIES

Just as our pets can develop allergies to pollen, dusts, and molds, they can also develop allergies to foods. We're mostly talking dogs here, but cats can have food allergies too. Food allergies can cause a host of gastrointestinal symptoms, but they can also cause signs very similar to environmental allergies: skin inflammation, ear infections, and secondary skin infections. The only difference is that skin inflammation due to food allergies is usually not itchy unless it gets infected, but as luck would have it, it often does. Fortunately, food allergies are relatively uncommon in pets, affecting only approximately 10 percent of allergic dogs.

The most common allergens are beef, chicken, dairy, egg, and fish (for cats, ironically). Most dogs are allergic to more than one of these. Corn, interestingly, is not a big problem for dogs despite all the marketing against it. In fact, you might be surprised to learn that grains in general are not unhealthy. This makes sense considering that most allergies are due to proteins, and grains contain very little protein.

A diagnosis of food allergies is not easy. There is no reliable skin test or blood test. Instead, we rely on food elimination trials using a diet containing a rare protein and carbohydrate your pet has never eaten before (for instance, rabbit and sweet potato, or kangaroo and barley). You'll need to feed your pet only this food for at least 21 days. That means no table scraps or treats. If new food eliminates the itching and at least starts to clear up the rash, you can keep feeding the diet to your pet long term. If not, your vet will ask you to try another diet or conclude that food allergy is not the problem. Most of the time, the culprit really turns out to be inhalant allergies.

SKIN ALLERGIES

Skin allergies, also known as atopic dermatitis, are woefully common in dogs and not unknown in cats. An allergy can occur when something touches the animal's skin (contact dermatitis) or through inhalation, which is the more common route and describes seasonal allergies. Atopic dermatitis (or "atopy") refers to a chronic, often seasonal rash caused by inhaled allergens. Dogs can be allergic to anything. Inhalant allergies can be caused by pollen, plants, house dust and mites, molds, trees, and yes, even cats. Signs include itching and rash localized to the paws, ears, muzzle, underarms, and groin. And atopic dermatitis

Typical dog hot spot

can also cause ear infections. Contact dermatitis is a bit different. In this, the skin reacts to the allergy source directly at the site of contact, not all over as in atopic dermatitis. It can be caused by many things, including fleas, poison ivy, or even flea medication. Dogs with contact and inhalant dermatitis are almost always itchy. We call this pruritus. Often, the itching is so severe that it causes worsening of the rash and even hot spots (see Chapter 32).

In cases of chronic pruritus and dermatitis, it's critical for your vet to determine exactly what your pet is allergic to, but this can be challenging as there is no definitive test to diagnose atopic dermatitis. Blood tests exist, but they are notoriously unreliable. The most accurate diagnosis requires a skin test. Done under a light sedative, a veterinary dermatologist will inject a tiny amount of up to 60 different antigens on a shaved section of your dog's side. Once the allergies are determined, the dermatologist will create a serum containing those antigens to start allergy shots for your dog. Less commonly, cats may also be tested and started on allergy shots.

Allergy hyposensitization, otherwise known as "allergy shots," have been around for pets for several decades now. You might think this is overkill, but I strongly recommend them. Anyone medicating a dog daily with drugs that may have copious side effects will attest to the benefit of a once-a-month allergy shot. Allergy shots do not always completely relieve allergic signs, but they often reduce the degree of signs and the amount of medication needed to control them.

Giving the shots is a breeze. Your vet will teach you how to do this. In increasing volumes,

YEAST SKIN INFECTIONS

Most dogs with chronic dermatitis have an overgrowth of *Malassezia pachydermatis,* a yeast that normally lives on the skin and in the ears of dogs. This happens due to a decrease in the immune defenses of the skin. Seborrhea, an increase in oils in the skin, can also allow yeast to overgrow. These dogs have a bad smell no matter how often you wash them. But wash them you must, preferably with a malassezia-reducing shampoo, or an anti-

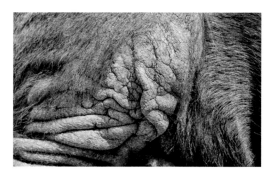

seborrhea shampoo to decrease the oil in the coat. An inexpensive but effective product for this is Head and Shoulders shampoo. In cases where you need a little more help, your vet can prescribe an antifungal medication.

Skin test

you simply inject 0.1 milliliter of allergy serum until you get up to 1 milliliter. After that, you give a booster shot once every 21 days or so. In one to two years, your pet will be less allergic to the substances—maybe not 100 percent, but you'll be giving less allergy medication and seeing far fewer ear infections and hot spots. It's well worth it.

Not all dogs need allergy shots of course. It depends on the severity and the time frame of the allergies. Allergy medications also have a downside, at least the older ones like prednisone, which can be hard on the organs. The newer immune-suppressing allergy medications are a different story. It's almost miraculous how they can stop allergic signs in dogs with no notable side effects (except the cost!). The new medication Apoquel (oclacitinib) made my shepherd, Jake, a different dog with virtually no side effects. Cats can also suffer from atopy, just not as often. Prednisone is routinely used to treat atopy in cats.

Atopic dermatitis normally raises its itchy head between puppyhood and six years of age. If you go the medication route, you could be dealing with a decade or more of allergy medications, which is also something to consider when deciding which treatment course to take. Use this rule of thumb: If your dog has significant allergies and itching for more than six months of the year, try the shots. You can always add the meds later and will probably be able to use fewer of them.

Regardless of the medication you use, always augment treatment with routine oatmeal baths and omega-3 fatty acid supplements. Research is spotty, but most vets agree that omega-3s make the skin healthier and more resistant to inflammation, plus they have other benefits like improving blood flow and brain function. ■

CHAPTER 25

Cardiac Disease

The prognosis for heart disease depends on its severity and how long it has gone untreated. This is why it's so important to see your vet for that annual physical exam and learn to recognize the signs of early heart disease. Some animals can be treated for congestive heart failure for years. For those with late-detected disease, treatment can only help whatever function remains. Signs of cardiac (heart) disease include exercise intolerance (a decrease in energy and endurance during physical activity), increased breathing rate, coughing, difficulty breathing, bluish gums, fluid in the abdomen, and fainting spells, which we vets call "syncope."

To diagnose cardiac disease, your vet will listen to your pet's heart and lungs, take chest x-rays, do an electrocardiogram (ECG), and possibly an echocardiogram, which is an ultrasound examination of the heart. Treatment for cardiac disease is highly dependent on the type of disease. Cardiac drugs have two possible targets. The first type of drug targets the heart itself, increasing heart rate or heart pumping force. Digoxin is a well-known example. The second type focuses on the blood vessels or volume of fluid the heart has to pump to make it easier for the heart to work. Enalapril and Lasix (furosemide) are well-known examples of these drugs. Often these two types of drugs are used together.

CARDIOMYOPATHY

Cardiomyopathy is an enlargement of the heart. This happens either because the heart builds up too much muscle (hypertrophic cardiomyopathy), and therefore has too little room for the blood, or because the muscle becomes stretched out (dilatative cardiomyopathy) to the point that it can no longer contract well. Either way, symptoms include signs of heart failure, such as weakness and breathing problems with cough. Cats are primarily affected, but other animals are also susceptible. In the dog world, sadly Doberman pinschers are too often afflicted.

One of the more miserable side effects of advanced hypertrophic cardiomyopathy in male cats is an aortic thromboembolism (blood clot). The failing heart cannot pump blood effectively, which causes erratic blood movement. This leads to clots, which careen around the body and often land in the lower abdominal aorta, stopping blood flow to the hind legs. Cats afflicted with aortic thromboemboli can't use their hind legs, resulting in very cold and extremely painful hind limbs. This is tragic to see and, unfortunately, when this happens, it usually means the cardiomyopathy has progressed too far to treat. Humane euthanasia is the most compassionate option for these cats.

CONGESTIVE HEART FAILURE

Congestive heart failure (CHF) affects all animals. It can be caused by valve disease, left-sided heart enlargement, or pulmonary artery disease. Since CHF affects the lungs, it usually shows up as breathing difficulty, rapid breathing, a chronic cough, and weakness.

Most commonly, heart disease affects the left side of the heart, where it can cause a syndrome where fluid builds up in the lungs, leading to CHF. If the disease occurs on the right side of the heart, it affects all the abdominal organs and can cause weakness, difficulty breathing, liver enlargement,

and fluid retention in the abdomen that results in abdominal distension. Heartworms can also cause right-sided heart disease. This is end-stage heart failure, but it can be managed, at least for a time, by treating the underlying cardiac disease with medications, including diuretics like Lasix (furosemide) to decrease overall fluid in the body, making it easier for the heart to pump blood.

HEART MURMURS

When we listen to your pet's heart, we're listening for irregular heartbeats, as well as sounds that don't belong there. Those sounds are called murmurs. Many young animals (under four months) have heart murmurs that go away by the time they're adolescents. For others, murmurs are an early indication of heart abnormalities, which must be watched, repaired, or treated.

Heart murmurs are especially common in dogs but also occur in other animals. If your vet hears a murmur in an adult animal, she will probably want to do an echocardiogram to determine the cause.

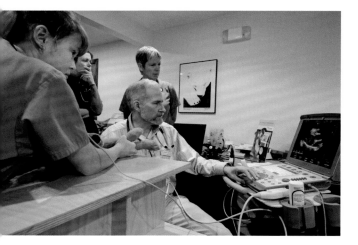

The most common problem by far is mitral valve prolapse. It manifests with a unique sound heard with a stethoscope. This can be congenital. It can also be due to adult heart disease, such as cardiomyopathy. It is also very common, and manageable, in older dogs, especially small and toy breeds. Sometimes only conservative treatment is necessary (prevent overexertion and cut down on salt). However, mitral murmurs may indicate that underlying heart disease exists, which must be diagnosed and treated with medication. Murmurs in cats are especially serious; all cats with murmurs should have an echocardiogram.

HEARTWORM

Heartworms (*Dirofilaria immitis*) can infect dogs (most commonly), cats, and ferrets. In rare cases, they can also infect humans. Transmitted by mosquitoes, heartworms enter the bloodstream through the mosquito's bite. These tiny baby worms, called microfilaria, grow into foot-long heartworms that end up in the heart and lungs. The adult worms then breed and make more microfilaria, which migrate to the pet's peripheral vessels and are picked up again when a mosquito bites. The microfilaria grow inside the mosquito until they're ready to be deposited into another dog. Heartworm is endemic to most of the United States and some parts of Canada. According to the American Heartworm Society, heartworm disease has been identified in all 50 states and is increasing in every area of the United States each year.

Heartworm disease is a great masquerader. It can cause respiratory problems like shortness of breath and cough, heart disease like weakness and

PDA, THE WORRISOME PUPPY MURMUR

A few years ago, a Samoyed puppy named Princess came to the San Diego Humane Society with a congenital heart problem called a patent ductus arteriosus (PDA). This puppy's heart murmur was concerning. It's caused when a small duct between the vessels leaving the heart fails to seal after birth. Without this seal, blood from the heart leaks backward between the pulmonary vessels, allowing nonoxygenated blood to be pumped out of the heart into the body. Without surgery, PDA puppies almost certainly die. The surgery, however, is very straightforward and successful. Princess had the surgery and today she's thriving with her new mom, who had a similar surgery when she was a child!

exercise intolerance, or even digestive problems like nausea and vomiting. It can also exist for years without any signs at all. Nearly all untreated heartworm disease is deadly, which is tragic considering how easy this disease is to prevent.

Approved by the American Heartworm Society, the following protocol will kill heartworms within one to three months:

1. Start a heartworm preventive. This won't kill the adult heartworms, but it will kill the babies before they grow into adults.
2. Give two Immiticide (melarsomine) injections 24 hours apart. A repeated course may sometimes be needed in severe cases once the microfilariae have developed into adults.
3. Restrict exercise; rest for at least two full months after the injections.
4. Retest for heartworms in six months.

The best treatment by far is prevention. Dogs should be on heartworm preventive their entire lives, starting by six months old. This magic number is when the microfilariae can develop into adult heartworms. Heartworm prevention has evolved greatly over the past 20 years. We've gone from a daily chewable tablet to monthly chews, and even four- and six-month tablets and injections. Today, many of these products also combine flea control, intestinal parasite treatment, and even tick and mange control. Unlike dogs, cats can't be treated for adult heartworms, so it's a good thing heartworm disease is relatively rare in cats. Talk to your vet about giving your cat a monthly preventive if you live in a highly endemic area.

Give monthly preventives at the same time each month. Regardless of where you live, use the preventive all year. All it takes is a warm spell in January to bring out the mosquitoes. This will also save you from having to come in for a heartworm test before restarting the medication every spring. With the multiple uses of heartworm preventives these days (intestinal worms, fleas, ticks, and heartworm), there's really no point in discontinuing the medication for a few months during the winter.

Heartworms develop so slowly that it can take years to show signs of the disease. All dogs, even those on year-round heartworm preventives, should be tested regularly for occult (hidden) heartworm disease so you can be sure the preventive is working. This routine test takes just a few drops of blood to identify if your dog is infected with adult worms. ■

CHAPTER 26

Ear and Eye Disorders

With ear and eye problems, your pet's hearing or vision could be at stake, so don't delay making a veterinary appointment when you suspect something might be wrong. Although it's often easy to see when something is amiss in the eyes (squinting, tearing, redness, or discharge), the ears can be trickier, especially if your pet has floppy ears. Make a habit of looking inside your pet's ears every week or so just to make sure everything looks okay. Normal, healthy ears should look clean and smell pleasant. If you notice any redness, heavy debris, or discharge in or around the ear canal or if you detect a foul odor, a vet visit is in order.

EAR ISSUES

Ear problems are among the most common issues that veterinarians see in dogs, cats, and rabbits. Your pet's ear is made up of three parts: external ear, middle ear, and inner ear. Problems can arise in each of these areas separately or in combination. Signs of a potential problem with the ear include swelling, redness, foul odor, heavy debris or crusting in the ear canal, head shaking or scratching at the ears, and hearing difficulty.

Aural Hematomas

Aural (ear) hematomas are pockets of blood that well up between the cartilage and skin layer of the ear flap (pinna) in dogs. We occasionally see these in cats and other animals. Most commonly, hematomas occur due to aggressive head shaking or ear scratching, which causes ruptures in the blood vessels within the ear flaps. Usually an underlying issue like an ear infection, allergies, or, in cats, ear mites causes the pet to shake his head or scratch at his ears, which then results in the hematoma.

Treatment for aural hematoma consists of addressing the underlying cause of the head shaking. If caught early, dog hematomas can be drained with a needle, after which a long-acting steroid is injected directly into the site on the ear. Usually, however, surgery is needed to open up the hematoma and relieve the pressure. The surgeon then sutures in a drain to keep the fluid from reaccumulating or sutures the inside of the ear together to keep the hematoma from re-forming. Neither is a whole lot of fun, and both require an E-collar for two to three weeks. Some vets do this surgery using lasers, in which case sutures might

not even be needed. Either way, this is not the most fun for you or your dog.

Deafness

We see a fair amount of deafness in dogs and cats. It can be caused by many things, including trauma to the ear canal, nerve damage, or chronic ear infections. Most often, though, deafness is passed on congenitally, meaning it's inherited. In cats, deafness is most common in white cats, especially white cats with blue eyes. Two pigmentation genes are often associated with deafness in dogs: the merle gene, seen in such breeds as Australian shepherds, collies, and dachshunds, and the piebald gene, seen in such breeds as bulldogs, Dalmatians, and English setters. Nearly 30 percent of Dalmatians might be deaf or partially deaf.

Older animals, like older people, may become deaf over time. If your dog seems unresponsive to his name, squeaky toys, or loud noises, he might be deaf. In cats, this isn't as straightforward since no self-respecting cat would acknowledge a mere

human calling her name. Neither dogs nor cats can control the subtle twitching of their ears when they hear a noise, so that's a big tipoff too. Finally, most deaf animals are very sound sleepers.

Sometimes only one ear is affected, which makes it harder to diagnose. In these situations, the brain stem auditory evoked response (BAER) test can help. This test is fairly expensive and usually available only through an internal medicine specialist. Since there's no treatment potential, the test is typically only administered to determine the breeding potential of animals prone to deafness.

YOUR RABBIT'S EARS

Rabbits can develop inflammation of the middle ear (otitis media) and the inner ear (otitis interna), usually due to a bacterial infection that spreads from the outer to the inner ear. These infections are most commonly caused by bacteria, fungal yeast, or ear mites. Left untreated, it can spread to the nasal passages, throat, and vestibular system (which affects balance). Infection of the middle or inner ear can cause a severe head tilt. Lop-eared rabbits are less affected, but any bunny can get an ear infection. Your vet will prescribe long-term antibiotics and antifungals to cure the infection. The best prevention is checking your bunny's ears weekly and cleaning them when needed.

Ear Infections

Ear infections (otitis) are common in pets. They are generally caused by a cycle of inflammation and itching that leads to scratching or head shaking, infection, and more inflammation. In dogs, most ear infections are caused by bacteria and yeast infections. Such infections often start because of allergies, which cause inflammation inside the ear and lead to an environment where bacteria and yeast thrive. In cats, most infections are due to ear mites (see "Mites" in Chapter 13).

You can be the first to identify an infection by examining your pet's ears regularly, especially if he's shaking his head, a major clue that an infection is present. If the inside of the earflap is red and has crusts or black wax in it, it's time for a vet visit. Your vet will look deeper into the ear to check the extent of the problem, as well as the health of the eardrum and sound apparatus. Inspect and clean your pet's ears at least weekly (more frequently depending on your pet's history), and you'll always be on top of a pending infection if it happens.

For most animals, ear infections are easy to treat. Your vet will do a deep ear cleaning in the clinic and usually send you home with ear antibiotics with steroid drops. At home, clean the ears once a day (see Chapter 14) and apply the medication as directed. Most infections clear up in a week or two.

For some dogs, however, an ear infection is anything but simple. Cocker spaniels especially are cursed with what seems like never ending infections in their ears. These chronic cases require routine ear cleaning followed by eardrops. It's vital to determine the underlying cause, such as seborrhea (see sidebar page 337), atopic

dermatitis, or food allergy. Depending on the extent of the infection, oral medications might also be necessary. New allergy medications work wonders in many of these dogs. In the worst cases, ablation surgery might be necessary to close up the ear canals and alleviate the symptoms permanently. That's nowhere near an optimal solution, but the relief it gives these poor dogs is worth it.

EYE PROBLEMS

The eye is a delicate organ. Irritation, allergies, infection, injuries, tear production disorders, and tumors can all cause the eyes to water, tear, or drip; in extreme cases, your pet can lose an eye. If you suspect an eye problem, it's important to see your vet as soon as possible so it can be treated before the damage is irreversible. Common signs of eye problems include squinting, rubbing at the eye(s), tearing or mucousy discharge from the corners, redness of the whites (sclera) of the eye(s), and swelling of the pink tissue (called conjunctiva) seen inside the lids.

Blindness

Never think you have to euthanize a pet simply because he's blind. Although blindness is a sad outcome for any pet, animals are very adaptive. Most blind animals continue to have a good quality of life and do very well if you don't make abrupt changes to their routine or the layout of your home. Blindness, which affects all species, can be present at birth or develop slowly over time. Some common genetic conditions you should be aware of are collie eye anomaly (CEA), progressive retinal atrophy (PRA), and sudden acquired retinal degeneration syndrome (SARDS).

CEA is a congenital and inherited disease caused by a simple autosomal recessive gene

defect in collies. It can be mild and manageable with medication, or it can cause full-blown blindness. Collies, Shetland sheepdogs, Australian shepherds, and other herding breeds should be tested for this gene to avoid breeding the disorder into their line. Ask your breeder if she tested the parents for this gene before buying a purebred puppy of one of these breeds.

PRA refers to a group of genetic diseases that affect many breeds, including cocker spaniels, collies, Labrador retrievers, miniature schnauzers, miniature and toy poodles, and Siberian huskies. Breeders of dogs known to be susceptible should test their dogs to determine if they carry the gene for PRA (ask to see the test results on the parents before buying a puppy). The first symptom is often a decrease in night vision, but many dogs with PRA are never diagnosed until their vision is nearly gone. Sadly, there is no treatment.

SARDS is a disease of older animals and particularly affects Brittanys, dachshunds, Maltese, miniature schnauzers, and pugs. Females are more than half as likely to be afflicted as males. With SARDS, the light-sensing cells of the retina, the rods and cones, suddenly die. This might be due to an autoimmune disease, a metabolic disease like diabetes, or an allergic reaction; we just don't know. There are no genetic or diagnostic tests to identify it. Blindness is the end result, and there's no treatment.

Cherry Eye

Cherry eye is the common term for a prolapsed gland of the third eyelid (nictitans membrane). Dogs and cats, as well as a few other animals, have a third eyelid that humans don't have; it protects the eyes from dust and other debris. You might see this small, whitish-tan eyelid roll diagonally up from the lower inside corner of the eye to the upper outside corner, much like a roman shade.

Cherry eye is so named because when the third eyelid gland prolapses, it looks like a red mass protruding from the lower inside corner of the dog's eyelid. It can affect one or both eyes. Cherry eye might be an inherited disease and certainly seems so due to its predisposition in beagles, bloodhounds, bulldogs, cocker spaniels, Lhasa apsos, and shih tzu. Theoretically, this syndrome can also affect cats, but it's rare.

Repair is fairly routine, but it's best done by someone with a lot of experience with this surgery. That can be your regular vet who has considerable experience with cherry eyes or a veterinary ophthalmologist. If the repair is done improperly, the suture can irritate or even damage the cornea. Even in the best of hands, the repair can fail and the gland can prolapse again. In the past, we used to advise cutting the gland out altogether. Since the third eyelid gland produces a great deal of healthy lubrication to the eye, it's better to leave it in. Dogs with cherry eye should not be bred to avoid passing on the trait.

Conjunctivitis

Conjunctivitis is inflammation of the tissues surrounding the eye. Commonly called pinkeye, it's the most common cause of eye discharge. In dogs, cats, and rabbits, it's commonly caused by allergies. Allergic conjunctivitis is treated with cortisone eye ointment or drops, but we first need to rule out a corneal injury or ulcer (see below) before starting treatment. If there's a corneal injury, cortisone will inhibit healing and possibly lead to a rupture in the cornea. For this reason, if your pet develops eye discharge or redness, never use eye medication leftover from his last bout of conjunctivitis without first seeing your vet for an exam. And certainly, never use your own!

Corneal Ulcers

The cornea is the transparent, clear membrane that covers the front of the eye. Composed of five layers, it's the major line of protection for the eye.

Injuries to this membrane can range from a small scratch to a full ulceration. Injury to the deepest layer of the cornea is called a descemetocele, and it's the most serious corneal ulcer because it can lead to a rupture.

Corneal ulcers can happen because of trauma, autoimmune disease, keratoconjunctivitis sicca (dry eye), or viral or bacterial infections. Rarely, endocrine diseases like diabetes mellitus and hypothyroidism can cause corneal ulcers. Short-nosed (brachycephalic) dog breeds are prone to corneal ulcers due to more prominent eyes with subsequent increased exposure of the cornea. Signs of corneal ulcers include redness, squinting (which we call blepharospasm), discharge, and pain.

Corneal ulcers are diagnosed through a simple test done by applying a drop of fluorescent green fluorescein dye in the affected eye. The dye is then gently rinsed out and the eye is observed for residual stain. Any remaining dye will stick to the

TEAR STAINING IN WHITE DOGS

I've been asked how to get rid of tear stains on white dogs for nearly 30 years. Unfortunately, there's no good answer. People have tried everything from hydrogen peroxide to baking soda to the antibiotic tetracycline, which was thought, somewhat correctly, to decrease pigmentation in the tears. These remedies rarely help. The best answer I have is to keep your dog as clean as possible with routine bathing and use a gentle cleaning solution like a baby wipe to clean underneath the eye daily. If you do use a specialty tear-stain product for this purpose, be very careful

to avoid the eyes. Many of these contain 10 percent hydrogen peroxide, which can severely irritate the eyes.

scratch or ulceration. The dye may also indicate how extensive and deep the ulceration is.

Treatment is antibiotic eyedrops or ointment applied often. Eye injuries are painful, so pain medication is also given, either orally or as eyedrops. Atropine drops are commonly used to calm the eye and decrease spasms. In severe cases, surgery might be necessary to either repair the ulceration itself by removing scar tissue or stimulate healing by doing a procedure called a keratectomy.

Since animals resist wearing eye patches to protect their eyes, it's sometimes necessary in severe cases to temporarily suture the inner lid tissue (conjunctiva) over the eyeball while the eye heals. This allows better blood flow to the cornea, as well as some serious protection for the eye. In most cases, corneal injuries heal readily, with scratches healing the quickest in three to five days and ulcers in about two weeks.

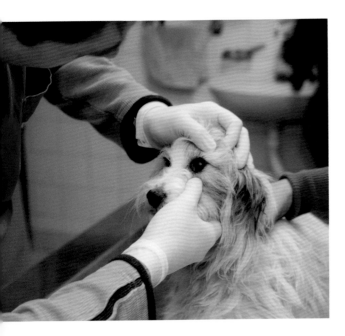

Ectropion

Ectropion is an eyelid disorder in which the lower or upper eyelid rolls outward, exposing the pink conjunctiva tissue of the eye. Ectropion is genetic in some breeds and normally occurs in young dogs and puppies. Typical breeds affected with ectropion include bassets and other hounds, mastiffs, retrievers, Saint Bernards, and spaniels. It's very rare in cats. Some of the complications of ectropion include overproduction of tears and facial staining caused by poor tear drainage, foreign object irritation because of lack of protection by the eyelids, and conjunctivitis (pinkeye).

In mild cases, no treatment is necessary. More severe cases are treated with eye lubricants and antibacterial or anti-inflammatory ointments or drops. In severe cases, the eyelids can be repaired surgically by shortening the eyelids and even doing a doggie face-lift to alleviate the droopiness.

Entropion

The opposite of ectropion is entropion, a genetic condition in which the eyelids are inverted (folded into the eye). This is a far more serious disorder than ectropion because the inverted eyelids can damage the eye. Eyelashes can scratch and irritate the corneas, leading to ulcers and scarring, which can affect vision. This disorder is nearly always diagnosed in young puppies.

Entropion rarely affects cats with the exception of a related disorder, feline eyelid agenesis, a congenital issue in which a kitten's eyelids don't grow correctly. The eyelids can be involuted and roll inward, shortened along the eye, or both, with lashes irritatingly inverted into the eye. This condition can cause enough damage to require the eye or eyes to be removed altogether. Don't let it get to this point.

Entropion is common in Chinese shar-pei and nearly always needs to be corrected to retain normal vision. Other affected breeds include basset hounds, bloodhounds, cocker spaniels, retrievers, and setters. All of the brachycephalic (short-nosed) breeds are prone due to their facial shape. Entropion can also affect giant breeds like great Pyrenees, mastiffs, and Newfoundlands.

Chronic eye discharge is one sign that entropion is present. The problem can be microscopic and is best diagnosed by a veterinary ophthalmologist. It's critical for breeders to pay close attention to their puppies to check for entropion. If a pup's eyes don't open by four or five weeks old, there's likely a problem with the eyelids.

Treatment is nearly always surgical. The eyelids are sutured so the lids and lashes face outward. Eye ointments are prescribed, and the result is usually good. In some very severe cases, facial surgery might be required.

Eyelash Disorders

The most common eyelash disorders are distichiasis, ectopic cilia, and trichiasis. Distichiasis refers to abnormal growth of lashes along the eyelid margins. These grow from tiny glands in the eyelids that shouldn't produce lashes. Ectopic cilia are lashes (cilia) that emerge from the underside of the lids on either the upper or lower eyelids. Trichiasis refers to normal lashes around the eye that poke into the eye. Lhasa apsos and shih tzu are the poster dogs for this problem. All three of these misdirected hair disorders can be extremely painful and cause damage to the eye. The best treatment is permanent removal of the involved lashes and

close grooming of all the hair around the eyes for breeds with trichiasis. Your veterinarian or a veterinary eye specialist can use laser or cryoablation (freezing) techniques to permanently remove these lash invaders, although sometimes the treatment must be repeated if new lashes emerge. Lasers should be used with caution as they might be too traumatic for the eyelids if multiple sites are treated.

Glaucoma

Glaucoma is defined as increased pressure in the eye due to the eye's inability to drain fluid normally. It can be the primary disease or secondary to other eye problems, such as lens disease, scarring, and tumors. Secondary glaucoma is much more common than primary. Increased pressure in the fluid of the eye causes pain, redness, bulging of the eye, increased discharge, uveitis (cloudy appearance to the eye), dilated pupil, and high pressure within the eye.

Glaucoma is extremely painful. Heartbreakingly, some animals even press their heads against furniture or a wall in an attempt to relieve the pain. Left untreated, glaucoma will damage the optic nerve and cause blindness. Certain dog breeds have a higher incidence. These include chow chows, cocker spaniels, poodles, Samoyeds, and Siberian huskies. Of all dogs affected with glaucoma, 40 percent will become blind regardless of treatment.

EYE REMOVAL

Removal of the eye, called enucleation, is a viable option to providing a good quality of life for animals who otherwise have chronic pain. The procedure is straightforward in experienced hands. See an ophthalmologist if you can, but most general veterinarians are comfortable with the surgery. (They'll tell you if they're not.) Animals do well after surgery, which has a fairly quick recovery. Most animals adjust extremely well to the loss of their eye or eyes, especially since they might have already had compromised vision long before the surgery happens.

If your vet suspects glaucoma based on the signs, she will measure the pressure within the eye using a handheld device called a tonometer. Treatment includes eyedrops and ointments to decrease the pressure. The goal is to treat before the optic nerve is damaged, but unfortunately, the disease might have been active for a while before owners recognize it. In cases where it's no longer possible to control the high pressure, the eye must be removed. That sounds terrible, but when you consider that this permanently stops the pain, it's a very good option.

Keratoconjunctivitis Sicca

Some dogs and cats produce too few tears. This is called keratoconjunctivitis sicca (KCS), otherwise known as dry eye. With KCS, the cornea dries out due to inflammation of the tissues of the eye. It is caused by either inadequate tear production or a change in the composition of the tears them-

selves. It can be genetic, caused by the environment (for instance, living in dry Phoenix rather than sultry New Orleans), or caused by medications. This can be an immune-mediated disease, in which the body attacks its own tear-producing cells, or caused by viruses like herpes in cats or distemper in dogs. Some drugs can also cause KCS. Your vet will be careful using these drugs in dogs with a predisposition to KCS (see below). Left untreated, KCS will cause conjunctivitis and even corneal ulceration.

The breeds most affected by KCS are bulldogs, hounds, Lhasa apsos, Pekingese, pugs, shih tzu, spaniels (cockers especially), and terriers. Cats and other species rarely get KCS, but it's possible for them to develop dry eye secondary to other diseases. Pannus is treated with lifelong topical corticosteroids or antibiotics, or both, to manage the condition. Most dogs do well with good management.

Signs of KCS include red, irritated eyes, with lots of blinking and squinting. KCS usually affects both eyes. Dry eye of any type is diagnosed via a Schirmer tear test. Your vet will place thin pieces of moisture-wicking paper inside your dog's lower eyelids to measure the production of tears. It takes only one minute for a diagnosis.

KCS is manageable, but treatment is lifelong, with the goal of stimulating tear production and replacing the tears with several

GIVING EYE MEDICATIONS

Here's a simple way to give eyedrops or ointment. Gently pull down the skin below the inside corner of the lower eyelid. You'll see a small cup form in the corner. Squeeze a small drop of liquid or ointment right in the cup and release the lid. The medication will spread over the entire eye when your pet blinks. If you have to, you can also put ointment on your index finger to apply the same way, although this isn't as clean. When administering eye medications, take care not to touch the tip of the dropper or tube to the eye.

eyedrops. In rare and intractable cases, surgery might be considered to transplant the duct from one of the salivary glands in the mouth to lubricate the eyes. This might sound strange, but salivary fluid is an excellent replacement for tears.

Pannus

Pannus, or chronic superficial keratitis (CSK), used to be considered a form of KCS. Today it's considered a separate, most likely immune-mediated disease that is inherited. It affects German shepherds more than any other dog, although other breeds can get it, including Australian shepherds, Belgian Tervuren, border collies, greyhounds, and Siberian huskies. It looks different from KCS in that a raised pink mass appears on the cornea of one or both eyes. Left untreated, it can spread and scar the eye, causing blindness. Pannus is typically treated with a combination of lifelong topical corticosteroids and other immunosuppressing drugs, and antibiotics as needed to manage the condition. Most dogs do well with good management.

Uveitis

Uveitis is a painful condition affecting the front of the eye underneath the cornea where the blood vessels are. It causes eye pain, redness, tearing, and squinting and might even lead to vision impairment. It can also lead to cloudy eyes and even glaucoma. Uveitis can have many causes, including autoimmune disease, viral and bacterial infections, parasites, injury, or tumors. There are two types of uveitis: anterior and posterior, which refer to the front or back of the eye respectively. Anterior uveitis is much more common than posterior. Treatment depends on the cause, but often an antibiotic or corticosteroid ointment or drops are prescribed. Uveitis can become a chronic disease. In those cases, a veterinary ophthalmologist can help with long-term treatment. ■

CHAPTER 27

Endocrine Disorders

The endocrine system affects nearly every organ system through hormones secreted by glands throughout the body. This complex system of chemical signals regulates every function of the body, including growth, blood sugar regulation, water retention, stress regulation, and sexual development. Many different glands make up the endocrine system, including the adrenal gland, ovaries and testicles, pancreas, pituitary gland, thyroid, and parathyroid. All of these glands secrete different hormones that work together to keep the body functioning. When hormones are lacking or not functioning properly, everything else breaks down.

Although different disorders have their own distinct symptoms, some common signs that something might be amiss with your pet's endocrine system include increased drinking and urination, increased hunger, panting, hair loss, potbellied appearance, muscle weakness, and lack of energy.

ADDISON'S DISEASE

Among all the disorders caused by hormone malfunction, none are more serious than Addison's disease (hypoadrenocorticism). All mammals have two adrenal glands, located near each kidney, that produce corticosteroids (stress hormones) and mineralocorticoids (hormones that regulate kidney and urinary flow). This disease is caused by alterations in the production of these hormones. We don't entirely know why this happens, but an immune-mediated destruction of the adrenal glands is suspected, especially when the disease affects young dogs. Later-onset cases might be caused by a tumor in the adrenal gland, certain drugs, or even overtreating Cushing's disease (hyperadrenocorticism).

Signs of Addison's disease are difficult to recognize, so diagnosis often occurs late. Typical signs include lack of appetite (anorexia), weakness, vomiting, dehydration, weight loss, and sometimes bloody stools. Although these symptoms can occur with many diseases, vets know that continual vomiting is a red flag and could indicate this disease. Addison's disease frequently affects young to middle-aged dogs, more often female than male. It's rare in cats. The disease is more common in standard poodles, bearded collies, Portuguese water dogs, soft-coated wheaten terriers, West Highland white terriers, and Rottweilers.

Addison's patients have abnormal electrolyte levels due to alterations in the kidney's ability to filter waste. This leads to a very high potassium level and low sodium level. The real diagnosis comes from an ACTH stimulation test, which measures an animal's cortisone response. A low response confirms the disease.

High potassium is not compatible with life, so the seriousness of Addison's disease cannot be overstated. The disease will progress to the point of shock if the dog is overly stressed. This is called an Addisonian crisis and is a true life-or-death emergency. Treatment is lifelong and involves an injectable medication to replace the mineralocorticoid that the adrenals can't produce. Oral prednisone is also often given to replenish the body's inability to make cortisol. This is not an easy disease, but it can be managed for a normal quality of life.

CUSHING'S DISEASE

The opposite of Addison's disease is Cushing's disease (hyperadrenocorticism), which is caused by excess production of corticosteroids by the adrenal glands. Cushing's affects middle-aged and older dogs, with a slight predisposition to female dogs over males. There are no reported cases of Cushing's in cats.

There are two forms of Cushing's disease. The more common form is pituitary-dependent hyperadrenocorticism (PDH). This form is caused by a usually benign tumor in the pituitary gland, which is attached to the base of the brain. The less common form is adrenal-dependent hyperadrenocorticism (ADH), which is caused by a tumor on the adrenal gland, which might be benign or malignant. PDH accounts for approximately 85 percent of all cases of Cushing's disease.

Signs of Cushing's disease include increased appetite, weight gain, panting, lethargy, a potbellied appearance, increased drinking and urina-

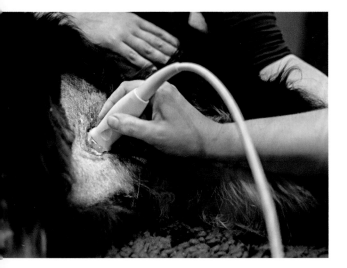

tion, skin rashes, and hair loss. A rare skin disorder called "calcinosis cutis" causes chronic inflammation due to deposits of calcium in the skin. Abnormal blood work or urinalysis tests are followed by a day-long blood test called a low-dose dexamethasone suppression test. Once your pet is diagnosed with Cushing's, the next step is determining what's causing the disease. This requires either another day's blood test or possibly an ultrasound examination of the adrenals.

Dogs with Cushing's can live normal lives. Treatment depends on the type. PDH doesn't always need to be treated. The pituitary tumor is usually benign, and the disease may cause minimal symptoms, so your vet might just want to monitor it. If symptoms are bothering you or your dog or they are progressing, it's time to treat. PDH can be treated with medication, either Lysodren, which must be given daily, or trilostane, which can sometimes be given weekly. The trick is to maintain the correct dosage by monitoring symptoms and checking blood work. With ADH where only one adrenal gland is enlarged, medication may be used to shrink the adrenal gland before surgery to remove it. If both adrenals are enlarged, the disease is most likely caused by a malignant tumor. Unfortunately, no treatment is possible since we can't remove both adrenal glands. This is extremely uncommon and very sad when it happens.

DIABETES

Diabetes mellitus is an all too common disease involving the hormone insulin, which is produced by the pancreas and is crucial in allowing

the body to use glucose (sugar) from food. There are two forms of diabetes: Type 1 diabetes is caused by a lack of insulin production. Type 2 diabetes is caused by a combination of impaired production of insulin, along with an inadequate response to it. In dogs, type 1 is more common; cats suffer more often from type 2 diabetes. The most common symptoms of diabetes are increased drinking and urination, along with weight loss over time. Other signs might be progressive and include weakness, vomiting and diarrhea, urinary tract infections, skin infections, and cataracts.

Causes of diabetes in dogs include genetics, autoimmune disease, chronic pancreatitis, obesity, and even some medications, such as long-term prednisone treatment. Female dogs older than six and certain breeds might be more predisposed to diabetes—dachshunds, golden retrievers, keeshonden, poodles, Samoyeds, and schnauzers—but any breed is susceptible. In cats, obesity is the most common cause.

Treatment includes weight reduction through diet and exercise because obesity inhibits the body from responding normally to insulin. If your diabetic pet is not spayed, it's recommended to do so because female reproductive hormones can have a profound effect on sugar levels.

Some early diabetes cases will respond to a high-fiber diet, which slows the production of glucose, and possibly oral medication. In cats, weight loss and high-fiber might be the complete treatment. Most diabetic dogs and cats, however, require daily or twice-daily insulin injections. Don't panic! Although insulin shots are certainly a commitment, it's much easier than it sounds. Your vet will show you how to give the injection

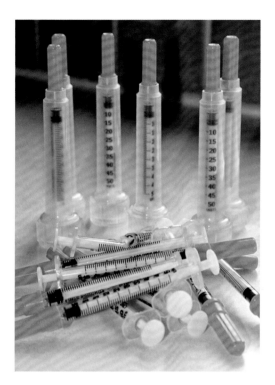

using a tiny insulin needle. Pets barely notice the injections. The biggest challenge is maintaining a consistent feeding schedule followed by the insulin injection.

If you notice your pet drinking and urinating more and losing weight, make an appointment to see your vet as soon as possible. Delaying could increase the chances your pet has a diabetic crisis, otherwise known as diabetic ketoacidosis. This is when glucose levels are high enough to affect electrolytes, the heart, kidneys, liver, and even the brain. This situation is truly an emergency. Diabetic crisis patients are weak, vomiting, and often near collapse. If this happens, your pet needs intensive care, IV electrolyte-repairing fluids, and insulin to regulate blood sugar. Normal sugar levels for dogs are about the same as ours—roughly 100 milligrams per deciliter. Cats

top out at between 150 and 250, especially when they're stressed. The best way to check glucose levels at home is by using a pet glucometer, a blood glucose meter that is made for dogs and cats. Your veterinarian can show you how to do this, and most diabetic pets tolerate it well. At-home blood sugar testing helps you and your vet monitor how well your dog or cat is responding to insulin treatment.

Diabetes is a complex disease that's potentially life-threatening. Proper diet and exercise are essential. Untreated diabetes causes chronic urinary tract infections, cataracts and blindness, electrolyte disturbances, and eventually death. When treated, dogs and cats can live normal, happy lives.

HYPERTHYROIDISM

Hyperthyroidism, an overproduction of thyroid hormone, is a common disease in cats. The number of affected cats is probably even higher than we realize since many are not diagnosed. (Dogs typically get hypothyroidism, an underproduction of thyroid hormone; see below.)

Thyroid hormone, which is produced by the thyroid gland located in the neck, regulates metabolism, energy consumption, growth, and even the production of other hormones. In cats, overproduction of this hormone is usually due to a benign tumor in the thyroid gland. Too much thyroid hormone can have devastating effects. Symptoms might include weight loss, increased appetite, increased heart rate, overstimulation, vomiting, and possibly increased thirst and urination. Often only the weight loss is typically evident. Hyperthyroidism frequently affects cats between five and 13 years of age, but cats of any age can be afflicted. Diagnosis is confirmed with a blood test to check for levels of the thyroid hormone T4.

Hyperthyroidism can be treated with a medication called methimazole, especially when concurrent kidney disease is involved. However, the gold standard treatment for feline hyperthyroidism is radiation: a single injection of iodine 131. This treatment requires a specialist. Cats get a one-time, one-week stay in the hospital for quarantine while the radiation is being excreted from the body. Radiation treatment, although relatively costly, is a permanent cure, so you never have to worry about thyroid medication (or its expense) again. In older cats, whose kidneys may be working overtime, radiation isn't usually advised since the treatment will permanently slow down what remains of effective kidney flow. This is a good discussion to have with your veterinarian.

HYPOTHYROIDISM

Hypothyroidism is an underproduction of thyroid hormones T3 and T4, usually due to an autoimmune disease in which the immune system attacks the thyroid gland. Rarely, it can also be due to a thyroid tumor. Hypothyroidism can affect any middle-aged dog, but we see it more often in cocker spaniels, Doberman pinschers, golden retrievers, and Irish setters. Spayed females and neutered males might also have a higher incidence, but we're unsure why.

Symptoms include weight gain, lethargy, poor coat and skin including chronic rashes, muscle loss, and cold intolerance. Most often, you'll just see weight gain and a dry coat. We use a combination of blood tests to diagnose hypothyroidism. It isn't life threatening, but treating it will dramatically improve the quality of your dog's life. Treatment consists of replacing the lacking thyroid hormone, available in regular or chewable pill form. ■

COMPOUNDED MEDICATIONS: LIFESAVERS FOR CATS

Cats love taking pills. Wait; no, they don't. They hate pills. And they hate anyone who tries to give them pills. Fortunately, specialty pharmacies can compound drugs that are easier to give to animals. Nearly every drug you'd have to give a cat is available as a liquid made cat palatable with fish or chicken flavoring. Some drugs can even be compounded into a topical gel that you simply apply to the skin on the neck or top of the head. These take some adjusting due to varying absorption rates, but they're a great way to ensure you and your cat remain BFFs.

CHAPTER 28

Gastrointestinal Issues

Digestion starts in the mouth and ends at the colon. Your pet cannot eat normally if something is wrong with his mouth or teeth, and problems of the digestive tract disrupt nutrient absorption. Whether suffering from a dental issue or gastrointestinal upset, signs can be similar, like inappetance (not eating or eating less) and weight loss. Even if your pet seems fine, make a habit of looking in his mouth once a week or so to check for issues like redness, bleeding, broken teeth, or a foul odor. Animals are masters at hiding pain and might continue to act normally when they have a sore mouth, even continuing to eat despite any discomfort they might feel.

THE MOUTH

Even though animals are good at hiding pain, dental issues can be seriously painful for them. General signs of a potential dental disease include painful mouth (your pet might vocalize when eating, drinking, or yawning), red gums, bleeding gums, salivating, eating on one side of the mouth, dropping food when eating, nasal discharge or sneezing, pawing at the mouth, and repeated snapping of jaws.

Broken Teeth

Broken teeth happen all the time, and you might not even know it happened until your vet discovers it at the annual exam. Although broken teeth can be repaired, many times we opt to extract rather than repair. Animals tolerate extractions well. Functionally, none of the teeth are irreplaceable for our pets. They even do fine without any teeth (as evidenced by the speed at which my German shepherd swallows treats whole). After an extraction, the pocket is either sutured closed or left open to heal on its own. Astonishingly, most animals act like nothing happened the next day. But since our pets can't tell us it hurts, always use the prescribed pain medications sent home afterward.

An extraction can be costly, but that sum pales in comparison with a complete repair. There are times, however, when you might not want to lose the tooth. If you elect to repair and restore the broken tooth, you'll need a veterinary dentist (see sidebar this page). With few exceptions, general practitioners don't have the training or equipment to restore teeth.

Retained Deciduous Teeth

Dogs and cats lose their deciduous teeth (baby teeth) around four months of age and usually have all of their adult teeth by six months. Sometimes the baby teeth don't fall out and become impacted in the gums, preventing the permanent teeth from developing. Baby teeth are considered retained if they persist longer than six months. This time line is convenient because it aligns nicely with the time to get your pet spayed or neutered. Retained teeth can be easily removed while a puppy or kitten is under anesthesia for that procedure. If you've missed the window at

VETERINARY DENTISTS

Your regular veterinarian can clean your pet's teeth and perform extractions, but when there's something more serious to evaluate or if you wish to save a tooth rather than extract it, a veterinary dentist can help. Dentistry is a credentialed specialty in veterinary medicine. Vet dentists are experts at extractions, root canals, reparative therapy, periodontal therapy, and oral surgical procedures. To find one near you, ask your regular vet for a referral, or visit the website of the American Veterinary Dental College: *avdc.org.*

the spay or neuter surgery, I prefer to wait until a dog or cat is at least six to eight months old to give the deciduous teeth a little more time to finally come out on their own.

Stomatitis

Stomatitis is a condition where the soft tissues of the mouth—the gingiva and tongue—become inflamed. If you've ever had an oral ulcer or canker, you know how painful these can be. Stomatitis can cause redness and bleeding, pain, bad breath, and drooling. In dogs, it's primarily caused by infections, abscesses, and tumors, but in cats, where it's much more common, it can be caused by bacterial, viral, or immune-mediated diseases. Treatment for stomatitis requires a visit to your vet for anti-inflammatories and antibiotics after the underlying cause is determined.

Feline stomatitis is severely painful and often chronic. If no underlying disease can be identified, we believe it to be an immune-mediated disorder. The treatment is long-term antibiotics in addition to steroid medications. In some cats, the severity and persistence of the disease require extraction of the premolars and molars, followed by the rest of the teeth if it continues. This sounds drastic, but the difference it makes in these cats' lives is profound.

Tooth Abscess

An abscess is a closed pocket of infection. At the risk of ruining your next meal, I'll just say it: An abscess is a pocket of pus. When abscesses occur in the teeth, they are truly horrible in terms of pain and severity. The carnassial teeth (the fourth premolar on both sides of the upper jaw) are those most prone to abscesses in dogs from bacteria entering the root canal. Cats, fortunately, don't get these abscesses often. Whenever we see a dog with a large swelling under the eye, the first suspect is a carnassial tooth abscess. If it's not treated, the abscess will eventually burst through the skin, but not until it possibly spreads infection throughout the face and eye.

CARING FOR YOUR RABBIT'S TEETH

Many rabbit health issues stem from poor dental health, including misaligned teeth and overgrown teeth. Rabbits' teeth grow continually, so have your vet check the mouth once a year. Some people think you should clip a rabbit's incisors when they get long. Please don't. This is painful and can lead to tooth fractures. Instead, let your vet grind the teeth down under general anesthesia. Any rabbit who is not eating well will develop overgrown teeth. A proper diet — pellets, hay, and vegetables — is essential in keeping teeth healthy and the proper length. Great information on rabbit care can be found on the House Rabbit Society website at *rabbit.org*.

TOOTH RESORPTION IN CATS

In tooth resorption, the bony substance called dentin that surrounds a tooth begins to erode, causing pain, exposed nerves, and eventually tooth destruction. We used to call these feline odontoclastic resorptive lesions, or, more simply, cervical line lesions, referring to the erosion of the area between the tooth and the gum. Over time the tooth deteriorates, causing more pain and inflammation. Tooth resorption can affect as many as 60 percent of cats, and most often, you'll never know your cat is suffering from it. They're masters at hiding pain and vulnerability, after all. Have your cat's teeth checked regularly by your vet, preferably with dental x-rays. Your cat won't thank you, because that would indicate gratitude. But her lack of pain will be all the thanks you need.

Extraction of the diseased tooth is a permanent cure. Root canal and restorative treatment are other options, albeit expensive ones. They're also not advised since extraction both removes the cause and allows for drainage. But if you opt to save the tooth, consult with a veterinary dentist (see sidebar page 303).

ESOPHAGUS, STOMACH, AND INTESTINES

For better or worse, we're intimately familiar with our pets' food processing—especially what's coming out. *Gastroenteritis* is the general term for stomachache, vomiting, and diarrhea (one or more of all of these)—basically anything from the stomach to the rectum. The gastrointestinal (GI) tract is full of "itises," the medical term for inflammation. For instance, enteritis is inflammation of the intestines, pancreatitis is inflammation of the pancreas, and colitis is inflammation of the colon.

Treatment of a GI issue depends on exactly where the problem occurs. In descending order from the mouth down, they are:

1. Esophagitis (inflammation of the esophagus)
2. Gastritis (inflammation of the stomach)
3. Pancreatitis (inflammation of the pancreas)
4. Enteritis (inflammation of the small intestine)
5. Gastroenteritis (inflammation of the stomach and intestines)
6. Colitis (inflammation of the colon)

Many GI issues result in diarrhea. It can be caused by dietary indiscretion (the medical term used for a pet who ate something he shouldn't have), infection, allergy, parasites, or endocrine disorders. Some common reasons pets get diarrhea include eating food that doesn't agree with them, eating too much food, eating nonfood, parasites, mold, and bacteria. All of these signs could also be signs of inflammatory bowel disease, endocrine diseases (hyperthyroidism, Cushing's, diabetes), toxins, and cancer.

Esophagitis

This is rare in animals, but any disorder of the esophagus is a serious problem because they are extremely difficult to identify. Signs include inappetence (not eating), regurgitation, vomiting, weight loss, coughing, and the biggest risk: aspiration pneumonia (pneumonia caused by inhaling food or liquid), which can be fatal. Regurgitation is not the same as vomiting; regurgitation is a quick return of food from the throat before it reaches the stomach, usually within seconds of ingestion.

Ask DR. GARY:

Why Do Dogs Eat Grass?

Why do some dogs, animals who would probably not eat salad greens even if their lives depended on it, eat grass like a herd of cows? Honest answer? Beats me. I can only guess that the strong smell of chlorophyll peaks their interest enough to chow down. The good news is it's a completely harmless activity. The old adage that dogs eat grass to make themselves throw up is all backward. Sure, the grass comes first and the vomit second, but that's completely unintentional on their part.

One rare esophagus disorder is megaesophagus, an enlargement of the esophagus. Generally it occurs because motility (which moves the food down the esophagus to the stomach) in the esophagus is disrupted, causing distention and enlargement. Megaesophagus is a neurologic disorder which occurs congenitally in certain breeds, including Chinese shar-pei, dachshunds, German shepherds, Labrador retrievers, great Danes, Irish setters, miniature schnauzers, and wire fox terriers, but it can occur in any dog.

Diagnosis is via endoscopy (a fiber-optic probe that examines the esophagus) or a contrast x-ray (the pet swallows a dye before the x-rays to better outline the esophagus). Treatment depends on correcting the underlying cause, but often no cause is found. Sadly, this is a disease with a poor prognosis requiring lifelong management: feeding small amounts of food, elevating the food bowl, and preventing aspiration pneumonia for as long as possible.

Gastritis

Gastritis is an inflammation of the stomach. The stomach's natural reaction is to get rid of the offender, otherwise known as vomiting. If your pet experiences a bout of vomiting, look to be sure there's not something unusual in the vomit, like a foreign object or flecks of blood. Blood generally just means that the vomiting was a bit violent, but if you continue to see blood in the vomit beyond the first day, call your vet. The usual plan of attack for continued gastritis is to withhold food for at least six hours to give the stomach a chance to calm down (you can give water), then feed a bland diet (see sidebar opposite) until all is well again. Your veterinarian might also prescribe an acid reducer

HOMEMADE BLAND DIET FOR DOGS

When your dog experiences a bout of vomiting or diarrhea, you can easily whip up a batch of food that will be
gentle on his stomach. Feed this only for a few days at
most; it's not a complete and balanced diet. If stomach
issues persist, see your vet.

1. Boil 1 pound of lean ground beef, turkey, or chicken.
   Then pour into a colander and rinse thoroughly to
   remove excess fat.
2. Cook some white rice and rinse to remove starch.
3. Mix the ground meat with the rice (1 part meat to
   2 parts rice)
4. Feed ¼ cup per 10 pounds of body weight.

Alternatively, combine plain cooked chicken breast with
rice. For cats, simply open a bottle of strained chicken baby
food and feed. When you get tired of this, ask your vet for a
few cans of special GI upset diets. These work wonders
and, dogs being dogs, I always keep a few cans on hand.

like Pepcid (famotidine). If vomiting continues for longer than a day, call your vet.

Pancreatitis

The pancreas sits between the top of the intestine (called the duodenum) and the stomach. This organ produces fat-digesting enzymes, insulin, and other compounds that the body needs to digest fats and regulate sugar. When the pancreas becomes inflamed (pancreatitis), your pet experiences vomiting, diarrhea, and lack of appetite. Painful cramps can also occur. This is much more serious than a simple gastritis.

One cause of pancreatitis is inappropriate diet, especially fatty foods. Other causes include tumors, autoimmune diseases, and inflammatory bowel disease. Pancreatitis can affect both dogs and cats, although dogs, with their proclivity for eating pretty much anything they can find, win this one by more than a nose.

Pancreatitis can range from mild lethargy and inappetence to full-blown vomiting and bloody diarrhea. When pancreatitis hits hard, it can cause so much inflammation that it starts to digest itself, something we call necrotizing pancreatitis. Rarely, it can lead to heart problems from toxins, diabetes, shock, and even death. More often, pancreatitis just causes a miserable, vomiting animal.

So how do you know if your pet is experiencing a dangerous attack of pancreatitis or something less serious like regular gastroenteritis? For one thing, pancreatitis makes pets feel very sick. They

don't eat, and they don't play. Usually this lasts for days or even longer. If your pet is vomiting or having diarrhea and acting lethargic, not eating, and just seems to be feeling really bad, visit your vet as soon as you can to rule out pancreatitis.

After diagnosis, treatment is all about giving the pancreas some down time; this includes supportive care to control symptoms like vomiting so that your pet will start to feel better and slowly begin eating again. Very sick animals need IV fluids in the hospital, but pets with mild cases go home on pain medication, anti-vomiting medication, antibiotics, an antacid, and a low-fat prescription diet. After a week or two, your vet will follow up with a recheck and blood work to make sure all is back to normal.

Pets who have had an episode of pancreatitis are prone to future episodes, so never feed high-fat foods like Thanksgiving leftovers, sausage, bacon grease, poultry skin, rich meat, and fatty scraps. You shouldn't feed these things anyway. Especially watch those counter-surfing dogs who go after anything you leave sitting out.

Enteritis

Enteritis refers to inflammation of the small intestine. It can be accompanied by both stomach upset (in which it's called gastroenteritis) or lower bowel irritation, known as colitis, or both. Signs include diarrhea and vomiting, painful abdomen, fever, and weight loss, depending on how long it's been going on. You might see blood in the diarrhea. As unpleasant as it is to see, it just means that the outer layer of cells in the intestines is sloughing.

Enteritis is common, and we don't always know why it occurs. Many things can cause it, including dietary indiscretion, parasites, bacteria and viruses, tumors, allergies, and immune-mediated diseases. Intestinal obstructions can also cause enteritis, which can complicate diagnosis and treatment due to damage to the intestines. Enteritis can be acute and short term or, unfortunately, chronic for which your vet will prescribe anti-inflammatories and diet change.

Because so many things can cause enteritis, we often lump them under the name inflammatory bowel disease (IBD) or irritable bowel syndrome (IBS). This can cause both upper or lower bowel inflammation (see "Colitis" page 310). Common in both dogs and cats, IBD can be caused by dietary intolerance to certain foods. In dogs, German shepherds, win this medal again, followed by soft coated wheaten terriers, basenjis, and Chinese shar-pei. This might be due to an allergy or because of an immune-mediated disease similar to Crohn's disease in humans. The most frequent symptoms are painful abdomen, decreased appetite, bloating, vomiting, and diarrhea with

mucus and blood. Just to confuse things, IBD can sometimes lead to constipation. Common causes of IBD include contractility issues in the intestines themselves, fiber deficiency, dietary intolerance, stress, bacteria like *Clostridia* and *E. coli,* and tumors of the GI tract.

The most definitive diagnosis is via endoscopy but this isn't always necessary; instead empiric treatment is usually chosen. Treatment of IBD is often lifelong and depends on identification of the underlying cause. If dietary intolerance is the suspected culprit, the cornerstone of treatment is avoiding compounds in the diet that are inflammatory, such as certain proteins and carbohydrates. Sometimes just eliminating one protein can change your pet's life. The goal for the life of your pet is to feed a very digestible food that is high in fiber. The trick is to identify which foods to avoid. Unfortunately, there's no simple test than can tell us this. That's why your vet will prescribe a limited-protein diet of ingredients your pet has most likely never eaten before, such as kangaroo and rabbit. Without previous exposure to these proteins, your pet won't have formed antibodies against them. The old recommendation of lamb and rice isn't good any longer. These ingredients are now common in pet food, so most dogs and cats have been sensitized to them.

If diet change alone doesn't control the disorder, medications can be used in conjunction with the diet change. For some dogs and cats, metronidazole, an antibiotic with antibacterial and anti-inflammatory properties, can resolve the major symptoms of IBD after only a few doses. Whether the disorder is due to an allergy or an autoimmune- or immune-mediated cause, immunosuppressive drugs like cyclosporine or

steroids like prednisone might help by decreasing the bowel's reactivity. Steroids are a double-edged sword, however. Long-term use can cause other bowel issues and even resistance.

IBD in cats is often immune mediated and very difficult to manage, requiring long-term prednisone therapy. Some cats don't tolerate steroids well; for them, immunosuppressants are a better bet. It's important to use the steroids in conjunction with

Ask DR. GARY:

How Can I Tell If My Pet Is Dehydrated?

If you're concerned your pet might be dehydrated, you can do a simple test. With your thumb and forefinger, gently pinch and lift the skin on the scruff of your pet's neck. Release the skin and time how long it takes to return to a normal position. In healthy dogs and cats, the skin takes less than two seconds to return to normal, but in dehydrated animals it can take two or more seconds to snap back. If you're still unsure how to do this, ask your vet to show you how.

diet change. When you find the diet that causes the least inflammation in the GI tract, stick with it. Whatever the cause, IBD is a chronic illness and needs to be managed for life.

Colitis

Colitis refers to any inflammatory disorder of the large intestine, otherwise known as the colon or lower bowel. The hallmarks of colitis are frequent, often small amounts of watery diarrhea, often with bright red blood or mucus. Don't panic: The blood is simply a sign of irritation to the colon.

In dogs, the most common causes are parasites like whipworms; bacterial infections from contaminated food, garbage ingestion, and other dietary indiscretions; immune-mediated disease; allergies to certain foods; blockages; and cancer. In cats, colitis is less common, but when it occurs, it is often caused by allergies or immune-mediated disease or, less frequently, parasites and bacterial infections.

Chronic colitis is often caused by an immune-mediated reaction to certain proteins in foods. We lump many of these into the category of food allergies or "sensitivities," referring to specific proteins that are not well or easily digested by our pets. That's why there are so many special diets for dogs that eliminate certain proteins or other ingredients that might cause bowel inflammation.

Acute colitis is treated the same way as any other form of gastroenteritis: a bland diet with no treats and something like Pepto Bismol or Imodium (loperamide) for dogs (ask your vet about these medications first but know that cats cannot have this medication). If the diarrhea continues, it's time to see your vet (bring a stool sample). Like enteritis, colitis responds well to the antibiotic metronidazole.

GARBAGE-ITIS

This sounds completely made up, but in fact, "garbage-itis" is a real diagnosis in dogs. Also called "garbage toxicosis," this is proof of a dog's ability to eat anything: the more disgusting, the better. When dogs eat old food that's been sitting in the trash, they also consume bacteria, molds, and other toxins. It's even worse if your dog eats something dead outside, as dogs will do (cats seem to  know better than to do this). The most common bacteria are *Clostridia, E. coli, Staphylococcus,* and *Streptococcus*. These cause normal gastrointestinal signs like diarrhea and vomiting, but in extreme cases, they might also cause seizures and even death. To keep your dog safe, always use garbage cans with tight-fitting lids and stow cans out of your dog's reach.

Gastroenteritis

Gastroenteritis is simply gastritis (stomach inflammation) and enteritis (small intestine inflammation) together. More a generic term, it's kind of the jackpot with vomiting and diarrhea. Gastroenteritis can occur because the GI tract is inflamed anywhere along its length, from stem to stern. It can also be due to IBD and it's pretty intense but usually short-lived. Treating gastroenteritis entails treating the vomiting and diarrhea in all the ways we've just discussed (see the sections on gastritis, enteritis, and colitis above).

Constipation

Constipation is no joke. It's a serious problem and a marker of overall health. Any animal can become constipated. A change in diet, a decrease in water consumption, a low-fiber diet, medication side effects, a decrease in exercise, and pretty much any other disease altering normal activity can all cause constipation. In cats, excessive grooming can lead to constipation because the swallowed hair slows digestion and can even cause an obstruction. Telltale signs of constipation are hard, dry stools; lack of stool; and straining.

Elderly pets are the most susceptible to constipation. Treatment includes a high-fiber diet, encouragement to drink more, stool softeners or laxatives, and increased exercise. In particularly difficult cases, enemas can help, but these should only be given by your veterinarian, not at home.

In the worst scenarios, no stool is produced. This causes abdominal pain, bloating, dehydration, and weakness. Dogs rarely suffer from this, but it's one of the worst issues to deal with for cats where long-term constipation is

FIBER: HELP FOR DIARRHEA AND CONSTIPATION

It might seem counterintuitive, but soluble fiber can help with both chronic diarrhea and acute or chronic constipation. Plain, unsweetened canned pumpkin is a great source of fiber for both dogs and cats, and many cats eat this readily with a spoonful or two mixed into their canned food. You can also use a teaspoon of Metamucil or any wheat-bran supplement mixed into wet food. Avoid citrus flavors; neither dogs nor cats like them. If your cat won't eat pumpkin or fiber supplements, try a flavored petroleum jelly supplement. These are marketed as hairball remedies.

called "obstipation" and can be life-threatening. Treatment often requires flushing out the colon under anesthesia. Since affected cats are pretty dehydrated even before this, we often keep them on IV fluids for a few days after the procedure. This also helps get things moving from a GI perspective!

Simply removing the stool might not be enough. The key is to discover why it happened. Common reasons are a dry food diet, decreased water intake, and just plain old metabolism changes. An early solution includes increasing fiber and fluids to prevent it from happening again.

LIVER DISEASE

Other than the skin, the liver is the largest organ in the body. The liver breaks down toxins and cleans the blood, metabolizes energy, makes bile acids for digestion, manufactures proteins for clotting, and metabolizes drugs. A hallmark sign of liver disease in any animal is inappetence, with the extreme version known as anorexia—lack of appetite entirely. This happens because liver disease can cause gastrointestinal inflammation and toxin buildup leading to inappetence and nausea. Other signs of liver disease are vomiting, diarrhea, increased drinking and urination, pot-bellied appearance, seizures due to excess ammonia in the blood, and jaundice (yellow discoloration in the skin, mucous membranes, and the whites of the eyes).

In puppies, we worry about a congenital malformation called a portosystemic shunt. In these cases, blood bypasses the liver instead of passing through it, which causes a dangerous buildup of toxins. Puppies with portosystemic shunts might suffer from seizures, disorientation, or stunted growth. Shunts can often be successfully repaired with surgery.

Any inflammation of the liver is called hepatitis. Older dogs get more secondary liver disease from disorders like Cushing's disease or diabetes. Cats can get liver disease from hyperthyroidism. The liver is also susceptible to bacterial and viral infections, most notably canine hepatitis, which we vaccinate against. Leptospirosis is another pathogen that can cause liver disease and is also preventable to some extent through vaccination. Finally, tumors are not uncommon, especially in retrievers, and they are often malignant since they arise as metastases.

Certain breeds are more likely to develop liver diseases than others. Chinese shar-pei are prone to amyloidosis, a metabolic nightmare of a disease in which a protein called amyloid builds up in the liver and brain, eventually causing death. Chronic hepatitis due to storage diseases is seen in other breeds, including Bedlington terriers, Doberman pinschers, Skye terriers, and West Highland white terriers. In these dogs, copper isn't metabolized correctly and builds up in the liver, causing liver failure. Sadly, there is no known treatment except supportive care.

Diagnosis of liver disease is made by blood test and ultrasound. Acute liver disease (sudden onset, called hepatitis) can be turned around, but chronic disease (ongoing) has a poor outlook. Most liver diseases are progressive and will eventually be fatal. Medical management includes lower-protein diets, antacids like famotidine (Pepcid), vitamin K supplements if needed for clotting, and omega fatty acids. Advanced cases may need chronic antibiotic therapy to control ammonia buildup due to bacteria growth.

Hepatic Lipidosis

Hepatic lipidosis, otherwise known as fatty liver disease, is common in cats, especially overweight male cats. We pretty much never see this in dogs. The condition occurs when triglycerides (fat) accumulate in the liver, shutting its function down. It can be fatal if not reversed quickly. Most cases are secondary to another health issue, such as diabetes, cancer, pancreatitis, kidney disease, or hyperthyroidism, but sometimes it happens because your overweight cat just won't eat. Ironically, this starvation results in fat accumulating in the liver, which in turn causes nausea and further inclination not to eat.

Signs of hepatic lipidosis include anorexia, lethargy, and jaundice, sometimes accompanied by nausea and vomiting. Diagnosis is made by physical exam, blood work, and x-rays. The most precise diagnosis requires a liver biopsy, but often these cats are too ill for that kind of procedure, which must be done under anesthesia. Getting nutrients in is the only way to turn around the disease, so treatment usually requires a feeding tube. Home care can take weeks to months, but most cats start to improve within days of tube feeding. Recurrent bouts are common unless the cat loses weight. No better incentive, I'd say. ■

CHAPTER 29

Musculoskeletal Disorders

Like kids, pets seem indestructible until they're not. They're more fragile than they realize. Some common signs of a musculoskeletal injury are limping or lameness, pain, refusing to jump up on a couch or bed, not running or playing normally, and not grooming themselves (cats). Some breeds are prone to certain musculoskeletal disorders like hip dysplasia or patellar luxation (slipped kneecaps). Injuries to the joints, tendons, or bones can be tricky. The key to resolving musculoskeletal issues is to seek treatment sooner rather than later. More damage can occur the longer a problem goes on. Treatment of musculoskeletal issues ranges from simple (anti-inflammatories, pain medications, and rest) to complex (surgery and rehabilitation). A universal way to prevent musculoskeletal problems is to keep your pet lean: Obesity puts more strain on the joints and tendons, increasing the chances of a problem.

LAMENESS

Lameness is a clinical sign that something is hurting, whether in the bones, joints, ligaments, tendons, or muscles. Other signs that your pet is feeling pain include lack of appetite, stiffness, muscle loss (atrophy), abnormal gait, or difficulty getting up or lying down. If your dog is limping after a romp at the dog park, do a quick check for anything obvious: a cut or thorn in the paw pad, a broken nail, or any obvious swelling.

Sprains and strains are the most common forms of limb injury in pets. A sprain is very different from a strain. Sprains are injured ligaments (which connect bones), and strains are injured muscles or tendons (which connect muscles to the bones). Sprains are more often seen in the wrists and knees, and strains are more common in the hips and thighs. Both sprains and strains can be acute, happening suddenly; they go away on their own with rest and medication, or they can become chronic and lead to arthritis.

If your dog is uncomfortable and it's after hours, you can safely give one dose of baby aspirin or enteric-coated aspirin like Ascriptin (5 milligrams per pound). Don't give aspirin to cats, and never give ibuprofen or acetaminophen. Better yet, if you have a veterinary nonsteroidal anti-inflammatory left over from a previous incident (Rimadyl or Metacam, for instance), give one dose for pain relief. This and a night's rest should resolve any minor limb pain from overexertion. If a problem is severe or continues, see your vet for a thorough physical exam and possibly some x-rays.

Treatment of lameness always includes rest. Sometimes it even includes strict cage rest, which means using a crate to keep your pet quiet and semi-immobile. Medications like nonsteroidal anti-inflammatories, other pain medications, and nutraceuticals can be a big help for lameness not requiring surgical repair.

SHOULDER INJURIES

Shoulder injuries are less common and affect dogs primarily. Tendon and ligament injuries make up

STEM CELL THERAPY

One of the most promising uses of stem cells is in the treatment of osteoarthritis in dogs, but stem cells are being used to treat other chronic diseases too, including injuries to bones and tendons, diabetes, and eye injuries. Stem cells are "unprogrammed" cells from the bone marrow, fat, or umbilical cords of the same species of animal. Often they're harvested from the patient and then injected back into the patient, where they move to the damaged area, decreasing inflammation and promoting healing by growing new tissue. We're just at the beginning of stem cell therapy in animals. As you'd expect, this is not cheap; one course of treatment can cost up to $2,000.

the majority of shoulder injuries and mostly affect medium to large breeds. These injuries can result from trauma or just wear and tear on the shoulder joint. They can also sneak up on you and your pet and become worse over time. Intermittent lameness after activity is common, and, like all orthopedic injuries, obesity will just make things worse. These injuries are best diagnosed with ultrasound or MRI (see Chapter 34). Treatment includes anti-inflammatories, rest, and sometimes a sling to restrict movement of the shoulder. Stem cell therapy can also be a big help. Severe cases require surgical repair. With physical therapy and rest, dogs do very well post-op.

Ask DR. GARY:

Should I Use Ice or Heat?

When your pet experiences an orthopedic injury, you can help by applying an ice pack or a hot compress, depending on how much time has passed. Use ice within the first 24 hours of any injury. Ice works to decrease inflammation to the injured area. A bag of frozen peas does the trick. By day two, start warm compresses. Use a warm washcloth or a warm heating pad set to low (make sure it's warm, not hot). Warmth helps by drawing blood flow to the injured area, which subsequently carries inflammatory fluid away. Ten minutes for either ice or warmth at least twice a day is sufficient in most cases.

ELBOW DYSPLASIA

Canine elbow dysplasia is caused by growth disturbances that can result in malformation and painful degeneration in the elbow joints. These might be due to genetics, development, or nutrition problems and are common in young (four months to a year) large-breed dogs, especially Bernese mountain dogs, German shepherds, golden retrievers, Labrador retrievers, Newfoundlands, and Rottweilers. One of the ways to avoid this disease is not to breed affected dogs and to avoid rapid growth during puppyhood (see "Hip Dysplasia" opposite).

This degenerative disease hurts, and dogs will tell you that quite clearly, if not consistently (the pain can fluctuate from great days to very bad ones), by holding up their leg, licking at their elbows, and, in heartbreaking cases, whimpering. Diagnosis requires x-rays or CT scan under anesthesia to fully manipulate the elbow joint. Surgery, often done arthroscopically, is the treatment of choice. In the most severe cases, the elbow can be replaced entirely.

Following surgery, physical therapy is a must to get these pups back on their feet. Pain medications and glucosamine will be prescribed. You'll also need to restrict activity for about a month except for the exercises prescribed by your vet or physical therapist. Once healed, most dogs get full mobility back within a few months.

HIP DYSPLASIA

With hip dysplasia, the ball-and-socket joints of the coxofemoral joint, otherwise known as the hip, are deformed. This results in rubbing and grinding instead of rolling and sliding, and it creates abnormal wear and tear on the joint. It's caused by genetic and environmental factors that cause the hips to develop improperly. Usually not identified until after four months of age, the joint gradually deteriorates, leading to pain and loss of function. Some early signs of hip dysplasia are decreased activity, muscle atrophy of the most affected side, bunny hopping, and reluctance to run, jump, or climb stairs. Diagnosis is made with x-rays, which are best done under anesthesia to properly position the hips. To minimize this problem in dogs, good breeders have their dogs' hips evaluated using Orthopedic Foundation for Animals ratings before breeding.

Hip dysplasia affects mostly dogs. Certain breeds are more likely than others to suffer from hip dysplasia, including German shepherds, great Danes, Labrador retrievers, and Saint Bernards. Due to the risk of developing hip dysplasia and other joint issues, we often recommend feeding large and giant breeds a puppy food that's lower in protein. The rationale behind this is to slow growth to allow the bones and joints to catch up with the rest of the body (see "Large Breed Growth" in Chapter 10). Small breed dogs and cats can also have hip problems, but they're

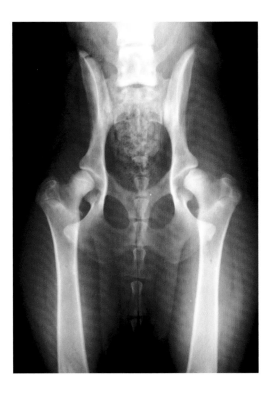

usually mild. Older dogs can also develop hip dysplasia due to degenerative changes in the hips.

Hip dysplasia has several treatment options. Many cases can be managed with medical treatment, including pain medications and nutraceuticals (food products that contain health-boosting properties) like glucosamine. Some prescription diets also help manage the progression of the disease with increased levels of glucosamine, vitamin E, and essential fatty acids. Joint massage, weight reduction, and physical therapy like swimming can help too.

Depending on the severity and progression of the disease, some cases can be treated only with surgery. You have two surgical options depending on the age of your dog. The first is a triple pelvic osteotomy (TPO) for puppies six months old or younger. This surgery rotates the hip sockets by

WHAT IS THE ORTHOPEDIC FOUNDATION FOR ANIMALS CERTIFICATION?

The Orthopedic Foundation for Animals (OFA) was founded in 1966 to promote the welfare of animals through reduction in genetic diseases. The OFA maintains a database for hip dysplasia, elbow dysplasia, eye certification, and cardiac disease, among others. Good breeders of purebred dogs most affected by these diseases will always have their animals certified before selling a puppy. If you're looking for a new German shepherd or collie, always ask your breeder before purchasing that pup. For more information, check out *ofa.org*.

cutting apart the pelvis and repositioning it with surgical plates. This creates a more functional, normal anatomical position for the hips, resulting in no more dysplasia. It's a time-tested and successful surgery for young dogs, but it must happen before the pelvis is fully developed. Since the pelvis is fractured and repaired during the surgery, recovery will take weeks. With a few weeks of nursing care at home and a few more weeks of activity restriction after that, these dogs do great. The recovery is not easy on the puppies or their families, but it's a lot better than the years of pain and lameness that would be in store for them without the surgery.

The second surgery is a total hip replacement (THR). This surgery is nearly identical to the surgery performed on humans and uses the same titanium implants. Unlike the TPO, total hips are usually done later in life unless the dysplasia is severe enough to warrant the surgery. The hip implant must be done in an entirely bacteria-free environment, so dogs are prepped weeks ahead of time by checking blood work and a urine culture to make sure they are free of any source of bacteria. Before the surgery, a dental cleaning is recommended to eliminate bacteria in the mouth. The surgery itself is a routine one for veterinary orthopedists. Dogs generally stay overnight in the hospital and are discharged the next day on antibiotics and pain medication. Dogs do terrific with a THR. This is good considering the many months of payments you'll be making on your credit card. For either surgery, physical therapy and therapeutic laser treatment are great postoperative treatments (see sidebar below).

A word of caution on orthopedics, particularly hip and knee surgeries. The good news is

THERAPEUTIC LASERS

Laser therapy treatment reduces inflammation and promotes healing in any damaged tissue. Most commonly used for postoperative adjunct treatment after orthopedic surgery, therapeutic lasers are painless and show improvement in healing in just a few sessions. The laser emits red or near infrared light, which penetrates deeply into tissue to lessen pain, relax muscles, and improve circulation. Today, more veterinarians are offering therapeutic laser as an adjunct therapy. If it's available to you, go for it. You'll get your pet back on his feet in half the time.

that animals have two of everything. The bad news is they have two chances for both limbs to become injured and need repair. This is very common in cruciate ligament injuries; fortunately, most hip replacement surgeries succeed by replacing only one hip.

LUXATIONS

A luxation occurs when a bone dislocates or pops out of place. It might completely break free of the joint, or it might slip in and out. Repairing luxations can range from replacing the dislocated limb and splinting it in place to full surgery. Surgery is much more effective in nearly every case and much easier for pet owners to manage than a splinted limb.

One of the most common luxations in dogs is hip luxation. This can happen due to trauma like a car accident, a congenital weakening of the ligaments holding the hip in place, or a degenerative disease like hip dysplasia. The luxation can be in any direction—above the hip, below the hip, or straight back—and it can be surprisingly subtle except for the dog's not bearing weight on the leg.

Hip luxation can be repaired in three ways. In the nonsurgical repair, called a "closed reduction," the surgeon pulls the femur back into place while the pet is under anesthesia. The real challenge in this approach is getting it to stay in place with an elaborate tape bandage and sling. In my experience, this is rarely successful in dogs. Much more effective, albeit costly, is an open reduction, in which the surgeon pulls the femur back into place and secures it with metal implants. This works nearly 100 percent of the time. In

some rare cases, a total hip replacement might also be considered. A third possibility, and one that is considered for cats and small dogs, is a femoral head ostectomy, which involves removing the head of the femur altogether.

After surgery, pets are usually up on their feet within days, although full recovery will take a couple of months, even with physical therapy. Pain medication and glucosamine are always prescribed. Animals usually do great after the repair.

Boston terriers, miniature pinschers, Pekingese, Yorkshire terriers, Chihuahuas, and other toy and miniature dog breeds are often afflicted with patella (kneecap) luxations. When buying a puppy from a breeder, ask if the parents of the litter were screened for this issue prior to breeding. I've never seen this happen in cats, but it's possible. A laxity in the ligament that holds the patella in place between the femur and tibia allows it to luxate or pop to the side. The kneecap will pop in and out of place frequently, especially after extensive exercise, going up or down steps,

or jumping. When this happens, it's painful for the dog, who will hold his leg up for a few minutes until the kneecap returns to its normal position. The chronic shifting of the patella causes damage to the knee joint, leading to degenerative arthritis in the knee.

Diagnosis is by physical exam with confirmation on radiographs, although it might not always show up on x-rays. Luxating patellas are graded 1 to 4. Fortunately, most cases are low grade and managed with glucosamine and occasional pain meds. Grades 3 and 4 are permanently luxated with increasingly degenerative changes in the joint. Surgery is reserved for these grades and includes deepening the groove in the tibia for the patella or surgically fastening it to the bone so that it can't move. Both surgeries are very successful. As in any orthopedic procedure, care after surgery includes pain medication, glucosamine, and physical therapy. Recovery takes about eight weeks.

CRANIAL CRUCIATE LIGAMENT TEAR

The most common cause of hind-leg lameness is an injury to the cranial cruciate ligament (CCL) in the front of the knee—or stifle, as it's called in animals. This ligament connects the back of the tibia (shinbone) with the front of the femur (thighbone). It's the same ligament that you know as the anterior cruciate ligament (ACL) in humans. These injuries occur more commonly in dogs than cats. Large-breed dogs are most commonly affected, including German shepherds, golden retrievers, Labrador retrievers, Newfoundlands, and Rottweilers. It's thought that neutering might increase a dog's chances of rupturing his CCL (see Chapter 15). Spayed female dogs are the most prone to both CCL tears and patella luxations. Like all orthopedic problems, obesity increases risk.

When the CCL ruptures, the stifle joint becomes extremely unstable. The rupture can be partial or complete. In some cases, partial tears can lead to chronic lameness and subsequent arthritis, so it's best to get these injuries evaluated as soon as possible. Dogs are usually not subtle when they have a CCL tear. They hold the affected leg up in a partially bent position. Another clue is muscle atrophy in the affected leg. Some dogs can improve with rest, but for others, lameness can last for months, then suddenly result in a complete rupture. A diagnosis is made through a physical exam, manual manipulation of the stifle joint, and x-rays of the affected leg.

Treatment for CCL rupture is usually surgical. In some cases, medical management with rest and pain medications might be recommended if

VETERINARY PHYSICAL THERAPY

Physical therapy, sports medicine, and rehabilitative medicine are all options for pets today. Especially for orthopedic surgeries, postoperative care is critical to expedite healing, alleviate pain, and get your animal back on his feet as quickly as possible. The physical therapy equipment used is impressive: ramps, balance balls, hydrotherapy, therapeutic lasers, and a host of other tools. If you can commit the time (often once or twice a week after surgery) and the cash, these specialists are well worth the effort.

the tear is partial and the joint is pretty stable. Medical management is often successful in dogs under 30 pounds. After a few weeks of rest and anti-inflammatories, many heal and no longer limp. In all but the smallest dogs, surgical repair is the preferred treatment to avoid arthritic changes later. In larger dogs and nearly all cats, surgery is inevitable.

Your veterinarian will determine the best surgical option for repair. Even veterinary orthopedists don't always agree on which technique to use. In general, the best technique is the one your surgeon has the most experience with. Two are most commonly used. The first is a decades-tested technique to replace the torn ligament with a very strong suture through holes drilled into the femur and tibia. This technique works best in small dogs and cats. The second technique is called a tibial plateau leveling osteotomy (TPLO). This procedure rotates the base of the tibia and secures it in a better position with a plate and screws. This technique is the gold standard in medium to large dogs.

Recovery takes at least eight weeks of rest, pain medication, and glucosamine. Physical therapy is strongly advised. Keeping your pup quiet during this period might seem more difficult than the surgery itself, but it's critical to the healing process. Unfortunately, many dogs with CCL tears rupture their other CCL within a year of the first injury. (Aren't you thankful for pet insurance now?) We believe some dogs have a genetic predisposition to these injuries, as well as the physical limitations imposed by their size and weight. ■

CHAPTER 30

Neurological Disease

Complex, vital, and indispensable, the nervous system is made up of the brain and spinal cord. The nervous system follows a specific and definitive pathway, so you just need to know all the routes to figure out what's going wrong. Some common signs of neurological issues are problems with balance or coordination, pain, paralysis, and seizures. The symptoms may come on suddenly and severely or more gradually over time. Discovering the root cause of a pet's neurological problem can be tricky. Often, advanced imaging like MRI or CT scans might be necessary. Neurological problems can be scary, but many treatments are available.

Ataxia

Your pets' balance and coordination are controlled by their vestibular system, which includes the many organs of the inner ear, which send signals to the brain. All mammals work this way. Vestibular disease, which affects dogs much more commonly than cats, disrupts the body's normal sense of balance, resulting in a lack of coordination of the head, trunk, limbs, or all three. This is known as ataxia, and is dependent on where the disease originates: the cerebellum of the brain, the vestibular system, or the peripheral nervous system in the spinal cord. No matter where the ataxia originates, it can affect one or both sides of the body.

The most severe type of ataxia is cerebellar ataxia, which causes uncoordinated movements in everything below the skull. The limbs, head, neck, and even the trunk have balance and coordination problems, along with weakness and tremors. Less severe but equally serious, is vestibular ataxia, which occurs when the vestibulocochlear nerve from the inner ear to the brain is damaged. This affects the position of the head and neck, causing a head tilt, as well as dizziness and a spinning sensation that can cause leaning and falling over. You might also see changes in eye movements, overall weakness, drowsiness, and even coma.

Ataxia can also occur due to trauma or a tumor in the spinal cord, in which case signals cannot pass from the brain to the limbs. This causes weakness and uncertainty when walking. For instance, rear paws in animals might cross each other or drag behind, or an animal will trip himself when walking and swaying.

Causes of ataxia include primary neurological disease, cancer, bacterial, viral and fungal infections, old-age degeneration, toxins, middle ear infections, trauma, and physiological abnormalities like sugar and electrolyte disturbances. The best way to help your vet narrow down the cause is with a good description of what's occurring at home, followed by a thorough physical exam, blood work, and urinalysis. Definitive testing might include sophisticated imaging with either a CT scan or MRI. These are the only ways to truly "see" into the nervous system to determine what's going on. These tests require anesthesia, which is something that might not be advisable in a severely debilitated animal. In most cases, your vet will stabilize your pet and then refer him to a neurologist for an MRI or CT scan.

Treatment depends entirely on where the problem lies. For example, a middle-ear infection can be diagnosed with x-rays or MRI and can be successfully treated with antibiotics. Other cases, like geriatric vestibular disease (see Chapter 36)

HOW TO NURSE A PET WITH NEUROLOGICAL DISEASE

If your pet is diagnosed with a nervous system injury, you will have to manage recovery at home. Set up a safe, comfortable place for your pet to rest, away from noise, activity, stairs, or other areas where he could further injure himself. You might even need a crate to restrict activity, at least initially. Set up puppy pads or use pet diapers if necessary because you might not be able to do walks. Place water and food bowls nearby. If necessary, turn your pet frequently to avoid bedsores, and try hand-feeding and treats.

WOBBLER SYNDROME

Cervical vertebral malformation, or wobbler syndrome, affects the cervical (neck) area of the spine in large-breed dogs. Doberman pinschers are the most affected, but it also appears in Bernese mountain dogs, German shepherds, great Danes, and Rottweilers. The disease might be genetic. It's caused by spinal-cord compression in the neck, which leads to neck pain and a wobbly gait in the hind limbs. Eventually all four legs can become affected. Diagnosis is made via MRI. Both medical treatment (rest and anti-inflammatory drugs) and surgical treatment may be effective depending on the disease's progression.

might improve on its own with time and supportive treatment. Unfortunately, some cases are also a sign of terminal disease, whether cancer, a fungal infection, or trauma. Localizing the cause of the ataxia is critical for devising a humane treatment plan with your veterinarian.

Epilepsy

Some manageable diseases manifest as chronic or lifelong seizures. The most common of these is epilepsy. Other causes of chronic seizures can be hypoglycemia, head trauma, developmental problems, and diabetes.

Epilepsy refers to nonspecific brain disease causing recurrent seizures. It affects dogs more than any other species and hits males more than females, usually beginning between six months and five years of age. Causes include toxins, tumors, and trauma, as well as metabolic diseases like diabetes. Most of the time, however, epilepsy occurs for reasons that are unknown. We call this idiopathic epilepsy and consider it an inherited disorder. Breeds commonly affected include beagles, Belgian Tervuren, Bernese mountain dogs, English springer spaniels, golden retrievers, Irish wolfhounds, Labrador retrievers, Shetland sheepdogs, and vizslas.

Dogs can have full, generalized seizures known as grand mal seizures or partial, focal seizures called petit mal seizures. Grand mal seizures are convulsion-type seizures affecting all four limbs. Usually a dog falls on his side, becomes stiff, loses bowel or bladder control, shakes, and salivates. This is often followed by a loss of consciousness. Grand mal seizures last between 30 and 90 seconds.

Partial seizures are more subtle, showing up as mild twitches, one limb at a time, or just facial twitching. Sometimes these can just manifest as a minute or two of staring. In time, partial seizures generally progress to grand mal seizures, so it's important to let your vet know early if your pet is exhibiting any of these signs. Recovery from either of these types of seizure can be immediate or take up to 24 hours.

If your dog has epilepsy, you'll become very attuned to signs that a seizure is coming. Watch for a change in mental state: looking worried or dazed, staring off into space, or hiding. Figuring out the triggers is key, but this isn't easy. Loud noises, stress, thunder, and bright light have all been hypothesized as triggers, but as these are specific to individual animals, they are not very reliable. Instead, pay close attention to any subtle

Ask **DR. GARY:**

Should I See a Veterinary Neurologist?

Neurologists are indispensable. Deciphering the exact cause of neurological disease in any patient is tough, requiring an encyclopedic knowledge of the neural pathways. It's doubly difficult if that patient is an animal who can't tell you what's going on. Veterinary neurologists go through at least five years of postgraduate veterinary education to hone these invaluable diagnostic skills. On top of that, neurologists have the equipment needed to aid in diagnosis – CT scans, MRIs – as well as the experience to decipher what those tests reveal and knowledge of the most current ways to treat.

their intensity, they can also cause liver and kidney problems, and their efficacy can wear off over time. Generally one or two seizures a year might be manageable without medication, but more than one seizure every other month probably needs medication. Common medications include phenobarbital, potassium bromide, and gabapentin. Your vet, or a veterinary neurologist (see sidebar this page), will tailor your pet's treatment based on severity and response to medications. Once on medication, set up a monitoring schedule with your vet to be sure your dog's levels are therapeutic and not causing harm to the liver or other organs.

Spinal Disorders and Paralysis

Injury to any part of the central nervous system of the spine can lead to paralysis. Paralysis can originate anywhere, from the peripheral nerves

pre-seizure clues your dog is demonstrating and then comfort your dog as much as possible. If you see signs of a seizure coming on, you can wrap your dog in a blanket and soothe him with gentle petting to try to head off a full seizure. This is good to do after a seizure too. Avoid sudden movements and noises. One of the biggest risks for epileptics is cluster seizures (more than one seizure per day). Seizures that don't stop require immediate emergency treatment.

If your pet's seizures are mild or infrequent, your vet might advise holding off on antiseizure medications. Once you start these, they usually need to be given for life. Although these drugs can help decrease the number of seizures as well as

DEGENERATIVE MYELOPATHY

Degenerative myelopathy (DM) can affect many breeds, including boxers, corgis, and soft coated wheaten terriers, but German shepherds suffer from this disease the most. The cause is unknown, but it affects the nerves of the thorax (chest) and lumbar (lower back) areas, which are referred to as the thoracolumbar spine. DM is a slowly progressive disease that looks a lot like Lou Gehrig's disease in humans. This nonpainful disease is mainly limited to the hind limbs, eventually causing paralysis and incontinence. Advanced DM will progress to the forelegs. There is no treatment except support. The disease is inherited, and a blood test is available to determine if a dog carries the genetic marker.

in the muscles all the way up to the brain. Sudden paralysis is a true emergency. The classic example is the middle-aged dachshund who wakes up one day dragging his back legs. Time is of the essence in getting these dogs to the vet as quickly as possible (see Chapter 20). But sometimes paralysis can come on more gradually.

The spinal column is composed of 24 vertebrae, which are separated by individual cushions of cartilage called intervertebral discs. Trauma to the vertebrae or their discs can injure the nerves within the spinal cord. Paralysis can happen by degree, however. Depending on the damage, paralysis might be total or partial. The number of limbs affected depends on where the trauma lies and how much of the nerve is damaged. In general, anything below the area of injury in the spine can be affected. Anything above the injury is okay. If the injury is in the brain, however, the entire body could be affected. Paralysis affects more than the legs. Damage to the lumbar spine can affect a pet's ability to urinate and defecate. It can even affect breathing and swallowing. Injury to these last functions has an extremely poor prognosis.

Aside from trauma to the spine and intervertebral disc disease (slipped disc), other causes of paralysis are brain or spinal infection, meningitis (inflammation in the brain) or meningomyelitis (inflammation of the spine), emboli (blood clots that can lodge anywhere in the body), tumors, tick disease (see sidebar opposite), or toxins. Finally, tumors of the spine, inflammation of the spine, spondylosis, or degeneration in the spine (see sidebar above) can also affect conduction of nervous system messages to the muscles.

To make a diagnosis, your vet needs a good background from you—where you've traveled

with your pet, how long the problem has been going on, any injuries or tick bites—and a great physical exam, including palpating the spinal column to localize the injury. Your vet will also test whether each limb has movement or feels sensation. A definitive diagnosis might require x-rays and a myelogram, which is a spinal x-ray with contrast dye injected into the spinal column to outline exactly where the issue is along the spinal column. Today, that procedure is more often replaced by a CT scan or MRI under anesthesia.

Treatment depends entirely on the cause and location of the injury or disease. In most cases, a diagnosis of paralysis requires a stay in the hospital and a consult by a neurologist. If the cause is intervertebral disc disease, conservative treatment

SUDDEN-ONSET PARALYSIS

A type of inflammatory disease called fibrocartillagenous emboli (FCE) can cause acute paralysis. FCE is caused by an embolism or blockage in the spinal cord's blood vessels. Usually we don't know why it occurs, but it often happens suddenly after exercise. Most often, FCE affects large-breed dogs between three and five years of age. It's also been reported in Shetland sheepdogs, miniature schnauzers, and even cats. Signs include partial paralysis of the hind legs. Dogs may cry out in pain when it strikes, then it becomes oddly painless. FCE nearly always occurs in males. Dogs and cats can recover with anti-inflammatories and strict rest, but it might take months depending on the extent of the injury.

TICK PARALYSIS

Ticks can cause an acute type of paralysis in dogs. This is a rare but very serious disease caused by a neurotoxin secreted by the salivary glands of the ticks. Cats, at least those in the United States, are immune to this toxin (not the case in Australia). The toxin causes paralysis that spreads from the lower to the upper limbs. The disease has also been known to affect people and can be fatal if it affects the diaphragm and therefore breathing. Symptoms come on quickly, usually within a few days of the tick bite. The best news? Once the tick is removed, paralysis resolves within a few days, which is another great reason to get ticks off your pets ASAP!

would be strict rest (possibly in a crate) and prednisone. This depends on how fast or how far the paralysis has gone. In some cases, only surgery will alleviate the pressure on the spine. Although these are serious surgeries, recovery is much improved from where we were just 10 years ago. Regardless of the treatment, once your pet has a spinal disease of any type, you must manage it for life. It can and often will come back. Prepare accordingly by being alert for potential trauma and not allowing your pet to overexert so you can protect that back for life.

Sadly, in some cases, we're too late, and the paralysis is permanent. Deciding what to do in these cases is a true quality-of-life decision, but if there is definite joy left in the life your pet will lead, a wheelchair is certainly a viable option. This is exactly the case for Jake, my German shepherd. ■

CHAPTER 31

Respiratory Disease

Many issues can affect your pet's lungs. Like humans, pets can get asthma, the equivalent of the common cold, and even pneumonia. Some common signs of respiratory disease are coughing (in pets, this can sometimes sound like gagging), sneezing, wheezing, runny eyes, runny nose, and rapid breathing (tachypnea). For mild symptoms like coughing or sneezing, seek veterinary treatment in a reasonable amount of time. If you suspect your pet is having trouble breathing, rush him to your vet or, if it's after hours, an emergency clinic. Difficulty breathing, known as dyspnea, evidenced by rapid respirations (more than 40 per minute in dogs and 50 in cats—see sidebar page 331), open mouth breathing, or flaring nostrils, is a true medical emergency.

UPPER RESPIRATORY DISEASE

The best thing you can do to prevent upper respiratory infections (URIs) is to keep your pets up to date on their vaccines. Cats are more susceptible to URIs than dogs. Most often, cats get viral URIs from herpesvirus and calicivirus, as well as from the retroviruses causing feline leukemia and feline immunodeficiency virus. These viruses are highly contagious between cats. Upper respiratory infections in dogs are caused by canine adenovirus, chlamydia, bordetella, and some pretty nasty bacteria (see "Lower Respiratory Disease" page 330). Symptoms include sneezing, congestion, runny nose, runny eyes, squinting, and sore or ulcerated nostrils, along with lethargy and loss of appetite.

Stress plays a critical role for URI more than almost any other illness. Stress can take many forms, such as abrupt changes in household routines, overcrowding of cats in animal shelters, and new stimuli or people. Some breeds are more affected than others, including flat-faced cat breeds like British shorthair, Himalayans, and Persians. Similarly, in dogs, brachycephalic breeds are the most afflicted (see sidebar below). Some cats are chronically affected. You might finally get your cat under control, and she comes down with another URI a month later. This is incredibly frustrating, and unpleasant for your cat. Your vet will help you manage this long-term.

If your pet has a URI, you don't always need to run to your vet. Much like the common cold in humans, the URI might just run its course with supportive care, including encouraging fluids (a little chicken broth in a bowl for your pets won't hurt) and decreasing stress. If the URI persists or symptoms are worsening, it's time to see your vet, who might prescribe antibiotics. Secondary

BRACHIOCEPHALIC AIRWAY DISEASE

Brachycephalic breeds (those with pushed-in faces like Boston terriers, French bulldogs, and pugs) struggle with upper airway abnormalities. These include narrowed nostrils, elongated soft palate, narrow trachea, and outpouchings of the larynx (voice box) into the trachea. Anatomic abnormalities make it harder for them to inhale air. Although the majority of these dogs grunt and snort their way happily through life, brachycephalic airway disease can be life threatening. Always avoid undue stress, high temperatures, and overexertion. In severe cases, surgery can help. Brachycephalic dogs should wear a harness and never use a neck collar. Keeping their weight down also helps.

bacterial infections are par for the course for cats with URIs. For chronic cases, your vet might also suggest supplementing with vitamins and the essential amino acid lysine, which we think might boost a cat's immune system. Dogs can benefit from antihistamines, but cats don't react well to these drugs. Instead, you can give cats some relief with saline nose drops.

LOWER RESPIRATORY DISEASE

Dogs get lower respiratory disease more often than cats, with the exception of feline asthma (see below). Lower respiratory disease includes tracheobronchitis (kennel cough), bronchitis, and pneumonia.

Kennel cough is more complicated than we used to think and even has a new name: canine infectious respiratory disease complex (CIRDC). In addition to a cough, clinical signs include sneezing and nasal and/or eye discharge. Interestingly, animals don't always cough. Severe cases can progress to pneumonia. CIRDC can be caused by viruses or bacteria or, most often, both. This debilitating disease is the scourge of shelters and easily spread from dog to dog.

Treatment includes stress reduction and supportive care. Many cases resolve on their own without treatment just like colds do for us, but if the cough is severe or prolonged and is

Ask DR. GARY:

Is My Pet Breathing Too Fast?

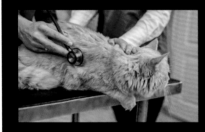

Rapid breathing can be an indication of lung disease. If you see your pet breathing faster than normal for a long period of time, count how many breaths he takes in 30 seconds and then multiply that number by two to get the respiratory rate. If it's higher than these numbers, see a vet right away:

Dogs: 10 to 35
Cats: 20 to 40
Birds (small): 30 to 60
Birds (large): 13 to 30
Rabbits: 30 to 60
Guinea pigs: 20 to 70
Reptiles: 5 to 20 (can often hold their breath for minutes)

accompanied by nasal discharge, your vet will likely prescribe cough suppressants and antibiotics. Ask your vet about using liquid Robitussin DM every four to six hours.

The complexity of this disease means that vaccination alone might not be fully protective. Some of the pathogens that cause CIRDC have no vaccine available, and others provide only partial protection. That said, all dogs who are boarded, go to day care, or will be exposed to lots of other dogs say, in dog parks, should have an up-to-date bordetella vaccine.

Bronchitis is an inflammation of the airways that deliver oxygen to the lungs. This is a loud, honking cough you won't forget in dogs, and it can last weeks or longer. Known causes are CIRDC, infections (bacterial, fungal, or viral), allergies, parasites, chronic obstructive pulmonary disease, and tumors.

Chest x-rays are critical in diagnosing bronchitis, but the most information can be obtained using bronchoscopy. This procedure is useful for many upper airway diseases. While the pet is under anesthesia, the vet can look at the inside of the airways with a bronchoscope to

FELINE NASAL POLYPS

Feline nasal or nasal pharyngeal (if also in the throat) polyps can cause chronic noisy and labored breathing in cats, along with sneezing, nasal discharge, and difficulty swallowing. These poor cats feel like something is stuck in their nose or throat but can't get it out. Nasal polyps may be caused by a previous virus or they can just happen. They can masquerade as a chronic URI, but they won't respond to medications. Once polyps are seen by eye or a scope under anesthesia, they can be surgically removed, curing your cat!

REVERSE SNEEZING

This common occurrence in dogs sounds like a full-fledged emergency; however, it's anything but. Reverse sneezing is a sneeze going the wrong way. Instead of sneezing out the nostrils, it is a forceful inhalation of air through the nose into the throat where it causes gagging and wheezing. We don't know why this happens—possibly an allergy or an irritation—but it's harmless and generally lasts just a few seconds or a minute. No treatment is needed except to comfort your dog (who is more alarmed by this than we are!). If it happens a lot, your vet might prescribe antihistamines. If it goes on longer than a few minutes, see your vet to rule out something else going on.

diagnose the cause of the cough. This is critical because treatment of bronchitis depends on the cause. Corticosteroids and bronchodilators may be used to open up the airways. Since bronchoscopy requires anesthesia for animals who may be too compromised for it, treatment is often begun empirically, which nearly always includes antibiotics.

The most dangerous lower respiratory disease is pneumonia, which occurs when the lower airways and lungs are inflamed or infected. It's often accompanied by, and may have developed from, bronchitis (called bronchopneumonia). Aspiration pneumonia is a life-threatening form of pneumonia that occurs when food or liquid is inhaled into the bronchi or lungs. This is precisely why we ask you to fast your pet before anesthesia so that the stomach is empty. Diseases like megaesophagus may predispose animals for aspiration pneumonia. Treatment for aspiration pneumonia includes hospitalization, IV or injectable antibiotics, and very close monitoring. In otherwise healthy animals who receive prompt treatment, the prognosis for recovery is good.

What Is Canine Flu?

Recently, we've encountered an increase in canine influenza across the United States. More often seen in large dog groupings, like shelters, this potentially deadly disease is thankfully rarely so. Much like human flu, annual outbreaks are marked by specific influenza subtypes, which cause the same symptoms as kennel cough and typically run their course with supportive care and antibiotics for secondary infections. A preventive vaccine is available but not given routinely; talk to your vet about whether this is a good idea for your dog.

FELINE ASTHMA

Asthma in cats is similar to asthma in people: a chronic inflammation of the small airways (bronchioles) that makes it difficult to breathe. The first sign is usually prolonged rapid breathing. A chronic cough can also be present, which people often mistake for hairballs. Wheezing and gagging can occur, as well as a shoulders-hunched posture.

Feline asthma is a form of allergic bronchitis, meaning your cat is reacting to something in the environment causing inflammation of the

PSITTACOSIS IN BIRDS

Psittacosis, otherwise known as parrot fever, is caused by an organism called *Chlamydophila psittaci.* It can cause multiple vague signs including decreased appetite, depression, watery green or yellow droppings, nasal discharge, pink eye, labored breathing, and even sudden death. Some birds carry it chronically and have no symptoms. This is a serious disease and one that is highly transmissible between birds through respiratory secretions, feces, and urine. It's also potentially transmissible to cats and people, most often immunosuppressed people. Diagnosis is by symptoms and confirmed with a blood test. Treatment with tetracycline by an avian veterinarian is critical, and birds must be isolated from other birds since infection, and reinfection, are common.

respiratory tract. Other things, including heartworm and heart failure, can also produce these signs, but nine times out of 10, it's asthma. This is good, because we can treat asthma. Usually feline asthma occurs in cats between one and eight years old. Often it hits females more than males.

Although feline asthma is treatable, it's not curable. The normal medication is prednisone, either given when signs occur for a period of days or weeks or even chronically over a prolonged period depending on the severity of the disease. We sometimes try to manage asthma with an inhaler, but I haven't met too many cats who tolerate this. The best thing you can do is to decrease the attacks by managing your cat's environment. This includes reducing your cat's stress, routinely testing for internal parasites (these can cause lung problems when they migrate from the digestive tract), and avoiding cat litter that produces a lot of dust. Humidifiers in dry winter months can help too. Most important, asthmatic cats should never be exposed to air sprays, room fresheners, scented candles, or cigarette smoke. ■

CHAPTER 32

Skin Disease

The skin is the body's best barrier against the dangers of the world. Any damage to the skin leaves your pet susceptible to infection. Skin issues range from infections and wounds to allergies, rashes, and more. Knowing what's healthy and what isn't can help your pet when things go wrong. Common skin symptoms include itchy skin; skin that is flaky or greasy; skin that has a foul odor; cuts, sores, or puncture wounds; scabbing or crusting; and lumps or bumps on or under the skin. Although skin problems are generally not emergencies, it's better to have your pet examined by a veterinarian as soon as you can reasonably get an appointment.

ABSCESSES

Put your lunch down for a minute. An abscess is a pocket of infection (pus) caused by bacteria in a closed space. Cats get a lot of abscesses since they tend to wrangle with each other and their sharp nails and teeth are full of bacteria. You can actually tell a lot about your cat based on where the abscess lies. If it's on the head, it means your cat stood up to the attacker. An abscess on the hind end means your cat turned tail and ran (or maybe she was just caught unaware). Dogs commonly get abscesses due to trauma, tumors, foxtails, foot dermatitis, and anal gland issues.

Once abscesses occur, your vet will need to lance the pocket, drain and flush the infected area, and start your pet on antibiotics and sometimes pain meds. A warm compress for 10 minutes every four hours helps relieve pain, bring down inflammation, and promote healing.

ANIMAL BITES

Animal bites are dangerous, whether from pets or wild animals. The danger comes from two directions: the teeth themselves, which can crush, tear, and slice, and the bacteria found in the mouth.

Given the choice between a bite by a domestic animal versus a wild one, I'll go with a domestic animal any day. Even so, companion animal bites are nothing to sneeze at. Dog or cat bites can result in abscesses. This is especially the case with cat bites. In fact, when people are bitten by cats, the normal medical protocol is to start them on antibiotics immediately. That's not necessarily

Ask DR. GARY:

Why Is My Pet Scooting?

When a pet scoots his butt on the carpet, most people think of worms, but worms don't generally cause scooting. Nine times out of 10, it's caused by full anal glands. Anal glands are two small sacs on either side of the anus that produce an oily, foul-smelling liquid that's expressed when the pet defecates. Cats won't admit it, but they have these too. Sometimes, the glands fail to empty and become uncomfortably full. Luckily, this is an easy fix – your vet can express the glands. If this happens a lot, ask your vet to show you how to do it. It's not difficult, but it's not exactly fun. Interestingly, ear infections often accompany itchy anal glands, so check both ends when one side is bothering your dog.

the case for dogs, but dog bites can really cause damage due to the sheer force of their jaws.

You may or may not see the bite itself, but clues to look for include limping if the bite is on the leg or shoulder, redness, and possible heat and drainage. Most animals with bite wounds also run a fever and are lethargic. If you find a bite wound on your pet, bring him in for a good cleanup and antibiotics. One final note of caution in cats: Bite wounds are an efficient method of spreading feline leukemia and feline immunodeficiency virus in cats. This is why we don't want cats with these infections to roam freely outdoors.

Pet entanglements with wild animals are heart chilling. Many wild animals can easily kill a pet, and if a pet escapes with his life, we worry about some really dangerous pathogens wild animals can pass along. Foremost among these is rabies (see sidebar below), but there are other scary pathogens like bacteria and rare parasites. Raccoons, which carry a parasite called *Baylisascaris,* are one of the more dangerous wild animals to tangle with (for your pet and you). But no matter the cause, if your pet is bitten by a wild animal, be thankful he is still with you and head immediately to your veterinarian or emergency clinic to clean and treat the wounds and start antibiotics and pain medications.

HIVES

You'd be surprised how often dogs get hives. In veterinary parlance, hives are called "urticaria." Unless you have a hairless dog, you might not even notice hives because of all the fur covering the skin. You're more likely to notice hives if you pet your dog and feel the bumps. If you part the hair, you might see tiny bumps along the skin at the hair shaft.

Hives in dogs are caused by an allergic reaction, which leads to an overreaction by cells in the skin, leading to fluid that pools inside the dermis. This creates those raised, swollen bumps. Hives are evidence that your pup is allergic to something. That can be an insect bite, a food, insecticides, plants (poison ivy or oak), or even medication. For dogs, you can try giving a dose of Benadryl (1 milligram per pound of body weight). If the hives don't resolve, see your vet for a stronger

Ask DR. GARY:

What Is My Pet's Risk of Rabies?

Four wild animal species have the highest incidence of rabies transmission to your pet: raccoons, skunks, bats, and foxes. Any bat found during the day is probably sick and might have rabies. Other animals, such as coyotes, are less common transmitters because they die of rabies before they can transmit it. Interestingly, squirrels, rats, and opossums are somewhat immune to the virus. Rabies is a far greater threat on the East Coast of the United States than the West where it is rarely seen in pets. Raccoons are the primary carrier. Rabies vaccination is mandatory for dogs and, in many jurisdictions, also for cats. No unvaccinated pet has ever survived a bite by a rabid animal.

medication and some help figuring out what's causing such a reaction in your dog. I take hives seriously. They aren't a big problem in and of themselves, but we don't want them to progress to a more serious allergic reaction (see Chapter 20).

HOT SPOTS

Hot spots, or moist dermatitis, are raw, red, usually circular skin rashes. These affect dogs but rarely cats. They occur when the skin becomes irritated, either because of chronic itching and inflammation, trauma, or an insect bite. The other component is moisture, which can come from swimming, a puddle, or, more often, self-licking

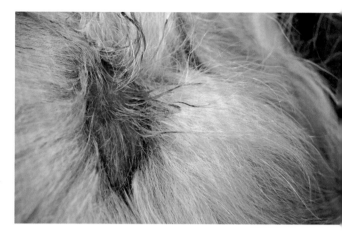
Dermatitis

the irritated skin. That's all it takes for bacteria to set up house.

Treatment is relatively easy, but it requires a vet visit for proper care and antibiotics. First, your vet will clip the fur around the affected area. Exposing the rash to air is essential. If the area is particularly dirty, your vet might clean it with warm, soapy water and then cleanse it with a dilute antiseptic solution.

Your vet may send you home with a combination antibiotic-and-steroid spray, antiseptic solution, antibiotics, and possibly an oral steroid. While the hot spot is healing, prevent your dog from licking it. That's what caused this in the first place. If needed, you can put a T-shirt on your dog or have him wear an E-collar (I like T-shirts better and so will your dog). Rinse the hot spot daily with a mild antiseptic like chlorhexidine solution (not scrub—that has soap in it) and apply the spray until healed.

If hot spots are caused by allergies, the ultimate cure is to discover the source of the allergy and avoid it. If it's seasonal allergies, ask your vet about allergy shots, frequent oatmeal baths, and allergy

SEBORRHEA IN DOGS

Seborrhea is a chronic skin condition in dogs that causes an increase in oiliness and flaking (dandruff). It often affects the ears. It's usually accompanied by an unpleasant smell and is particularly common in Chinese shar-pei, cocker spaniels, English springer spaniels, and West Highland white terriers. It causes itching, hair loss, and chronic skin infections. Treatment is frustrating because it's long term. In addition to treating with medication, a lifetime of nutritional support with fatty-acid supplements and medicated shampoos is necessary. (I love the human product Head and Shoulders for dogs with seborrhea.) With proper care, seborrhea is usually very manageable in dogs.

medications. Keep your dog especially well groomed, possibly even shaved down, to allow more airflow over the skin and therefore less of a moist environment.

LUMPS AND BUMPS

Some pets, especially dogs, seem to grow lumps and bumps apparently overnight as they get older. I affectionately make fun of my pit bull, Betty, who, in her old age, even has bumps on her bumps. If you find a lump on your pet, don't panic; not every lump and bump is a tumor. In fact, the great majority of them aren't.

The only way to know for sure what's brewing inside the skin is to collect a sample and check the cells under a microscope. Your vet will do this with a fine-needle aspirate, which uses a tiny needle to extract some cells from a skin lump. This may be done right in the exam room with you by your pet's side. These cells can then be looked at under a microscope. Sometimes we luck out and make the diagnosis based on the fine-needle aspirate, but if the results are inconclusive, your vet will recommend a full biopsy of the lump under anesthesia.

Ask DR. GARY:

What Are All These Cysts on My Dog?

As dogs age, they get a lot of bumps, tags, and cysts. Among the most insidious are sebaceous cysts, which are plugged oil glands in the skin. Small dogs produce these with a vengeance. They're benign and nothing to worry about unless they get infected. But they can burst, leak fluid, bleed, and make a real mess. In most cases, they rupture, and you never see them again. Your vet will clip the fur around them, clean them, and prescribe oral antibiotics and an antibiotic ointment. Sometimes they need to be surgically removed, and in rare cases, they can develop into a benign tumor called a sebaceous adenoma. Once removed, the cyst will not cause problems again. If your dog has a lot of them, you can ask your vet to remove some the next time your dog has a dental cleaning.

One of the most common lumps in dogs is the lipoma. These harmless deposits of fat are soft, round, nonpainful, and usually lie just under the skin. In some cases, they can grow between muscle sheaths where they might present a little more of a problem. Lipomas are benign and, in most cases, don't need to be removed so don't rush into surgery for these. In fact, the empty space created by remov-

ing them can become more of a problem than the lipoma itself. When we do remove these, it's usually because the mass was large and impeding movement of a limb, or it was growing into a problematic version called an infiltrative lipoma. In rare cases, lipomas can become liposarcomas, which is the malignant form, but this happens infrequently. Like any other skin bump, if there is a sudden change in the look of the lump, see your vet.

Other skin masses include skin tags, which are common and nothing to worry about, skin cancers (see Chapter 35), and sebaceous cysts (see sidebar opposite).

PODODERMATITIS

Pododermatitis, an inflammation of the paws, can be caused by infection, allergies (food and environmental), immune-mediated disease, or tumors. Generally a disease of dogs more than cats, pododermatitis can be mild and short-lived or severe and chronic. German shepherds are particularly affected by chronic pododermatitis, but boxers and bulldogs also suffer from these. Signs include red and inflamed feet, ulcers, and even cysts and abscesses between the toes. In the case of allergies, itching can be a constant problem, made worse by chewing on the inflamed areas.

Diagnosing these can be challenging and is based on clinical signs and history of what your pet might have been exposed to, such as molds in certain parts of the country. Your vet will then do skin scrapings, cultures, and even biopsies. Treatment is based on the cause and a sound understanding that in most cases, management rather than cure is the goal. Short-term treatment consists of antibiotics and corticosteroids.

Typical ringworm lesion

Long-term treatment consists of avoiding triggers and possibly allergy shots, which can help tremendously.

PUPPY TUMORS AND WARTS

Puppies and young dogs (under five years old) can develop quarter-size, flattened skin masses called histiocytomas. These benign tumors seem to pop up almost overnight on the face, head, muzzle, and nose. They're alarming to see, but they are entirely harmless and can go away on their own. Don't have them removed unless your vet is concerned. A fine-needle aspirate can

diagnose these. We don't know why they occur, but it might be due to some stimulus that causes these cells to overgrow. When that stimulus is gone, the mass goes away. The usual time frame from appearance to disappearance is about five weeks. Just keep an eye on it, and let your vet know if something changes. In no time at all, that puppy face will be beautiful again.

Typically, dogs get papillomas (warts) only in the adolescent phase of life (between four months and one and a half years). Caused by the canine papillomavirus, they show up on the skin, usually around the face, or they can turn up inside the mouth. They pop up all over the gums and tongue and are quite startling to see but are entirely harmless (although there are very rare accounts of them progressing to cancer). The warts typically go away on their own in about three weeks. There is no risk to people, but they are contagious to other young dogs, so keep your pup away from his friends until they're completely gone.

RINGWORM

Despite the name, ringworm is not a worm; it's a fungus that infects the skin. In people, it's called tinea pedis, otherwise known as athlete's foot. In veterinary medicine, we call ringworm "dermatophytosis." It's a highly contagious disease that often causes circular areas of hair loss and inflammation, usually on the head, ears, and forelimbs. Cats get ringworm more than dogs do, although dogs, especially puppies, can get infected with either the cat varieties or their own. Ringworm can spread to other animals and humans too so it's zoonotic. The spores can live for up to a year on walls, air vents, furniture, and pretty much anything else they come in contact with. Kittens are especially susceptible.

Ringworm is diagnosed based on its appearance (the characteristic ring-shaped lesion) and by turning off the lights and looking at it with a black light (the spores are fluorescent green). Diagnosis is confirmed with a culture. Treatment depends on the severity of the infection. The best course is a medicated sulfur dip to kill the spores and an oral antifungal for about a month or more until cultures are negative. Thorough cleaning of the home and discarding contaminated objects is essential to prevent reinfection to the pet or

people in the house. This is not the time to hang onto that carpeted cat tree. People are also at some risk, but the infection won't live long on us since we're not a natural host. But as long as it's still in the environment, people can develop recurrent infections. ■

Ask DR. GARY:

Did My Dog Just Give Me Poison Ivy?

You managed to get poison ivy on your last hike, even though you never stepped off the path. But your dog did. That's right, dogs can pick up urushiol oils from poison ivy, poison oak, and poison sumac and pass them on to their hapless owners. The dogs usually don't react to the oils, but we do. If you've ever been given this gift by your dog, put on gloves, get him into the bath, wash off the oils using dishwashing liquid, and follow up with a gentle shampoo. Next time, keep your pup on a leash for that portion of the hike.

CHAPTER 33

Urinary Tract Disease

Urinary problems can be complicated and frustrating to live with, especially if your pet is having accidents in the house or waking you up at night to go outside to urinate. Some common signs of a urinary issue are frequent urination, urinating very large or very small amounts, inability to urinate (squatting to go but not producing any urine), blood in the urine, pain when urinating (the pet might cry or lick the area), and accidents in the house (dogs) or going outside the litter box (cats). If your cat starts going outside the litter box or your formerly housetrained dog suddenly starts having accidents in the house, don't assume it's a training issue.

It might be but schedule an appointment with your veterinarian to rule out a medical cause for the problem.

BLADDER STONES

Both dogs and cats can get bladder stones, otherwise known as uroliths. Other animals can surely get bladder stones, but we either don't diagnose them or they don't occur as frequently as in dogs and cats. Uroliths can occur anywhere along the urinary tract, from the kidneys, through the ureters, to the bladder, and finally the urethra. In dogs, most stones occur in the bladder. In cats, these often occur in both the bladder and the urethra. Bladder stones are composites of minerals. They start out small, but can grow very large in time. The type of minerals depends on the mineral content in the bloodstream, pH of the urine, and frequency of urination. Diet can also play a part.

The first sign of stones might simply be urinary accidents in the house. Many animals just lick around the urinary opening, which is a sign of discomfort. Other signs include blood in the urine, straining to urinate, and even inability to urinate. This final symptom is a true emergency that warrants a middle-of-the-night trip to the emergency clinic.

Diagnosis is relatively straightforward: urinalysis, urine culture, and x-rays. Most stones are made up of the mineral struvite, which is magnesium ammonium phosphate. Others might be composed of calcium oxalate, cystine, or urate crystals. Urates are particularly a problem in Dalmatians. Some stones show up on x-rays, while others require an ultrasound to visualize.

Struvite stones are readily seen on x-rays, but cystine stones are almost transparent on x-rays, and urates are entirely transparent.

Treatment of bladder stones can be medical or surgical. The decision is based on the type of stone (only some dissolve with medical treatment) or the number of them. Medical management involves antibiotics for infection, which may have even caused the stones, and a prescription diet to modify the acidity of the bladder to make it a less desirable place for that particular stone to develop. Surgical removal is called a cystotomy. The advantage to doing a cystotomy is that the stones can be completely removed as well as analyzed for composition. In medical management, we have to make an educated guess based on urinalysis results. Many stones are composed of more than

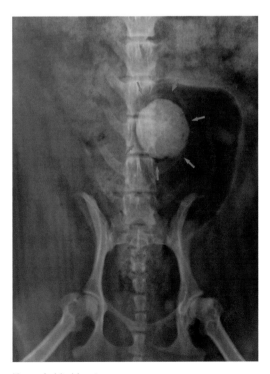

X-ray of a bladder stone

one mineral and so might not dissolve with medical treatment. Once the stones are removed, antibiotics and a therapeutic diet are prescribed to prevent them from recurring.

FELINE LOWER URINARY TRACT DISEASE

Feline lower urinary tract disease (FLUTD) is a broad diagnosis covering a wide range of urinary problems in cats. Signs include the usual symptoms of urinary disease—urinary accidents, straining, blood in the urine, and licking of the urinary region—and can be quite serious.

FLUTD is a complex syndrome in cats with more than a single cause. Infections, diet, and even inflammation with no perceived cause can all be culprits. The biggest scare with FLUTD is urethral obstructions in male cats (these almost never occur in females). If you notice that your male cat is straining and not producing any urine, go immediately to your vet or an emergency clinic. For cats, stress can also be a factor, especially in households with intercat aggression or too many cats. With FLUTD, inflammation occurs in the bladder (called cystitis). This can be due to infection or it can be caused by something called feline idiopathic cystitis (see opposite) in which no bacteria are seen.

Crystals are the particulate minerals that make up stones. They just haven't had enough time or chemical inclina-tion to aggregate into stones. Both crystals and stones might also occur in feline lower urinary tract disease. These are composed of minerals that accumulate in the urine and may form blockages in the urinary tract of male cats especially. In cats, the two most common types of crystals are magnesium ammonium phosphate (struvite) and calcium oxalate.

Diagnosis is made by urinalysis and x-ray or ultrasound. Treatment may either be medical through a prescription diet to rebalance the acid-base constitution of the urine, or surgical removal of the stones. Surgery is less common in cats than in dogs. Medical management using a stone- or crystal-dissolving diet is much more common, especially for cats with struvite crystals. Struvites form in a very alkaline environment, so decreasing the pH of the bladder to make the urine more acidic can dissolve these crystals before they can form stones. For calcium-oxalate crystals, just the opposite: Increasing the urinary pH is necessary, although they are very difficult, if not impossible, to dissolve; using diet and surgery is more common in these cats. Regardless, any cat with a history of crystals or stones needs lifelong management since recurrence is likely. This includes feeding the appropriate diet (a food that maintains a urine acidity that won't promote the stone you removed) and feeding more canned food for better hydration and more dilute urine. Sometimes medications are also prescribed to keep the urine at the appropriate pH to prevent crystals from forming. Management is key to preventing future stones.

FELINE IDIOPATHIC CYSTITIS

Feline idiopathic cystitis (FIC) is a wide-reaching but vague term. Cystitis is merely inflammation of the bladder. Idiopathic means "of unknown cause," which is a confession that we don't really know what's going in cats with this disease. What we do know is that it's prevalent and seems to be a complex syndrome that includes frequent urination, pain on urination, and bloody urine. Cats may genetically be predisposed to FIC, but stress and even obesity can be key factors. We used to believe these were ordinary urinary tract infections since they often clear up on antibiotics. We also used to think that diet contributed. Neither of those assumptions seems true now. FIC tends to strike and then clear up on its own. Our treatments and preventives, while making cats more comfortable, were mere coincidences. In some cases, infection and crystals were secondary and needed treatment, but neither caused FIC. Relieve your cat's stress, keep the litter box clean, and offer as much wet food as possible, and you might luck out and never see this disease again.

KIDNEY DISEASE

If you're lucky to have a cat live long enough, you'll probably learn all about kidney (renal) disease. Nearly every cat older than 14 years will develop some type of renal disease. It's just the natural course of events. The same goes for dogs and our

KIDNEY TRANSPLANTS IN CATS

Kidney transplants have been done in cats since the late 1990s, and the procedure has gotten better with time. Cats must otherwise be in good physical health, have no infectious diseases, and, since stress is a pretty good guarantee of transplant rejection, must be amenable to frequent medication. Younger cats are the best candidates, but they're usually not the ones in need. The procedure is still relatively uncommon, and most programs require that the donor kitty be adopted by the receiving kidney cat's family. Then there's the cost. At $10,000 to $15,000, this isn't a treatment chosen lightly. But who can put a price tag on all that extra time with your cat?

other pets, although cats develop kidney disease more frequently. We can't cure kidney disease (except with a kidney transplant), but we can hope to slow its progression.

There are two types of kidney disease: acute (sudden onset) and chronic (ongoing). Acute kidney failure can be caused by toxins, infection, trauma, cancer, and physiologic shock, which occurs with heatstroke for example. It can also be caused by bladder stones. The most common cause of acute kidney failure in pets is toxins. Toxic plants, some human medications, antifreeze, some household cleaners, and pesticides are highly toxic to the kidneys, which filter the blood. Some toxins are species specific; others are toxic to all animals. Acetaminophen is extremely toxic to all pets, but even a slight dose will cause almost certain liver failure and death in cats. Make sure your home is safe for your pets by keeping medications and cleaning products safely out of their reach. With prompt treatment, acute renal failure can be reversed. There are two kidneys after all, so we have a good chance of saving at least some of the normal kidney function.

Chronic kidney failure is a disease of older animals and especially common in cats. These senior cases are difficult to treat but can be managed with diet and increased fluid intake, including giving subcutaneous fluids if necessary. There are many signs of kidney disease; two of the most common are increased drinking (polydipsia) and increased urination (polyuria). This is why it's so important to pay attention to your pet's normal water consumption and output. Other signs include urinary-tract infections, dilute-looking urine, bloody urine, decreased appetite, vomiting and diarrhea, weight loss, weakness, an unkempt or dry coat, and oral ulcers and bad breath.

Diagnosis of renal disease is based on physical exam, blood work, and urinalysis to see how well the kidneys are concentrating urine. On a blood profile, the creatinine and blood urea nitrogen (BUN) levels are key indicators of kidney function (see Chapter 34). Phosphorus will also be elevated in severe renal cases.

Treatment for acute kidney failure is all about fluids. Lots and lots of fluids are administered in the hospital to flush out the damaged kidneys. Chronic kidney failure might require a stint in the hospital for IV fluids upon diagnosis or when symptoms flare up. Management includes a diet low in phosphorus and protein that's enriched with vitamin D and omega-3 fatty acids. Access to lots of freshwater is essential, and canned food is always preferred (Have I said this enough? Feed cats canned food!). In some cases, augmentation with subcutaneous fluids is necessary to keep your pet well hydrated. These can easily be given at home, and your veterinary technician will show you how to administer them. If vomiting is an issue, maintaining hydration levels will help greatly, but you can add an H_2 blocker like famotidine (Pepcid) or another acid blocker like

omeprazole (Prilosec) once a day to decrease stomach acid (see Appendix B).

URINARY INCONTINENCE

Incontinence (loss of bladder control) is a problem in many pets. Although common in seniors, it can affect younger pets too. Incontinence is an indiscriminate leaking of urine and can be just a little leakage or more like Niagara Falls. It's different from urinary accidents, in which the pet assumes the normal "potty" stance. In dogs, for which it is relatively common, incontinence can be caused by congenital malformation of the urinary tract; low estrogen, which is common secondary to spaying; weak bladder sphincter; fear or anxiety, or both; urinary tract infections; bladder stones; endocrine diseases like hypothyroidism, diabetes, and Cushing's disease; and certain medications. It's thought that estrogen-insufficient urinary incontinence occurs in somewhere between 10 and 20 percent of spayed female dogs.

CAN CATS GET HYPERTENSION?

Pets are not as cursed as we are when it comes to hypertension, or high blood pressure. The exception is cats. Cats can develop high blood pressure due to obesity, heart disease, hyperthyroidism, or kidney disease. The most common problem we see in hypertensive cats is vision problems. We can measure a cat's blood pressure with a Doppler device. Amlodipine, a human hypertension medication, can work well for these cats. Treating the underlying cause, like renal disease, is key.

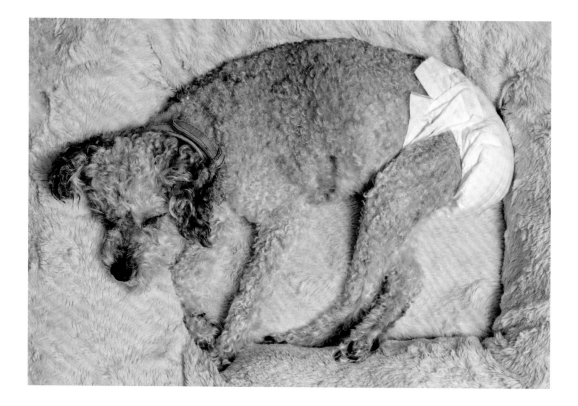

Diagnostically, the most important thing to rule out is a urinary tract infection—something curable. Otherwise, most incontinence situations are chronic and require extended, even lifelong management. This is, unfortunately, not uncommon in senior pets. If infection is not the cause, the majority of dogs with incontinence suffer from hormone-related incontinence. But for cats, it's almost always behavioral.

Once we rule out infection, you can do several things to help your pet and protect your floors. First, never make your pet wait too long to relieve herself—no 12-hour waits between walks. A few medications can also help tremendously, including phenylpropanolamine, which helps tighten up the urinary sphincter. Estrogen therapy is another option. Estrogen has a few side effects

that we don't love, so most vets recommend trying phenylpropanolamine first. If medications aren't helping, pee pads and doggie diapers are an important part of the arsenal. Keep the urinary outflow area clean to prevent sores and urinary tract infections. Chronic leakage can lead to bacteria ascending up the urinary tract from the skin and causing a UTI. Never limit water intake, no matter how frustrated you are cleaning up.

URINARY TRACT INFECTIONS

Urinary tract infections (UTIs) occur when bacteria enter the urinary tract, usually from the area on the skin in contact with the urethra. Rarely, descending infections can occur from bacteria that

are deposited into the urine from the kidneys. These painful infections mostly affect females, with the exception of FLUTD in cats. Certain health issues can predispose a pet for a UTI, including diabetes, bladder stones, tumors, incontinence, and immune system compromise. Prostate problems can also cause, and complicate, UTIs in dogs.

Signs of UTI might include one or more of the following: increased drinking, increased urination, straining to urinate, painful urination, dribbling or loss of bladder control, blood in the urine, and cloudy or bad-smelling urine. Some animals with UTIs can become systemically ill with fevers, lethargy, and poor appetites, especially those that originate from the kidneys.

To diagnose a UTI, your vet will run a urinalysis, as well as a urine culture and sensitivity, to identify the correct antibiotic for the bacteria growing in the bladder. Treatment for UTIs also includes treating any underlying cause like diabetes or uroliths. UTIs are relatively easy to treat. They can also be very painful for your pet, so don't delay in getting her checked out. There's also a risk of ascending infections to the kidneys and the formation of bladder stones if you don't. That will make a relatively easy problem to fix become one you'll be living with, and making payments on, for years. ■

EGG BINDING IN PET BIRDS

All female birds can lay eggs, even when there is no male. Egg binding occurs when a bird fails to expel her egg. This occurs due to a poor diet deficient in calcium, such as seeds. Birds usually pass two to four eggs, one to two days apart. If a bird doesn't pass eggs in more than two days, she might be egg bound. Egg-bound birds are lethargic and depressed, often have a swollen abdomen, and stop eating. Most birds lay eggs around dawn, so any bird straining to lay an egg during the day is probably egg bound. Paralysis of one or both legs can occur when the egg stuck in the canal presses on nerves. Diagnosis is via x-ray. Treatment is to first stabilize the bird and then replenish the

needed nutrients like calcium and vitamin D. The egg is then manipulated or sucked out from the canal—a lot of work that a balanced diet might have prevented.

PART 6

Diagnostics, Aging, and Holistic Medicine

Staying on top of your pet's health is the key to a happy, long life together. As pets age, they might need more routine lab testing and some pets develop chronic issues that require advanced care. Such care may come from your regular veterinarian or a specialist, or you might seek the help of a holistic vet who uses a combination of natural and conventional methods.

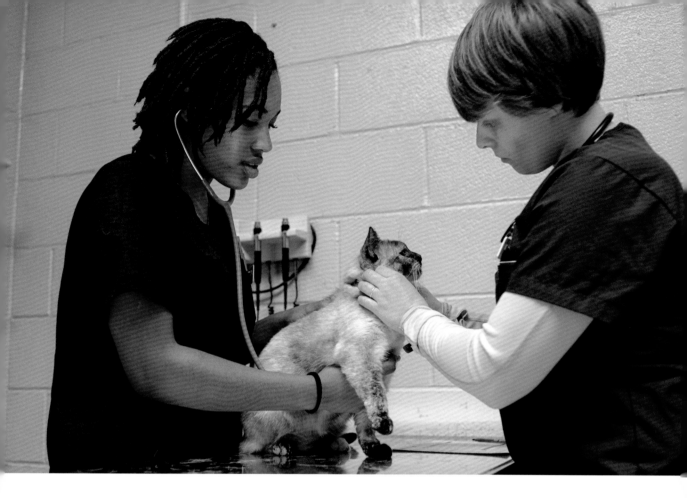

CHAPTER 34

Diagnostics

A big challenge in veterinary medicine is learning what's normal for so many species, especially when each pet's "normal" can vary considerably. That's where lab work and other diagnostics come in. These tests are a window to the inner workings of an animal's body, cluing us in to what might be ailing them. Whether your pet is ill or you just want to ensure their aging bodies are in tip-top shape, diagnostic tests provide the information your vet needs to help them. Some tests require just a little blood or urine; others capture images of the inside of your pet's body to reveal issues that would otherwise go undiagnosed.

BLOOD TESTS

Most baseline lab work consists of two blood tests (blood chemistry panel and complete blood count) and a urinalysis. Together, these tests can tell us what's going on in your pet. The blood chemistry panel, otherwise known as a blood profile, contains about 20 individual tests that cover every major organ system, plus protein, fats, and electrolytes. They can be tailored to add or subtract tests. For instance, a geriatric profile is tailored for organ changes consistent with older animals. Geography and species play a part too by adding tests more specific for that patient. Your vet might want to add a thyroid level in your seven-year-old cat (see sidebar below), or another heartworm test if you live in the southern United States. In addition to times of illness, we often run blood profiles prior to anesthesia and surgery. Blood profiles can also be helpful during annual exams, so we have a baseline to refer to if your pet becomes sick later.

Blood samples are obtained via a prominent vein. In dogs and cats, the most widely used are the cephalic vein running along the top of the foreleg

CAT THYROID PANELS

All cats over seven and any cat with suspected thyroid disease (see Chapter 27) should have a thyroid panel added to her routine blood work. This is a simple test run with the same blood drawn for chemistry analysis. A high T4 or free T4 (which means it's unbound in the blood) level, will confirm hyperthyroidism and get you your cat onto a very successful course of treatment.

IN-HOUSE ELISA TESTING

Even if they don't do full blood work in-house, nearly all veterinary hospitals perform some common blood testing in the clinic. ELISA blood tests, which stand for "enzyme linked immunosorbent assays," use an enzyme color test much like pregnancy tests for humans. All that's needed is a drop of blood, and results appear in minutes. Common in-house tests include heartworm, feline leukemia, feline immunodeficiency virus, parvovirus, Lyme disease, tick-borne infections like anaplasma, and Ehrlichia. Incredible information available in minutes that can add years to your pet's life.

or the jugular vein in the neck. Your vet might need to shave the area, but often a squirt of alcohol to wet down the fur does the trick. For most pets, obtaining blood is no big deal. The one thing some pets don't like, however, is the restraint required. Your vet might need to muzzle your dog or wrap your cat in a towel. In some cases, blood samples must be collected under sedation. It's never acceptable to strong-arm an animal. In addition to that, stress can affect blood work results, especially in cats.

Most vets send blood out to a lab with a turnaround time under 12 hours. Some vets have in-house labs and can get a result in less than an hour. Blood chemistries do come at a cost and can ramp up your charges for any diagnosis or procedure. But there's no more valuable data than a blood chemistry panel. Once your pet reaches seven years of age, consider a blood panel at least once every couple of years.

The partner to the blood chemistry is the complete blood count (CBC). The CBC measures hydration status, infection, anemia, some aspects of blood clotting, and the immune system response. Specifically, it measures the amount, size, and shape of red blood cells and the number of white blood cells and platelets. The CBC is vital when diagnosing symptoms of fever, vomiting, diarrhea, bleeding disorders, and anemia.

URINALYSIS

The urinalysis measures hydration status and helps identify kidney or bladder disease, infections, and metabolic diseases like diabetes. A urine sample from your pet can be obtained by free catch into a clean cup at home or in your vet's office. Alternatively, your vet can express the bladder or insert a needle straight though the abdominal wall into the bladder, a procedure called a cystocentesis. Sometimes, this is even done with ultrasound to make it even more precise. Collecting a urine

FECAL EXAM

The fecal exam measures your pet's stool quality like color, consistency, and the presence of mucus or blood. It's also the best way to check for intestinal parasites. If your pet needs a fecal exam, you can either bring in a small sample of fresh stool or your vet can collect a stool sample in the office using a tool called a fecal loop. It's a good idea to check a stool sample at least once a year.

sample this way ensures that it's sterile—any bacteria seen came from the urine itself and not the cup you collected it in. A sterile sample like this is especially important if your vet wants to culture the urine. Although some pets don't like to be held still for the procedure, it's quick and relatively uneventful for your pet.

X-RAYS

X-rays are best at visualizing areas of the body that have contrast, like bones and muscles or lungs and air. Although x-rays do transmit ionizing radiation, which can be harmful in large amounts, kept to a minimum, they're safe and irreplaceable in visualizing what a good physical exam can only suggest. Even better, they're digital and can be immediately manipulated and enlarged to help with diagnosis.

Today, x-rays are even used in veterinary dentistry. Rather than guess what's happening beneath the gums, we can now actually see the whole tooth and root. X-rays are one of the best diagnostic tools we have and well worth the cost if your pet needs them.

CT SCANS

Computed tomography (CT) scans are similar to x-rays but far better at visualizing three-dimensional images of the body. CT scans collect multiple x-ray images or "slices" of the body. These slices are then put back together via computer. Certain parts of the body—for instance, the nasal cavity, inner ear, and joints—are much better visualized with CT than ordinary radiographs. Dense objects and air are better seen with CT scans because they are highly contrasting with the body's tissues.

All veterinary hospitals perform x-rays, but only specialty hospitals do CT scans. The methods and equipment are the same as those used in humans with one exception: Animals require anesthesia to keep them still during the scan. That means patients must be fasted, anesthetized, and monitored while in the CT chamber. The full session takes about 45 minutes to an hour. In general, CT scans run between $1,000 and $3,000 depending on geographic location.

MRI

Unlike CT scans, magnetic resonance imaging (MRI) is not at all like x-rays. MRI employs a different technique using magnetic fields and radio waves. As such, it's even safer than x-rays in that no radiation is used, but it does require that your pet be anesthetized. MRIs are great for visualizing soft tissues like the brain and spinal cord. MRIs take about 45 minutes to complete. In veterinary medicine, the MRI is king of all diagnostic techniques and is available only in specialty hospitals. The price can be high though, around $2,000 to $2,500.

ULTRASOUND

Ultrasound is great for visualizing organs, even eyes, as well as for lameness examinations in dogs and horses, pregnancy checks, or examining the real-time functioning of the heart where it's called an echocardiogram. Ultrasound waves are considered very safe.

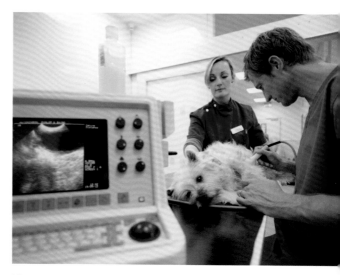

Ultrasound

Besides being versatile and noninvasive, the other advantage to ultrasound is that almost all pets can be examined without anesthesia. Some pets might need a sedative if they can't be convinced to stay still. The exam usually takes less than 45 minutes and only requires the pet to lie on his side or back in a soft, cushioned cradle. The vet will shave the area he wishes to view, apply a special sound-transmitting gel, and hold a probe against the area. The images come up immediately on a screen next to your pet.

Ultrasound is pretty reasonably priced at about $400 to $500 per examination, and many private practices have ultrasound. The real key to getting your money's worth, however, is to be sure your veterinarian is highly experienced interpreting the wavy-washy black-and-white images. Your vet should refer you if she or he thinks you should work with a specialist. That may be the case for more complicated diagnoses. For the best ultrasound diagnosis using the best equipment, a specialist or specialty hospital is often preferable. ▪

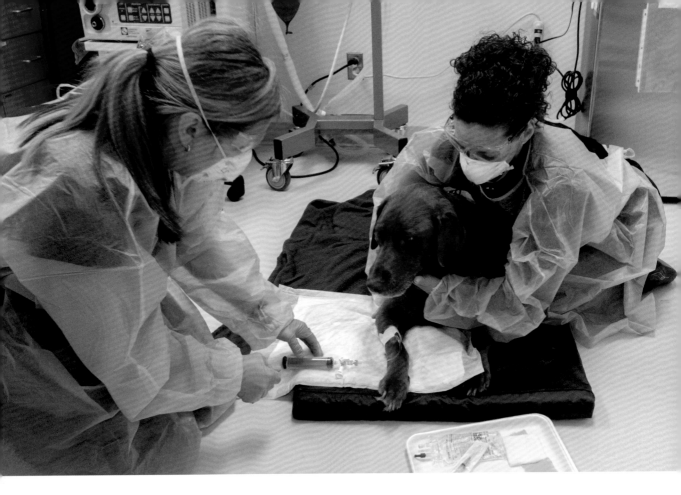

Cancer

No one wants to hear the word cancer. Cancer rates in dogs are similar to humans; cats are somewhat less likely to get cancer, but when they do, it tends to be more aggressive. According to the Veterinary Cancer Society, one in four dogs will develop cancer during their lifetime and 50 percent of dogs older than 10 will develop cancer. In dogs, cancer is the leading cause of death, and in cats, it's the second biggest cause of death. The good news is that we have many cutting-edge treatments and palliative care options for cancer in pets, many of them as sophisticated as the treatments available for cancer in humans.

BREED PREDISPOSITION

Although cancer can occur in any animal, some breeds are more frequently affected than others. In general, we're talking dogs; specific cat breeds aren't as prone to cancer. Of course, cancer doesn't just affect purebred dogs. It also strikes mixed breeds.

A lot of cancer research is done with purebred dogs, which might misleadingly increase the statistics of cancer in certain breeds like golden retrievers, Labrador retrievers, and German shepherds. This is because the genetic pool for most purebred dog breeds is very limited, which helps researchers study the causes and treatments for certain types of cancer. Understanding genetic links to cancer might someday lead to treatments and even cures.

COMMON CANCERS IN PETS

Although pets can get many different types of cancer, certain cancers are seen with greater frequency. Some cancers are more likely to affect dogs or cats or certain breeds; others affect all animals equally.

Adenocarcinoma

Adenocarcinoma, sometimes just called "carcinoma," is a malignant tumor affecting the epithelial tissues that line the stomach, intestines, and rectum. As with most other cancers, older animals are at more risk. Signs are gastrointestinal, including vomiting and diarrhea, lack of appetite, weight loss, and possibly blood in the stool or vomit. This is a tough cancer to diagnose as it requires an endoscopy or colonoscopy under anesthesia along with a biopsy. Treatment includes surgical resection of the tumor. Unfortunately, this is rarely successful since most carcinomas have already spread by the time they are diagnosed. Chemotherapy is not very effective and is not usually recommended. Radiation, however, may sometimes give pets more time with us.

Fibrosarcoma

Fibrosarcomas are tumors of the connective tissues beneath the skin. They have many variations, but most are caused by an injury to the tissues from which they arise. For example, a bone fracture can affect the connective tissue around the bone leading to fibro- or osteosarcoma. Like all other cancers, fibrosarcomas are multifactorial and hard to avoid. Most are seen in large-breed, middle-aged to older dogs. Cats can also be affected and when this hits them, the prognosis is grim (see "Feline Injection Site Sarcomas" below).

These slow-growing tumors rarely metastasize to other organs, so the prognosis is hopeful. The exception to this rule is vaccine-induced fibrosarcomas in cats. The prescribed treatment is surgery, ranging from removal of the mass to removal of the limb. Radiation is often recommended for this type of tumor and is a successful adjunct to ensuring the cancer is eradicated for as long as possible. Sometimes, "as long as possible" is all we need.

Feline Injection Site Sarcomas

Vaccines are responsible for saving more lives than almost any other discovery in medicine. However, like all other medicines, they can have their downsides. One of the most significant of these is the feline injection-site sarcoma (FISS), which we started seeing with alarming frequency in cats in the late 1990s. This malignant version of the fibrosarcoma occurs at the site of certain vaccines, most commonly, the feline leukemia vaccine. Although less common, it has also been linked to the rabies vaccine. Sarcomas can develop at the injection site weeks to years after the vaccination is given.

We don't know exactly why, but some vaccines cause inflammation at the injection site because of certain ingredients in the vaccine, namely, aluminum containing adjuvants used to increase the effectiveness of the active ingredients in the vaccine. Some cats might also have a genetic predisposition for this abnormal reaction. Even though these sarcomas are limited to a single area in the skin, they are usually fatal because they're nearly impossible to completely remove. They can also metastasize to other organs. Radiation therapy is recommended after surgery, but in many cases, cats succumb to this cancer regardless of treatment.

The risk of FISS is estimated at less than 1 in 10,000 to 30,000 cats. Still, that's of little solace if your cat is one of them. The American Association of Feline Practitioners advises only vaccinating cats for feline leukemia virus (FeLV) who are at great risk for exposure: cats who go outdoors, cats commonly involved in cat fights, or those who live with FeLV-positive cats. If your cat is an indoor cat, most vets will recommend skipping the FeLV vaccine. The rabies vaccine is required by law, but that's a discussion you should have with your vet if your cat never leaves the house. If your vet recommends the FeLV vaccine, a nonadjuvanted vaccine is available that's much safer for cats. Removing the ingredients thought to cause inflammation has nearly eliminated the sarcomas. After initial vaccination, revaccinate one year later, then every three to four years. Always ask for the FeLV and rabies vaccines to be given in the lower leg. In the rare chance that your kitty gets a sarcoma, it's much better to deal with a limb amputation than losing your cat. We don't want either of these outcomes to happen, of course.

CANCER TERMINOLOGY

Neoplasia, another word for cancer, goes by a lot of names: *cancer, tumor, malignancy, mass*. Here's a quick decoder ring on cancer:

All masses are **tumors.**

All tumors are **cancer.**

Tumors can be **benign,** meaning they don't **metastasize** (spread to other tissue).

Tumors can be **malignant,** meaning they will dangerously invade adjacent organs or metastasize. Malignant tumors are deadly, often even if treated.

Hemangiosarcoma

Hemangiosarcoma, a blood cancer, is not a good one to get. By the time it's diagnosed, it has usually already metastasized to other locations in the body. This cancer is often discovered in tumors of the spleen or liver of large dogs. These tumors usually don't bother the dog until they get big enough to press on other organs (they can be basketball size) or start bleeding into the abdomen. The first sign something is wrong could be when the dog collapses from blood loss.

Boxers, English setters, German shepherds, golden retrievers, great Danes, and pointers are predisposed to this cancer. It also seems more common in male dogs. Like most other cancers, hemangiosarcoma is usually seen in dogs between eight and 10 years of age. Since they're a blood vessel cancer, hemangiosarcomas quickly metastasize to other organs like the liver, lungs, heart, and brain. Once the tumor does this, we generally do not recommend any further treatment.

If the cancer has not spread, surgical removal is recommended. Problem is, it's impossible to know if it's spread or not. Many of these tumors are in the spleen, and we can all live without our spleen. A small percentage of these are even benign, called a hemangioma. If the mass turns out to be malignant, it's likely that it has already spread. The real challenge then is to determine if chemotherapy is an option. Sadly, in most cases, chemotherapy does not lengthen survival time. This aggressive tumor generally takes its toll within weeks to months of surgery. This tumor is very bad news.

Lymphoma

Lymphoma is one of the most common types of cancer in dogs and cats. This is a cancer of the lymphocytes, white blood cells that function as part of the immune system. All cats with lymphoma should be tested for feline leukemia and feline immunodeficiency virus, which are associated with lymphoma. Symptoms include weight loss, lack of appetite, and enlarged peripheral lymph nodes in dogs. In cats, the cancer typically affects internal organs more than peripheral lymph nodes, so the external nodes are generally not enlarged.

Treatment can extend a pet's life, but it's not easy and requires a very strong commitment. You'll need

to rearrange your schedule to accommodate frequent visits to your vet, monthly or more frequent blood checks, and chemotherapy. Treatment is also expensive. But dogs with peripheral lymphoma might get years of good-quality life during and after treatment. In cats, the prognosis is not as cheery, but even they may have a few years after diagnosis.

Mammary Cancer

Tumors of the mammary glands are one of the most common forms of cancer in dogs (occurring most commonly in unspayed females). Males can also develop mammary tumors, although it's rare. Mammary cancer is also common in cats and can affect rodents and rabbits, as well. Tumors are either mammary adenomas (which are benign) or mammary adenocarcinomas (which are malignant). Pets have eight mammary glands, so these masses have four times as many options to become cancerous than they do in humans.

Most affected dogs are small breeds like cockers and other spaniels, dachshunds, and poodles. Obesity may also be a factor. We don't see much breed influence in cats, although some think that Burmese, Siamese, and other Asian breeds are more affected.

Diagnosis is straightforward since these masses are clearly visible. What's not as easy is determining whether they are benign or malignant. In cats, most mammary tumors are malignant and aggressive. This is generally not the case in dogs, but certain types are malignant. Surgical excision, which is recommended along with

spaying, decreases the estrogen and progesterone that stimulate these tumors to grow. This is why we recommend spaying dogs and cats before they ever go into heat, generally around six months of age. No hormonal stimulation means a negligible chance of developing mammary carcinoma.

In cats, most of these tumors are carcinomas and will recur despite removal, so radiation and chemotherapy may be recommended. Dogs can live for years after their mammary tumors are removed as long as they've also been spayed. That is especially the case with smaller tumors, which have a better prognosis than larger ones.

Mast Cell Tumors

Mast cells contain histamine involved in allergic reactions. They're primarily found in connective tissues just below the skin, mouth, nose, and lungs. Most often, mast cell tumors, or mastocytomas, show up on the skin. Any animal can develop them, but we see them more in Boston terriers, boxers, and pugs than other breeds. Mast cell tumors are graded 1 to 3 in increasing order of malignancy or metastatic potential. Their appearance varies greatly, so diagnosis requires a fine-needle aspirate (see Chapter 32).

Treatment is removal. Your vet will cut a wide periphery around the tumor to make sure all cancer cells are removed. If the grade is low enough, this can mean a cure. In higher-grade mast cell tumors or those that are not amenable to a wide excision, radiation or chemotherapy, or both, might be recommended after surgery.

Melanoma

Melanomas are malignant skin tumors made up of pigment-containing cells called melanocytes.

IS IT SKIN CANCER?

Pets grow skin lumps and bumps all the time. Many times they're nothing to worry about. Noncancerous lumps and bumps include cysts and warts. Miniature poodles and cocker spaniels in particular develop a lot of benign skin cysts. A client once brought in her poodle for a routine dental appointment and asked if I could remove some cysts. She had circled about two dozen with a blue Sharpie. Needless to say, I removed only the worst-looking ones, leaving the harmless majority alone. Any questionable lumps should always go to pathology.

They're most commonly found in the mouth or on the paws. Some melanomas are benign; others can be highly aggressive and metastasize to other organs. They can affect all species, including humans. Light-colored pets, especially those exposed to a lot of ultraviolet radiation from the sun, are at higher risk for melanoma. In cats, the benign form of the disease, melanocytoma, is more common and occurs around the eyes and on the toes.

If you see an unusual spot on your pet, have your vet check it. If it is indeed melanoma, surgical removal of the tumor with wide margins is necessary. This can be challenging if the tumor is in the mouth, and chemotherapy and radiation may be recommended. In 2010, the Food and Drug Administration approved a vaccine for canine melanoma. It's not widely used but has shown potential for helping dogs with melanoma live longer lives. Prevention is the best treatment. Limit your pet's exposure to direct sunlight, and consider sunscreen especially if he has a short, thin coat and is white or light colored.

Osteosarcoma

A diagnosis of osteosarcoma, or bone cancer, is devastating. These tumors have usually already spread by the time they're diagnosed. These are cases where we wish animals could speak and tell us their legs are hurting before it becomes obvious due to a limp. Large-breed dogs are most affected. This cancer is rare in cats and when they do get it, it's generally less aggressive and can be entirely cured by amputation. Sadly, this is not the case for dogs.

I've lost two dogs, both greyhounds, to this aggressive cancer. My first dog, Sophie, lived for five years after her amputation and chemotherapy. My second greyhound, Lucy, died within eight months. There doesn't seem to be a genetic link, but large dogs, especially athletes like greyhounds between the ages of eight and 10, are the primary target. Treatment is tough. Most cases require amputation and chemotherapy with variable, mostly poor, results. In general, osteosarcoma is fatal.

Perianal Cancer

Perianal adenocarcinoma, including anal sac cancer, is seen in dogs but is very rare in cats. It's highly invasive with a poor prognosis. It manifests as a visible, or palpable by your vet, anal growth that might cause dogs to have trouble defecating. Perianal cancer can cause high calcium levels in the blood, which can be a big tipoff to this cancer. Unfortunately, by then it has often

MY RAT HAS A TUMOR

The most common tumor in rats is the mammary fibroadenoma, a benign tumor that affects unspayed female rats. There is also a malignant variant called the fibroadenocarcinoma. These masses can look beastly. They show up anywhere along the belly from the throat to the tail and grow like wildfire. Surgery can be curative unless the tumor is malignant. To prevent your female rat from developing mammary tumors, have her spayed.

spread to neighboring lymph nodes. Surgery can give your dog more time but not a cure. Radiation can help, but this tumor does not have a good prognosis. Perianal furunculosis, which is a chronic inflammatory disease affecting German shepherds primarily, can look like perianal cancer but has very good treatment success.

Prostate Cancer

Prostate cancer is seen mostly in unneutered dogs. We don't see enough unneutered cats to know its incidence in felines. Prostate adenocarcinoma is the malignant form that metastasizes quickly and is more common in large-breed dogs between the ages of eight and 12. Signs include difficulty and pain urinating, often with visible blood in the urine. Treatment involves radiation and chemotherapy. Unfortunately, neutering after diagnosis is not beneficial. Prostate cancer has a poor prognosis. If you need one more reason to neuter your pet, this is it.

Squamous Cell Carcinoma

Squamous cell carcinoma (SCC) is typically seen in the mouth, nose, skin, and paws. Both dogs and cats are susceptible, but cats are much more commonly affected. In cats, these tumors start off as nonhealing sores on the nose, eyelids, above the lip, and on the ear tips. Masses can look like anything, but often develop raw, painful-looking centers. These tumors invade and spread. Finding one is a race for diagnosis and immediate treatment.

SCC is a real problem in cats. Long exposure to ultraviolet light is a known cause. White or light-pigmented cats should not sunbathe (the same goes for light-pigmented dogs). If possible, limit sunbathing time to avoid the hours between 10 a.m. and 2 p.m. Pet-safe sunscreen is a good idea too, especially on white muzzles and ears.

Tumors on the skin are usually surgically removed. If the tumor involves a toe, it's best to simply amputate. Where surgery is not possible,

UTERINE CANCER IN RABBITS

Uterine adenocarcinoma, a malignant tumor of the uterus, is one of the most common cancers in rabbits. It occurs in up to 60 percent of rabbits over three years old. Common signs include blood in the urine, vaginal discharge, and cysts or tumors in the mammary glands. Behavioral changes such as aggression have also been noted. Anemia from blood loss is common and can be helpful in making a diagnosis. Treatment, if  caught before metastasis, can be successful and includes spaying your bunny, something we recommend for all female rabbits to prevent development of this aggressive cancer.

radiation and chemotherapy may be recommended. Cats are more prone to nose and ear tip SCC. For the former, radiation is recommended; for the latter, your vet will surgically remove the affected side of the ear, sometimes even the entire ear. Radiation is not an easy treatment for your cat, but if we can get to these tumors early enough, a full cure is possible.

CANCER TREATMENTS

If your pet is diagnosed with cancer, you have some decisions to make. Although you may choose to have your regular veterinarian treat your pet, another option is finding a veterinary oncologist, who is board-certified in diagnosing and treating cancer. They have specialized training beyond what all veterinarians learn in vet school. All they see are cancer patients, so they're very familiar with specific cancers, the most effective treatment options, and managing side effects. Depending on the type of cancer, your pet might require chemotherapy, immunotherapy, radiation, or surgery (or any combination of these) and might end up with a team of veterinarians treating him. A veterinary oncologist can act as your pet's point person, managing and coordinating his care. In addition, a vet oncologist might be able to enroll your pet in a clinical trial if he qualifies.

Treatment outcomes may vary considerably. When each of my greyhounds Sophie and Lucy developed osteosarcoma, it was the same tumor, same breed, same age, and same treatment. Each dog had completely different outcomes. My poor Lucy survived only eight months, but Sophie had five years.

Chemotherapy

Even saying the word *chemotherapy* causes us to imagine the worst: pain, nausea, vomiting, weakness, and hair loss. In people, oncologists shoot for a five-year survival time. In pets, whose lives are much shorter, we try to slow the cancer to give pets more quality time with us. That's why chemotherapy in animals is generally milder than in people. We're not trying to cure what can't be cured; we're just trying to get some more quality time.

In animals, we don't tolerate side effects with veterinary chemotherapy. It's not fair to expect them to go through nausea, vomiting, weight loss, and exhaustion just to give us more time with them. According to Dr. Lisa Barber, assistant clinical oncologist at the Cummings School of Veterinary Medicine at Tuft University, most pets have no side effects from chemotherapy and less than 5 percent of animals get very sick during this process. If they do, we dial back the chemo.

Although your regular vet might be able to administer chemotherapy, it's well worth it to see an oncologist for this. They're the masters at titrating doses, avoiding side effects, and changing

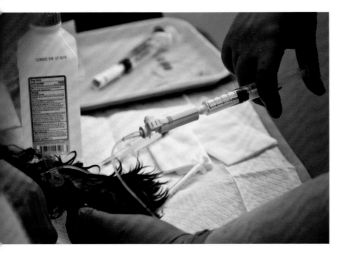

drugs if needed. They are up to date on all the latest and greatest in treatment options, and know the prognosis, chances of survival, and the exact amount of chemotherapy your pet can tolerate.

Whenever anyone asks me if they should consider chemotherapy for their pet, I have one answer: If there's a good chance to capture a reasonable amount of quality time with your pet, go for it. One proviso: Stop the chemotherapy if your pet ever realizes he's having it.

Radiation Therapy

The difference between chemotherapy and radiation therapy is that radiation is localized and chemotherapy is systemic, meaning it affects the whole body. The goal of radiation is not to completely eradicate a tumor (we would if we could) but to limit the impact it's having on our pets in order to gain some quality of life. According to a 2011 study by researchers at the University of Pennsylvania's Ryan Veterinary Hospital, 75 percent of the study dogs who received radiation therapy had an overall positive response.

A good friend once called me to talk about her cat who was diagnosed with nasal squamous cell carcinoma. After consulting with her vet, she planned to start radiation the next weekend. I was torn. I knew she loved her cat, but I also knew she'd never want to hurt him. Radiation is tough. It can knock out the tumor cells, but treatment usually involves general anesthesia and daily radiation five days a week for three to four weeks. Although the treatments are painless, the tissue damage from the radiation surrounding the tumor may be uncomfortable or even painful. That's a month of stress, anesthesia, and swelling. Imagine that in the face and you'll understand how I felt about giving that advice to my friend.

When contemplating radiation, consider the chances of remission, quality of life, and the discomfort of the treatment. That's a conversation for you and your vet. If the equation comes out positive, for instance, 30 days of unpleasantness for three years of normal life, radiation might be something to seriously consider. I recently had this experience with my own dog Jake, who went through five days of radiation for a carcinoma we discovered. The treatments were a breeze but the recovery was tough for a week afterward. He's doing well now and we're treasuring every extra month we get in remission.

Immunotherapy

New techniques in our fight against cancer are in development. One of the most promising is immunotherapy, or using antibodies to treat tumors. The idea is to redirect the body's normal defenses against cancer cells, which are usually not recognized as foreign (since they arose from normal cells). The goal is to get normal defense cells to attack the cancer cells but leave healthy cells alone.

A referral oncology clinic might offer immunotherapy using low doses of daily oral or injectable medications. Although immunotherapy is less available than chemotherapy or radiation therapy, we're making some headway with this treatment.

TO TREAT OR NOT TO TREAT

Most of the time, cancer in pets is ultimately terminal. Knowing how far to go depends on the possible outcome. Generally pets with metastases are given less than six months to live. The question to ask your vet is not, "Can you cure my pet?" but, "Can you give my pet a good quality of life with what time remains?"

I often hear people criticize friends or relatives for "spending so much money on an animal" or "making the pet suffer" by choosing chemotherapy. This is unfair. First, choosing to spend your own money on an animal is nobody's business but yours. Second, the assumption that you're putting your pet through a huge amount of discomfort is just a plain misunderstanding of chemotherapy in animals.

Sure, treating cancer delays the inevitable, but that's not all you're doing. You're making a controlled, deliberate plan with your vet to give your pet more quality time. Sometimes you might even luck out and get a cure. Cancer is just like any other chronic disease—you manage it. As long as your pet is still experiencing a good quality of life, the chance for more life might be worth the risk. It's a controlled risk that you can start and stop.

In the end, it's always about quality of life. That's the only thing that ultimately matters and the Five Freedoms are a good place to start. Every answer to the question of quality of life is individual, as is every cancer treatment plan. But if you still see some happy potential—dinner, walks at the park (even if you drive there now instead of walking there), a good brushing, cuddles on the couch, all without pain, then you and your pet still have some quality time left together.

But if you decide, for whatever reason, not to treat the cancer, don't feel guilty. This is your choice and all that matters is to prevent discomfort. For that reason, don't prolong the inevitable. The more advanced the cancer gets, the more discomfort your pet will experience, including nausea, inappetence, and worse. Don't wait too long. ■

Ask DR. GARY:

How Much Does Cancer Treatment Cost?

No question, treating cancer is costly. Between surgery, specialists, chemo, radiation, rechecks, and blood work, expect costs to be in the thousands. Before starting treatment, ask for an estimate, even if it's just a ballpark one. There's no way to predict exactly how your pet's cancer will respond to treatment, but at least you'll have an idea of where to start. If you decide not to go the treatment route, your vet will help your pet with pain medication and other ways to maintain quality of life as long as possible. Unfortunately, since animals truly show signs of cancer so late, that may not be much time.

CHAPTER 36

Aging Pets and Death

If we're lucky, old age awaits us all. Depending on the species, breed, and size, pets are considered "senior" between seven and 10 years of age. Today, veterinary services for senior pets include geriatric care, specialized hospice services and end-of-life care. Once your pet passes seven years old, plan on bringing him at least once a year for a physical exam, senior blood work, and urinalysis. Your senior pet skipping one year is like you not seeing your doctor for a decade. That's too much time between physical exams. Annual exams give your vet a running start on senior problems before they ever show up.

COMMON ISSUES IN AGING PETS

If your pet lives long enough, he'll likely develop one or more age-related medical issues. Hearing and eyesight diminish, joints become arthritic, and sleep-running becomes the most exercise your pet might get. Knowing what to look for and seeking treatment early can help you manage any problems so your pet can live out his golden years without pain or discomfort.

Animals, like people, slow down. This isn't about physical activity alone; pets' behaviors also change as they get older. These changes can be the first sign of aging. Less interest in favorite activities like running at the park or playing with a favorite ball and decreased appetite are normal behavioral changes that go along with aging. Drastic changes, though, are something to speak to your vet about. The most common of these is cognitive dysfunction syndrome (see page 368).

Arthritis

The technical term for osteoarthritis, or simply arthritis, is *degenerative joint disease,* which means the lubricating surfaces between the bones aren't effective. This causes instability in the joint and erosion of the cartilage between the bones. In time, this erosion causes bone to rub on bone, causing pain. In dogs, the most commonly affected joints are the shoulder, elbow, carpus (wrist), hip, and stifle (knee).

Arthritis is an old-age disease. On the one hand, it's great that pets are living long enough to get it. On the other hand, it can negatively affect pets' quality of life, and occasionally pops up at a relatively young age. Arthritis is seen a lot in large- and giant-breed dogs, including Bernese mountain dogs, German shepherds, golden retrievers, Labrador retrievers, Rottweilers, and Saint Bernards. We used to think that cats didn't

Ask DR. GARY:

Should You Get a New Pet for Your Senior Pet?

I get asked this question a lot. There is no one answer, but in many cases, a younger pet can bring back some of the energy you thought was gone in your older pet. I saw that myself years ago when I got a greyhound puppy for my 10-year-old girl, Max. It really depends on your pet. If he's always been a social animal, a young pet might be just the thing to put that spark back in his eyes. If not, this might cause stress. If you do decide to bring home a new pet, make sure your senior pet always has a quiet, comfortable place to retreat to on those occasions when the youngster becomes a little too much!

suffer from arthritis, but today we know that our feline friends, rabbits, rodents, and even reptiles can suffer from joint degeneration and arthritis.

A diagnosis of degenerative joint disease can be delayed for months to years since animals tend to hide their pain. The most obvious sign of arthritis is limping, but pets might be subtle, moving more slowly or avoiding stairs. Cats might stop using the litter box, self-groom in excess, or stop jumping up on the couch or bed.

A plethora of treatment options are available for arthritis, including nutraceuticals (nutritional supplements), anti-inflammatory drugs, stem cell therapies, therapeutic lasers, and even surgery. The key is to reduce inflammation and eliminate pain.

Weight reduction is one of the best ways to treat arthritis. The less an animal weighs, the less strain is placed on her joints. Talk to your vet about a diet and exercise plan to help your pet trim down.

Just 20 years ago, we only had aspirin to help dogs in pain. Today, there are more than 20 different veterinary-specific nonsteroidal anti-inflammatory drugs (NSAIDs) for pets. NSAIDs decrease pain and inflammation. Other pain medications might be used in combination with NSAIDs or as an alternative to them if a pet doesn't tolerate NSAIDs well.

Some of these include nutraceuticals, which are safe and effective and may be given at the earliest signs of stiffness. We aren't entirely sure how these work, but glucosamine and chondroitin sulfate appear to help some pets with arthritis feel better and are safe to use. A veterinary-specific product is best. In fact, Adequan (poly-sulfated glycosaminoglycan) is an FDA-approved, injectable glucosamine-like arthritis drug used in difficult cases of degenerative joint disease in dogs. It is given as an intramuscular injection by your veterinarian twice a week for a month. Other nutraceuticals, including omega-3 and omega-6 fatty acids, reduce inflammation and pain. Methyl-sulfonylmethane (MSM) might also help some animals with pain.

Today there are many options to help pets suffering from arthritis. And that includes cats as well as dogs. Talk to your vet about starting your pet on these and you could have many more years of quality play time with your senior friend.

Cognitive Dysfunction Syndrome

Aging doesn't spare the mind for pets any more than it does for us. Animals don't forget where they left their phone or keys, but you might notice changes in how they react to their normal routines. Similar to dementia in humans, cognitive dysfunction syndrome (CDS) results in problems with memory, awareness, and learning. Whether it's from protein accumulations in the brain like Alzheimer's or some other neurophysiological change, it's extremely common in pets as they age. You might see symptoms of CDS in dogs 11 years and older and in cats 10 years and older.

CDS can come on so slowly that you might not notice it's happening. What seems like deafness (your dog doesn't respond when you call) might in fact be confusion or disinterest. One help is to break down signs into five categories using the acronym DISHA, which stands for Disorientation, (altered) Interactions, Sleep cycle changes, House soiling, and Activity (level changes). Heading out the door for a walk but turning in the wrong direction might indicate disorientation. Head pressing against a wall can be altered interaction. Up all night panting or pacing indicates sleep cycle changes. Even personality can change.

Most of the signs of CDS can also be symptoms of other issues. For instance, excessive vocalization in a cat could be a sign of dementia or a sign of arthritis (pain can cause cats to vocalize). Additionally, confusion or "spacing out" could indicate a neurological disorder. For this reason, if your older pet starts acting off, bring him in to your veterinarian for a complete physical exam. If the symptoms are

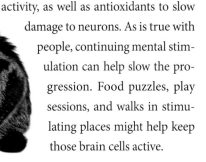

COMMON SIGNS OF CDS IN DOGS AND CATS

Cognitive dysfunction syndrome can take many forms. No one knows your pet better than you do, so tell your vet if you see any of these signs:

Sleep pattern changes (for instance, pacing at night rather than sleeping)

Vocalization changes

Anxiety or nervousness

Disorientation or confusion

Staring at walls

Eating or drinking less

House soiling

Irritability

Not responding to voice commands

Circling

Wandering away from home

No longer self-grooming (cats)

caused by something other than CDS, it might be treatable.

No proven medications really turn things around, although one drug is on the market for canine cognitive dysfunction—Anipryl (selegiline hydrochloride). To be honest, I haven't found this helps a great deal. Some pet foods contain high levels of omega-3 fatty acids to support brain activity, as well as antioxidants to slow damage to neurons. As is true with people, continuing mental stimulation can help slow the progression. Food puzzles, play sessions, and walks in stimulating places might help keep those brain cells active.

DOG UP ALL NIGHT?

I hear it all the time. Senior dogs up all night panting, pacing, or asking to go out at 2 a.m. This type of behavior can be caused by cognitive dysfunction syndrome, discomfort, or both. Talk to your vet about the following:

1. Consider Benadryl before bed. This doesn't have quite the sleep-inducing properties it has for humans, but it can help.
2. Treat arthritis. If your dog has arthritis, keep it under control with anti-inflammatories and glucosamine.
3. Consider trazodone. This antianxiety medication has been around for a long time for people. It's safe to use in pets, so ask your vet if it might help your dog.

Geriatric Vestibular Disease

Geriatric vestibular disease (GVD) primarily affects dogs in their senior years and shows up as a severe head tilt, unsteady gait, and even vomiting. A hallmark sign is "doll's eye" movement, where the eyes flick back and forth uncontrollably. We're not entirely sure what causes GVD, but the signs develop suddenly, often in less than an hour. You must see your vet when this happens, but it generally goes away in time with rest, motion sickness medication, and antinausea medication. The most tragic thing I hear is that someone euthanized their dog too soon because of this. As challenging as this disease is, it often gets better.

Hearing Loss

It's not uncommon for older pets to develop partial or complete hearing loss. You might notice that your older pet sleeps through loud sounds or stops responding when you call his name. Age-related hearing loss is not reversible, but you should always have your pet examined by a vet to make sure it's truly age related and not something else like a bad ear infection. To help your deaf pet, keep his daily routine consistent so he knows what to expect and always approach your pet from the front or side to avoid startling him.

Congestive Heart Failure

Congestive heart failure (CHF) is end-stage heart disease. This can occur due to pre-existing heart disease advancing to CHF or undiagnosed heart disease finally becoming evident. Pets don't routinely develop vascular heart disease or cholesterol problems like humans do, but valvular disease can occur, mostly in dogs.

The most common heart disease in dogs is mitral valve disease (see Chapter 25). Detected at a younger age, it's a congenital disease, but in seniors it's considered a degenerative change and is called endocardiosis. This occurs because the valves thicken and can't close properly. We treat this conservatively in senior pets as it's an almost normal development. Some pets never develop heart disease but it's a good idea to watch them closely for signs to begin.

Cats rarely get valvular disease but might get worsening of a previously diagnosed cardiomyopathy (see Chapter 25). This enlargement in the heart can also lead to leaking in the mitral valve, especially in dilated cardiomyopathy. We don't see this as often because many cats with dilated cardiomyopathy don't make it to their senior years. When either cardiomyopathy in cats worsens in their senior years, we're on the lookout for congestive heart failure.

Signs of congestive heart disease are exercise intolerance, weakness, panting, and a cough. If these symptoms begin, treatment includes a diet change to reduce sodium intake and exercise restriction (don't go running together). If a pet is coughing, fluid is accumulating in the lungs and it's time for medication. If no signs of congestive heart failure have begun, under the careful care of your vet, pets can live for years with heart disease.

Age-Related Incontinence

Signs of incontinence include accidents in the house, dribbling, bloody urine, and soaked beds. When we talk of incontinence, it's not just the urinary variety. Impaired muscle control of the rectum and anus due to neurological and musculoskeletal diseases also cause fecal incontinence. Senior pets develop incontinence for a variety of reasons, some of which are treatable. Your vet will first rule out urinary tract infections, metabolic diseases, and hormone-related incontinence in spayed female dogs (see Chapter 15).

If none of those are the cause of your pet's incontinence, it's likely caused by normal aging.

The most common condition leading to incontinence is arthritis. Difficulty walking, squatting, lifting a leg, or hopping into a litter box can occur when your pet is experiencing joint pain or entrapment of a nerve by degenerative bone changes in the spine. Renal insufficiency, which is common in older cats, might lead to increased urination. Many older animals might be on medications for other issues, and many of these can lead to incontinence. Cognitive dysfunction can also be a cause of incontinence.

NEW DEVELOPMENTS IN SENIOR PET HEART TREATMENT

Heart disease treatment in veterinary patients is catching up to human cardiology treatment in both surgery and medicine. The cardiac drug pimobendan is showing great promise in the treatment of mitral valve disease in dogs, with multiple studies demonstrating significant improvement in both dogs and cats. In addition, new surgical valve replacement techniques are currently being developed in animals. That's good news for the thousands of animals with mitral and tricuspid valve disease who may never have to risk developing CHF in their senior years.

LIVING WITH AN INCONTINENT PET

Management is the key to keeping your older pet comfortable and maintaining your own sanity. Here are a few things that will help:

1. Frequent walks for your dog
2. Late-night potty trip before bed
3. A shallow litter box
4. Washable pet bedding
5. Pee pads inside your dog bed (you can wash the covers easily but that insert is a nightmare)
6. Doggie diaper or belly band
7. Keeping your pet clean and dry
8. Keeping calm and understanding it's never their fault; in fact, your pet might be as stressed as you are by this
9. Never restricting water
10. Asking your vet for help

Unless there is a treatable underlying condition, there's no cure for age-related incontinence, but it can be controlled. The drug phenylpropanolamine can help tighten up the external urinary muscles, and this has been used for years. For female dogs with estrogen-responsive incontinence, the gold standard is a naturally occurring estrogen called Incurin. This synthetic version of estriol (a short-acting estrogen) has been shown to be very effective in controlling urinary incontinence in spayed dogs without the risk of the bone marrow suppression we faced with diethylstilbestrol, an estrogen derivative vets used for years. Unfortunately, there are no medications for cats, but treating mobility issues will help all animals. Using a litter box with low sides can make it easier for old cats to get in and out. Cement-mixing trays, sold at home improvement stores, are perfect for this.

Renal Disease

Older animals are more susceptible to renal disease, or kidney failure. It's very common in senior cats as we've discussed. We've all seen that skinny-as-a-rail old cat with unkempt fur gingerly walking around her home. You can bet she's dehydrated and has kidney disease. Pets with renal disease have poor appetites, lose weight, urinate frequently, and get immensely dehydrated. The goal is to keep them comfortable and slow the progression with fluids and a senior diet. A lower protein, low-phosphorus diet can help slow the progression of renal disease, but only if your cat will eat it. This isn't the time to impose serious diet changes on your elderly feline. We just want her to eat. Even if the kidneys are failing, with good management and compassionate care, you might get some pretty good quality time with your pet.

RECOGNIZING SENIOR KIDNEY DISEASE IN YOUR CAT

Kidney disease in senior cats can be subtle. Here are the common signs to look for:

Increased drinking
Frequent urination
Dehydration
Loss of appetite
Weight loss
Vomiting or diarrhea
Bad breath
Mouth ulcers

Vision Loss

Blindness can develop naturally in aging pets from hypertension due to chronic kidney disease or from diabetes and its resultant cataracts. Cataracts are an opaque thickening of the lens in the center of the eye. Unlike in humans, cataracts in pets are relatively uncommon, but dogs are afflicted the most. Untreated diabetes can lead to cataracts too. Cataracts are entirely treatable once the underlying cause is controlled. Treatment consists of laser surgery that dissolves the lens using an ultrasonic probe. This has the great name "phacoemulsification." It's then removed (along with the cataract that formed over it) and an artificial lens is inserted. The procedure is safe and effective. The price tag for this cure is high, but it's a terrific thing to do for your pet (yet another good reason to invest in pet insurance).

WHAT IS QUALITY OF LIFE?

I've been asked my entire career to define "quality of life." This isn't an easy question to answer because it's all about happiness, which is different for everyone and every animal. You know your pet better than anyone else. What does he love doing? Is food the most important thing on the planet, or chasing after a favorite tennis ball? Sitting high on a window sill watching birds or sleeping in the sun?

Alice Villalobos, veterinary oncologist and former president of the American Association of Human Animal Bond Veterinarians and leader in veterinary oncology and pet hospice care, has developed a quality-of-life scale that includes identifying behaviors that provide happiness and comfort for your pet. This is important because

Ask DR. GARY:

Do Gray Eyes Always Mean Blindness?

Many owners mistake cloudy eyes for cataracts in their pets, especially dogs. Called nuclear lenticular sclerosis (NLS), this is a normal aging change in senior animals characterized as a bluish-gray haze in the lens of the eye. We're not entirely sure why it happens, but the lens appears to get thicker as pets age. Unlike cataracts, NLS is transparent. Light passes through it, so it doesn't significantly impair vision. Your vet can easily tell the difference. Another clue is that NLS always affects both eyes, whereas cataracts may affect one eye more than the other.

as pets age, "normal" moves further away from what it once was. According to Dr. Villalobos, keep track of any red flags and when you see one, reassess how your pet is doing. Her scale specifically addresses terminally ill pets, but it can also be used to get a sense of how your senior pet is doing. The HHHHHMM Scale refers to seven objective criteria to assess: hurt, hunger, hydration, hygiene, happiness, mobility, and more good days than bad days. The scale runs from 1 to 10 (worst to best). A score above five on most of these criteria is considered good.

I wish there was an easier answer, but there's not. Even having a good appetite is not the best indicator as many animals will eat right up until their euthanasia appointment. Your answer to quality of life is simply a painless, comfortable pet who has at least a few moments a day when you recognize that young animal you fell in love with so many years ago. That's the most any of us can wish for.

END OF LIFE CARE

Along with pets living longer come the challenges those years carry. Geriatric or rehabilitative care treats not only the pet but also the pet parent. It acknowledges how alone people feel when left to deal with the most difficult part of their beloved pets' lives. Veterinary geriatric care includes pain management, mobility support,

physical therapy, holistic medicine, and, when the time is right, euthanasia.

Hospice

Sometimes pets are diagnosed with a terminal illness but still feel pretty good. They might have days, weeks, or even months of good-quality life left. You might be reluctant to elect euthanasia yet, and that is where veterinary hospice services come in. Hospice is an in-home service that provides supportive care to make sure the pet is not in pain or suffering, helping your pet comfortably enjoy his last days at home with his family. Your regular vet might offer in-clinic or at-home hospice services. Some specialty mobile veterinarians only practice hospice care. They will come to your home to treat your pet, giving fluids, medications, nutrition, and anything else he needs.

Hospice care doesn't mean you don't treat your pet. It just means you don't do anything to decrease his quality of life. Sometimes that means avoiding aggressive treatment. Pursuing aggressive treatment when the prognosis is poor is not in the best interest of your pet. Age is not a disease, yet it can preclude rigorous treatment when there are limited gains. For instance, we've made great advances in cancer treatment, yet is an aggressive amputation and chemotherapy the right thing for a 13-year-old Labrador retriever with osteosarcoma? Probably not.

Hospice care provides the best quality of life possible for terminally ill pets until the pet dies or you make the decision to euthanize. Hospice gives you quality time with your pet while allowing you to slowly adjust to the fact that your pet's life is coming to a close. Hospice might not change the outcome that lies ahead for your pet, but it will give you peace knowing you gave your pet every chance for happiness until the very end.

Helping with the euthanasia decision is one of the most valuable roles hospice practitioners play. When the times comes, most hospice vets will also do the euthanasia themselves, either at the clinic or in your home. We all want our pets to pass peacefully on their own at night in their sleep. A good hospice vet will help you aim for this, but please don't wait to intervene if it becomes necessary. More often than not, that is past the point of comfort for your animal.

Euthanasia

Euthanasia is by far the most difficult thing you can go through with your pet. It's also the most unfair. Not only do you lose your best friend, but you have to make the decision. We make a contract with pets the moment we take them into our homes. That contract is to maintain the Five Freedoms and ensure their happiness. The day that contract is no longer possible is the one we all dread. One of the privileges of being a veterinarian is to ensure that the decision to euthanize is not made prematurely, and that it's done in the most compassionate, humane manner for both pet and human.

I've euthanized every one of my pets myself. I always get them their favorite thing to eat, whether it's a bag of McDonald's hamburgers or doggie ice cream. Then we go the next step together. Being there during the euthanasia procedure is something everyone should consider. I realize this isn't possible for everyone, but if you can, it's the ultimate gesture of love and commitment you can give your pet. It also helps with closure: You were there at the end.

Once the decision is made, what exactly happens? A good vet will make sure it's painless for

Ask DR. GARY:

Should You Show Your Other Pets Your Deceased Pet?

Like people, pets grieve. They notice that their companion is gone. I've heard many people, even vets, say they want to let their other pets see their deceased pet. I don't agree. Dogs and cats don't understand the concept of death. It's far more likely they'll pick up on your stress and grief than on the fact that their friend has died. Better to simply give copious attention to the animals who are left with you. That will do them, and you, the most good.

the pet and peaceful for you. Although not always possible, my preference is to do this in your home, where your pet is most comfortable. Many veterinarians offer this service, even if they don't ordinarily do house calls. Either way, it should be in a quiet, calm, and soothing environment.

Whether at home or in the clinic, your pet can lie in his bed or on a soft blanket on the table or floor. First, a sedative is given through an IV catheter or simply an injection. This allows your pet to fall asleep peacefully. Then an injectable barbiturate anesthetic is given. Death occurs within a few seconds to minutes and doesn't appear to be painful or uncomfortable for your pet.

It's important to know that animals do not close their eyes when they die. Sometimes vets stroke the eyelids down into a closed position, just as human physicians do for people. Animals might also vocalize during euthanasia. This doesn't mean they're in pain. It's just an excitable period during the process of full anesthesia caused by the barbiturate. A twitch or a final few gasps might occur, but this is normal and doesn't mean your pet was in pain. All of these activities are much less likely with a pre-euthanasia sedative so I recommend them every single time.

Your Pet's Remains

One of the hardest things for me to talk about with clients is what they'd like to have done with their deceased pet. There are a few options depending on your preferences. Your vet will typically make all the arrangements.

Cremation is the most common option. If you elect a private cremation, you'll have your pet's ashes returned to you within a few days in an urn or box, sometimes with a clipping of fur or a paw print as well. Costs range from $100 to $500 or more depending on the size of your animal. If that isn't important to you, you may choose a group cremation, which is the most cost-effective method. In a group cremation, your pet is cremated with other pets. You don't get your pet's ashes back if you choose this option.

Burial at a pet cemetery or crematorium is another option. Either ashes from a private cremation or the body itself is buried. This option can be a good one because it provides a permanent, serene environment for your pet to rest. In my experience, this option is relatively uncommon because there aren't many pet cemeteries to choose from. If you do decide to go this route, ask your vet for help locating a pet cemetery in your area or check with the Association of Pet Cemeteries and Crematories, which maintains a national list.

Depending on jurisdictional regulations, pets may be buried on your property. The downside to this is your pet will remain behind if you move. When burying an intact body, a big challenge is ensuring that your pet isn't dug up by another animal. Always check on your local, county, or state ordinances before electing to do this.

WHAT TO DO IF YOU FIND YOUR PET DECEASED

We all hope for a peaceful end for our pets, simply going in their sleep. If you think your pet has passed away at home, but you're not sure, check for breathing. If none is detected, lightly tap the inside corner of one eye to check for a blink reflex. If you see no response, wrap your pet in a blanket and go to your veterinarian, where staff will make arrangements for you. My recommendation is to do a private cremation, bring home the remains, and keep them until you can choose a final resting place, whether it's your home garden or bringing them along with you on your own final journey. That's what I'm going to do.

Pet Loss Support

Perhaps the loneliest person on Earth is the individual who has just lost his pet, tormented by a mix of emotions, including pure grief and guilt at having made the euthanasia decision, compounded by the fact that many people don't understand the impact of pet death. Fortunately, the sentiment that losing a pet is something you just

HOW TO COPE WITH THE LOSS OF YOUR PET

This pain is intense, no two ways around it. Here are a few suggestions that might help:

1. Realize you're not alone. Lots of people have experienced the pain of losing a beloved pet.
2. It's okay to be upset and you have every right to mourn.
3. Don't let others dismiss your feelings, and seek others who understand.
4. If you can, take at least a day off work.
5. Don't feel guilty. If you chose euthanasia, you maintained your contract with your pet by not letting him suffer.
6. Get the ashes and keep them in a place you can visit.
7. When you're ready, get another pet. You're not replacing your lost pet, but a new animal will distract you in the best way possible.

"get over" is changing. Memorial services are more common, employers are recognizing the need for bereavement time, and friends and family seem to be more understanding. Animals aren't humans for sure, but they are our friends, family, and children. They're our perpetual dependents and their absence is painful beyond belief.

At my shelter, the San Diego Humane Society, we host monthly pet loss support groups. We're not the only ones. These groups, typically run by professional grief counselors, allow people to share their grief with others who are experiencing the same thing. There's even an Association for Pet Loss and Bereavement, a group of professionally trained pet bereavement counseling volunteers, and the Pet Loss Grief Support Center, which offers resources to help people mourn, and heal from, the loss of their furry family member. ■

TALKING TO YOUR CHILDREN ABOUT PET DEATH

When talking to your kids about the death or imminent death of a pet, be honest and don't underestimate them. According to child psychiatrists, it's important not to suggest their pet just "ran away," which they might believe was because of them. It's also important not to refer to euthanasia as "put to sleep" as this term is confusing to young children who may develop fears of sleeping. This is an opportunity to teach about the value of animals and the sanctity of all life, and to grow as a family by going through a difficult situation together. The most important thing is the chance to teach compassion and how no animal should ever suffer. Recognize that your children will grieve, just as you will. It's better to do it together.

CHAPTER 37

Holistic Veterinary Medicine

Holistic veterinary medicine, also called natural, integrative, or alternative medicine, takes a whole-picture approach to treating patients. Holistic veterinarians look at nutrition, living environment, medical history, genetics, stress factors, and your pet's relationships with other family members. Most holistic vets use a combination of conventional treatments (including medications and surgery) and natural treatments including nutritional therapy, acupuncture, supplements, and more.

Some pet owners use holistic veterinarians as their pet's primary vet; others seek holistic vets to help with chronic medical conditions that aren't responding to conventional treatment. Holistic veterinarians commonly treat cancer, arthritis, diabetes, autoimmune diseases, chronic pain, allergies, kidney disease, chronic ear infections, heart disease, and gastrointestinal disorders.

HOW TO FIND A HOLISTIC VET

Depending on where you live, it might be difficult to find a holistic veterinarian. The American Holistic Veterinary Medical Association (AHVMA), which publishes the only peer-reviewed journal on integrative medicine, maintains an online database to find vets and practitioners certified in their practice (visit *ahvma.org*). Another organization, the Veterinary Institute of Integrative Medicine, also offers a search on its website (*viim.org*). If you don't have a holistic veterinarian in your area, some practitioners will do consultations over the phone or via video chat. One thing to keep in mind is that specialty licensure is not required for veterinarians to practice holistic medicine, but clinicians might be certified in acupuncture, herbal medicine, homeopathy, and chiropractic. You should definitely require this of any practitioner you employ to treat your pet.

COMMON ALTERNATIVE TREATMENTS

Many treatments fall under the natural or alternative umbrella. Results will vary with such treatments. Some pets see dramatic improvement; others have little to no change. Some of these treatments have been studied by researchers, and others are considered traditional treatments with anecdotal evidence of their efficacy. Most holistic veterinarians combine one or more natural treatments with or without one or more conventional treatments.

Acupuncture and Acupressure

Acupuncture has been around for more than 5,000 years, but only recently have scientists started to understand the mechanisms behind this ancient treatment. It involves placing very tiny needles into specific places on the body to stimulate the body to heal itself. Acupuncture is said to increase blood flow and circulation, reduce nausea, and decrease inflammation and pain. It can strengthen the immune system, which can have profound benefits. Some forms even use electric stimulation with the needles to gently increase the effect of the treatment. Arthritis pain is the most common use for acupuncture. Some practitioners believe it to be as effective as nonsteroidal anti-inflammatories, and without the side effects.

A variation of acupuncture is acupressure, which uses pressure rather than needles to stimulate a healing response. Reiki is a related healing method that originated in Japan in which energy is channeled through to the animal through a light touch or from a distance. Scientific confirmation of the effects of these therapies has been inconclusive. Proponents are devout about the

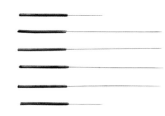

Acupuncture needles

benefits; I love the calming attention it gives to pets. For animals suffering terribly with osteoarthritis in their later years, a safe and calming treatment is nothing to dismiss.

Aromatherapy and Essential Oils

Aromatherapy is used particularly in relieving stress. Animals can smell from seven to 40 times better than we can; imagine the efficacy of aromatics in treating stress and anxiety. Lavender is an effective scent to calm pets and people alike. Even if this is mostly anecdotal, it's a safe and easy way to calm everyone around you. Caution must be exercised with essential oils, especially with cats, who are more sensitive to them. Certain essential oils can even be toxic to pets, especially if they are not properly diluted. Always work with a holistic veterinarian if you want to explore aromatherapy for your pet.

Chiropractic

Chiropractic care is often used to treat degenerative joint disease, chronic pain in the neck or and back, intervertebral disc disease, musculoskeletal weakness, and incontinence. In North America, the American Veterinary Chiropractic Association certifies both animal chiropractors (a human chiropractor certified to treat animals) and veterinarians certified in animal chiropractic (a licensed veterinarian certified to practice chiropractic). This certification is critical in finding an experienced, and safe, practitioner.

Herbal Therapy

Holistic vets use many herbs, often in combinations of 20 or more. Among the most common are chamomile, valerian root, cava, and milk thistle. The right dosages are critical, as are the correct combinations to avoid interaction problems with

DON'T BECOME YOUR OWN HERBAL PHARMACIST

Used to treat everything from stress to colitis, herbs are compounded by practitioners of herbal therapy in combinations based on their unique ingredients. Getting results takes expertise so don't try this at home! It's important to know which herbs might react with any medication prescribed. Herbal therapies are not approved or standardized by the FDA. That's why it's so important to seek the advice of a trained holistic vet when going green. Commonly used herbs include:

Alfalfa for arthritis and allergies

Aloe vera juice for ulcers, acid stomach, arthritis, and more

Black walnut as a natural dewormer and treatment for fungal infections

Chamomile for pain and inflammation in the intestines and stomach

Colloidal silver for rashes, cuts, and burns as well as a natural alternative to antibiotics

Corn silk for incontinence

Echinacea to fight infections and improve the immune system

Garlic as a natural antibiotic

Green tea as an antioxidant aid to your dog's immune system

Slippery elm tincture to deal with diarrhea and stomach problems

other herbs and Western drugs. Some herbs might have a deleterious effect on diseases so let your holistic professional prepare the right herbs and combinations for your pet.

Dried or fresh herbs are given as powders, capsules, tablets, teas, tinctures, oils, or extracts. Herbal therapy is often used as an adjunct to other therapies. There are more uses for medicinal herbs than you can shake a milk thistle branch at. Some of the herbs commonly used may surprise you (see sidebar opposite).

Veterinary Homeopathy

Veterinary homeopathy is based on the theory that like cures like, meaning if a lot of a substance causes disease, then a little bit of that same thing will cure it. Homeopathy uses remedies, either pills or liquids, that contain very tiny amounts of certain plant or mineral ingredients such as gold and arsenic. Many different remedies are available to treat a wide variety of issues, including allergies, arthritis, skin disease, inflammatory bowel disease, asthma, cancer, and liver problems. Like herbal therapy, homeopathy is frequently used in combination with other therapies.

This 200-year-old field needs proven data, which will come in time. For now, homeopathic clinicians will continue to treat their patients and gather data that can be used for the greater good, both veterinary and human.

Nutritional Therapy

Many holistic vets include nutritional therapy as part of a pet's treatment plan since diet can affect many different aspects of health. This might be as simple as choosing a prescription diet to help treat a certain disease or as complex as Chinese food therapy in which different food "energies" are balanced to provide relief of symptoms or disease. Today both traditional and Western-trained veterinarians ascribe to a "one health" approach to illness. Nutrition is a major facet of the belief that "food is medicine." Diet and nutrition, exercise and enrichment, work together with medicine to keep our animals well.

Traditional Chinese Veterinary Medicine

Traditional Chinese veterinary medicine (TCVM) is an ancient natural medical system that has been practiced in China for thousands of years. The other branches of TCVM are acupuncture, herbal medicine, food therapy, and *Tui na* (massage). Chinese medicine is based on the Taoist worldview that the physical body is just a small part of the surrounding universe and therefore governed by forces that influence the external world. Those forces are called "qi" (pronounced "chi").

Like other types of integrative medicine, TCVM focuses on a holistic approach to the body and is best used in conjunction with Western medicine. According to practitioners, one of the best uses of TCVM is the treatment of chronic illnesses. ■

Epilogue

Animals inspire compassion in me every single day. They make me a better person and teach me how to better care for people, as well as pets. Protecting and caring for these special creatures gives all of us a chance to truly show our humanity. Making sure our pets are healthy and happy is how we repay them for the joy they bring us. I hope this book has given you some ideas and tips on how to better care for your own pets. At the very least, I hope I've inspired you to develop a meaningful relationship with your pet's veterinarian because that partnership is truly the best way to ensure your pet stays healthy, as well as the best way to care for him when he's not.

It has been more than 50 years since Roger Brambell set the stage for the minimal level of care we need to ensure our animals thrive. When he conceived of the Five Freedoms for a 1965 U.K. government investigation on livestock production, he summed them up in one sentence: "An animal should at least have sufficient freedom of movement to be able without difficulty, to turn round, groom itself, get up, lie down and stretch its limbs." This short statement became known as Brambell's Five Freedoms. These were soon adopted in a report issued by the U.K. Animal Welfare Council to outline the five basic requirements all animals need, and they remain the best road map to inspire the compassionate treatment of animals:

1. Freedom from hunger or thirst by ready access to freshwater and a diet to maintain full health and vigor
2. Freedom from discomfort by providing an appropriate environment, including shelter and a comfortable resting area
3. Freedom from pain, injury, or disease by prevention or rapid diagnosis and treatment
4. Freedom to express (most) normal behavior by providing sufficient space, proper facilities, and company of the animal's own kind
5. Freedom from fear and distress by ensuring conditions and treatment that avoid mental suffering

From diet and behavioral enrichment to surgery and euthanasia, these five rules are the pillars on which we base the humane treatment of animals. Everything we do to, for, and with animals should be tested in terms of how well we are adhering to these five tenets.

Today we know that chickens have complex social structures, dolphins "talk" to each other, and dog brains are emotionally wired much like ours. Adhering to the Five Freedoms is only the beginning of what we owe our animals. Respecting them, loving them, and valuing their happiness is nonnegotiable in an advanced society.

The biggest gift of running an animal shelter is spreading the happiness that animals can bring. I'll always remember the day I walked into the main entrance of the San Diego Humane Society and passed a young woman who was dressed very smartly in business attire. She was holding a cardboard cat carrier up in the air at eye level and peering into it. She was so focused on her precious cargo that she nearly walked into me. When our eyes met, I saw the biggest, purest smile I had ever seen on a human face. She was in seventh heaven because she had just adopted two kittens. I never take for granted the privilege I have in working somewhere that can make people feel that good. That bond, whether it's about oxytocin release or just elation in having these special creatures occupy some part of our lives, is something I'll never stop marveling over.

If I could, I'd add a sixth freedom to Brambell's list: the freedom to experience happiness. Nine times out of 10, what makes your pet happiest is you. Okay, food is a strong competitor, but years of domestication have truly evolved in strengthening the bond that holds humans and animals together. I can't look at an animal without smiling. How could any of us bear to have them not feel the same way about us? Taking remarkable care of them is just the start. Adding the love and compassion we feel for them every single day would make Dr. Brambell more than proud. ■

Acknowledgments

This book is the distillation of 30 years of providing veterinary advice, both solicited and not, in public (radio) and in private (practice). I've given copious amounts of off-the-cuff veterinary advice to friends, family, and even animal shelter supporters who ask me about their pets whenever I see them. I've also had the more structured opportunity to work with thousands of veterinary clients who truly care about their pets.

Throughout my career, it's always bothered me that animals have no voice in what happens to them, even when it may happen with good intent. That's why this book is based on the 50-plus-year-old Five Freedoms, which is probably the closest thing we have to a blueprint for caring for animals. We have a big challenge today in veterinary medicine in terms of cost and accessibility, but I never doubt that providing top care for all animals is something every veterinarian wants to achieve. No one goes to vet school for the pay.

Over the past three decades, I've had plenty of opportunity to help both homed and homeless animals, and I've learned that veterinary medicine is as much about people as it is about animals. To be an effective veterinary practitioner, you have to want to help people as much as animals. That's the only way it works. It's a true partnership in the best sense of the word with a team made up of veterinarian,

veterinary staff, and the families who love, worry, and really want to care for their animals. The spirit of this book relies on the partnership you have with your own veterinarian to work together to help and heal your pets. This guide is an adjunct to that irreplaceable partnership.

This book would not have been possible without the support of my family, especially Randy Loewenstein, my partner in crime who has been the most patient inheritor of the worst dog ever, my animal-loving friends, and, most important, my shelter colleagues who demonstrate compassion in everything they do. This book started as the conceptual brainchild of Bridget E. Hamilton, my editor at National Geographic, who had coffee with me one cold winter morning in Washington, D.C., in 2015 and has kept it on course over the years since then. The words themselves would never have gotten onto the page without the very talented Jackie Brown. Jackie worked on countless drafts and spent hours on the phone going over details with me. She not only organized the text in a superhero kind of way; she got things going when it didn't seem as if they ever would. Jackie knows nearly everything there is to know about animals. For all of them and my two humbling dogs Jake and Betty, who have taught me how defenseless even a vet can feel when your pet is sick, I say a heartfelt thank you.

Appendix A:
The Status of Animal Welfare

Humans love animals. Thank heaven for that. Just log onto Facebook or Instagram, and you'll be inundated with clips and posts about animals—everything from philosophical questions about how we treat the animals we live with to how we hurt those we don't. We cringe over videos of our oceans filling up with plastic and other garbage affecting some of the largest animals in the world. And we despair over photos of hunters posing with their prey as though they just saved a village of children from attack. In spite of our burgeoning consciousness about animals, we are a confusion of emotions about how we as a society view animals. Truly, animals make

our world a far better place and transfix us in a way that few other things do. But how many of us understand the real issues about animal welfare and how we regard these living, sentient, beautiful beings who share a planet with us?

ANIMAL ETHOS: DO ANIMALS FEEL?

In the 17th century, René Descartes, convinced that animals don't experience pain, conducted gruesome experiments on dogs and other animals in ways that can only be described as monstrous now. More recently, humans

BREED-SPECIFIC LEGISLATION

In 2016, Montreal passed a terrible ordinance banning pit bulls. It was put in place after a woman was fatally mauled by her dog. According to the adoption records, however, the dog was allegedly a boxer. Breed-specific legislation (BSL) exists in many North American cities, and in every case it's the wrong solution. In fact, it can actually make things worse. Today, BSL is being repealed on a national scale, and I hope it will be eliminated. Laws work only if you can identify what you're regulating. In this case, what dogs are we talking about? Genetically tested American Staffordshire terriers? Pit bulls, which aren't even a breed at all? All big-headed dogs? Additionally, it's had an adverse effect on animal welfare because people who fear retaliation don't license their dogs, don't seek out veterinary care, and don't spay or neuter their dogs. BSL just makes people less able to be responsible pet owners. A better alternative is laws that help people take care of their dogs, readily access spay and neuter options, and become more responsible pet owners.

believed that the only animals that showed evidence of conscious thought were Old World primates, cetaceans, and cephalopods (the big three in terms of intellect in the animal world). Today, animals ranging from marine shrimp to chickens, pigs, dogs, and parrots exhibit evidence of thought, reasoning, and feeling. We've certainly come far since those dark days of Descartes, and yet for many animals, namely those raised for food in commercial production facilities, the world is not all that different from what it was in Upton Sinclair's day when he wrote *The Jungle*, his epic novel that exposed the horrific truth about the meat-packing industry in New York City.

In our modern era, we know that animals have thoughts and feelings, and they register pain, grief, love, joy, and sadness. We know that chickens and fish can have complex social structures. There are even legislative debates about how "human" primates may be and whether we have the right to keep orcas in captivity for entertainment purposes (we don't).

You have only to scroll through Facebook for a few minutes at most to see posts and videos about dog emotion, reasoning, and communication or cat attitude and behavior. A more rigorous approach is to turn to peer-reviewed journals, such as the journal *Animal Behavior,* to find studies that open our eyes to the fact that domesticated animals have feelings much like ours; they experience loneliness and make choices to increase happiness or demonstrate selflessness, just as we eternally hope humans do. To be the best pet owner, it's important to consider what happiness you can give all animals you bring into your home.

ANIMAL RIGHTS VERSUS ANIMAL WELFARE

According to the American Veterinary Medical Association, animal welfare is a human responsibility encompassing all aspects of animal well-being, including proper housing, disease prevention and treatment, responsible care, humane handling, and, when appropriate, humane euthanasia. In short, animal welfare seeks to improve the humane treatment and well-being of animals. Animal rights, on the other hand, are not the same thing as animal welfare.

Animal rights is a philosophical view that animals have implicit rights as living beings. True animal rights advocates believe that humans have no right to use animals at all—not for food, not for labor, certainly not for entertainment, not even for companionship. Animal welfare is the objective concern for the physical and emotional well-being of animals. The terms *animal welfare* and *animal rights* cannot be used interchangeably, although they frequently are. This is a dangerous equivalency that holds back improvements to the Animal Welfare Act, as well as more humane methods of animal handling. Equating the two terms means that you cannot love and appreciate animals if you eat a hamburger at a Labor Day picnic. Such inflexible doctrine can alienate and separate animal advocates and, in the long run, slows our progress with an all-or-nothing ultimatum that may at times hinder progress in improving animal welfare for the animals we all love.

The Much Used "Human-Animal Bond"

Over the past four decades a trendy phrase has entered the vernacular of nearly every animal welfare organization. Entire graduate programs have been established to study this topic, and policies have been created to honor and promote the concept. Simply stated, "human-animal bond" has become a slogan covering every positive interaction we have with animals. Although I wholly appreciate the concept and enthusiastically celebrate the philosophy, it strikes me as an ironic, sometimes overused term that may actually reduce the value of animals to a relative measure based on their relationship to humans. The risk being that non–animal lovers may conclude that animals, on their own, can't be appreciated for what they are unless their value is related to human perception. I'd much prefer we simply say that we have a "bond" with animals, which is very real and doesn't need any more qualification than a bond between people would have. After all, we don't talk about the human-human bond. It's just a bond. The ultimate trophy in our relationship with animals is the very fact that animals mean something to us, and us to them. Regardless of the name of that relationship, we should always strive to exhibit it. Do we ever refer to a married couple's relationship in terms of one partner's perception of the other? No. We call it love. And hopefully, respect. That's what we strive for in our relationship with animals, and most probably, why you're reading this book in the first place.

The Pit Bull Divide

There is no greater divide among dog lovers (and nonlovers) than that between pit bull fans and pit bull foes. There is good reason for this. Pit bulls are involved in an inordinate number of attacks on dogs and people. Some of these attacks are tragic. The breed itself isn't even a breed but a description of a certain type of dog. Sure, pit bulls are strong dogs. But so are Rottweilers, Dalmatians, and Newfoundlands. The problem is that pit bulls have an appeal for some people who raise them to fight, guard, and attack. That is no more their fault than, say, training a Doberman pinscher to guard an estate. Add to that equation a lack of socialization in the wrong hands and you've created a real problem.

Most well-raised, well-trained pit bulls are actually sweet, loving, and friendly pets. I have one myself. The only thing I need to worry about with my dog Betty is feeling guilty about not giving her enough snacks. Still, in many shelters and rescues nationwide, especially near cities, pit bulls make up a tremendous percentage of dogs in residence. They may not be for everyone, but banning them doesn't solve the problem. In fact, that, along with renting prohibitions, has become part of the problem and why so many end up in shelters. Sensible breeding, good training, a loving home, and accessible spaying and neutering are the solution here.

Closing Comments

Some may argue that you must be a vegan to do the right thing by animals. I see where they're coming from, but I disagree. While I respect that choice, I don't believe it's practical to expect the whole planet to become vegan or even vegetarian, not when we're hardwired to be carnivores (or omnivores who like meat). But we're carnivores with brains capable of more than just hardwired programming. That means we can exercise compassion in all we do, from how we treat our best animal friends, to being conscious of what animals go through to become part of our diet. Jonathan Safran Foer wrote in his book *Eating Animals,* "We live in a world in which it's conventional to treat an animal like a hunk of wood and extreme to treat an animal like an animal." Recognizing the truth regarding animal consciousness, suffering and joy, and teaching others the most humane way to live with animals will go far to make our world, and theirs, a far better place.

HUMANE CERTIFICATION

Humane Farm Animal Care (HFAC) is a nonprofit dedicated to improving the lives of food animals. Its goal is to shine a light on humane farm animal practices and help people to make more responsible, and more compassionate, food choices. Confusing and often misleading labels such as free range, cage free, and other platitudes may make us feel better about what we're eating, but HFAC's certification is the one to really look for in terms of humane farm animal treatment. If it says "Certified Humane," you can be sure we've done the best humanly possible (besides not eating them) that we could in keeping to the Five Freedoms for farm animals.

Appendix B:
Over-the-Counter Drugs and Dosages for Dogs

It is possible to occasionally treat your pets with an over-the-counter remedy. If you do so, always check with your vet first and use only the pure medication and not combination drugs, as many include decongestants and other ingredients that are not safe for pets. Although the medications listed here are mostly safe, the key word is *mostly;* use with caution and note if your pet has any reactions. Always head to the hospital if your pet seems very ill. Here are a few common over-the-counter meds you might want to give your dog. These medications are for dogs only; they are not safe for cats, guinea pigs, birds, and rabbits. Check with your vet before using any medication, including over-the-counter medications.

Aspirin (use an enteric-coated aspirin like Ascriptin)—
for musculoskeletal inflammation/pain
5 mg/lb up to twice a day

Diphenhydramine (Benadryl)—antihistamine for
allergies
1 mg/lb up to twice a day

Chlorpheniramine (Chlortrimeton)—antihistamine
for allergies
2-4 mg/10 lb up to twice a day

Loratidine (Claritin)—antihistamine for allergies
5 mg daily under 15 lb; 10 mg daily (or 5 mg twice daily)
from 15 to 39 lb; 10 mg twice daily if over 40 lb

Loperamide (Immodium)—for watery diarrhea that
occurs more than once a day
0.04 mg/lb two to three times a day

Bismuth subsalicylate (Pepto Bismol)—for diarrhea
¼ tablet/20 lb every six to eight hours

Famotidine (Pepcid)—antacid for decreasing gas,
nausea, and inappetence
0.25-0.5 mg/lb twice a day

Cimetidine (Tagamet)—antacid for decreasing gas,
nausea, and inappetence
3-5 mg/lb two to three times a day

Dimenhydrinate (Dramamine)—for motion or car
sickness
2 mg/lb up to twice a day

Appendix C:
Common Behavior Drugs for Dogs and Cats

Over the past 15 years, we've seen a real rise in behavioral drugs for pets. They should always be paired with behavior modification and hopefully reduced or eliminated once the behavior starts to change. Be sure to visit your vet and not your own medicine cabinet if you think your pet needs a behavior medication. Some of the most common medications include the following:

- Alprazolam (Xanax): Benzodiazepine sedative for anxiety (dogs and cats)
- Diazepam (Valium): Benzodiazepine sedative for anxiety (dogs)
- Trazedone: Antidepressant for anxiety (dogs)
- Clomipramine (Clomicalm): For separation and other anxiety disorders (dogs and cats)
- Amytriptyline (Elavil): Tricyclic antidepressant for separation and other anxiety disorders (dogs and cats)
- Fluoxetine (Prozac): Selective serotonin reuptake inhibitor (SSRI) for separation and other anxiety

disorders, dog aggression, and obsessive-compulsive disorders (dogs and cats)

- Buspirone (Buspar): For mild anxiety and fear (dogs and cats)
- Lorazepam: Benzodiazepine used in advance of anxiety-causing event (dogs)
- Sertraline (Zoloft): For anxiety (dogs)

- Holistic Medications (dogs and cats):
    Rescue Remedy: A popular anxiety treatment made from diluted flower essences (star of Bethlehem, rock rose, impatiens, cherry plum, and clematis)
    Homeopet Anxiety Relief Drops: Valerian root, jimson weed, and other botanicals

Resources and Further Reading

Resources

Throughout this book I have often made reference to many of the organizations listed here. These are just some of the dedicated organizations devoted to animal health and well-being. Check them out to learn more about them and the work they do.

American Kennel Club (AKC.org)

American Red Cross (redcross.org)

American Society for the Prevention of Cruelty to Animals (ASPCA.org)

The Association for Animal Welfare Advancement (theaawa.org)

Association of Shelter Veterinarians (sheltervet.org)

Cat Fanciers' Association (CFA.org)

Certification Council for Professional Dog Trainers (ccpdt.org)

Compassion Over Killing (COK.net)

Family Paws (familypaws.com/resources)

Hill's Pet Nutrition (hillspet.com)

Humane Society International (HSI.org)

Humane Society of the United States (Humanesociety .org)

International Fund for Animal Welfare (IFAW.org)

Mercy for Animals (mercyforanimals.org)

Morris Animal Foundation (morrisanimalfoundation .org)

Nestlé Purina Pet Care Company (purina.com)

Orthopedic Foundation for Animals (OFA.org)

People for the Ethical Treatment of Animals (peta.org)

Petco Foundation (petcofoundation.org)

PetSmart Charities (petsmartcharities.org)

San Diego Animal Welfare Coalition (SDAWC.org)

San Diego Humane Society (sdhumane.org)

The International Cat Association (TICA.org)

United Kennel Club (ukcdogs.com)

World Animal Protection USA (worldanimalprotection .us.org)

Further Reading

There are hundreds of thousands of books and articles on animal welfare. A few of them are acknowledged in this book. Many more, like the ones listed here, should also make their way into your library. Check them out to learn more about where we are in animal welfare today and more important, where we want to be.

Aiello, Susan, Michael Moses, and Dana Allen. *The Merck Veterinary Manual.* Kenilworth, NJ: Merck, 2016.

Bradshaw, John. *The Animals Among Us: How Pets Make Us Human.* New York: Basic Books, 2017.

Dodman, Nicholas. *The Well-Adjusted Dog: Dr. Dodman's Seven Steps to Lifelong Health and Happiness for Your Best Friend.* Boston: Mariner Books, 2009.

Drimmer, Stephanie Warren. *Cat Breed Guide: A Complete Reference to Your Purr-fect Best Friend.* Washington, D.C.: National Geographic, 2019.

Foer, Jonathan Safran. *Eating Animals.* New York: Little, Brown, 2009.

Grandin, Temple, and Catherine Johnson. *Animals in Translation: Using the Mysteries of Autism to Decode Animal Behavior.* Orlando, FL: Harcourt, 2005.

———. *Animals Make Us Human: Creating the Best Life for Animals.* Boston: Houghton-Mifflin Harcourt, 2010.

Horowitz, Alexandra. *Inside of a Dog: What Dogs See, Smell, and Know.* New York: Scribner, 2009.

Katz, Jon. *Soul of a Dog: Reflections on the Spirits of the Animals of Bedlam Farm.* New York: Random House, 2010.

Lindner, Lawrence, and Nicholas Dodman. *Good Old Dog: Expert Advice for Keeping Your Aging Dog Happy, Healthy, and Comfortable.* Boston: Mariner Books, 2012.

Marra, Peter P., and Chris Santella. *Cat Wars: The Devastating Consequences of a Cuddly Killer.* Princeton, NJ: Princeton University Press, 2016.

Miller, Lila, and Stephen Zawistowski. *Shelter Medicine for Veterinarians and Staff.* Hoboken, NJ: Blackwell, 2016.

Natterson-Horowitz, Barbara, and Kathryn Bowers. *Zoobiquity: The Astonishing Connection Between Human and Animal Health.* New York: Vintage Books, 2013.

Newman, Aline Alexander, and Gary Weitzman. *How to Speak Dog: A Guide to Decoding Dog Language.* Washington, D.C.: National Geographic, 2013.

———. *How to Speak Cat: A Guide to Decoding Cat Language.* New York: National Geographic, 2016.

Pacelle, Wayne. *The Bond: Our Kinship with Animals, Our Call to Defend Them.* New York: William Morrow, 2012.

Pelar, Colleen. *Living with Kids and Dogs.* Woodbridge, VA: Dream Dog Productions, 2013.

Resler, T. J. *Dog Breed Guide: A Complete Reference to Your Best Friend Furr-ever.* Washington, D.C.: National Geographic, 2019.

Safina, Carl. *Beyond Words: What Animals Think and Feel.* New York: Picador, 2016.

Sources

Part 1

American Pet Products Association. *2015-2016 National Pet Owners Survey—Generational Report.* 2015.

Andics, Attila, et. al. "Voice-Sensitive Regions in the Dog and Human Brain Are Revealed by Comparative fMRI." *Current Biology* 24, no. 5 (March 2014): 57–578.

"Dog Bite Prevention." American Veterinary Medical Association, accessed April 12, 2018, https://www .avma.org/public/Pages/Dog-Bite-Prevention.aspx.

"History of the Domestication of Animals." History World, http://www.historyworld.net/wrldhis/Plain TextHistories.asp?historyid=ab57.

"How Many Pet Rabbits Are There in the U.S.?" House Rabbit Society, July 6, 2014, https://rabbit.org/how -many-pet-rabbits-are-there-in-the-u-s/.

"How Much Does It Cost to Raise a Dog?" American Kennel Club, May 19, 2015, http://www.akc.org/expert -advice/lifestyle/did-you-know/cost-to-raise-dog/.

Lord, Linda K., Walter Ingwersen, Janet L. Gray, and David J. Wintz. "Characterization of Animals With Microchips Entering Animal Shelters." *Journal of the American Veterinary Medical Association* 235, no. 2 (July 15, 2009): 160–167. https://doi.org/10.2460/javma.235.2.160.

"Microchipping of Animals FAQ." American Veterinary Medical Association, accessed April 12, 2018, https:// www.avma.org/KB/Resources/FAQs/Pages/Microchip ping-of-animals-FAQ.aspx.

Nagasawa, Miho, et al. "Oxytocin-Gaze Positive Loop and the Coevolution of Human-Dog Bonds." *Science* 348, no. 6232 (April 17, 2015): 333-336. https://doi.org/ 10.1126/science.1261022.

Wells, Deborah L. "The Effects of Animals on Human Health and Well-Being." *Journal of Social Issues* 65, no. 3 (September 2009): 523–543. https://doi.org/ 10.1111/j.1540-4560.2009.01612.x.

Part 2

Beauvais, W., J. M. Cardwell, and D. C. Brodbelt. "The Effect of Neutering on the Risk of Mammary Tumours in Dogs—a Systematic Review." *Journal of Small Animal Practice* 53, no. 6 (June 2012): 314–322.

Cooley, Dawn M., et al. "Endogenous Gonadal Hormone Exposure and Bone Sarcoma Risk." *Cancer Epidemiology, Biomarkers & Prevention* 11, no. 11 (November 2002): 1434–1440.

Diesel, Gillain, D. Brodbelt, and C. Laurence. "Survey of Veterinary Practice Policies and Opinions on Neutering Dogs." *Vet Record* 166, no. 15 (April 2010): 455–458. https://doi.org/10.1136/vr.b4798.

Duerr, Felix M., et al. "Risk Factors for Excessive Tibial Plateau Angle in Large-Breed Dogs With Cranial

Cruciate Disease." *Journal of the American Veterinary Medical Association* 231, no. 11 (December 2007): 1688–1691. https://doi.org/10.2460/javma.231.11.1688.

Duval, J. M., S. C. Budsberg, G. L. Flo, and J. L. Sammarco. "Breed, Sex, and Body Weight as Risk Factors for Rupture of the Cranial Cruciate Ligament in Young Dogs." *Journal of the American Veterinary Medical Association* 215, no. 6 (September 1999): 811–814.

Egenvall, A., et al. "Incidence of and Survival After Mammary Tumors in a Population of Over 80,000 Insured Female Dogs in Sweden From 1995 to 2002." *Preventive Veterinary Medicine* 69, nos. 1-2 (June 2005): 109–127. https://doi.org/10.1016/j.prevetmed.2005.01.014.

Fossum, Theresa Welch, and Laura Pardi Duprey. *Small Animal Surgery.* St. Louis: Mosby, 2002.

Glickman, Larry, Nita Glickman, and Roland Thorpe. *The Golden Retriever Club of America National Health Survey (1998–1999).* Oklahoma City, OK: Golden Retriever Club of America.

Greene, Craig E. *Infectious Diseases of the Dog and Cat.* Philadelphia: Saunders, 1990.

Grumbach, Melvin M. "Estrogen, Bone, Growth and Sex: A Sea of Change in Conventional Wisdom." *Journal of Pediatric Endocrinology and Metabolism* 13 (2000): 1439–1455. https://doi.org/10.1515/jpem-2000-s619.

Hart, B. L., L. A. Hart, A. P. Thigpen, and N. H. Willits. "Long-Term Health Effects of Neutering Dogs: Comparison of Labrador Retrievers with Golden Retrievers." PLoS ONE (July 2014). http://journals.plos.org/plosone/article?id=10.1371/journal.pone.0102241.

Hart, Benjamin L. "Effects of Gonadectomy on Subsequent Development of Age-Related Cognitive Impairment in Dogs." *Journal of the American Veterinary Medical Association* 219, no. 1 (July 2001): 51–56. https://doi.org/10.2460/javma.2001.219.51.

Kaplan, E. L., and Paul Meier. "Nonparametric Estimation From Incomplete Observations." *Journal of the American Statistical Association* 53, no. 282 (June 1958): 457–481.

Kasström, Hakan. "Nutrition, Weight Gain and Development of Hip Dysplasia: An Experimental Investigation in Growing Dogs With Special Reference to the Effect of Feeding Intensity." *Acta Radiologica Supplementum* 344 (1975): 135–179.

Kent, Michael S., Jenna H. Burton, Gillian Dank, Danika L. Bannasch, and Robert B. Rebhun. "Association of cancer-related mortality, age and gonadectomy in golden retriever dogs at a veterinary academic center (1989-2016)." PLoS ONE (February 2018). http://journals.plos.org/plosone/article?id=10.1371/journal.pone.0192578.

Khanna, C., et al. "The Dog as a Cancer Model." *Nature Biotechnology* 24 (2006): 1065–1066.

Kubinyi, Eniko, Borbala Turcsan, and Adam Miklosi. "Dog and Owner Demographic Characteristics and Dog Personality Trait Associations." *Behavioural Processes* 81, no. 3 (July 2009): 392–401. https://doi.org/10.1016/j.beproc.2009.04.004.

Prymak, C., L. J. McKee, M. H. Goldschmidt, and L. T. Glickman. "Epidemiologic, Clinical, Pathologic, and Prognostic Characteristics of Splenic Hemangiosarcoma and Splenic Hematoma in Dogs: 217 Cases (1985)." *Journal of the American Veterinary Medical Association* 193, no. 6 (September 1988): 706–712.

Root Kustritz, Margaret V. "Determining the Optimal Age for Gonadectomy of Dogs and Cats." *Journal of the American Veterinary Medical Association* 231, no. 11 (December 2007): 1665–1675. https://doi.org/10.2460/javma.231.11.1665.

Rothman, Kenneth, J., and Sander Greenland. *Modern Epidemiology,* 2nd ed. Philadelphia: Lippincott Williams & Wilkins, 1998.

Ru, Giuseppe, B. Terracini, and Larry T. Glickman. "Host Related Risk Factors for Canine Osteosarcoma." *Veterinary Journal* 156, no. 1 (July 1998): 31–39. https://doi.org/10.1016/S1090-0233(98)80059-2.

Sallander, Marie H., Ake Hedhammer, Malin Rundgren, and J. E Lindberg. "Demographic Data of Population of Insured Swedish Dogs Measured in a Questionnaire Study." *Acta Veterinaria Scandinavica* (March 2001): 71–80. https://doi.org/10.1186/1751-0147-42-71.

Salmeri, K. R., M. S. Bloomberg, S. L. Scruggs, and V. Shille. "Gonadectomy in Immature Dogs: Effects on Skeletal, Physical, and Behavioral Development." *Journal of the American Veterinary Medical Association* 198, no. 7 (April 1991): 1193–1203.

Slattery, M. L., et al. "Estrogens Reduce and Withdrawal of Estrogens Increase Risk of Microsatellite Instability-Positive Colon Cancer." *Cancer Research* 61, no.1 (January 2001): 126–130.

Teske, E., et al. "Canine Prostate Carcinoma: Epidemiological Evidence of an Increased Risk in Castrated Dogs." *Molecular and Cellular Endocrinology* 197, nos. 1-2

(November 2002): 251–255. https://doi.org/10.1016/S0303-7207(02)00261-7.

Trevejo, Rosalie, Mingyin Yang, and Elizabeth M. Lund. "Epidemiology of Surgical Castration of Dogs and Cats in the United States." *Journal of the American Veterinary Medical Association* 238, no. 7 (April 2011): 898–904. https://doi.org/10.2460/javma.238.7.898.

Vail, D. M., and E. G. MacEwen. "Spontaneously Occurring Tumors of Companion Animals as Models for Human Cancer." *Cancer Investigation* 18, no. 18 (2002): 781–792.

Villamil, J. Armando, et al. "Hormonal and Sex Impact on the Epidemiology of Canine Lymphoma." *Journal of Cancer Epidemiology* (2009): 1–7. http://dx.doi.org/10.1155/2009/591753.

Ware, Wendy A., and David L. Hopper. "Cardiac Tumors in Dogs: 1982–1995." *Journal of the American Veterinary Medical Association* 13, no. 2 (1999): 95–103. https://doi.org/10.1111/j.1939-1676.1999.tb01136.x.

White, Carrie R., Anne E. Hohenhaus, Jennifer Kelsey, and Elizabeth Procter-Gray. "Cutaneous MCTs: Associations With Spay/Neuter Status, Breed, Body Size, and Phylogenetic Cluster." *Journal of the American Animal Hospital Association* 47, no. 3 (2011): 210–216.

Witsberger, T. H., et al. "Prevalence of, and Risk Factors for, Hip Dysplasia and Cranial Cruciate Ligament Deficiency in Dogs." *Journal of the American Veterinary Medical Association* 232, no. 12 (June 2008): 1818–1824.

Zatlouka, J., et al. "Breed and Age as Risk Factors for Canine Mammary Tumours." *Acta Veterinaria Brno* 74, no.1 (2005): 103–109. https://doi.org/10.2754/avb2005 74010103.

Part 3

Cattet, Jennifer. "Reactivity and Aggression in Dogs—Managing and Treating." *Pet Tutor*, April 15, 2014. http://blog.smartanimaltraining.com/2014/04/15/reactivity-and-aggression-in-dogs-managing-and-treating/.

"Dog Bite Risk and Prevention: The Role of Breed." American Veterinary Medical Association, May 15, 2014. https://www.avma.org/KB/Resources/Literature Reviews/Pages/The-Role-of-Breed-in-Dog-Bite-Risk-and-Prevention.aspx.

Duffy, Deborah L., Yuying Hsu, and James A. Serpell. "Breed Differences in Canine Aggression." *Applied Animal Behaviour Science* 114, no. 3–4 (December 2008): 441–460. https://doi.org/10.1016/j.applanim.2008.04.006.

Overall, Karen L., Arthur E. Dunham, and Diane Frank. "Frequency of Nonspecific Clinical Signs in Dogs with Separation Anxiety, Thunderstorm Phobia, and Noise Phobia, Alone or in Combination." *Journal of the American Veterinary Medical Association* 219, no. 4 (2001): 467–73. https://doi.org/10.2460/javma.2001.219.467.

Pappas, Stephanie. "Dog's Closest Wolf Ancestors Went Extinct, Study Suggests." *LiveScience,* January 16, 2014. https://www.livescience.com/42649-dogs-closest-wolf-ancestors-extinct.html.

Simpson, B. S., G. M. Landsberg, I. R. Reisner, J. J. Ciribassi, et al. "Effects of Reconcile (Fluoxetine) Chewable Tablets Plus Behavior Management for Canine Separation Anxiety." *Veterinary Therapeutics* 8, no. 1 (2007): 18–31.

Part 4

Aronson, Lillian R., Daniel J. Brockman, and Dorothy Cimino Brown. "Gastrointestinal Emergencies." *Veterinary Clinics of North America: Small Animal Practice* 30, no. 3 (2000): 555–579. https://doi.org/10.1016/s0195-5616(00)50039-4.

Glickman, L. T., et al. "Analysis of Risk Factors for Gastric Dilatation and Dilatation-Volvulus in Dogs." *Journal of the American Veterinary Medical Association* 204, no. 9 (May 1, 1994): 1465–1471.

Mackenzie, George, et al. "A Retrospective Study of Factors Influencing Survival Following Surgery for Gastric Dilatation-Volvulus Syndrome in 306 Dogs." *Journal of the American Animal Hospital Association* 46, no. 2 (2010): 97–102. https://doi.org/10.5326/0460097.

Part 5

American Heartworm Society. "Heartworm Incidence Maps." Pet Owner Resources, accessed April 12, 2018. https://www.heartwormsociety.org/pet-owner-resources/incidence-maps.

"Any Kernels of Truth to Claims That Corn Is Bad for Your Dog?" *Your Dog*, August 2013. http://www.tuftsyourdog.com/issues/19_8/features/Any-Kernels-of-Truth-to-Claims-That-Corn-Is-Bad-for-Your-Dog-228-1.html.

Chew, Dennis J. "Diagnosing and Managing Urinary Incontinence in Dogs (Proceedings)." dvm360, October 1, 2011. http://veterinarycalendar.dvm360.com/

diagnosing-and-managing-urinary-incontinence-dogs
-proceedings.

Freeman, Lisa M., Deborah E. Linder, and Cailin R. Heinze. "What Every Pet Owner Should Know About Food Allergies." In Clinical Nutrition Service, a blog of the Cummings Veterinary Medical Center at Tufts University, January 27, 2017, http://vetnutrition.tufts.edu/2017/01/food-allergies/.

Gelatt, Kirk N. "Cornea." In Merck Veterinary Manual Online, accessed April 12, 2018, https://www.merckvetmanual.com/eye-and-ear/ophthalmology/cornea.

Greco, Deborah S. "Cushing Disease (Hyperadrenocorticism)." In Merck Veterinary Manual Online, accessed April 12, 2018, https://www.merckvetmanual.com/endocrine-system/the-pituitary-gland/cushing-disease-hyperadrenocorticism.

Nelson, Thomas, "AHS Board Speaks Out: Get the Latest Guidelines Now." American Heartworm Society, 2012, https://www.heartwormsociety.org/veterinary-resources/veterinary-education/ahs-board-speaks-out/256-get-the-latest-guidelines-now.

Strain, George M. "Breed-Specific Deafness Prevalence in Dogs," August 17, 2017, www.lsu.edu/deafness/incidenc.htm.

———. "Hereditary Deafness in Dogs and Cats." Lecture at Tufts' Canine and Feline Breeding and Genetics Conference, October 2003.

Part 6

Eckstein, Sandy. "Cancer in Cats: Types, Symptoms, Prevention, and Treatment." WebMD, accessed April 12, 2018, https://pets.webmd.com/cats/guide/cancer-in-cats-types-symptoms-prevention-and-treatment.

"Facts." FETCH a cure, http://www.fetchacure.org/resource-library/facts/.

Lee, Y. J., et al. "Prognostic Factors and a Prognostic Index for Cats With Acute Kidney Injury." *Journal of Veterinary Internal Medicine* 26, no. 3 (2012): 500–505. https://doi.org/10.1111/j.1939-1676.2012.00920.x.

McCarthy, Carol. "Chemotherapy for Dogs." PetMD, accessed April 12, 2018, https://www.petmd.com/dog/general-health/chemotherapy-dogs-everything-you-need-know.

Ogilvie, Gregory. *Managing the Cancer Patient*. Yardley, PA: Veterinary Learning Systems, 1997.

Reina-Doreste, Y., et al. "Case-Control Study of the Effects of Pimobendan on Survival Time in Cats With Hypertrophic Cardiomyopathy and Congestive Heart Failure." *Journal of the American Veterinary Medical Association* 245, no. 5 (September 2014): 534–539. https://doi.org/10.2460/javma.245.5.534.

Rosenthal, Karen L., Neil Forbes, Fredric L. Frye, and Gregory A. Lewbart. *Rapid Review of Small Exotic Animal Medicine and Husbandry: Pet Mammals, Birds, Reptiles, Amphibians and Fish*. London: Manson Publishing/Veterinary Press, 2008.

Tollett, M. A., L. Duda, D. C. Brown, and E. L. Krick. "Palliative Radiation Therapy for Solid Tumors in Dogs: 103 Cases (2007–2011)." *Journal of the American Veterinary Medical Association* 248, no.1 (January 2016): 72–82. https://doi.org/10.2460/javma.248.1.72.

Veterinary Cancer Society. "Frequently Asked Questions," http://vetcancersociety.org/pet-owners/faqs/.

Withrow, Stephen, and E. Gregory MacEwen. *Clinical Veterinary Oncology*. Philadelphia: Lippincott, 1989.

Contributors

Contributors

Jackie Brown, contributing writer

Pet expert Jackie Brown has spent 20 years following her passion for animals as a writer and editor in the pet publishing industry. She is a regular contributor to pet and veterinary industry media and is the former editor of numerous pet magazines, including *Dog World, Natural Dog, Puppies 101, Kittens 101,* and the Popular Cats Series, and author of the book *It's Raining Cats and Dogs: Making Sense of Animal Phrases* (BowTie, 2006). Before starting her career in publishing, she spent eight years working in veterinary hospitals, where she assisted veterinarians as they treated dogs, cats, rabbits, pocket pets, reptiles, birds, and one memorable lion cub. She lives in

Southern California with her husband, son, and miniature poodle, Jäger.

Board of Advisers

Sherman O. Canapp, Jr., DVM, MS, CCRT, DACVS, DACVSMR

Sherman Canapp holds a combined DVM/MS from Kansas State University. He completed an internship in small animal medicine and surgery at the University of Missouri and a three-year residency in small animal surgery at the University of Florida. He is a diplomate of the American College of Veterinary Surgeons and a charter diplomate of the American College of Veterinary Sports Medicine and Rehabilitation and former president of the college. He currently practices orthopedic surgery and sports medicine at the Veterinary Orthopedic and Sports Medicine Group in Annapolis Junction, Maryland, where he is owner and chief of staff. Dr. Canapp routinely receives referrals for sports-related injuries, arthroscopic procedures, and regenerative medicine treatments from domestic and international sources. He is also the president and CEO of Orthobiologic Innovations, where he is actively engaged in concept and product design and development for orthopedic and arthroscopic devices, instrumentations, medical systems, biologics, and regenerative medicine technologies.

Todd R. Cecil, DVM, DABVP-Avian, Cert AqV

Todd Cecil's journey working with avian and exotic patients began as a zookeeper for the San Francisco Zoological Society after receiving a college degree in biology. He received his doctorate in veterinary medicine from the University of California, Davis in 1994. For the past 24 years, he has treated and administered to a wide variety of "special species" family members, including birds, small exotic mammals (ferrets, rodents, rabbits, primates, exotic cats), reptiles, amphibians, wildlife, and fish, just to list a few. He is also the head veterinarian of Avian and Exotic Veterinary Services at the Pet Emergency and Specialty Center in California, where he and his team are dedicated to improving the lives of their "special species" patients and their relationship with their human family members.

Amanda Kowalski, MS, CPDT-KA

Amanda Kowalski serves as the behavior center director for the San Diego Humane Society, where she leads a team of animal trainers and caregivers who provide specialized behavior plans for shelter animals, as well as behavior support to members of the San Diego Community. She has specialized in behavioral care in shelters across the country for over 10 years. She holds a master's in animals and public policy from the Cummings School of Veterinary Medicine at Tufts University, is a Certified Professional Dog Trainer, and serves on the board of directors for the Certification Council for Professional Dog Trainers.

Jennifer Zeisse, DVM

Jennifer Zeisse has spent nearly 20 years in veterinary clinical practice. After graduating from the University of Illinois in 1999, she spent three years in private clinical practice before she found her true calling as a shelter veterinarian. She is currently a hospital director for the San Diego Humane Society and divides her time between mentoring, teaching, and shelter practice. She resides in the San Diego area with her husband, three children, and several furred and feathered family members. Her favorite dog breed is the American Shelter Dog.

Illustrations Credits

Stock Photo; 25, GlobalP/iStock/Getty Images; 26, © Marco Bottigelli/Getty Images; 27, cynoclub/iStock/Getty Images; 28, Pekic/Getty Images; 29, GlobalP/iStock/Getty Images; 30, Johner Images/Getty Images; 31, Debra Bardowicks/Getty Images; 32, Annie Otzen/Getty Images; 33 (UP), Veera/Shutterstock; 33 (LO), EEI_Tony/iStock/Getty Images; 34, FatCamera/Getty Images; 35, oksana2010/Shutterstock; 36, Courtesy of San Diego Humane Society; 37, Courtesy of San Diego Humane Society; 38, Photo by Casey Dean; 39 (UP), Marc Henrie/Getty Images; 39 (LO), LJSphotography/Alamy Stock Photo; 40, Andrew_Deer/iStock/Getty Images; 41, Alex Mladek/Shutterstock; 42, cynoclub/iStock/Getty Images; 43, DebbiSmirnoff/Getty Images; 44, MorePixels/iStock/Getty Images; 45, Kevin Oke/Getty Images; 46, Panther Media GmbH/Alamy Stock Photo; 47, vladans/iStock/Getty Images; 48, Zharinova Marina/Shutterstock; 49 (UP), Alexander_Evgenyevich/Shutterstock; 49 (LO), Dorottya_Mathe/iStock/Getty Images; 50 (UP), Yuriy Golub/Shutterstock; 50 (LO), jhorrocks/Getty Images; 51, a katz/Shutterstock; 52, Tracy Morgan Animal Photography/Dorling Kindersley/Getty Images; 53, Weekend Images Inc./Getty Images; 54, MaraZe/Shutterstock; 55, Kitoo/Shutterstock; 56, Aarontphotography/Shutterstock; 57, Anna Hoychuk/Shutterstock; 58, YuriF/Getty Images; 59, LWA/Getty Images; 60, Photo by Casey Dean; 61, ballyscanlon/Getty Images; 62, Fertnig/Getty Images; 63, Susan Schmitz/Shutterstock; 64, JackF/iStock/Getty Images; 65, Nenov Brothers Images/Shutterstock; 66 (UP), BookyBuggy/Shutterstock; 66 (LO), Jaromir Chalabala/Shutterstock; 67, Kelvin Wong/Shutterstock; 68, CBCK-Christine/iStock/Getty Images; 69, Sergey Lavrentev/Shutterstock; 70 (UP), 135pixels/Shutterstock; 70 (LO), Nature Art/Shutterstock; 71, GlobalP/iStock/Getty Images; 72, Capelle.r/Getty Images; 73, DenisNata/Shutterstock; 74, absolutimages/Shutterstock; 75, Editor77/Alamy Stock Photo; 76, stockelements/Shutterstock; 78 (UP), jclegg/Getty Images; 78 (LO), vetkit/iStock/Getty Images; 80, Charlotte Banfield/Alamy Stock Photo; 81, Jeffrey Coolidge/Getty Images; 82, anetapics/Shutterstock; 83, Courtesy of Finding Rover; 84, Dave and Les Jacobs/Getty Images; 85, Anton Tyagniy/EyeEm/Getty Images; 86-87, Karan Kapoor/Getty Images; 88, Gumpanat/Shutterstock; 89, Sergio Azenha/Alamy Stock Photo; 90, Per Dahl/Getty Images; 91, Yulia Reznikov/Getty Images; 92, irencik/Shutterstock; 93, gradyreese/Getty Images; 94, GlobalP/iStock/Getty Images; 95, Steve Teague/Getty Images; 96, Jo Bradford/Green Island Art Studios/Getty Images; 98, Spiky and I/Shutterstock; 99 (UP), adogslifephoto/iStock/Getty Images; 99 (LO), Jordan Siemens/Getty Images; 100, Nataliya Sdobnikova/Shutterstock; 101, Image by Chris Winsor/Getty Images; 102, LexiTheMonster/iStock/Getty Images; 103, Melounix/Shutterstock; 104, Nick Ridley/Getty Images; 105, Akitameldes/Shutterstock; 106, w-ings/iStock/Getty Images; 108, Martin Leigh/Getty Images; 109 (UP), Zave Smith/Getty Images; 109 (LO), Susan Schmitz/Shutterstock; 110, PeopleImages/Getty Images; 111, Hero Images/Getty Images; 112, wundervisuals/iStock/Getty Images; 113, Serhiy Kuzmin/Alamy Stock Photo; 114, Nenov/iStock/Getty Images; 115, Inti St Clair/Getty Images; 117,

Svetlana Foote/Alamy Stock Photo; 118, Irina Kozorog/Shutterstock; 119, Tatyana Nikitina/Alamy Stock Photo; 120, Phasin Sudjai/Alamy Stock Photo; 121, Tierfotoagentur/Alamy Stock Photo; 122, Africa Studio/Shutterstock; 123, Svetlana Popova/Alamy Stock Photo; 124, humonia/iStock/Getty Images; 125, Martina_L/Shutterstock; 126, Inti St Clair/Getty Images; 127, SharafMaksumov/iStock/Getty Images; 128, Plamena Velikova/EyeEm/Getty Images; 129, Tom K Photo/Alamy Stock Photo; 130, F16-ISO100/Shutterstock; 131, GCapture/Shutterstock; 132, cynoclub/iStock/Getty Images; 133, Jasmin Sachtleben/EyeEm/Getty Images; 134, onetouchspark/iStock/Getty Images; 135, Highwaystarz-Photography/iStock/Getty Images; 136, Norman Chan/Shutterstock; 137, Viacheslav Blizniuk/Shutterstock; 138, Ariel Skelley/Getty Images; 139 (UP), GOODLUZ/Alamy Stock Photo; 139 (LO), Nejron Photo/Shutterstock; 140, LWA/Getty Images; 141, Westend61/Getty Images; 143 (UP), GlobalP/iStock/Getty Images; 143 (LO), oksana2010/Shutterstock; 145, DjelicS/Getty Images; 146, John Donges/University of Pennsylvania School of Veterinary Medicine; 147, John Donges/University of Pennsylvania School of Veterinary Medicine; 148, sematadesign/iStock/Getty Images; 149, Pamela Webb/EyeEm/Getty Images; 150, Littlekidmoment/Shutterstock; 151, BanksPhotos/iStock/Getty Images; 152, BanksPhotos/iStock/Getty Images; 153, CREATISTA/iStock/Getty Images; 154, Faba-Photography/Getty Images; 155, coopder1/Getty Images; 156, Okssi68/iStock/Getty Images; 157, K_Thalhofer/iStock/Getty Images; 158, sasel77/iStock/Getty Images; 159, Ed Reschke/Getty Images; 160, BanksPhotos/iStock/Getty Images; 161, GlobalP/iStock/Getty Images; 162, CNRI/Science Source; 163, DigitalAnimals/Alamy Stock Photo; 164, AntonGrachev/Shutterstock; 165, Diego Moreno Delgado/Shutterstock; 166, Markus Gann/Shutterstock; 167, Imagination-Photography/iStock/Getty Images; 168, PRESSLAB/Shutterstock; 169 (UP), dusanpetkovic/iStock/Getty Images; 169 (LO), Denis Felix/Getty Images; 170, alexsokolov/iStock/Getty Images; 171, RichLegg/Getty Images; 172, harpazo_hope/Getty Images; 173, grase/iStock/Getty Images; 174, Balzs Kemendi/EyeEm/Getty Images; 175, Kalamurzing/Shutterstock; 176, GlobalP/iStock/Getty Images; 177, Jon Paciaroni/Getty Images; 178, alexeys/iStock/Getty Images; 179, Pedro Martinez/EyeEm/Getty Images; 180, Mitskevich Uladzimir/Shutterstock; 181, CasarsaGuru/Getty Images; 182-183, CBCK-Christine/iStock/Getty Images; 184, Anna Hoychuk/Shutterstock; 185, Studio-Annika/iStock/Getty Images; 186, karen roach/Shutterstock; 187, Jessica Peterson/Getty Images; 188, Boris Zhitkov/EyeEm/Getty Images; 189, SolStock/Getty Images; 190, cmannphoto/Getty Images; 191, Life On White/Getty Images; 192, richcano/iStock/Getty Images; 193, Colleen Gara/Getty Images; 194, Filip Jedraszak/Shutterstock; 195, Parilov/Shutterstock; 196, Africa Studio/Shutterstock; 197, Doug Menuez/Forrester Images/Getty Images; 198, Westend61/Getty Images; 199, Matej Kastelic/Shutterstock; 200, Michelle D. Milliman/Shutterstock; 201, WilleeCole Photography/Shutterstock; 202, Photo by Casey Dean; 203, Photo by Casey Dean; 205, Alex Potemkin/iStock/Getty Images; 206, Eric Isselee/Shutter-

Index

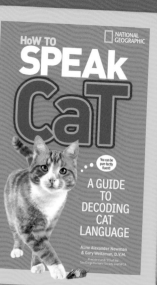